MIAMI
CONTEMPORARY ARTISTS

Paul Clemence & Julie Davidow

Foreword by Elisa Turner

Schiffer Publishing Ltd

4880 Lower Valley Road Atglen, Pennsylvania 19310

Other Schiffer Books by Paul Clemence:
South Beach Architectural Photographs
Mies van der Rohe's Farnsworth House

Library of Congress Control Number: 2007931608

Front Cover Image: *The Sleep of Reasons Breeds Monsters*, 2006, vinyl tape and resin on panel, by Gavin Perry, *Courtesy of Gavin Perry and Frederic Snitzer Gallery.*

Back Cover Image: *Illegal Zone,* 2002, graphite on marble, by Glexis Novoa, *Collection of Dr. Martin and Jeri Zaiac*.

Type set in Zurich BT

ISBN: 978-0-7643-2647-9
Printed in China

Published by Schiffer Publishing Ltd.
4880 Lower Valley Road
Atglen, PA 19310
Phone: (610) 593-1777; Fax: (610) 593-2002
E-mail: Info@schifferbooks.com

For the largest selection of fine reference books on this and related subjects, please visit our web site at **www.schifferbooks.com**
We are always looking for people to write books on new and related subjects. If you have an idea for a book please contact us at the above address.

This book may be purchased from the publisher.
Include $3.95 for shipping.
Please try your bookstore first.
You may write for a free catalog.

In Europe, Schiffer books are distributed by
Bushwood Books
6 Marksbury Ave.
Kew Gardens
Surrey TW9 4JF England
Phone: 44 (0) 20 8392-8585;
Fax: 44 (0) 20 8392-9876
E-mail: info@bushwoodbooks.co.uk
Website: www.bushwoodbooks.co.uk
Free postage in the U.K., Europe; air mail at cost.

DEDICATION

To Stephen Anderson, for being a great friend, supporter and initiating the friendship that made this book possible.

Paul Clemence

This book is dedicated to the memory of my father, Melvin Davidow, whose passion for life, and endless curiosity of the world taught me to keep my eyes and heart open, and revel in its diversity.

Julie Davidow

ACKNOWLEDGMENTS

We would like to extend our deepest thanks and appreciation to everyone who has helped in the realization of this project and its publication. First and foremost we thank all of the artists in these pages. *Miami Contemporary Artists* would not have been possible without the inspiration and generosity of these artists. Our gratitude goes to their galleries, representatives, assistants, and the many museums, private collections, and nonprofit arts organizations of Miami for their invaluable contributions to the production of this book.

Genaro Ambrosino, Ambrosino Gallery
Daniel Aubry (photography for Purvis Young)
Nikki Beem, Curatorial Assistant, Miami Art Museum
Cora Bettcher, Bettcher Gallery
Damien Boisseau, Director, Damien B. Contemporary Art Center (for Reeve Schumacher)
Claire Breukel, Curator
Kimberley Brown, Zach Feuer Gallery (LFL) (for Luis Gispert)
David Castillo, Castillo Fine Art (for Pepe Mar and Quisqueya Henriquez)
Jeremy Chestler, Executive Director, ArtCenter/ South Florida
Bonnie Clearwater, Executive Director, Chief Curator, MOCA
Mark Coetzee, Curator, Rubell Family Collection
Douglas Congdon-Martin, Schiffer Publishing
Silvia Karman Cubiña, the Moore Space
Carol Damian, Florida International University, Dept of Art and Art History
Denise Delgado, Curator of Exhibitions, Miami Dade Public Library – Main
Gilliane Duval-Carrié (for Edouard Duval-Carrié)
Donna Fields, Special Projects Manager, Museum of Contemporary Art, North Miami
Roni Feinstein, art critic, Miami correspondent for Art in America
Richard Fendelman (for Purvis Young)
Skot Foreman (for Purvis Young)
Paul Gaeta (for Cristina Lei Rodriguez)
Noelle A. Galperin (for Pablo Cano)
Stephanie Garcia, Chelsea Galleria
Alexander Heria
Katherine Hinds, Director of the Martin Z. Margulies Foundation
Nina Johnson, Bernice Steinbaum Gallery (for Glexis Novoa)
Helen L. Kohen, the Vasari Project, Miami Dade Public Library – Main
Leila Leder-Kremer, Administrative Assistant, ArtCenter/ South Florida
Rosa Levy, R&R Studios (for Roberto Behar & Rosario Marquardt)
Dorothy Long, Director, Chelsea Galleria (for Tina Spiro)
Lee Materazzi, the Margulies Warehouse
Andrea Navarro, Programs and Marketing Coordinator, Miami Art Central and CIFO
Wayne Northcross, Lehman Maupin Gallery (for Teresita Fernandez)
A. Palmer (for Carlos Betancourt)
Gavin Perry
Valerie Ricordi, Public Relations, Museum of Contemporary Art North Miami
Ana Maria Sarlat, Alonso Art Gallery
Peter and Nancy Schiffer, founders of Schiffer Publishing Ltd.
Peter N. Schiffer, Schiffer Publishing
Richard and Ruth Shack
Tina Skinner, Editor, Schiffer Publishing Ltd.
Stephanie Smith, Lehmann Maupin Gallery (for Teresita Fernandez)
Frederic Snitzer, Frederic Snitzer Gallery
Mitchell Snow, Communications Coordinator, Miami Art Museum
Anthony Spinello, Spinello Gallery
Chip Steeler, Director Martin Z Margulies Sculpture Park at FIU
Bernice Steinbaum, Bernice Steinbaum Gallery
Elisa Turner, art critic, The Miami Herald and Miami ARTnews correspondent
Juan Valdez, Registrar, the Rubell Family collection (for Cristina Lei Rodriguez)
Christopher Vasquez, Frederic Snitzer Gallery

CONTENTS

PREFACE

The idea for this book came from the enjoyment and excitement that two friends (coauthor Julie Davidow and I) share of this most fertile moment in the arts that we are experiencing in Miami today. It's a moment that says "Look where we are, look how far we've come, look where we can go." It is a moment full of pride, accomplishments, and promise. So inspired by this, we decided to put together our passions – Julie's for the arts, mine for building books – to try to capture and celebrate the people making the art that fuels this moment.

We came to this project from quite different backgrounds. Julie is a Miami native, for years involved in the arts, and an accomplished artist. I was raised in Brazil, educated as an architect, and am now a photographer. This meant that, although we had the same vision of this project, we came to it from different perspectives. This proved to be very helpful, as it allowed us a wider range of resources with which to tackle such an ambitious project.

From the start, the concept for the book was to be a very inclusive showcase of Miami artists. Featuring not only the best, or the more recognized or talked about names, but to reveal a vertical slice of this community and present artists in different stages of development, or who took different career paths. We wanted to show the stars with international careers whose work is in museum collections, along with the ones just beginning to make a name for themselves; the artists who inspired and taught others, and the countless artists with no gallery representation at all, hidden away in their studios, doing their art, getting out there and breathing creative energy into the city.

Of course, it would have been physically impossible to feature all of the artists that could have been in these pages. We had, somehow, to limit the number of entries. In doing so, unfortunately, many well deserving artists were excluded. So we take this opportunity to apologize to all the talented people who we were not able to include in this volume. It was never a question of merit only, but rather that we kept to the variety we intended the book to represent.

Another trying selective process, but this one highly enjoyable, was curating the artwork. Our approach here was not only to choose what was most representative of each artist, but also what would maintain that quality on a five by seven inch photo on a book page, within the flow of the book. This flow was also a deciding factor for each layout design and length.

In addition, each artist was asked to submit a written statement about their work as well as their experience being an artist in Miami, thus revealing a more personal insight into their ideas and response to the city.

Through all of our decisions, a lot of time was spent poring over the images to allow a unique appreciation of these artworks. This time offered an intimate opportunity to relate to each piece, to learn more about each artist, to enjoy and examine the work, then enjoy and examine it again. I come away from this experience feeling this incredible artistic energy that challenges easy, stifling definitions, but is nonetheless very present. And I have a renewed respect and gratitude to these artists and their dedication to their craft.

To give the readers some perspective on how this current moment came to be, we invited renowned South Florida art critic Elisa Turner to write the foreword. Her writing is at once historic and informative. Her insightful text helps piece together the various people, institutions, collectors, philanthropists and, of course, the artists who are essential to creating the conditions in which this creative burst could flourish.

"*There is no cultural life in Miami!*" some like to say. Certainly we might still lack the scale of venues and institutions that other more traditional cities have in abundance. But, hopefully, this book will help the world to see that here, also, in our very young city, culture is very much alive and well. Although our cultural "apparatus" is still a work in progress, we already have the most essential requirement: a vibrant, talented, clever, and original group of artists seriously dedicated to create art.

Paul Clemence

INTRODUCTION

Miami is a natural playground for inspiration. A collision of land, and sea, and sky at the edge of the continent; dipping its geographical thumb into the Caribbean, testing the waters of possibility. Steamy days and sultry nights set the stage for endless narratives. An expansive sky radiates with brilliant light, casting a sparkling spell on Biscayne Bay, glancing off the rising towers of downtown. Its glow sweeps the streets of its inequities, if only for a brief moment. This is the magic hour in Miami that captivates everyone. Lush and tropical, the surrounding vegetation wraps its tendrils through the concrete, defying encroaching development to overcome its true, natural state.

This is a city of endless contradictions. The economic disparities between its neighborhoods combine with a convergence of peoples and cultures to create a rich, didactic brew. The flavors, sights, colors, and sounds spill onto the streets from these diverse neighborhoods, and seep into the work of its many artists. Obsessively, compulsively, instinctively, like archaeologists these artists unearth the origins and complexities of our humanity to expose the infinite diversity of self. They are our conscience and our mirror – exposing our hopes, our dreams, our frailties and our mortality. They are our cultural ciphers, divining truth from a cacophony of influences. Ultimately, when the politics of our culture fails, the vision of the artist prevails.

Miami has always provided safe haven for artists. Existing for decades outside of the forces of the art market, the city has been a frontier where artists staked claim to blighted neighborhoods, responding to the streets, the climate, the decadence and despair, and each other. A freedom to explore and experiment has been an intrinsic part of this culture. Here, artists have been able to create their own definitions. Not only defining their work while finding their voices, but defining the kinds of environments in which they wanted to see their work exhibited. With a tenacious, entrepreneurial spirit, a growing population of Miami artists set forth to establish venues outside of the limited gallery system in the city.

The evolution of a city is impossible without the existence of a core of creativity. There is a symbiosis that develops amongst its inhabitants, and like any natural system, it requires all of the elements to be in place in order for it to function, thrive, and survive. We need the pioneers, the innovators, the teachers, the students, the stars, the renegades, the clowns, the transients, and the outsiders. The pioneers forge new ground, in new neighborhoods, and generate interest and excitement where before there was none. The entrepreneurs boldly set their own course, thus showing the way for the more tentative to do the same. The ebb and flow of artists moving in and out of the city impart bursts of energy to spark continued growth. All play an undeniable role in fostering the character of our creative community.

Miami is my hometown. My history is wrapped up in its streets. The countless transformations to its distinctive, colorful neighborhoods can not silence the whispers of its past or mine. And the foundations of its future, gleaming new skyline are built on its legacies, as are mine. My father first came to Miami in the late thirties, and moved here with my grandfather and uncle in 1947. My great-grandmother and mother came to Miami Beach in 1958. I heard endless stories of the heyday of Miami Beach, soldiers training on the sands off of Ocean Drive, tanks that rumbled past our home during the Cuban Missile Crisis. And I would sit on our porch with my grandfather, an artist turned businessman who had attended Cooper-Union in New York, and receive my first drawing lessons. My parents exposed me to every possible cultural experience they could find in the city. The Bass Museum, the early FIU Gallery, Virginia Miller and Dorothy Blau galleries, theatre at the Coconut Grove Playhouse and Jackie Gleason Performing Arts Center, symphonies and opera at the Dade County Auditorium. Early on they enrolled me in art classes at the Metropolitan Art Museum Center where I visited resident artists in their studios. I knew then what I wanted to be.

There was not much art going on here growing up, so it has been with great pride that I have watched my city mature to this point. After many fits and starts, and years of hearing *"Miami has so much potential,"* I believe that we are finally reaching a momentum that will fulfill that potential. Many of the artists in these pages I know personally. Some were my teachers, others fellow students – their energy and spirit played a role in realizing my own potential as I transformed, from business owner to artist. Some are my close friends – whose confidences I enjoy daily, and who support me in my own struggle to evolve as an artist. Others are newer acquaintances, and some I know by name and reputation only. They challenge me, inspire me, confound me, and humor me. Their tireless commitment to their work, developing their craft, and constantly pushing to excel motivate me to do the same. But it is the diversity of the human experience as revealed through the work of the artists in these pages which is most profound. The infinite perspectives and interpretations that can be had of our world remind me that we are all valid and thriving here in Miami.

Julie Davidow

FOREWORD

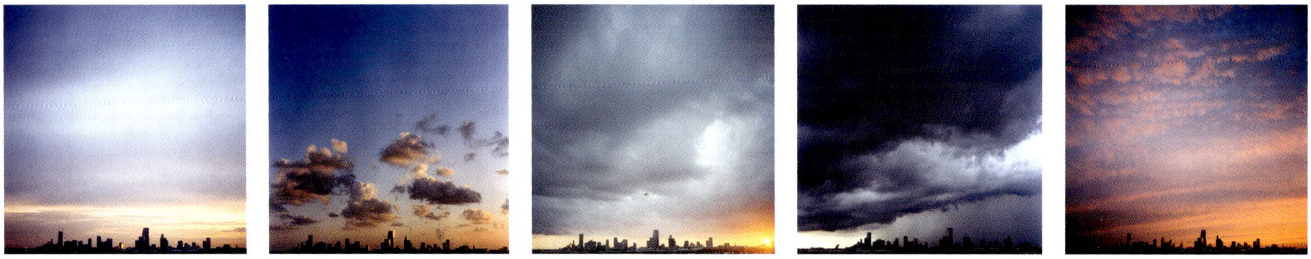

City Sky Series, 2005, C-Print,10" x 10." *Courtesy of Alex Heria.*

As I write these thoughts on how the Miami art scene has flourished in the last few years, glaring sunshine broils our summer days. It's that time of year when people who live in South Florida often check weather reports, wondering when the next hurricane will tear our way. Experts say we are in the midst of an unusually active storm cycle, following the devastating hurricane season of 2005.

As the intensity of South Florida's stormy weather accelerates, another kind of acceleration surrounds us. Miami is experiencing a building boom and an attendant surge in real estate prices. Construction cranes, with their skeletal lop sided structures, jab the sky. Construction on office and apartment towers snarls traffic all over town.

Miami's art scene, once considered a backwater, is in the midst of a boom as well. Galleries and art venues continue to set up shop in Wynwood and the Design District, neighborhoods near downtown that are enjoying a renaissance. Property values climb. Art galleries with national and international reputations move to Miami. A few homegrown galleries are reaping international cachet.

The city's evolving art district does not match the bustle of New York's Chelsea neighborhood, but all kinds of markers, such as this very book, point to a swiftly maturing art scene, one that's sparking international attention well beyond the intense days of Art Basel Miami Beach. This art fair, in existence since December 2002, has rapidly climbed the charts in terms of its fevered popularity for an international crowd of contemporary art collectors. A sure sign of the fair's success is the way it has attracted an expanding flotilla of smaller art fairs that migrate here in early December. They aim to take advantage of the moneyed museum and collector crowd that Art Basel Miami Beach attracts like a dazzling 21st century lighthouse.

Some, especially those looking from the outside, tend to think that the Miami area's boom owes virtually everything to the vision of Art Basel organizers, and to their decision to make Miami Beach the site of the first Art Basel organized art fair located outside of Basel, Switzerland, where the annual fair in June has enjoyed years of popularity and prestige as the best of its kind in the world.

That perception regarding Miami is false. Basel organizers were interested in Miami because the art scene here was already percolating and productive. In January 1999, I reported in the Miami Herald that Lorenzo Rudolph, at the time the director of Art Basel, had been introduced to Miami Beach city officials by collector Mera Rubell to discuss organizing a major art event in the city. "Art Basel is convinced that there is great cultural potential in the Miami area," said Samuel Keller, then an Art Basel spokesman, in January 1999. No doubt about it, the Basel fair gave the art scene here – an expanding core of artists, collectors, museums, galleries, critics, and writers – a considerable surge, one that those in Miami continue to witness.

I've been asked to write about milestones paving the way for the accelerated art scene we are now witnessing. South Florida has been famous for years for its warm and sunny winter weather. But warm winter weather was not enough to make Samuel Keller, the current director of Art Basel Miami Beach and Art Basel, want to invest in a startup art fair in Miami Beach. He and others in the Art Basel organization were looking for a place receptive to art, artists, and art lovers. They found such an artful spot in the balmy winter destination of Miami Beach.

Certainly the support of Miami collectors has been integral to the success of the fair and the growing art scene. Beginning with the first year of the fair, Miami collectors have opened their private homes and collections to fairgoers hailing from this country, Latin America, and Europe. Visitors to the fair flock in droves to these opportunities to see private, sometimes internationally famous collections of 20th and 21st century art. This kind of access has been virtually unheard of in Basel and the rest of Europe. Collectors have also been active here in local museums, by serving on boards, participating in fundraising events, and making loans and contributions to permanent collections. Among these active Miami collectors are Norman and Irma Braman, Paul and Estelle Berg, Mireille Chancy-Gonzalez, Ella Fontanals Cisneros, Carlos and Rosa de la Cruz, Jeff Gelblum, Tony Goldman, Maggie Hernández, Steven and Rochelle Lanster, George Lindemann, Martin Z. Margulies, Peter Menéndez, Rafael and Marijean Miyar, Javier and Monica Mora, Arturo and Liza Mosquera, Jorge and Darlene Perez, Carl and Toni Randolph, Craig Robins, Donald and Mera Rubell, Marvin and Ruth Sackner, Dennis and Debra Scholl, Richard and Ruth Shack, and Marty and Cricket Taplin.

The city is a very different place from the one I came to know when I moved here from New York in the early 1980s. The television show "Miami Vice" was all the rage then. People joked about how life in Miami could fry your brain. For years the rest of the country said Miami Beach and its nearby cities was a place of sun and fun, a place "where summer spends the winter," to quote an old tourist brochure promoting Coral Gables. Yes, South Beach celebrity sighting is still fodder for gossip columns. But there is a difference. Now the Miami area flashes its cultural credentials, particularly in the visual arts.

How did it happen? There were lots of steps along the way.

In the early 1980s, the art scene was made up primarily of the Lowe Art Museum at the University of Miami, the Bass Museum of Art in Miami Beach, and a handful of veteran gallery dealers, including Barbara Gillman in the Design District, Gloria Luria and Dorothy Blau on Kane Concourse in Bal Harbour, and Virginia Miller in Coral Gables. The Visual Arts Gallery was founded in 1977 at Florida International University, although the institution really started to show promise in 1980 when Dahlia Morgan was hired to direct the gallery, and even more so in 1985 when its name was changed to Art Museum at FIU. That institution now is called The Patricia & Philip Frost Art Museum. It's outgrown its location on the ground floor of a building at FIU, and in 2008 it will open an impressive new building of its own on the campus.

Although the Miami area was still considered a sleepy place for culture, new places took shape throughout the 1980s. Artists renovated blighted areas around town, lured by low cost rents. In 1984, the South Florida Art Center was founded by forward thinking artist Ellie Schneiderman on the west end of Lincoln Road Mall in Miami Beach. She secured grant money from the City of Miami Beach to make the art center happen; it offered studio spaces and a cooperative gallery. Another initiative evolved in Wynwood two years later. A group of affordable art studios, the Bakehouse Art Complex held an open house in May 1986, while renovations continued on the building, a former bakery that had been vacant since the early 1980s. By February of the following year, it was fully open. Visionaries Helene Pancoast and Faith Atlass found the finances to make the Bakehouse a reality.

In 1984 the Center for the Fine Arts opened in downtown as a non-collecting art museum in a complex with the Main Library and the Historical Museum of Southern Florida. The complex was designed by architect Philip Johnson. This was the same year that an "artist colony," as the *Miami Herald* sometimes called the South Florida Art Center, was slowly transforming Lincoln Road.

Also throughout the 1980s, several generations of Cuban-born artists drew attention to Miami. Many had left Cuba shortly after dictator Fidel Castro seized power in 1959. In 1983, the now defunct Cuban Museum of Arts and Culture presented "The Miami Generation" an exhibit of work by nine artists born in Cuba and educated in Miami. Artists making art in exile in Miami included Carlos Alfonzo, Mario Algaze, Maria Brito, Humberto Calzada, Pablo Cano, Ramón Carulla, Demi, Silvia Lizama, Connie Lloveras, María Martinez-Cañas, Arturo Rodriguez, Lydia Rubio, Rafael Soriano, and César Trasobares. In ways ranging from subtle to overt, their art reflected the anguish of being uprooted from their homeland, and their art sometimes got caught up in the city's volatile exile politics.

In the 1990s, changes occurred more swiftly as the decade came to a close. By the early 1990s, another generation of Cuban artists was finding their way to Miami, sometimes leaving Cuba by first moving to Mexico. These artists had belonged to Cuba's noted "80's generation," artists who had generally eluded censorship while being the first in a group to exhibit beyond the island and receive positive attention in the mainstream art world. Artists who had come of age as artists in 1980s Cuba finding their way to Miami included José Bedia, Florencio Gelabert, Tomas Esson, Glexis Novoa, and Rubén Torres Llorca.

Of this group, Bedia had the most stature when he arrived here around 1994. His art had already been included in two landmark exhibitions: "Magiciens de la Terre" in 1989 at the George Pompidou Center in Paris, and "Latin American Artists of the Twentieth Century" in 1992 at the Museum of Modern Art in New York.

In 1990 the art fair Art Miami was established. In 1994, the Martin Z. Margulies Sculpture Park was founded at FIU with long term loans of Margulies' vaunted monumental sculpture collection. A year later, Suzanne Delehanty arrived to direct the Center for the Fine Arts, which changed its name the following year to Miami Art Museum (MAM). MAM not only had a new name, but a new mission as a collecting museum. As MAM's website explains, its mission is "to exhibit, collect, preserve, and interpret international art with a focus on the 20th and 21st centuries." More historical shows, which are often more accessible to members of the public bewildered by cutting edge art, are not ruled out if they fit with this focus. The website adds that the museum may present "works of art outside this time frame when appropriate."

A critical point in Miami's recent art history was the opening in February 1996 of the new building designed by architect Charles Gwathmey for the Museum of Contemporary Art (MOCA) in North Miami. MOCA's heavily publicized inaugural exhibition brought Miami and Miami based artists to the art world's surprised and somewhat grudging attention with "Defining the Nineties: Consensus making in New York, Miami, and Los Angeles," curated by MOCA director and chief curator Bonnie Clearwater. Regrettably, this show did not travel to other cities, but it still had a major impact on this city's art community by presenting Miami artists in the company of national and international figures. Artists with ties to Miami in this show were José Bedia, Robert Chambers, Teresita Fernández, the late Felix Gonzales-Torres, Quisqueya Henríquez, and Rubén Torres Llorca.

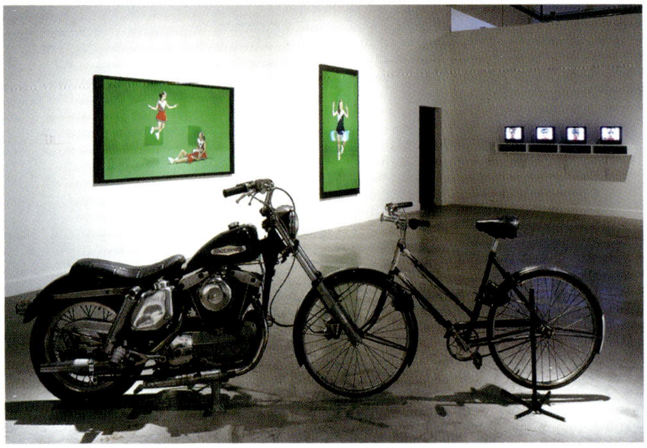

From *"Making Art in Miami: Travels in Hyperreality,"* 2000, installation view *"Motoshag"* by Robert Chambers and *"Untitled (Three Asian Cheerleaders)"* by Luis Gispert. *Museum of Contemporary Art, North Miami.*

Not surprisingly, there was grumbling about the Miami artists who did not make it into this inaugural exhibit. The show was nevertheless a major step in highlighting Miami artists in a significant institutional space in greater Miami.

That "local" artists were rarely exhibited in the major institutions here, except possibly during the broiling summers when tourists stayed away and the few Miami collectors were not in town, had been a sore point for years between the artists and museums here. In current parlance, "Miami-based" has replaced the more provincial sounding adjective of "local." As Robert Thiele told me in 2000, there was an earlier time when he and other artists here "were doing our work but not aiming at a larger audience, when museums....generally had a hands-off policy in terms of the home-grown product."

Since its inaugural exhibit, MOCA has played a leading role in showcasing Miami based artists in a variety of inventive ways, in both group and solo shows. Some artists are discovering that it's no longer always the case that they need to move away from Miami to find recognition elsewhere, especially in New York, to get attention on their home turf. Or they are discovering that being from Miami now has a cachet that once only belonged to places like New York, London, and Los Angeles.

"Everywhere we go there is interest in Miami. Miami has an amazing mystique outside of Miami. It's a new hub," says Neraldo de la Paz. De la Paz, with Alain Guerra is part of an artist team known as Guerra de la Paz.

In the summer of 2005, I met with Hans Ulrich Obrist, who was in Miami to choose artists for a group show he was co-curating for the Astrup Fearnley Museum of Modern Art in Oslo, Norway. The show was "Uncertain States of America: American Art in the 3rd Millennium," which has traveled in Europe and the U.S. It first opened in Norway in the fall of 2005. Miami artists in that show were Jiae Hwang, Cristina Lei Rodriguez, and the TM Sisters. Miami artist, curator, and critic Gene Moreno and I contributed essays to the show's catalog. Obrist asked me to put together a "collage" of articles I had written for the Miami Herald about the growing scene here. "We are interested to know how this 'Miami miracle' happened," he told me.

After MOCA opened in 1996, as I later noted in my "collage," the "Miami miracle" grew. In December 2000 an important show contributing to that miracle or mystique (call it what you want) was "Making Art in Miami: Travels in Hyperreality" at MOCA. It was the museum's fifth anniversary show. It brought together work in a range of media by twenty two artists. The artists in "Making Art in Miami" were Hernan Bas, Natalia Benedetti, Robert Chambers, Westen Charles, Cooper, William Cordova, John Espinosa, Naomi Fisher, Robert Flynn, Dara Friedman, Luis Gispert, Adler Guerrier, Mark Handforth, Jason Hedges, Beatriz Monteavaro, Gene Moreno, Jorge Pantoja, Norberto Rodriguez, David Rohn, Eugenia Vargas, Annie Wharton, and Elizabeth Withstandley.

The research that curator Bonnie Clearwater prepared for this show underscored the growing strengths of Miami's art community. In her catalog essay "Making Art in Miami," she discussed the importance of artist-run exhibition spaces and the presence of strong private collections. She notes how the city's emerging artists were often taught in various Miami art schools by a previous generation of artists, particularly Carol Brown, Robert Huff, Karen Rifas, and Robert Thiele. In her catalog essay "Navigating the Hyperreal," she links art in the show to the area's long tradition of creating fabulous fantasies, from Vizcaya, industrialist James Deering's Renaissance styled villa built in 1916 on Biscayne Bay, to the theme park of Disney World in nearby Orlando. Further, she connects the art and fabulous tradition to an essay by Italian novelist Umberto Eco called "Travels in Hyperreality," in his book by the same title.

Also in late 2000, the Miami art community became more self aware, when an invaluable archive, The Vasari Project, was created with the Miami Dade Public Library by former Miami Herald art critic Helen L. Kohen and now retired librarian Barbara Young. With oral histories, ephemera, and all kinds of documents, The Vasari Project records the Miami art scene from 1945 to the present. The Miami Art Exchange, a loose coalition of artists and their supporters, was also set up this year with support from Miami dealer Bernice Steinbaum. The Miami Art Exchange is now a website, newsletter, and blog thanks to the tireless efforts of Onajide Shabaka.

At the Miami Art Museum a series of solo shows dedicated to eight Miami artists began in 2001. Curated by Lorie Mertes and Amy Rosenblum, it was launched with fanfare. This series was called "New Work Miami." Dividing MAM's downstairs "New Work" gallery in half for each artist, the series gave solo shows to Frank Benson, Consuelo Castañeda, Robert Chambers, Naomi Fisher, Dara Friedman, Adler Guerrier, Glexis Novoa, and Robert Thiele.

Another pivotal museum show from this year was at the Bass Museum of Art on Miami Beach. This show was "globe>miami>island" in December 2001. It was titled with a typographically quirky title that seemed to suit the quirkily creative mind of the man who provided the globally generous and effervescent organizing spirit for the some thirty artists in this show. Many, but not all, worked in Miami. The show came with a strong catalog essay by Amy Capellazzo, an early director of the Rubell Family Collection. It was curated by Robert Chambers, who has been pivotal in his own right in the city's maturing art scene. Not only has he been featured in the noteworthy shows of Miami artists at MOCA, MAM, and Miami Art Central, the museum founded here in 2001, but he has been a catalyst by encouraging other artists to exhibit and produce their best work, particularly while he was teaching in the art department at University of Miami. One of his many students, artist Annie Wharton, fondly remembers his "patient" way of working with and nurturing aspiring artists. He's also had a significant networking influence by helping artists to make contact with out of town venues, such as the alternative space Exit Art in New York.

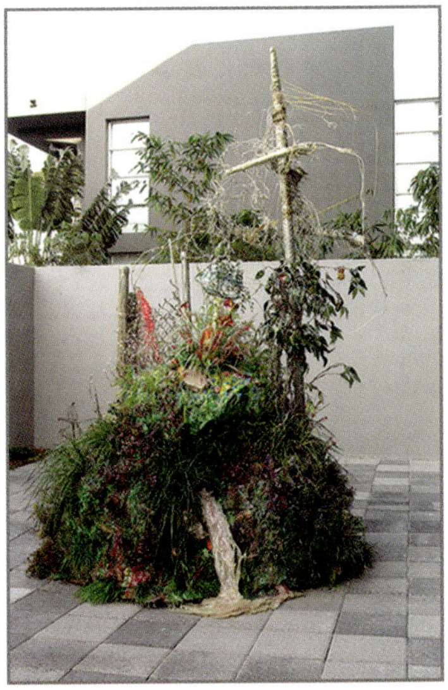

From *"At this time: 10 Miami Artists from the Rubell Family Collection,"* 2005, installation view of Cristina Lei Rodriguez, *Reclaiming Ruins,* 2004, plastic, resin, and selected objects, 72" x 72" X 144".

Reflecting highly memorable moments for an art scene rapidly in flux, these shows do point to a mixed legacy. The Bass has not since mounted a show of the ambition and scope of "globe>miami>island." Some of the featured artists in these shows at MOCA, MAM, and the Bass have since moved to other cities, and new talents are now receiving attention. Especially notable is Teresita Fernández, who grew up here and now works in New York. She won a Macarthur Foundation "Genius Grant" accompanied by a $500,000 award in 2005. Her art was part of MOCA's inaugural exhibition and she has had a solo show at MAM.

In particular, "New Work Miami" at MAM illustrates this mixed legacy. For example, Frank Benson no longer works in Miami, and Consuelo Castañeda seems to have kept a relatively low profile here since her solo show at MAM. MAM curators didn't anticipate the rapidly rising star of Hernan Bas, although Bas's early, grainy drawings in Slimfast were a part of "Making Art in Miami: Travels in Hyperreality" at MOCA. In the MAM series, Chambers, Fisher, Guerrier, Friedman, Novoa, and Thiele have continued to turn out solid work, although they have not enjoyed the same levels of recognition. Both Fisher and Bas have seen their "star power" in the art market rise considerably, and they have both been championed by internationally known Miami collectors Donald and Mera Rubell.

While extremely important to Miami's recent art history, these shows at MOCA and MAM did contain hits and misses. For instance, neither the MAM series nor the MOCA show included photographer Maria Martinez-Cañas. By 2000, her distinctively manipulated, mostly black and white photography was in the permanent collections of the Museum of Modern Art in New York, the Museum of Contemporary Art in Chicago, and the Los Angeles County Museum of Art. The MAM series and the MOCA show also didn't include the collaborative team of artists Rosario Marquardt and Roberto Behar, although Marquardt and Behar have since had a solo show at MAM curated by Cheryl Hartup, and Maria Martinez-Cañas has since been exhibited at both museums.

The three MAM curators just mentioned are not working in the city now. Amy Rosenblum left the museum soon after "New Work Miami" was launched; Cheryl Hartup left in 2005 to become chief curator at the Museo de Arte in Ponce, Puerto Rico; and Lorie Mertes left in 2006 to head the Fabric Workshop and Museum in Philadelphia. Remaining at MAM is senior curator Peter Boswell.

Other curators now having an effect on shaping the kinds of shows that present Miami based artists among the national and internationally known artists are Mark Coetzee, director of the Rubell Family Collection, and Silvia Karman Cubiña, director of the Moore Space.

In 2005, Coetzee showed "At This Time: 10 Miami Artists from the Rubell Family Collection." They were Hernan Bas, José Bedia, Pablo Cano, Cooper, Naomi Fisher, Mark Handforth, Jiae Hwang, Norberto Rodriguez, Cristina Lei Rodriguez, and Purvis Young. Karman Cubiña curated "metro pictures" in 2006 at the Moore Space and at MOCA with Miami artists Adler Guerrier, Susan Lee Chun, Beatriz Monteavaro, and George Sánchez-Calderón. Also in the show was work by Quisqueya Henríquez, who now lives in the Dominican Republic but who had previously lived in Miami and was part of MOCA's inaugural exhibit, "Defining the Nineties."

The Moore Space resulted from an effort in 2001 spearheaded by influential Miami art collector Rosa de la Cruz, who had approached Craig Robins, a Design District developer and collector, about putting together a show that would spotlight Miami artists for the first Art Basel Miami Beach. Although that fair was postponed, the show was still mounted in a space that later became known as The Moore Space, a lively exhibition space for international concerns in contemporary art that has, through initiatives like its guest curator program, helped Miami artists be more in touch with wider circles in the art world.

That first show at the Moore Space was "Humid," curated by Dominic Molon of the Museum of Contemporary Art in Chicago. It brought together twenty-six artists working in Miami, Chicago, London, Los Angeles, New York, and Pittsburgh. Miami artists in that intriguing exhibit included Kevin Arrow, Hernan Bas, Natalia Benedetti, Cooper, William Cordova, John Espinosa, Naomi Fisher, Luis Gispert, Mark Handforth, Jason Hedges, Norberto Rodriguez, and Elizabeth Withstandley.

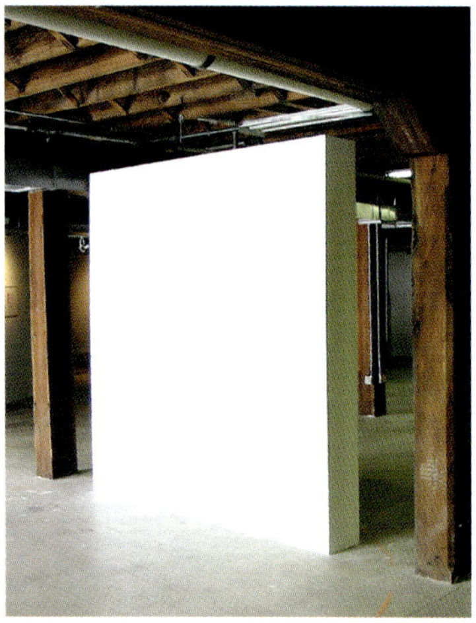

From *"Humid"* at The Moore Space, 2002, installation view, *A wall I built with my Father, wood, drywall, metal, ongoing project of variable dimensions and locations* by Norberto Rodriguez.

In non-profit spaces around town, it's important to note the prescience of shows at the Centre Gallery of the downtown Wolfson Campus for Miami Dade College (formerly called Miami Dade Community College) and the ArtCenter/South Florida in Miami Beach (the renamed South Florida Art Center). The shows were put together by curators Goran Tomcic and Tami Katz-Frieman, who also are no longer in Miami. They made a notable impact while they worked here chiefly in the mid 1990s to around 2000, calling attention to artists who have since enjoyed international recognition. These curators worked outside the more entrenched bureaucracy of museums. Their contributions were important in setting the stage for today's expanding art scene.

In "Currently: Art Focus I, Summer 1999" at the ArtCenter, curators Tomcic and Katz-Frieman put together a show that I described at the time as one that "bristles with urban grit and glamour, fashion and foolishness." It included works in photography and other media by Frank Benson, Luis Campos, Ximena Carrion, Leslie Merry, and Wendy Wischer. That show coincided with "Booty Bass," an exhibit at the Centre gallery curated by Tomcic featuring early photography by Naomi Fisher and installations that imaginatively reinvented blasting car stereos by Luis Gispert. That summer in 1999 offered another show of work by yet another significant artist in town who no longer works here. Complementing these shows was a solo show by that artist, John Espinosa, at Frederic Snitzer Gallery. It's important to note that Gispert, Fisher, and Espinosa have been featured in group shows at MOCA, while Bas had a solo show at MOCA in 2002 and Espinosa had one in 2004.

"I think right now there's a very special moment in the young art scene in Miami," Katz-Frieman told me that summer of 1999. She is now chief curator at the Haifa Museum of Art in Israel. When she made those remarks, she was referring in particular to William Cordova's experimental narrative drawings shown earlier that year at Ambrosino Gallery, and to the work of John Espinosa. "I consider the show we curated [at the ArtCenter] as a continuation of this very special moment....Now, there are young people who are very talented and have a clear, crystallized voice. They're working at a very high level."

Josh Levine, a former Miami based artist who now works in Los Angeles, also did his part to contribute to the percolating activity here in the visual arts. He curated a summer show, "2 x 2" at the ArtCenter and included drawings by William Cordova and Nina Ferre, as well as other work by Annie Wharton, Luis Gispert, and by Levine himself. The show was part of the center's ongoing efforts to highlight homegrown talent. These efforts have been decidedly uneven, and even though curators from prestigious out of town museums have been regularly stopping in Miami for years to visit major private collections and museums, they have rarely made the ArtCenter/South Florida a must see stop.

The current director of the ArtCenter/South Florida, Jeremy Chestler, recognizes that the center has needed to become less set in its ways and attract fresh, new talent in order to remain relevant to the art community here. He says that over time the center had become insular. It had a number of resident artists who were traditional painters, even though younger artists work in more experimental media. Some artists had kept studios in the center for as long as twelve to nineteen years. Now juried artists can have a studio for three years, applying for a second three year term; but six years is the limit. "The quality of the artists-in-residence and the exhibitions are starting to get more people's attention. We are reinventing ourselves and becoming more relevant,' he says. The center is also hosting more seminars, talks, and other events that are professional resources for the art community.

A show timed to coincide with Art Miami in January 2000, and was really planned to set the stage for the galvanizing art event that this art community believed would be The Big One, the much talked about Art Basel Miami Beach likely to debut in December 2001, truly surprised collectors, artists, curators, and other art supporters with the enthusiastic response it generated. This show was "Departing Perspectives." It was loosely curated by dealer

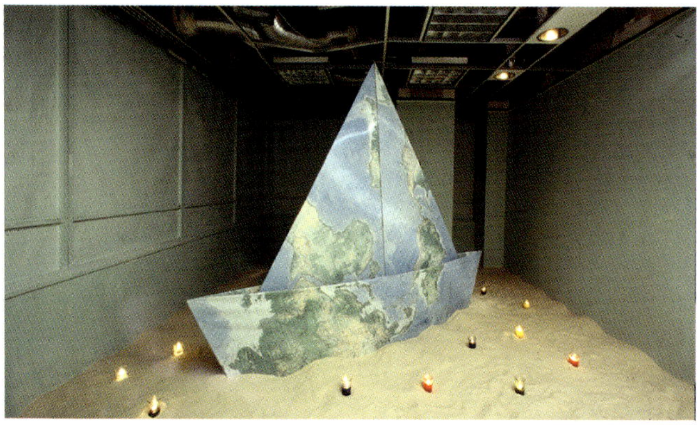

From *"Departing Perspectives,"* 2000, Installation view of *The Dimension of our Hope (detail),* mixed media, variable dimensions by Roberto Behar and Rosario Marquardt.

Frederic Snitzer in a building on Brickell Avenue slated for demolition, the old Espirito Santo Bank Building. "Departing Perspectives" was one of many well attended art exhibits on view around Miami during that week. It coincided with cutting edge exhibits at the Rubell Family Collection, located in the Wynwood warehouse before it was fashionably renovated and expanded in 2004, and with the newly installed contemporary photography collection of collector Martin Z. Margulies, also located in a Wynwood warehouse that's since been expanded.

I called the enthusiastic response for those exhibits of contemporary art "a milestone in the area's coming of age saga." The response "demonstrated a clear desire for innovation in the visual arts and a real hunger for challenging exhibition spaces."

A reported 1,200 visitors showed up for the opening night gala of "Departing Perspectives," which raised funds for the New World School of the Arts, where Snitzer has taught since 1993. In the event's three-day showing, another 1,200 visitors walked through the building. Although these attendance figures are not huge, I recall an unprecedented feeling of electricity in the crowd exploring that transformed building. I remember that Karen Rifas told me then that the spirit of the crowd reminded her of the "high after Christo." She was referring to the sense of community Miami experienced nearly twenty years before, when "Surrounded Islands" by Christo and Jeanne-Claude was completed in Biscayne Bay in May 1983. In eight floors of abandoned office cubicles and hallways, NWSA students exhibited their art alongside more seasoned Miami artists like Karen Rifas and Carol K. Brown, also teachers at NWSA, and Robert Chambers, Maria Martinez-Cañas, Lydia Rubio, Rubén Torres Llorca, and Annie Wharton.

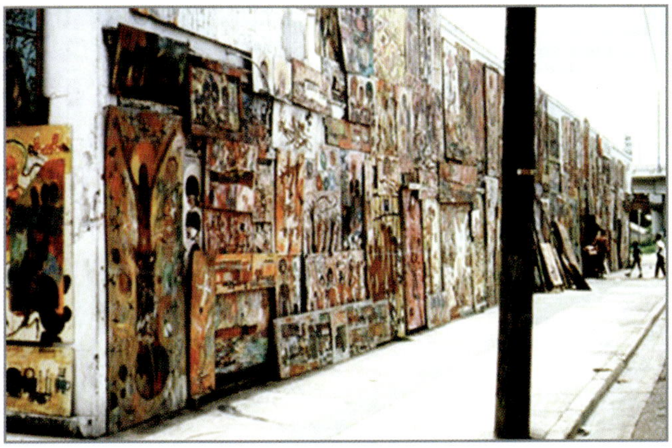

Purvis Young's *Goodbread Alley*, 1972. Overtown, Miami.

On the sleek marble surfaces of this abandoned corporate interior, Purvis Young painted his signature rearing horses. It was startling to see his work in this corporate environment, but of course Young is an artist with special links to Miami's urban growth.

Young is a self taught artist championed for years by Miami Dade Public Library System librarians Margarita Cano and Barbara Young (no relation) after he made astonishing works of impromptu public art in the early 1970s by plastering dozens of painted boards along "Goodbread Alley" in Miami's Overtown. This historic black enclave fell into swift decline when construction for Interstates 95 and 395 destroyed homes and displaced businesses there in the early 1970s. For years Young has been a chronicler of Overtown's fate, obsessively painting weeping Christ figures, pregnant women, rearing horses, and rumbling trucks. As an outsider artist, he was often included in museum and gallery shows beyond Miami, but in 1999 Miami collectors Don and Mera Rubell acquired a studio full of thousands of his paintings, putting his art in the ranks of major cutting edge contemporary artists.

In "Departing Perspectives," there were some forty artists showing works in all kinds of media. Hernan Bas turned in a coy reference to Felix Gonzalez Torres' cascading piles of candy; Bas's piece was made with strawberry flavored Slimfast cascading from a corner. Bhakti Baxter, an artist who went on to be part of the influential alternative exhibition space called "The House," and has since received attention outside Miami, made a striking collaborative installation with light with Jay Hines and Julian Picaza. As I wrote at the time, "Eugenia Vargas also played with local allusions to airy esprit de vivre with her glass enclosed room billowing with constant, mechanically produced bubbles, a spectacle that charmed viewers as they stepped out of a stairwell." Vargas summed up the work then to me in this way: "Bubbles are happy and they also describe Miami, I had a lot of fun with this. It's not about the frenzy of 'We have to make a great piece and see if we sell it." It's about the pure pleasure of making."

By the spring of 2001, art supporters in Miami could see how emerging contemporary artists were doing something that differed significantly from the past. Instead of complaining about how galleries and museums were not showing their works enough or at all, bold minded artists were taking things into their own hands. They were making their own spaces to show their work. These spaces were a far cry from the glamorous spaces like Galerie Emmanuel Perrotin, a Miami offshoot of the Paris gallery that's located in Wynwood today, although most of these adventurous, chiefly artist run spaces were either in a still unfashionable Wynwood or a short drive away.

An early example of this "can do, make do" spirit afoot in Miami's art scene took place in another part of town, considerably south of Wynwood. This was at a space known as Box, first located in the warehouse district near Tropical Park, and then in downtown Miami.

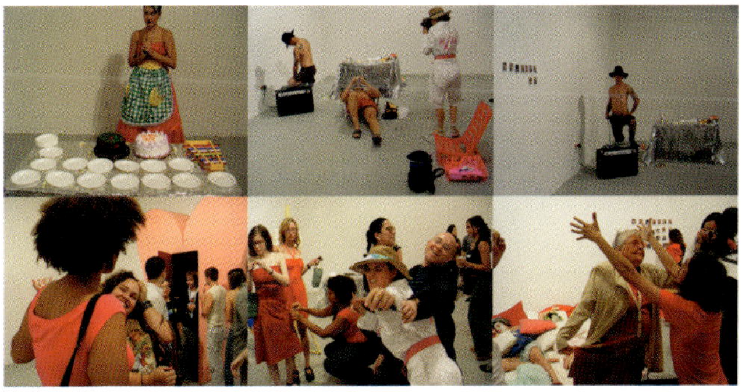

Front and Center, 2003, opening at BOX.

It was founded in 1997 by artists Manny Prieres, Jose Reyes, and Leyden Rodriguez-Casanova, and continued through 2004. It was started, as Rodriguez explained to me, "because of frustration. All three of us were looking for a venue to exhibit in those days and we weren't having any luck." The first show at Box was made up of the founders' own work. He recalls that over time they showed over forty artists, including Hernan Bas, the artists' collaboratives FeCuOp and Friends With You, John Espinosa, Naomi Fisher, Luis Gispert, Jiae Hwang, Gean Moreno, Kyle Trowbridge, Stella Rey, David Rohn, the TM Sisters, and Pedro Vizcaino.

Another example of this innovative spirit took place north of Wynwood, near Miami Shores. These were the "Home Shows" staged by Eugenia Vargas. Beginning in 1999, Vargas intermittently invited fellow artists to take over her one story home. She gave them free rein to convert nearly every room into an impromptu gallery for showing all kinds of work, including sculpture, photography, installation art, video, and painting. It was in her living room that I first saw a colorful mound of used clothing assembled into what seemed to be an indoor volcano by Guerra de la Paz.

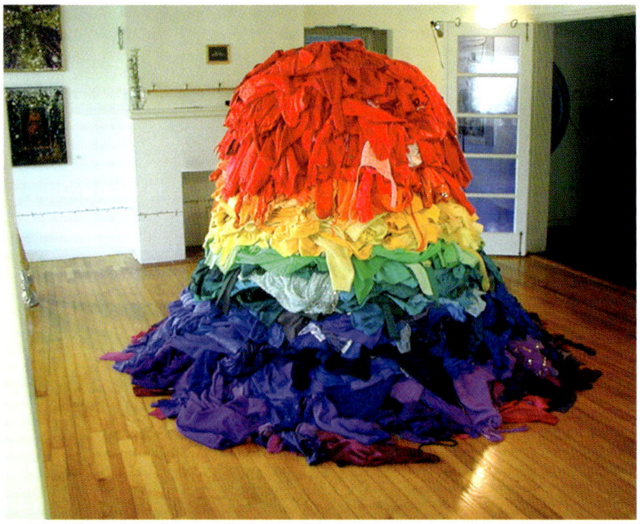

From "*The Home Show,*" 2002, installation view of *Tribute*, recycled garments, variable dimensions by Guerra de la Paz.

"Isn't it beautiful?" I remember her asking me with a swift grin. Other artists who took part in these home Shows" included Westen Charles, Lou Anne Colodny, Denise Delgado, Gean Moreno, and Chuck Ramirez. She recalls that William Cordova curated one of these "Home Shows," and Robert Chambers curated the last one in September 2002, which she kept up until January 2003, making it the one that ran the longest.

Vargas explained to me in 2001 why she did these "Home Shows." Her answer resonates now more than ever at a time when the art market seems especially pervasive and powerful. An opportunity like a "Home Show," she said, "gives artists more independence. People can do whatever they want without pressure. I think it really stimulates young people."

Private collectors Don and Mera Rubell, along with their adult children Jason and Jennifer, were catalysts in the change taking over the city's art community. A vital Wynwood pioneer is their impressive Rubell Family Collection, focused on art from the 1960s to the present, which opened to the public in 1996 in a 45,000 square foot former DEA warehouse for confiscated goods. After it opened, other spaces sprung up in Wynwood in converted warehouses to present edgy, emerging artists, some from Miami and some not. These included Locust Projects, founded on a shoe string budget by artists Westen Charles, Cooper, and Elizabeth Withstandley with much of their own money in 1999; they first rented the space a year earlier. In 2002, Locust Projects formally acquired non profit status, and in 2005 it became one of twelve alternative art spaces around the country to receive a "Warhol Initiative" grant from the Warhol Foundation.

Dorsch Gallery, a commercial space run by Brook Dorsch, first started in a modest walk-up apartment on Coral Way in 1991. It moved to a Wynwood warehouse in 2000, and has played an important role in exhibiting up and coming Miami artists. Diaspora Vibe Gallery, founded in 1996 in rented space at the Bakehouse by Rosie Gordon Wallace, later moved to the Design District and gives artists of Caribbean descent a valuable forum. Edge Zones in Wynwood is an artist-run exhibition space offering artists opportunities to show work and network with out of town curators.

The House, in the nearby Edgewater neighborhood, was particularly important in giving shape to this "Miami miracle." The House was felled by a developer's wrecking ball in 2004. But for the previous four years, it had created novel exhibits in its two-story, white frame house, mixing edgy if uneven work by artists from Miami and other cities with work by the artists who actually lived there, Martin Oppel, Tao Rey, and Bhakti Baxter. Daniel Arsham was another gifted artist who played a strong curatorial role for The House, and Robert Chambers curated a memorable show there. "The camaraderie they've built helped in a great way to create an artists' community here that expands beyond Miami," said Bonnie Clearwater for a story I wrote for the Miami Herald in June 2004. By that time, the artist community here was starting to flourish in the wake of Art Basel Miami Beach. (The House artists' next step was to start a gallery in the Design District, Placemaker.)

When the first Art Basel Miami Beach was postponed, galvanizing effects of this camaraderie and "make do, can do" spirit were clear. Intense disappointment followed the postponement of the first mega art fair in 2001. Although they had planned the fair long before the terrorist strikes on the World Trade Center of September 11, 2001, fair organizers decided that December 2001 was not the time to launch a new art fair. Collectors were leery of flying. Insurance prices for dealers shipping art works skyrocketed. Miami's art community rallied, and went on with most locally planned events. One event planned for that fateful month of December 2001 was greeted with spectacular enthusiasm. This was the wildly innovative "globe>miami>island" at the Bass.

When the first and long awaited Art Basel Miami Beach took place in December 2002, it enjoyed a critical and commercial success that in large measure continues, and the fair capitalizes on the current strong market for contemporary art. The fair sparks more initiatives in the city, which compete for attention in an increasingly hectic week. Private collectors in Miami use the Art Basel Miami Beach week to launch their own exhibits

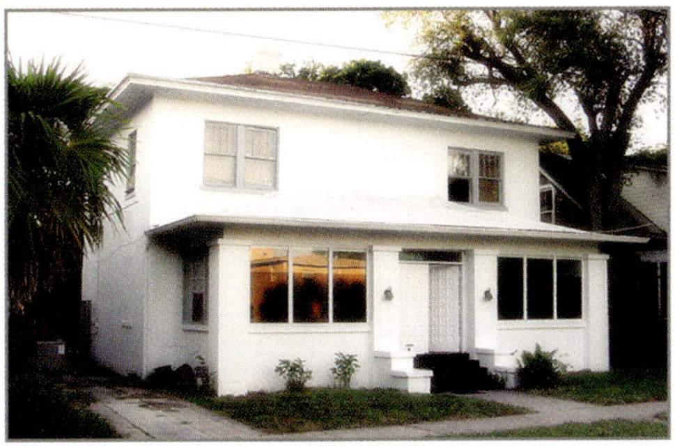

The House, 2000.

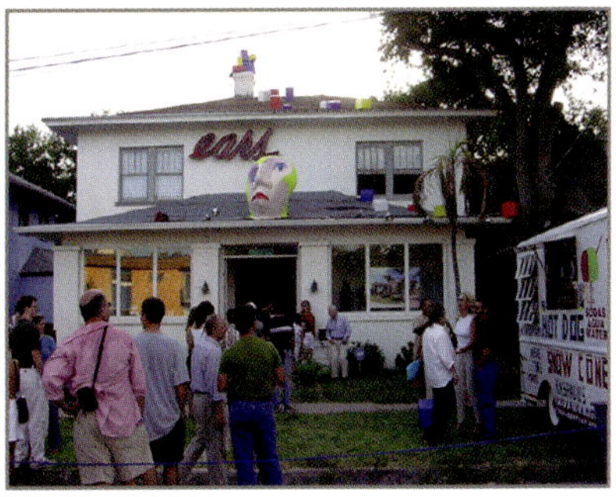

Sears Building at The House, 2001, curated by Robert Chambers.

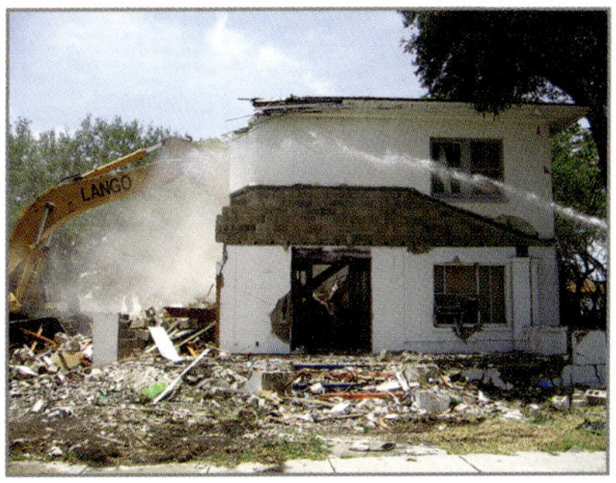

The House Demolition, 2004.

and programs in order to attract international attention, but many of their efforts benefit the art community here throughout the year.

A promising new institution, Miami Art Central (MAC) founded by collector and philanthropist Ella Fontanals Cisneros, opened in December 2003 during the second Art Basel Miami Beach. It opened with a vote of confidence in the Miami art scene. MAC's inaugural show was called "10 Floridians," but nine of the Floridians worked at the time, or had worked, in Miami. The artists in this show were José Bedia, Robert Chambers, Dara Friedman, Jacin Giordano, Luis Gispert, Adler Guerrier, Mark Handforth, Gean Moreno, Glexis Novoa, and Sergio Vega. In an important step to expand networking between the Miami art community and the international art world, well-connected out of town curators were asked to select the artists for this inaugural exhibit. Only one curator for this exhibit was working in Miami at the time. That curator was Paula Harper, the art professor at the University of Miami who has for years been a vital player here in the art community. She chose Robert Chambers.

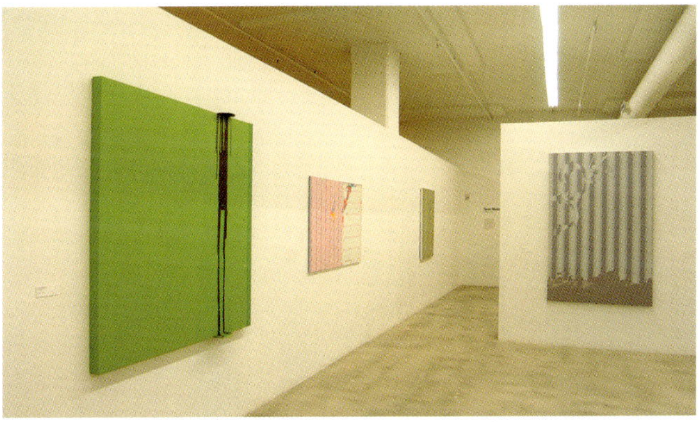

From *"10 Floridians,"* 2003, installation view of paintings by Jacin Giordano. Miami Art Central.

The following year, The House collapsed and another artist run space started up in the Design District in response to its demise. This is the Bas Fisher Invitational, founded by Hernan Bas and Naomi Fisher. "We just wanted to provide space for people to really do absolutely whatever they want, for and by themselves," Fisher explained to me. "We prefer to offer solo shows to artists….it is hard to get a good sense of an artist if you just see an artwork in a group show here and there, and we felt that many people we knew who were interesting artists were only publicly experienced piecemeal." She expresses a belief in the importance of cultivating creativity without art market pressures. Her remarks recall those made by Eugenia Vargas about her Home Shows and the landmark "Departing Perspectives." Says Fisher: "We believe that having the forum for a solo show without the pressure of a commercial debut would allow an artist to blossom." She relates that in the summer of 2005 Bas Fisher Invitational hosted its first group show. This was a collaborative show organized by Bhakti Baxter and Jason Hedges. "Many great dialogues resulted from it," she recalls, adding that Hans Ulrich Obrist saw a video there by the TM Sisters, and chose it for the exhibit "Uncertain States of America."

Two years after MAC opened near the University of Miami, the Cisneros Fontanals Art Foundation (CIFO) opened in downtown, just blocks from where construction continued on the Carnival Center for the Performing Arts. Again CIFO opened during what some now like to call "Basel Week," The building was designed by architect Rene Gonzalez. Walking into CIFO is a bit like walking through a bamboo forest transplanted into the heart of Miami. Visitors are greeted by a beautiful façade of glass Bisazza tiles depicting bamboo thickets. The vibrant green façade can be seen to symbolize how Miami is becoming a breeding ground for culture and the arts. CIFO develops exhibits based on emerging artists from Latin America.

The story of Miami's growing art scene continues as the city's cultural profile rises. The legendary and pioneering choreographer Merce Cunningham, who has worked over the years with visual artists Robert Rauschenberg, Jasper Johns, and others hailed for their own pioneering contributions, premiered a new work at Miami's Carnival Center for the Performing Arts in early 2007. The work involved collaborations with a host of cultural organizations in the city. Specifically, Daniel Arsham, recommended to Cunningham

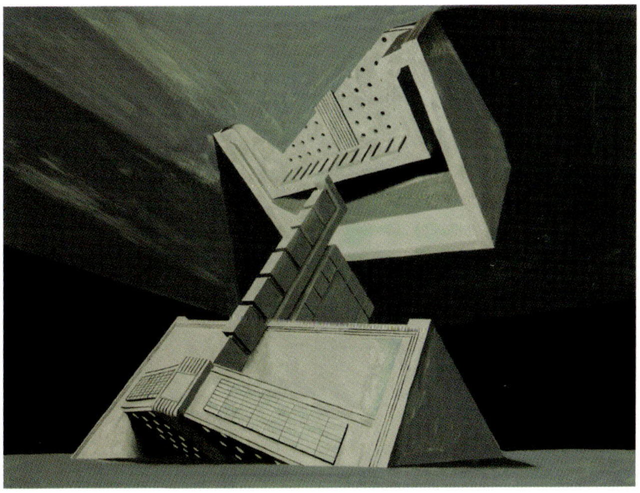

Daniel Arsham, *Downstage Left*, 2007,gouache on mylar, 25" x 33" set design for Merce in Miami at The Carnival Center for Performing Arts. Courtesy of Galerie Emmanuel Perrotin, Paris/Miami.

by Bonnie Clearwater, collaborated with the choreographer in the creation of sets and costumes. Cunningham also worked with composer David Behrman. In 2007, MOCA presented an exhibition of Cunningham's collaborations with visual artists, including Arsham of course, from 1998 to the present, to coincide with the performance. MAM is planning a new building within walking distance of the Carnival Center for the Performing Arts. When Suzanne Delehanty stepped down as MAM director at the end of 2005, the museum chose Terence Riley to be the new director. He came to MAM from the Museum of Modern Art in New York, where he was chief curator for architecture and design. An architect himself, he began this position in March of 2006. His job will be to steer MAM into the next stage, expanding the private collection and giving it an appropriate home in a new building.

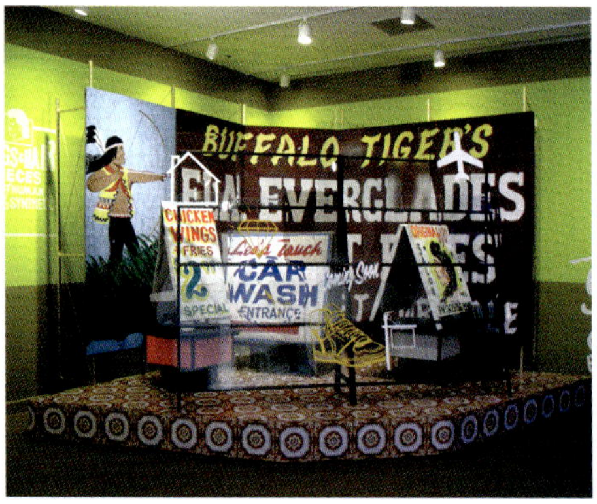

From *"Miami in Transition," Development Opportunity For Sale,* 2006, mixed media installation, variable dimensions, by Michael Loveland. Commissioned by the Miami Art Museum.

In the first follow up to its "New Works Miami" shows, MAM presented a provocative group show that is directly inspired by Miami's current building boom, with the transformation of downtown and the gentrification of surrounding neighborhoods. Luxury condos proliferate and affordable housing becomes harder than ever to find. The show was mounted in the spring of 2006, and was called, aptly enough, "Miami in Transition." It was curated by Lorie Mertes and curatorial research assistant René Morales, and came with a brochure featuring an important essay by Morales. The range of work and artists in the show touched on many aspects of Miami's recent and accelerating art scene. Artists in this show were Daniel Arsham, Natalia Benedetti, Vicenta Casañ, Xavier Cortada, Patricio Cuello, Andres Ferrandis, Mark Handforth, William Keddell, Leila A. Leder Kremer, Nicolas D. Lobo, Michael Loveland, Glexis Novoa, Martin Oppel, Placemaker, Tao Rey, Leyden Rodriguez-Casanova, George Sánchez-Calderón, Tina Spiro, Ivan Toth Depeña, Thomas Brian Virgin, and Purvis Young.

Just because art is made in Miami does not guarantee that it's worth looking at more than once. But a number of strong works being created here do make intriguing statements about current strands of multi-faceted contemporary art and culture. These works do that in a significant range of media.

There's a lot of talk now about whether the city's art community is witnessing a "Miami style," and what such a hard to define phenomenon would look like. I think back to a story written during the Basel Week of 2005 by my Miami Herald colleagues Enrique Fernandez and Fabiola Santiago.

Once so much art made here seemed preoccupied with exiles' experience of a lost homeland in Cuba or in other Caribbean and Latin American countries suffering tumultuous politics. Miami, as a city of immigrants, has become an adopted home for so many artists who've migrated here permanently or for extended stays. Like so many things about the community here, this conversation is changing. In the November 30, 2005 Miami Herald story I just mentioned, dealer Fred Snitzer speaks of today's Miami generation. Such a term is years removed from the "Miami Generation" identified in 1983 by the Cuban Museum of Arts and Culture exhibit, with a show by nine Cuban-American artists reviewed by the previous Herald art critic Helen L. Kohen.

Many of the current Miami generation of up and coming artists attended New World School of the Arts. Snitzer points out that these artists grew up in times molded by effects of the Mariel Boatlift of 1980, the memory of Biscayne Islands shimmering in pink plastic in Christo and Jeanne-Claude's "Surrounded Islands" of 1983, the chaos of Hurricane Andrew of 1992, and the emigration crisis over Elian Gonzalez of 1999 and 2000. These artists also grew up seeing shows and installations by José Bedia. Bedia is known for his riveting and utterly distinctive way of mixing ordinary objects with painting, drawing, and elements of Afro-Cuban ritual.

Other elements making up today's Miami style, look, or generation: To suggest what a place is like where the sun and fun are inextricably mixed with grimmer realities, Cooper is quoted as having coined the term "sunshine noir" in jest. Influential private collectors here have spurred interest in contemporary art. Artist and Frost Museum curator Elizabeth Cerejido notes the rise of artist-run spaces in recent years. This "can do, make do" spirit, as I have called it, has further contributed to the new levels of creativity we are witnessing. But to confine those new levels of creativity into one label? So far, I don't know anyone who has come up with a lasting label. As Elizabeth Cerejido says at the end of the Miami Herald story, "This city is up for grabs." The city is still defining and re-inventing itself, and artists here contribute to that essential, evolving process.

August 2006, Miami

Elisa Turner

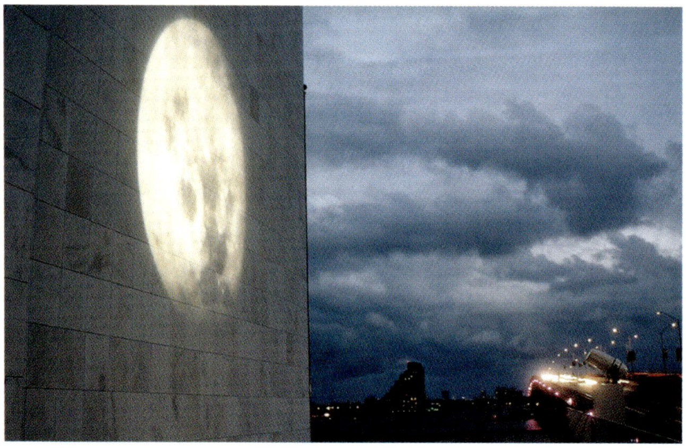

Full to Wailing and Back Again, 2002/2004, outdoor installation, projected light using a source four light and gobo pattern, approx 26' diameter, by Wendy Wischer.

ARTISTS

KEVIN ARROW

My work as a visual artist fuses various elements: humor, the sacred, found objects, and obsolete media. This reflects a personal quest, whereby I continually seek the sublime within the mundane experience, and the mundane within the sublime, in addition to investigating the interchangeability of both. This interchangeability of the mundane and the sublime is encapsulated in the Buddhist story of the "dog tooth relic." This story tells of a young man who goes on a religious pilgrimage, promising to return with a relic of the Buddha for his elderly and very devout mother. However, he forgets until just before he arrives home. Realizing he cannot return empty handed, he pulls a tooth from a dead dog on the roadside, cleans and wraps it carefully, and presents it to his mother as a precious relic of the Buddha. Delighted and believing it to be genuine, the old woman prays devoutly to the dog tooth until she attains enlightenment. The moral of the story? The viewer confers value on an artifact, not vice-versa. Perceiving an object as sacred is a blessing in itself. In many ways, my drawings, paintings, and projected work are a very personal attempt to extend the life of otherwise ephemeral experiences, a way of marking time and illustrating its existence, always reminding us of the fleeting passage of time.

Being an artist in Miami continues to be a rewarding experiences for me. I have specifically enjoyed watching and participating as Miami's art community has developed and matured over the past twenty-five years. I've witnessed the emergence, growth, and sometimes the passing, of many great artists, galleries, scenes, neighborhoods, districts, collectors, critics, and institutions. In Miami, I have been able to live and create with relative ease. Through my position as Registrar at the Museum of Contemporary Art in North Miami I have been fortunate enough to meet many of the world's greatest living artists, and be in the presence of their art for months at a time. Prior to this, the generosity of a local arts patron enabled me to run an independent photographic exhibition space and Art Center on Española Way in Miami Beach for six years. The benefits of these experiences can not be put into words. Everything in Miami is built upon constantly shifting sand. Depending on your outlook, this suggests instability or a sense of boundless opportunity. For me, things seem possible here which might seem impossible in the granite and concrete worlds of Chicago, New York, Los Angeles, or the great, historic European cities. Perhaps this is why the past decade has seen ever greater numbers of people from these once distant places flocking to Miami, as they finally turn toward the light that makes this city so magical.

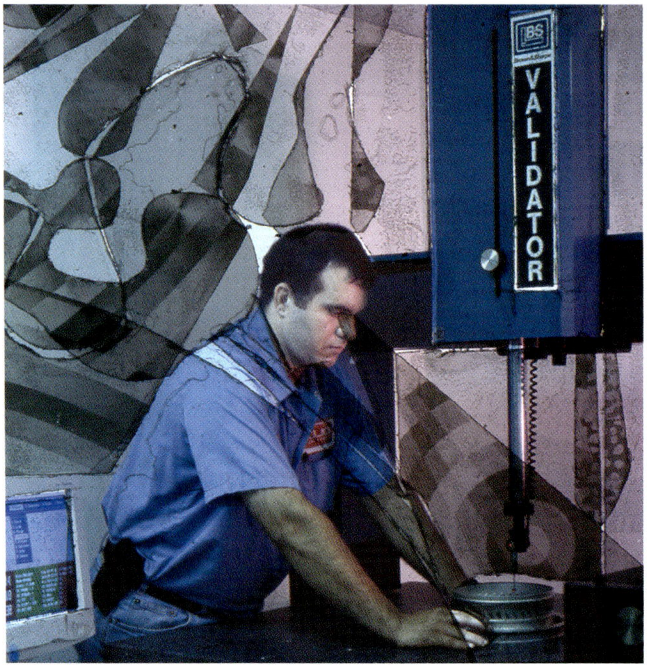

Untitled (Validator), 2005. Polarized transparency [projection],Variable dimensions. *Collection of the artist.*

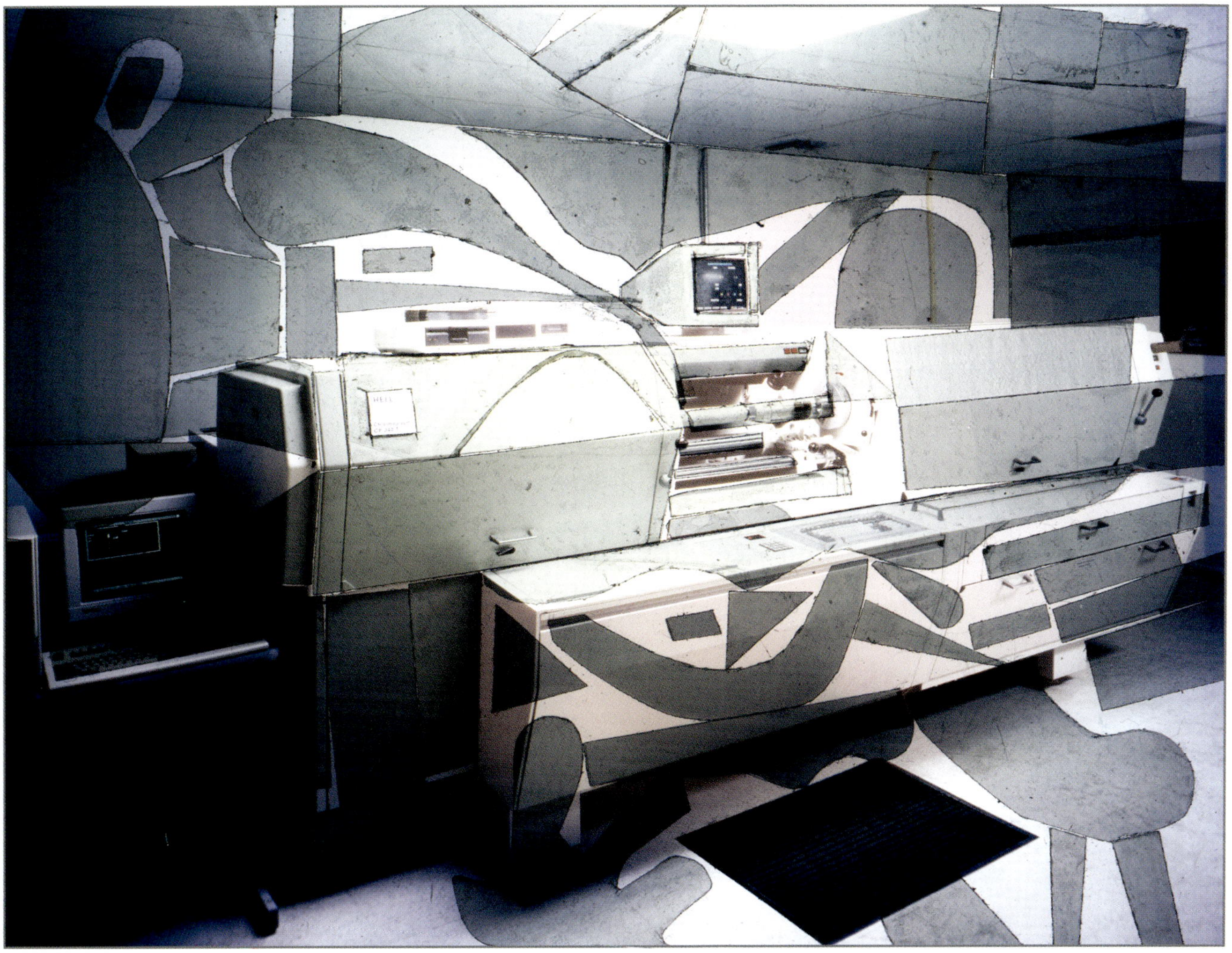

Untitled (Hell), 2005. Polarized transparency [projection], variable dimensions. *Collection of the Museum of Contemporary Art, North Miami*

DANIEL **ARSHAM**

Diane Dispar: *How would you characterize work that is being made in Miami right now, and do you feel as if the city has had an impact on your work?*

Daniel Arsham: I think that this city is in a period of drastic change, the kind of change that happens only 30 or 40 years in a city of this size. There are so many high rise buildings being put up and so much other construction going on that from certain vantage points, the entire city looks like a construction site with a forest of cranes moving about. I have lived in many different places in this country, some urban and others more rural, and the spectacle of construction here is greater that I have seen anywhere. I think its greatest impact on me is that it causes me to notice things about the landscape that were not necessarily apparent before. It can make areas that were once completely familiar to me, completely foreign. I used to live in a house that was demolished to make way for a large condo project. There were things about that block that you would know about only if you lived there. Small inconsequential marks in the pavement become landmarks of some event, and more than anything it showed me that my memory of that place is so bound up in the way that it was put together, I mean the physical nature of the house, its proximity to the next building, and all of the strange architectural anomalies that happened inside. There is also a kind of architectural chance that happens in a block populated by multiple structures that is often lost in complete urban planning. I don't know, these things affect you.

DD: *You mention there were architectural anomalies. What do you mean by that?*

DA: The house I lived in was supposedly built by the DuPont family. They owned a larger house on the corner and in 1930 they built the house I lived in for their daughter. It was a typical Miami Bungalow type house, nothing extraordinary, but pleasant. The front of the house was completely symmetrical. In 1999, a few friends of mine rented the house with the intention of converting it into an exhibition space. They tore down a few walls and added others in order to create a more refined space. In doing so they covered up portions of the exterior architecture, things like the fireplace, windows, closets, electrical outlets etc. In many places you could see the remnants of the previous physical space, emerging from a wall, or making a room appear smaller than it felt like it should have been, but in others those remnants were invisible. There were all kinds of interruptions like this. I love that kind of thing. The sort of impromptu alteration of space, and the remnants that it leaves.

DD: *When we were in New Mexico you described the forms that were in your most recent work as being in a space between building and ruin, hinting at a larger structure that is either under construction or that has been lost. It occurs to me now that Miami is somewhat like that.*

DA: I don't think that is just this city, but you are right that there are places here that have these kinds of ambiguous structures. Some of them have obvious purposes, either already executed or for the future. One thing that happens here with all the construction is that you have a building under construction, and right next to that you have a building being demolished. You can have this kind of moment where the two are the same, indistinguishable from one another. That space exists in the drawings, but for me they are this kind of study of built forms, nothing too complicated but starting with a simple block and evolving into more complex structures that can be used, structures that have some type of physical relationship with a person. The drawings were also looking at the relationship between an organized group of forms that could be used, like a staircase for instance, and built forms that don't appear to have any organization, like a pile of blocks.

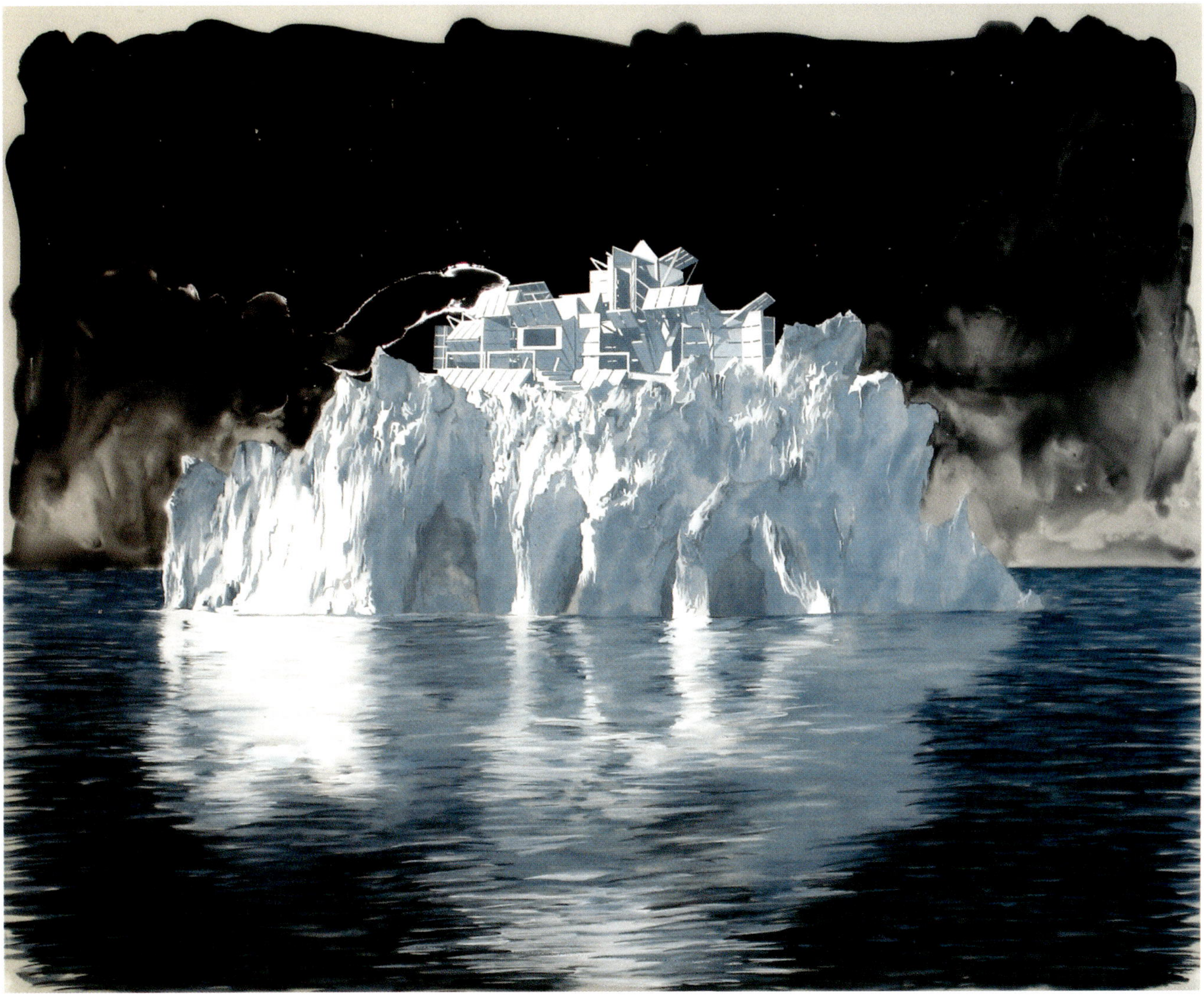

The M House got lost and found itself floating on the sea affecting salination levels in the North Atlantic, 2004. Gouache on Mylar, 24" x 36".

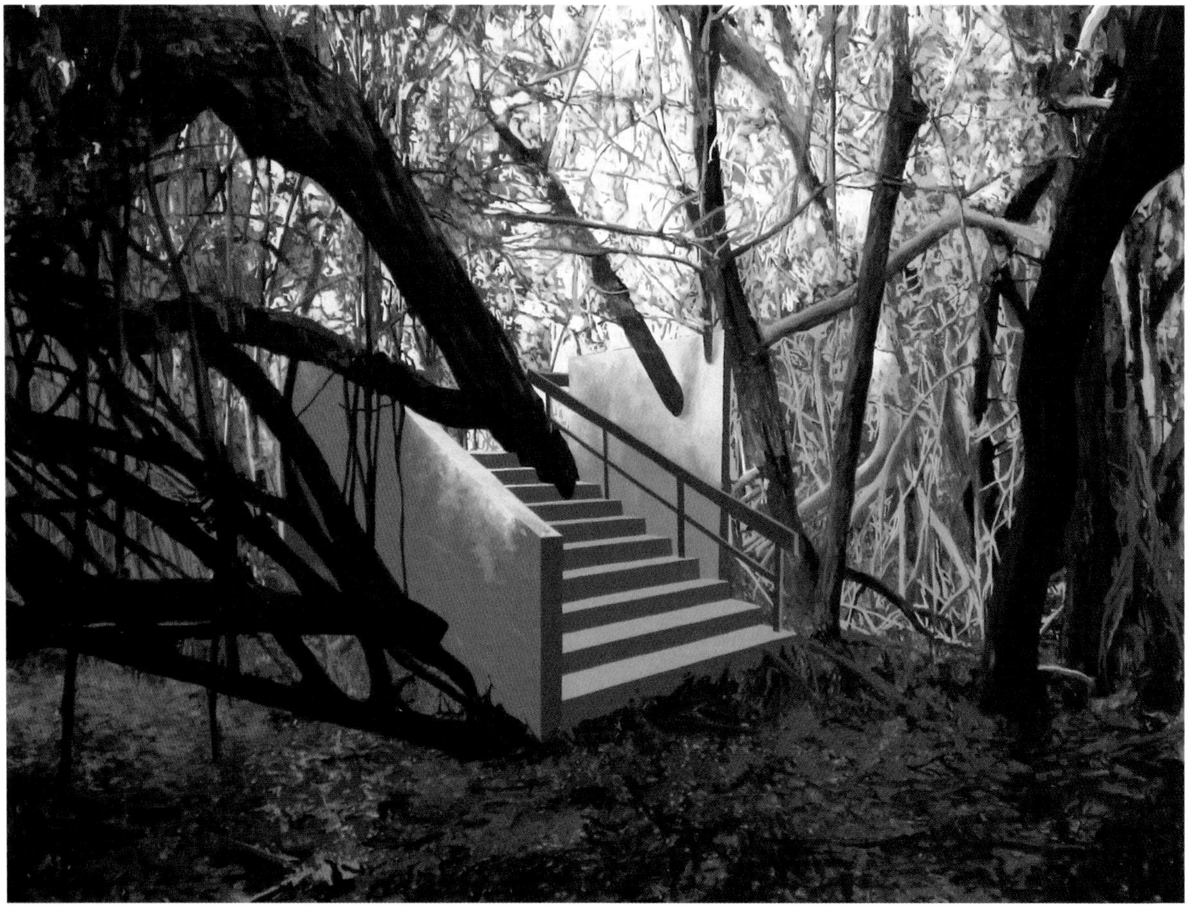

The Return #1, 2005. Gouache on Mylar, 30″ x 40″.

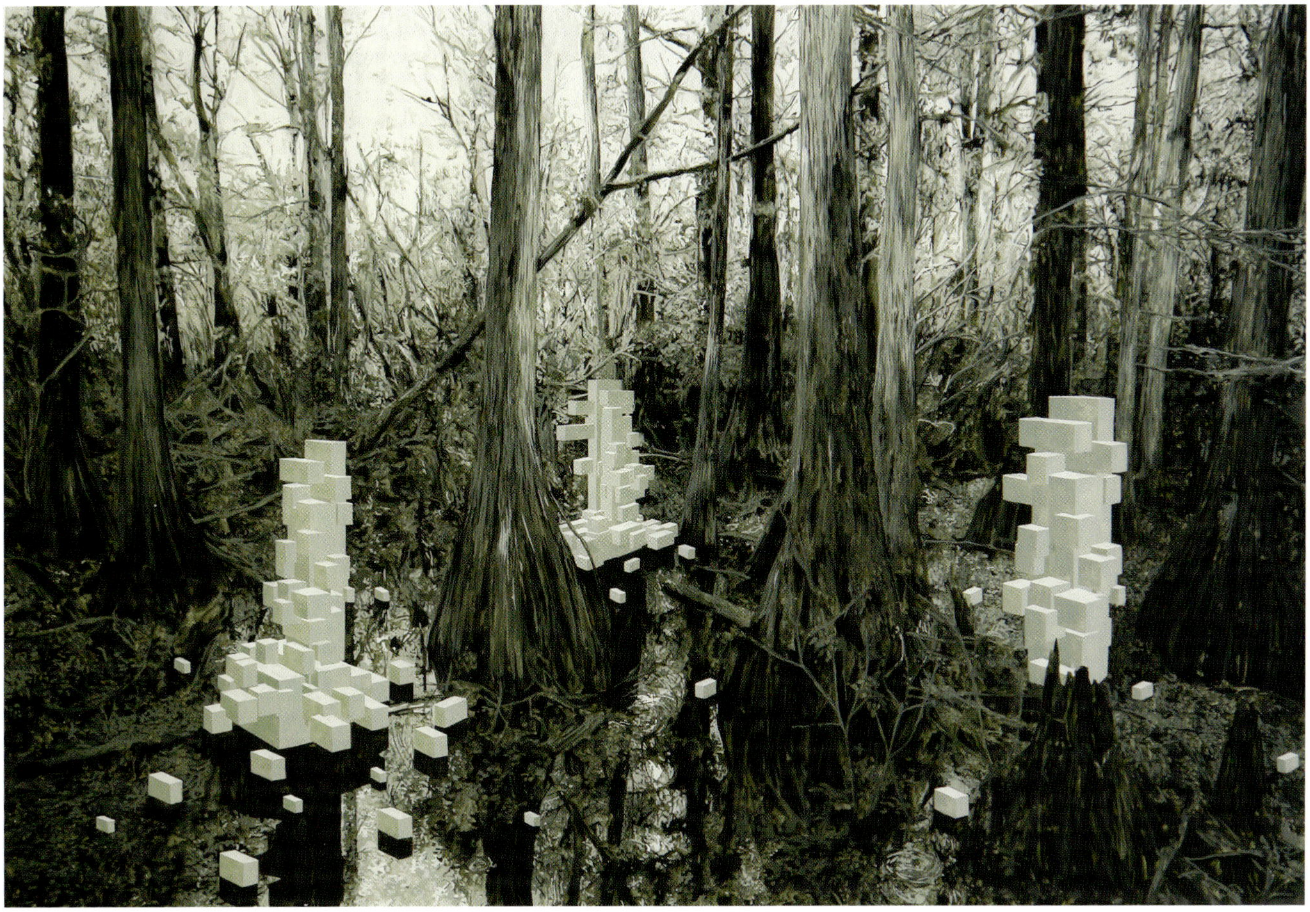

Cypress, 2006. Gouache on Mylar, 40" x 60".

ASANDRA

I want my art to touch the soul. Although we live in an age where art trends lean towards the politics of our time, I choose instead to reflect on the timeless, soul-inspired reality. My personal inspiration as an artist is sourced in all cultures and epochs with the evocation of spirit the desired aim. Representational and abstract symbols: stamped, drawn, or collaged, coexist with balanced design elements to create an overall visual harmony. Bold geometries suggest an archetypal language spoken in unseen dimensions. To interpret the symbols, one must use cognitive powers based on intuition rather than analysis or logic. As art is considered to be subjective, so too is the capacity to translate a symbolic meaning such as that experienced in dreams. In other words, we innately understand its meaning without having to be literal. The intention of the work is to suggest an expanded realm wherein our consciousness not only already dwells, but also innately comprehends. Each painting can be experienced for both its surface beauty, as well as being a visual meditation reflecting larger, abstract realities.

Arriving in Florida from the gray toned metropolis of New York, I was immediately struck by the abundance of brilliant sunshine. Light is an artist's collaborator. It determines the saturation and intensity of how one paints. The thing I had avoided most as an artist, color, became my muse. For the first time I dared to venture into the usage of bright, primary hues in my paintings. It had never been my oeuvre to use color so boldly and yet I began to fall in love with the process as I imagine Matisse had. In my recent rediscovery of the nuances of a gray palette, I have come full circle, returning to its subtle beauty. And yet I take with me what I have learned as a colorist inspired by the bright Miami sun.

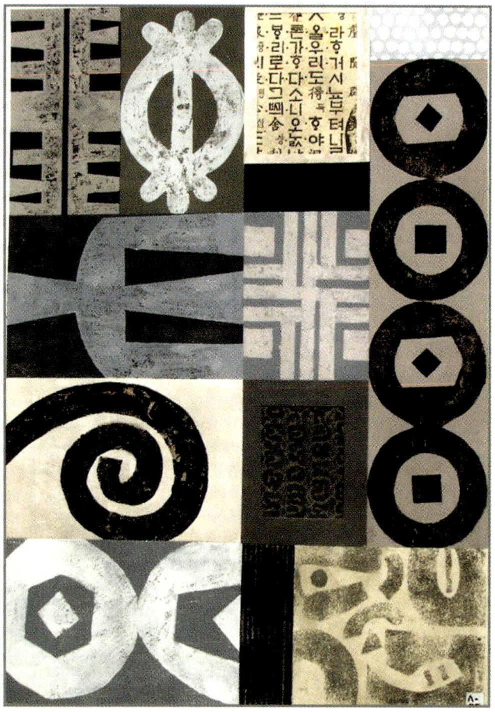

The Forgotten Language XIII, 2005. Mixed media on paper, 18.5" x 26".

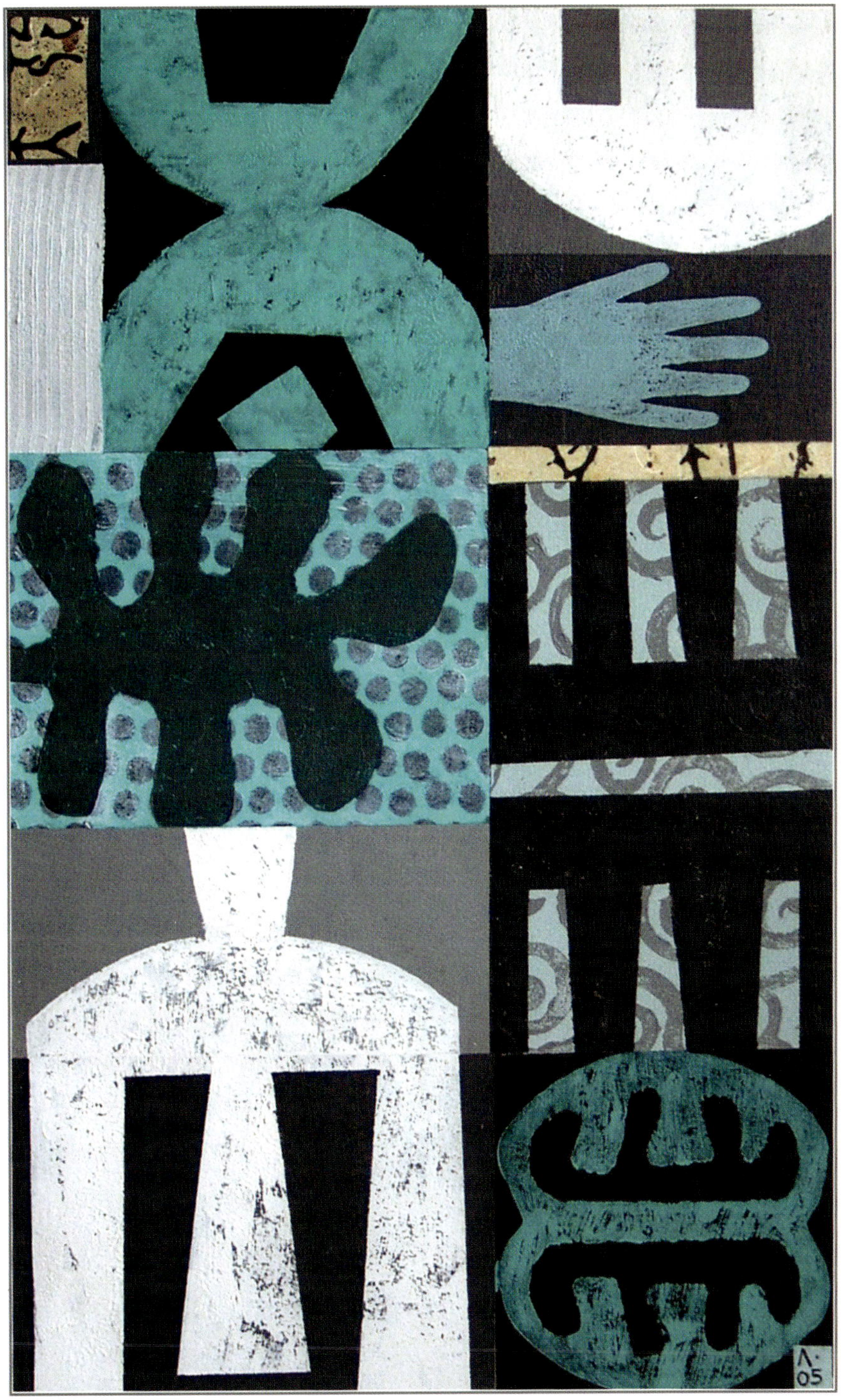

The Forgotten Language IX, 2005. Mixed media on paper, 11.5" x 19".

JOHN BAILLY

"Most information has long stopped being useful to us."
Neil Postman

The work I have developed over the past six years stems from my growing suspicion of the legitimacy of information and systems. The very idea of understanding the nature of objects or events has become impossible for me. Rather, everything has become random. There seems to be no order to events, nor is anything more than it is. This perspective has resulted in a departure from my previous paintings, and in many ways contradicts them. No tradition remains dominant, and the "truth" is no longer my premise. Although this allows everything to be an inspiration, it also entails the abandonment of any conceptual structure. While this is liberating, it also presents new difficulties. A shift towards a more investigative approach has broadened the subject of my work. Using methods inspired by Dada poets, I aim to abandon control of form. I draw symbols randomly and reconstruct them by chance, as Tzara did with phrases. For example, in *Metropolitan Transit*, the background consists of approximately 250 heads. In front of these sits a contour portrait of Paul Robeson, with representations of the Roman Coliseum behind him. The whole is then intermingled with colored lines that represent a map of the NYC subway system. The assimilation of new methods and subjects are integral to my work, as I attempt to reflect the abundance of information we process and explore its legitimacy. Ultimately, the data determines the composition and becomes an end in itself.

Miami is one of the few places I feel both at home and abroad. As an artist whose work focuses on juxtapositions of unrelated data, Miami is perfect for me. This city is random, chaotic, and beautiful. I feel part of Miami, yet everyday I see something I have never seen before. I was born in Slough, UK in 1968 of a French father and American mother. I was raised in Slough, Long Island, Paris, Aix-les-Bains, Epersy, Lyon, and finally Miami. My wife is Cuban. Her ancestors include Spanish, Norwegians, and Chinese. Our three children are French, Chinese, Irish, Savoyard, Norwegian, English, German, Cuban, Spanish, American native Miamians. Culture feeds art, and Miami has an abundance of subcultures that influence Miami's art. The diversity of Little Haiti, Sweetwater, Bal Harbor, Little Havana, Goulds, etc transforms itself into a diversity of form. This is particularly true for me, as my work involves contrasts: naturalism to abstraction, glazes and painterly sections; figures rendered loosely, others in proportion; achromatic, monochromatic, and extensive palettes. For example, in *Ocean Currents*, I first painted and scraped off several figures. I then transferred a map of Rhodes in contour, painted the periodic table in opaque colors, glazed on a trans-Atlantic trade map, and finally painted ocean currents in abstract arrows. Robert Farris Thompson described Miami as "the hippest city in the U.S. you guys are the future." In this sense, Miami hints at a homogeneous world undergoing a creolization. I can think of no other place I would rather paint.

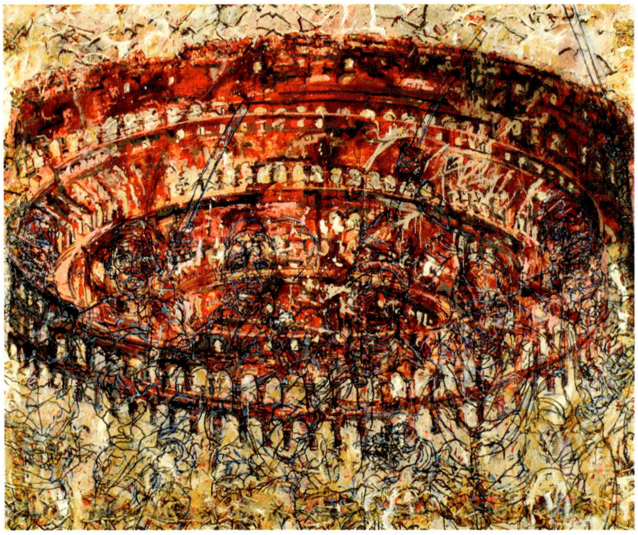

Umkhonto we sizwe, 2003. oil on canvas, 80" x 100".

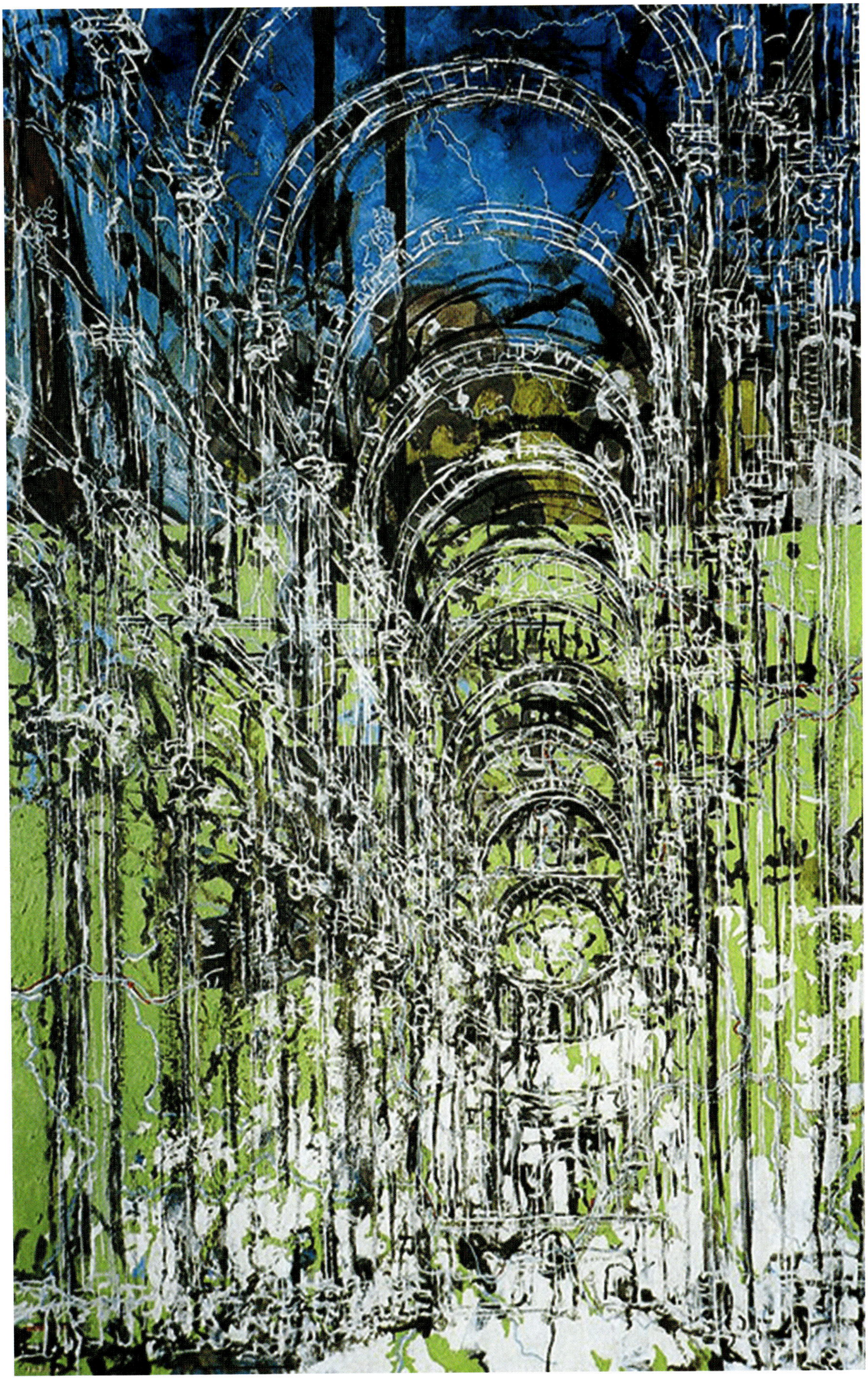

Lewis and Clark, 2005. Oil on canvas, 55.5″ x 36″.

HERNAN **BAS**

Hernan Bas is a New World School of the Arts graduate who has achieved a level of international success that has eluded many seasoned artists. Painting and drawing narratives which include young slender boys, he has created bodies of work that speak of sentimental longings and paradoxical identity concerns. Almost overnight, Hernan's work captured the attention of some of the most prestigious gallery and museum directors. In 2004, he exhibited an impressive collection of drawings at the Victoria Miro Gallery in London and at the 2004 Biennial at New York's Whitney Museum of American Art. Among his exhibition credits are *First Comes the Blood, Then Comes the Boys*, Fredric Snitzer Gallery, Miami, FL; *Love in Vein*, Sandroni Rey, Venice, CA; *It's Super Natural*, Museum of Contemporary Art, North Miami, Fl; *Young Miami*, Wooster Projects, New York, NY; *TRANScontinENtal*, Galerie, Montreal, Quebec; *Superfantastic 7*, The Dirt Room, Kansas City, Ohio; Frank: an adj. Connoting....Superfantastic, Baltimore, Maryland; *Making Art in Miami: Travels in Hyperreality*, Museum of Contemporary Art, Miami, FL; *Friends and Family*, Lombard-Fried Fine Arts, New York, NY; and *Herman's Merit and the Nouveau Sissies*, Fredric Snitzer Gallery, Miami, FL. During Art Basel, Miami Beach, 2003, Hernan's gallery dealer, Fredric Snitzer sold out all of his drawings and paintings to highly respected international collectors. His work is in the prestigious collections of Donald and Mera Rubell and Rosa and Carlos de la Cruz. He currently lives and works in his studio in the Design District in Miami.

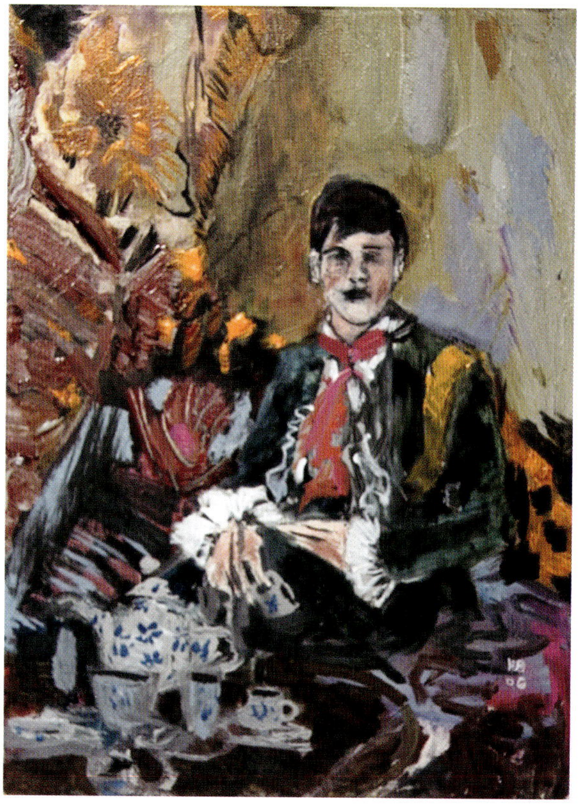

Untitled 2, 2006. Oil on canvas, 12′ x 9″.

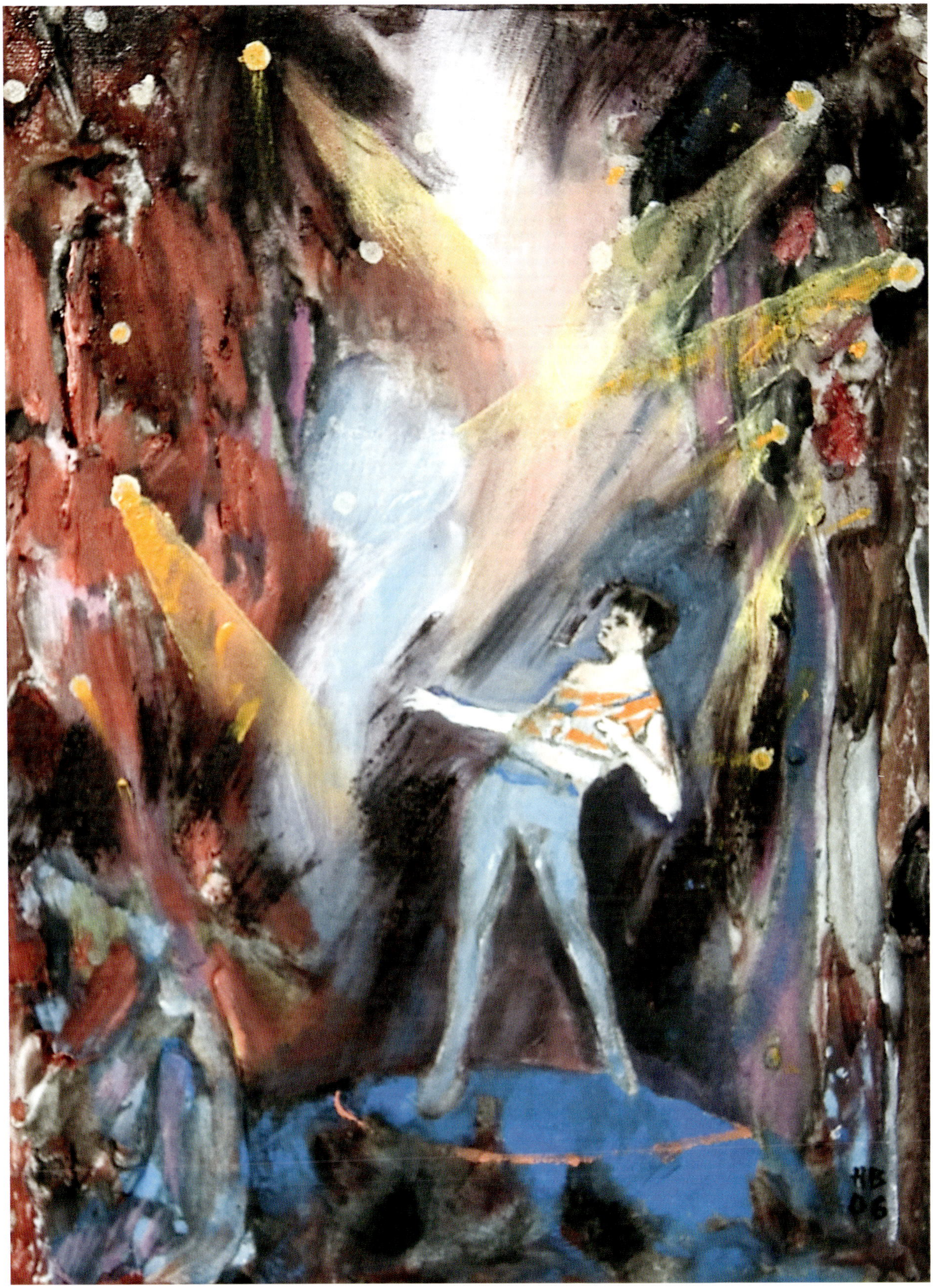

Untitled 3, 2006. Oil on canvas, 12" x 9".

BHAKTI BAXTER

For many years I have been making work that seeks to echo the divinity, or infinity, found in nature. Observing nature, one becomes amazed at what appears to be a series of systems working in unison without division on multiple levels of our universe; Spirals, spheres, branches, waves, and grids are all precise design paths for life to flourish, innumerable in variety, in constant flux with each other, always. Throughout time, people have taken these patterns and built entire civilizations with them; from the symbols they appropriated to the stones that were laid, all things were given an order and the more that order agreed with nature, the better it worked. There were those who used them for political power, but others crafted some of the world's greatest treasures out of these geometric forms for the sake of uplifting the soul. Among them are places of worship and intricate mandalas, gardens and fountains arranged for a spiritual purpose. Regardless of the origin, they all tend to embrace proximity and proportions to send you to the stars, smells and sound that open new doors of experience, and above all a play of light within spaces so sublime they have the ability to house heaven itself. To this day these works of art dispersed throughout the world transport mankind into other dimensions over and over again. These marvelous works of art, along with nature, inspire what I do within a contemporary mind frame. The work is driven by the human need to understand oneself and in turn the universe of which we are a part.

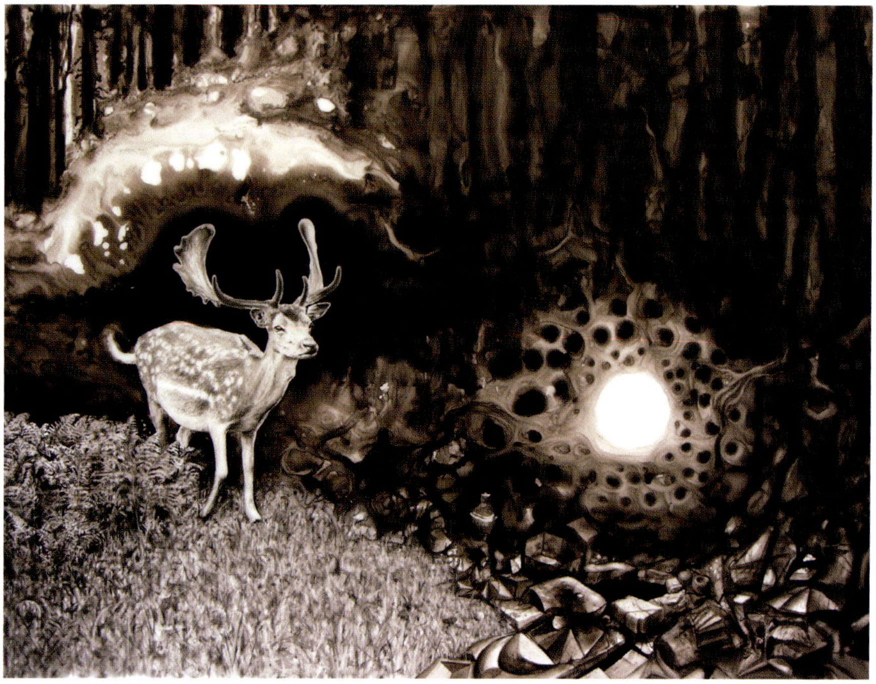

Deersphere, 2005. India ink on mylar, 36" x 28".

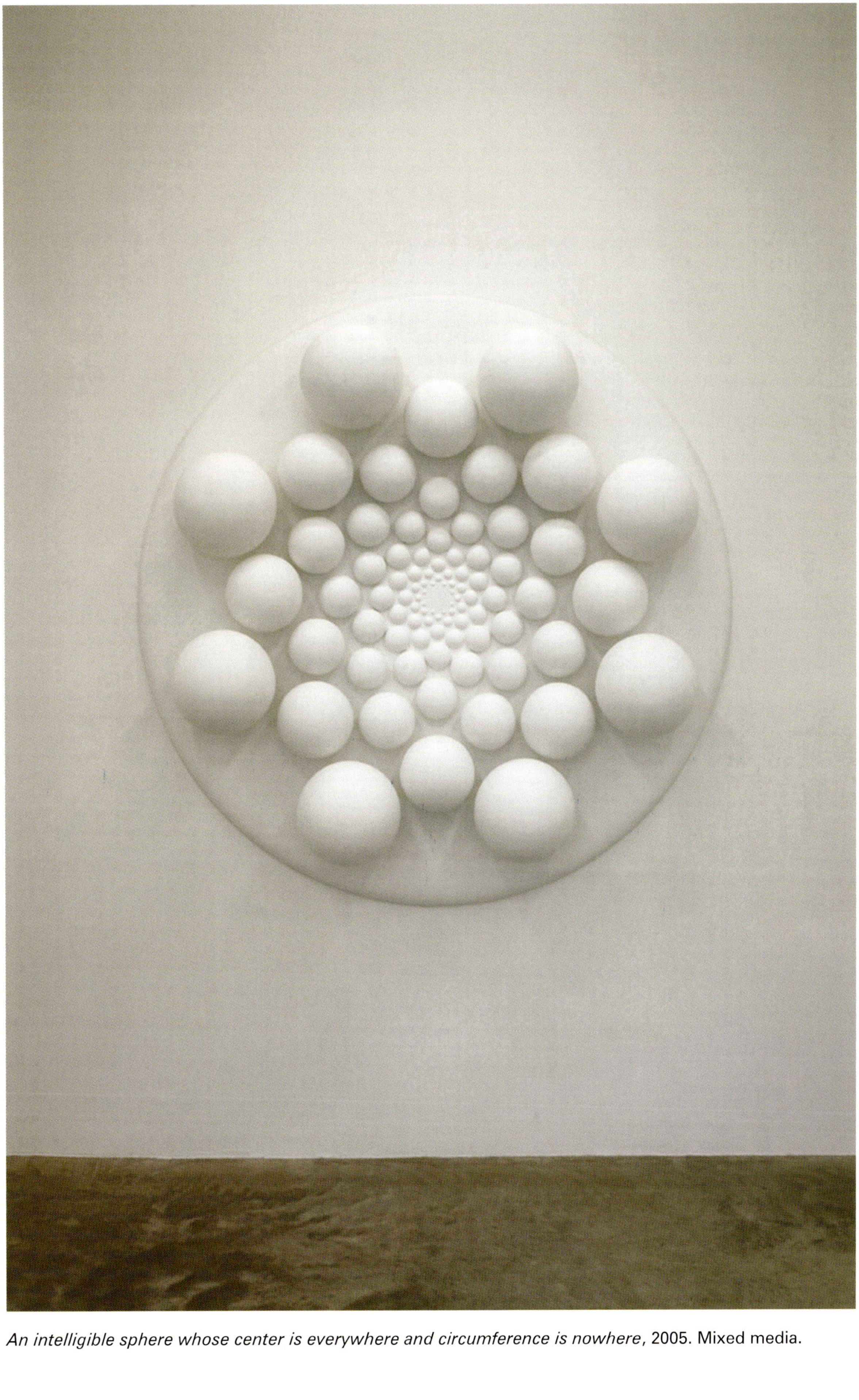

An intelligible sphere whose center is everywhere and circumference is nowhere, 2005. Mixed media.

JOSÉ BEDIA

José Bedia's work brings together the sociological and cultural observations he has made throughout his travels in life and books. His paintings have roots in native arts' production and in the Afro-Cuban religion Santería. The themes of his work apply to the relationships between the First and Third World. He shows in his work where the modern and technological first world collides with the spiritual and primitive third world. Ships and machines embody first world cultures – cold, empirical, and smoky – while beasts, tricksters, and active spirituality are signs of the third world. In Bedia's work both sides have incredible power and terrible flaws. The moments Bedia conveys are points of contact which have no easy explanation.

José Bedia was born in Havana, Cuba in 1959 and immigrated to Mexico in 1991. From Mexico, he immigrated to the United States in 1993. Bedia currently lives and works in Miami, FL. Bedia's works are in the permanent collections of the Tate Modern, London; the Museum of Modern Art, New York; Whitney Museum of American Art, New York' the Museum of Contemporary Art, Los Angeles; MARCO (Museo de Arte Contemporanéo), Monterrey, México; the Hirshorn Museum and Sculpture Garden, Washington, DC; the Museum of Contemporary Art, San Diego, CA; and the Philadelphia Museum of Art, among others. He is the recipient of numerous awards, including the Cintas Foundation Fellowship and the Guggenheim Memorial Foundation Grant.

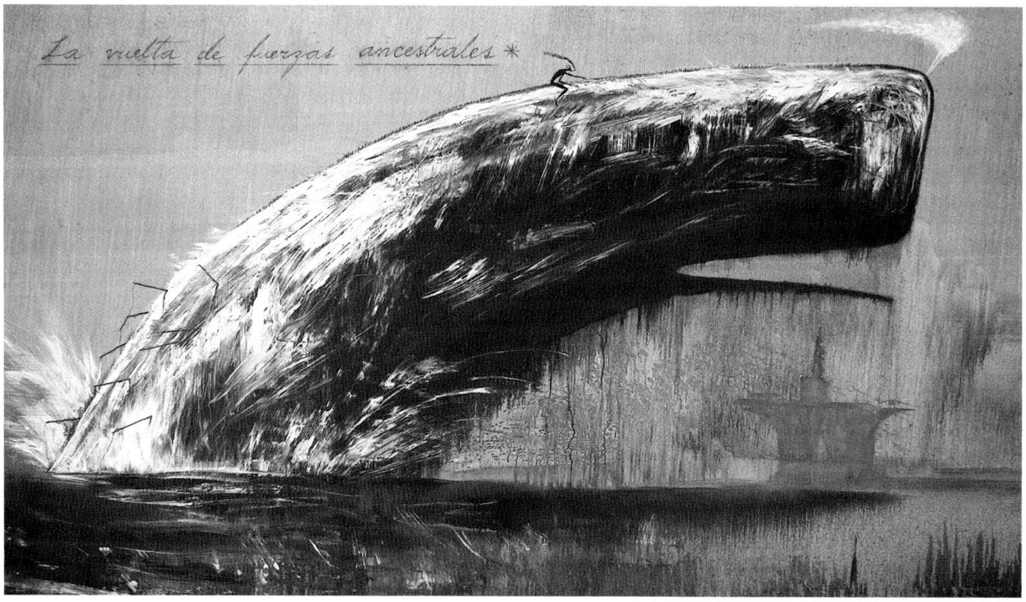

La vuelta de fuerzas ancestrales (The return of ancestral forces), 2006. acrylic on canvas, 71" x 121".

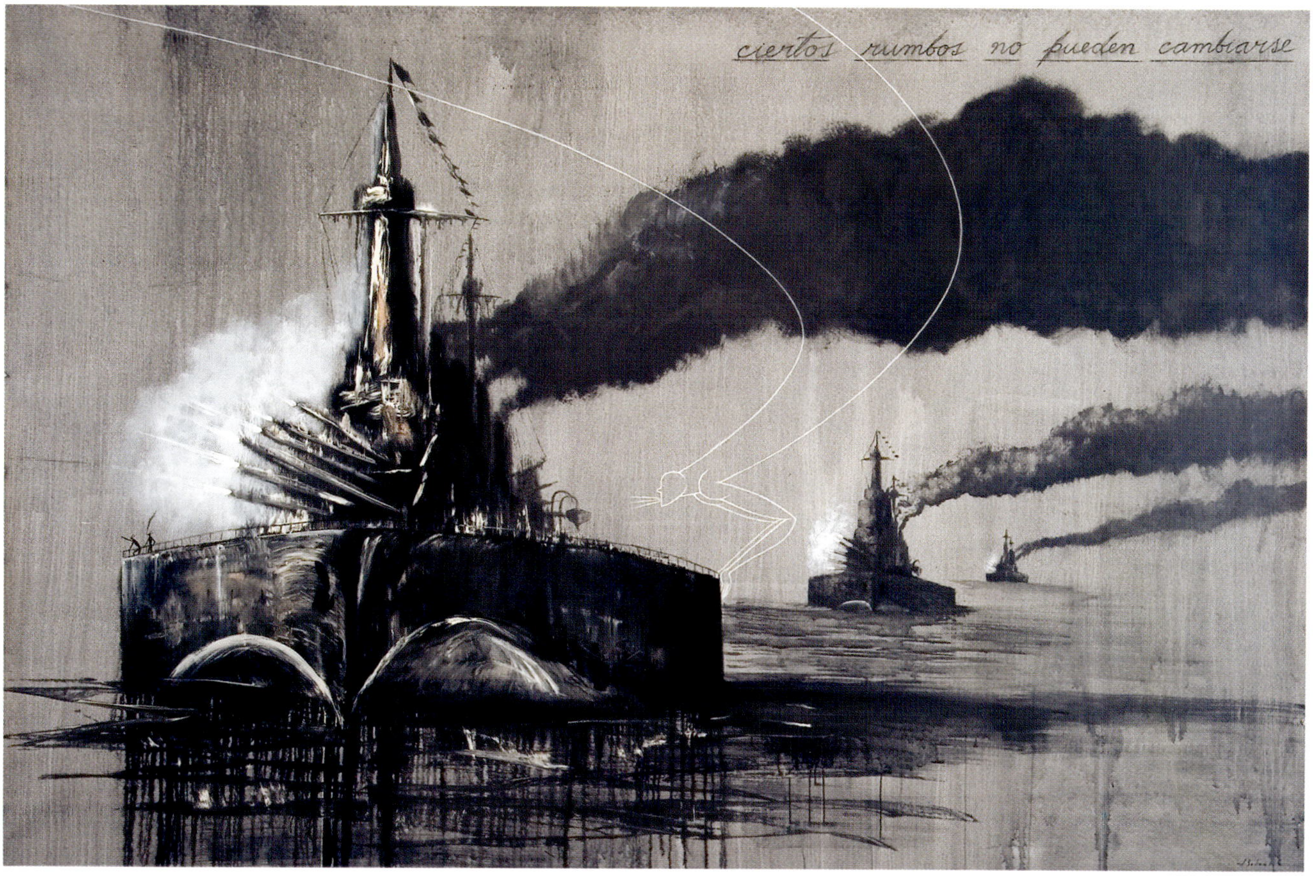

Ciertos rumbos no pueden cambiarse (Certain routes cannot be changed), 2006. *A*crylic on canvas, 71.125" x 107".

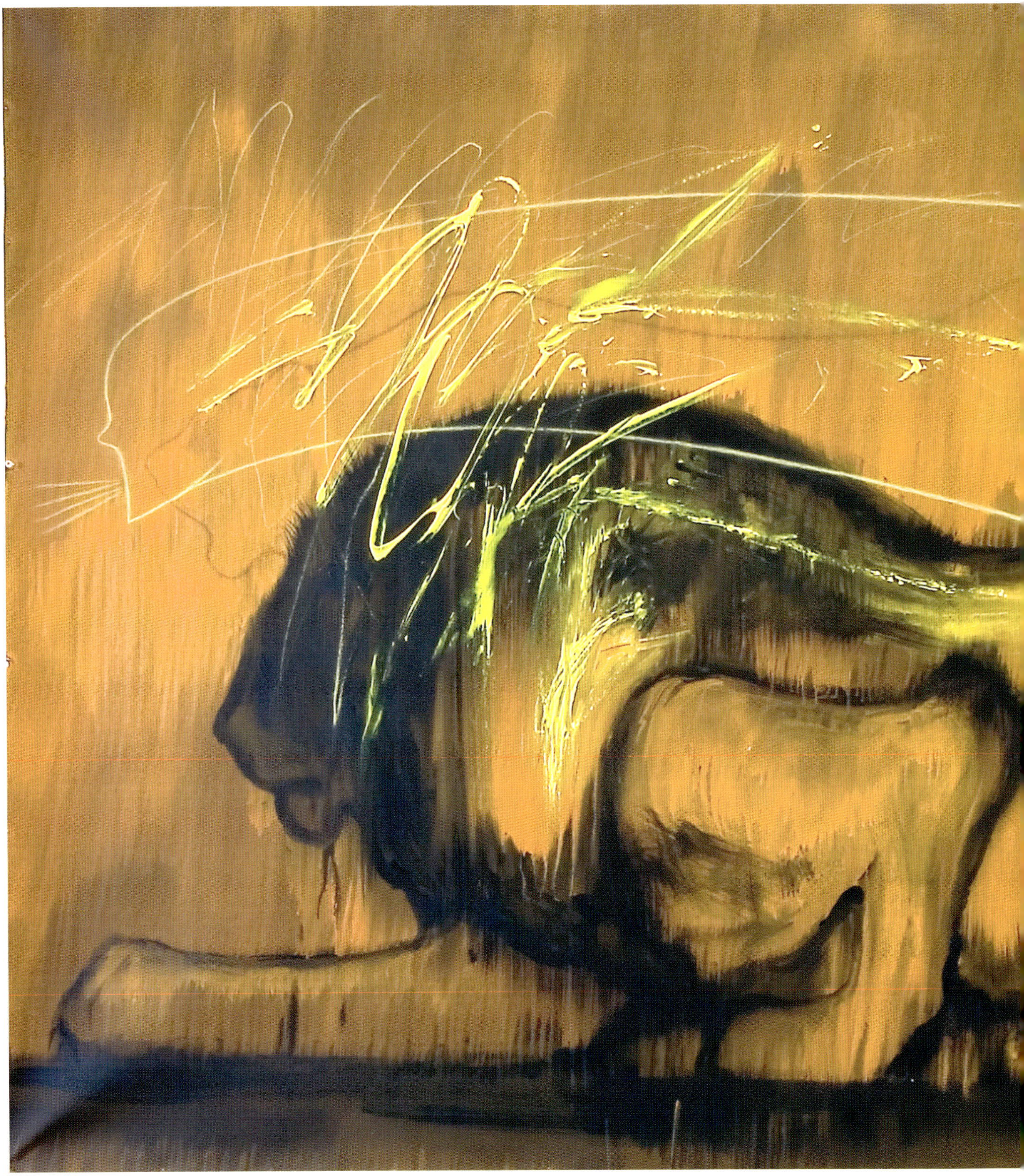

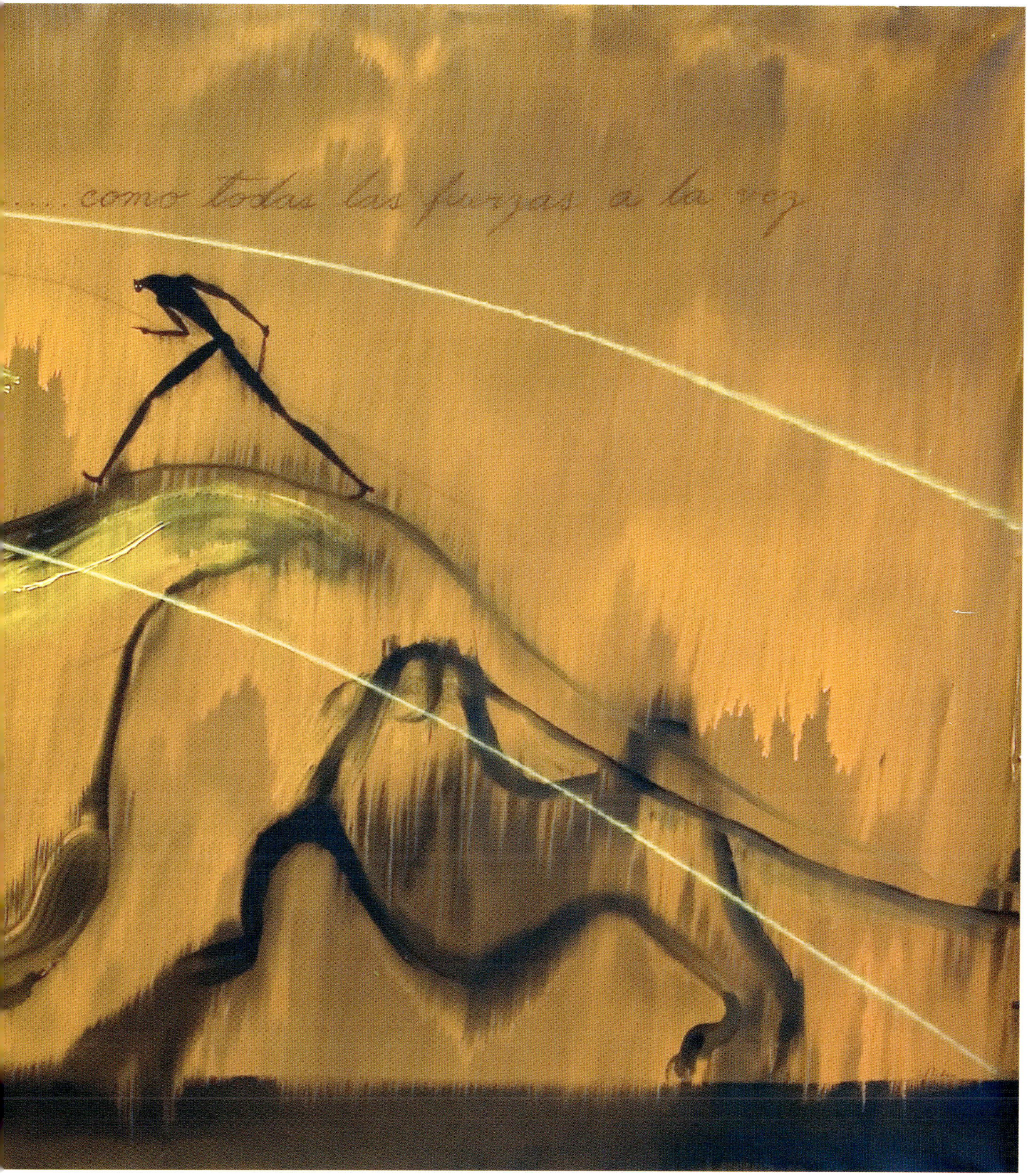

Como todas las fuerzas a la vez (With all the forces at one time), 2006. Acrylic on canvas, 71" x 121".

ROBERTO **BEHAR** AND ROSARIO **MARQUARDT**

Roberto Behar and Rosario Marquardt have been working together since 1996 when R & R Studios was created. They live and work in Miami Beach. Their work travels from painting to the urban realm stretching and diffusing the boundaries between architecture and the visual arts. Their projects; either as drawings, models, or architecture, always stimulate possibilities. They are models in a state of anticipation and are part of a web of interconnected ideas, changing scale, acquiring new meaning, raising new implications and becoming something else. Their collaborative work dwells upon the interrelationship between art and everyday life, popular culture and contemporary art, the city in which we live, and the one that has been invented. For Roberto and Rosario, paintings, installations, and urban interventions are but three different expressions of the same idea: an idea that proposes encounters of stories and spaces which oscillate between the city and the home, between fiction and reality, between play and critique. Perhaps because they live in Miami, their work mirrors contemporary conditions and elaborate upon a unique equilibrium between belonging and strangeness presenting themselves as unfinished poetic events.

Miami is a city in constant flux, simultaneously a metropolis and a frontier town. The city alternates between the first and the third world, and is the anticipated capital of the "fourth world." A world of the present and tomorrow where almost everyone comes from somewhere else; offering each other a culture of cultures to discover. Here we meet, at the crossroads of the North and the South, to build a home away from home. We are actors and spectators of the invention of Miami. Miami as an extraordinary place of encounters informs our work. We invent a parallel world through imaginary solutions. They oscillate between utopia and reality, the natural and the manmade, one language and another. They suggest the city as home, social sculptures, the possibility of public pleasure, an architecture of hope.

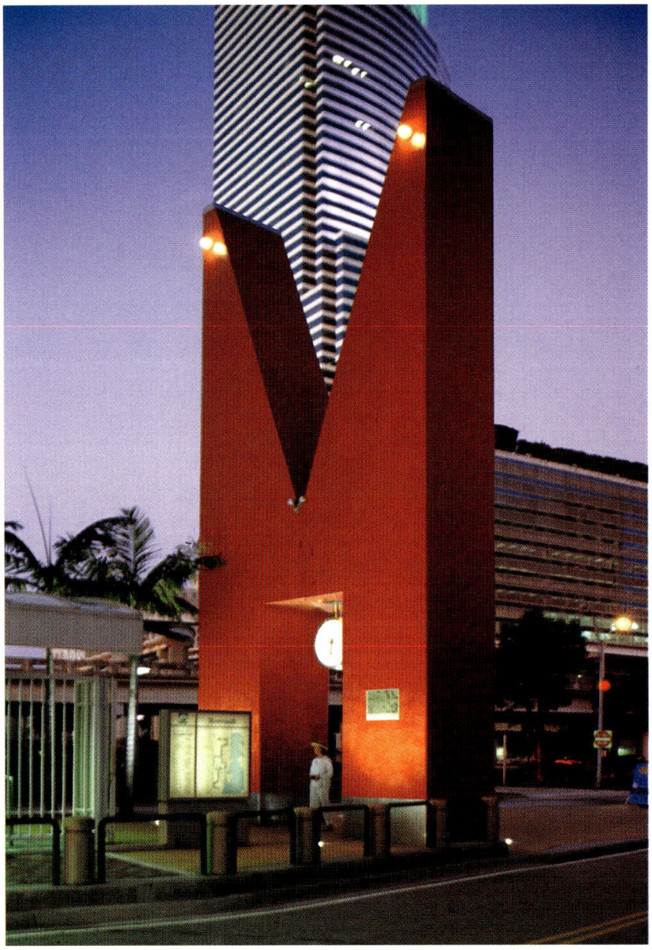

M, 1996. Concrete, stucco and metal, 45′ x 20′ x 6′. Miami, FL.

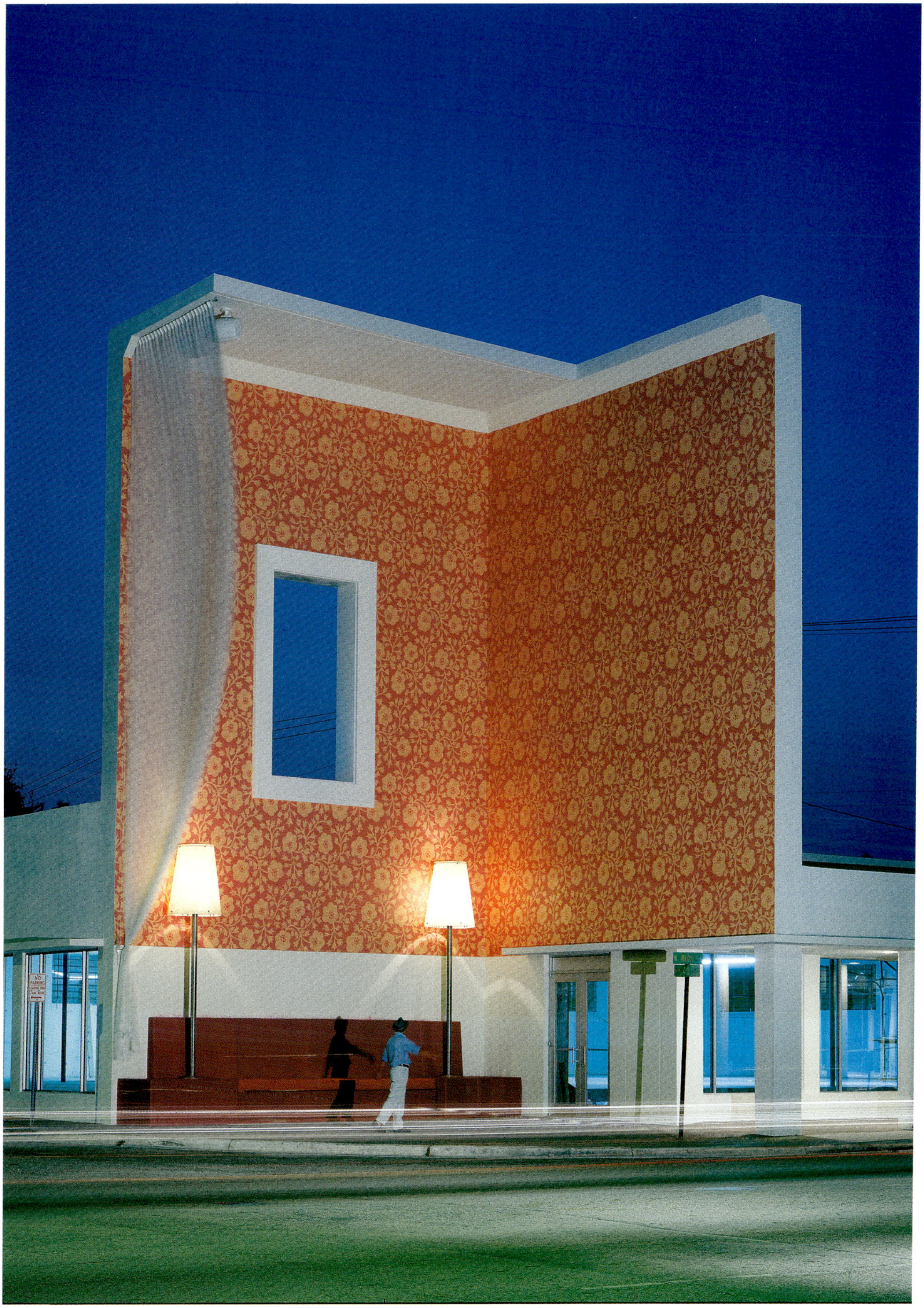

The Living Room, 2001. Concrete, stucco, glass, fiberglass, metal and fabric, 42′ x 100′x 100′, Miami, FL.

NATALIA **BENEDETTI**

Dreams are as real as our awakened states, but we take the latter much more seriously. One distinct difference between them is that we experience dreams in the privacy of our minds while our conscious states are experienced collectively with billions of beings. The joys of our existence have the potential of becoming limitless when we share them with everyone else; the more happiness and insight we give to others, the more richness we will experience. Therefore, in consciousness we have a wonderful opportunity to transform every situation into a meaningful event. While most joyful encounters involve other people, there are beautiful moments in between thoughts when we can stumble upon an instant of clarity. *Every Atom, An Ocean and Many Waves, Love Dust,* and many other works reflect such experiences. Video has consistently allowed for a clear and spontaneous documentation of each perfect moment, and possibly as a result, many individuals will discover that this freshness and potential can be found at any time.

Artists here are repeatedly asked what it is like to be an artist in Miami and why they choose to stay. Radio, television, newspapers, art critics, book authors, panelists and audiences, they all want to know. Do artists in New York, Paris and Berlin get asked these questions as often as we do? Although it is probably quite difficult to be an artist in those cities, I mention them because they can be so attractive for artists. Being an artist in Miami, I think, is not so difficult. So maybe this is why we stay and why so many are coming. We also really enjoy the warm weather, the excessive light and space everywhere, and all the friends from around the world. While we are asked this question over and over again, we also benefit from a long list of exhibitions dealing with this subject matter: *Miami in Transition, Miami Nice, Making Art in Miami, Made in Miami, Young Miami, Miami: Visions of Now.* It would seem as if Miami had been a well kept secret that was just discovered. But it really is great that everyone is so excited about this city. I love it here too. I also look forward to what will come, and a time when being an artist living in Miami will not be all about being a Miami artist.

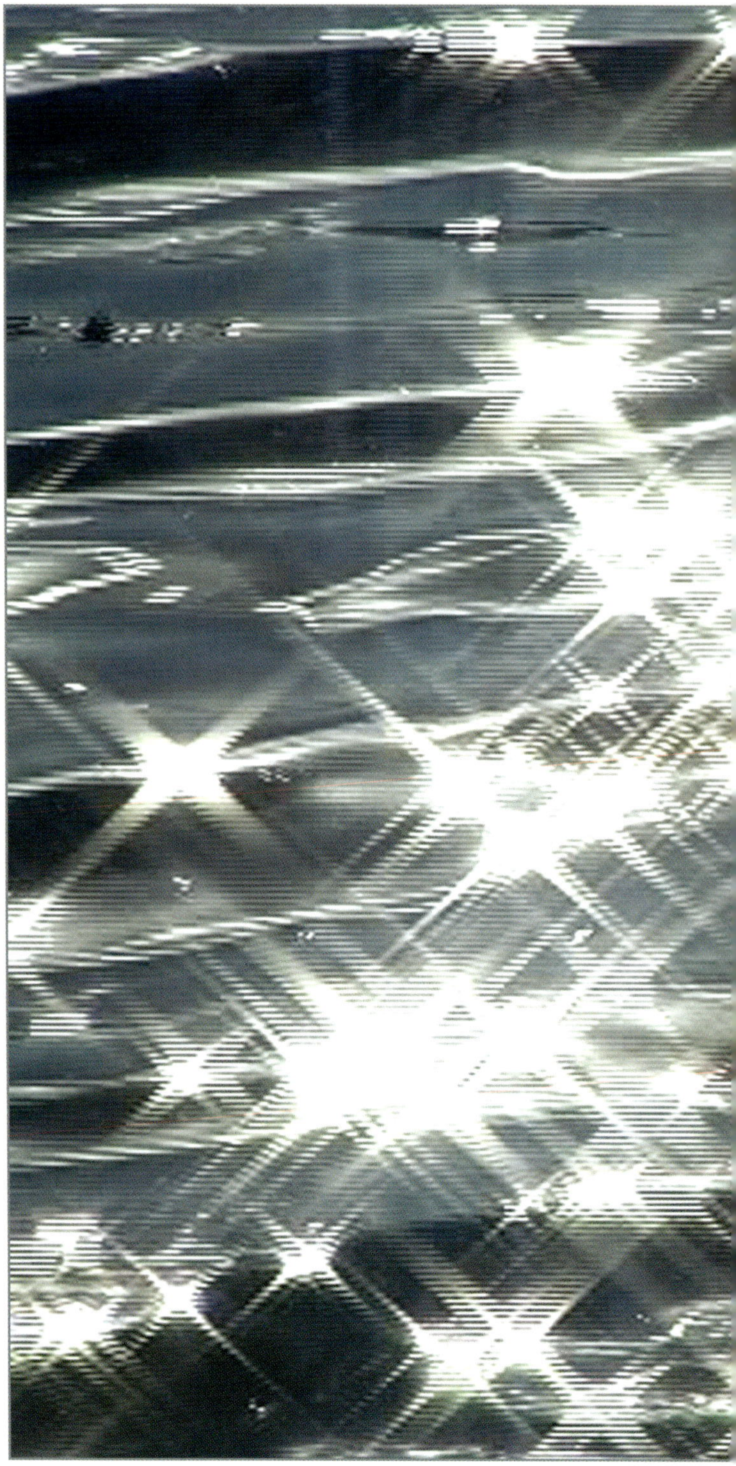

Luminosity, 2005. Video installation, variable dimensions.

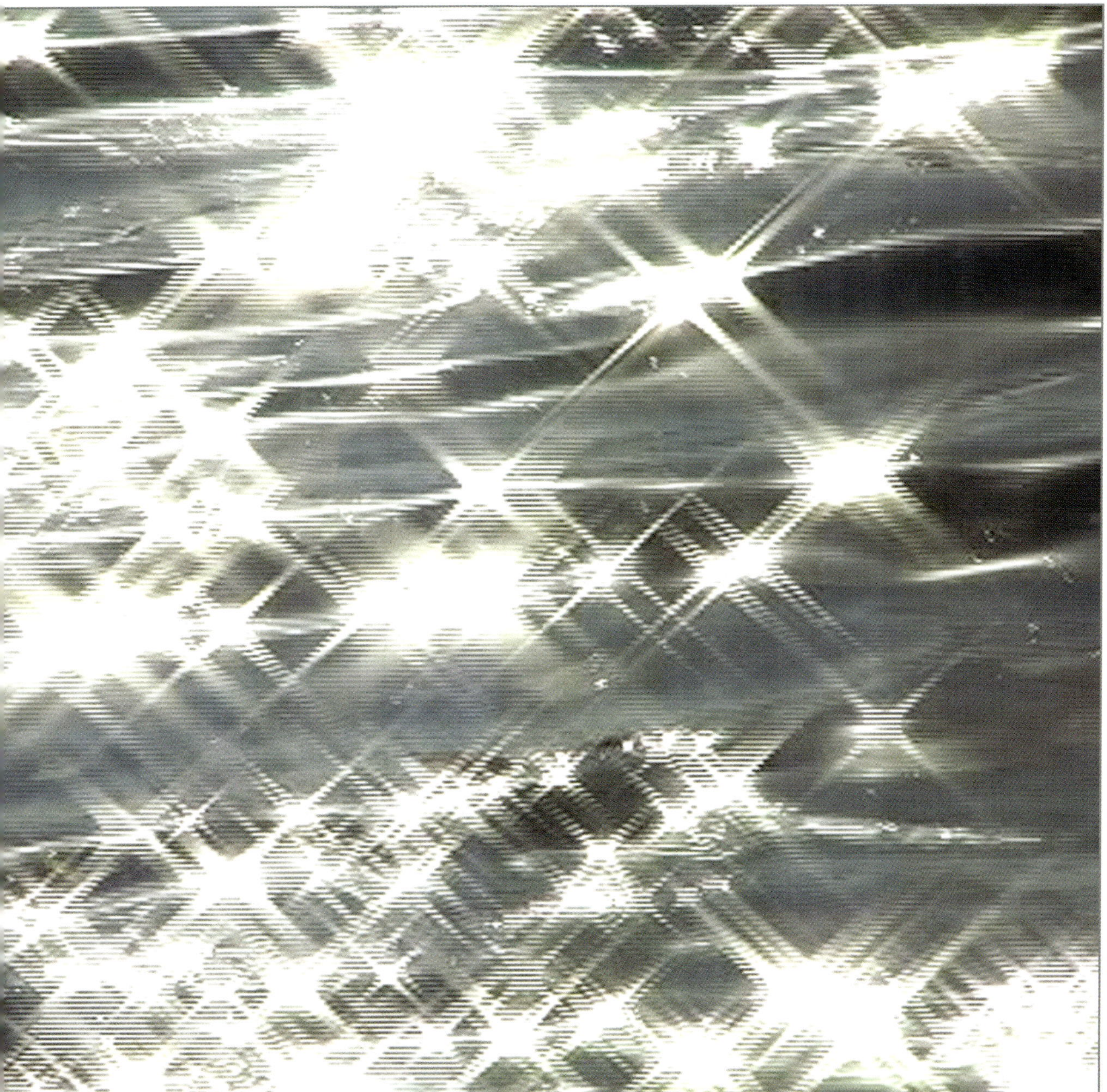

RAKEL BERNIÉ

Through the process of gathering and constructing objects, I am constantly revising memories and exploring personal anxieties. George Botaille in his "Language of Flowers" of 1929 supported his theory of plants as entities that are rooted in the earth and yet seek light, occupying a space between profanity and sanctity. In the series, "*Altered States of Flora and Fauna*," the focus is on the illusion that I can create an alternative protective space. Each piece becomes a quiet protest, a subtle theatrical scenario where I can develop my narrative. The process of weaving, layering, and sewing are the tools I use to piece together my history. Moving from the past to the present, I leave a trail of fragile constructions that represent my artistic search.

Ten years ago I moved to Miami. I had been living in England for more than eighteen years. One day my husband told me that we would be moving to America for his new job. The word that best describes how I felt about this move is "reluctant." I thought that I had my life all figured out, so I began this journey in an unhappy mood. I arrived in Miami and tried to settle into this new place. I went through all of the stages of what can be described as 'Culture Shock": denial, desperation, and more. One day, I was reading about the impact of exotic plants and the destruction that these plants can have on a fragile environment like the Everglades. I compared these plants to myself, because as an artist my focus is very much upon nature. Upon reflection, I have learned that Miami is a magic experiment full of different forces that have combined to help this place grow with a strength that does not happen in many other places. Miami, like the Everglades, will embrace and nurture anyone that arrives here to be part of this great adventure. For me, Miami has been a place where I have grown as a person and as an artist, because I came to understand that being an "exotic plant" here is perfectly fine – as long as one does not forget to give back and be part of this good community.

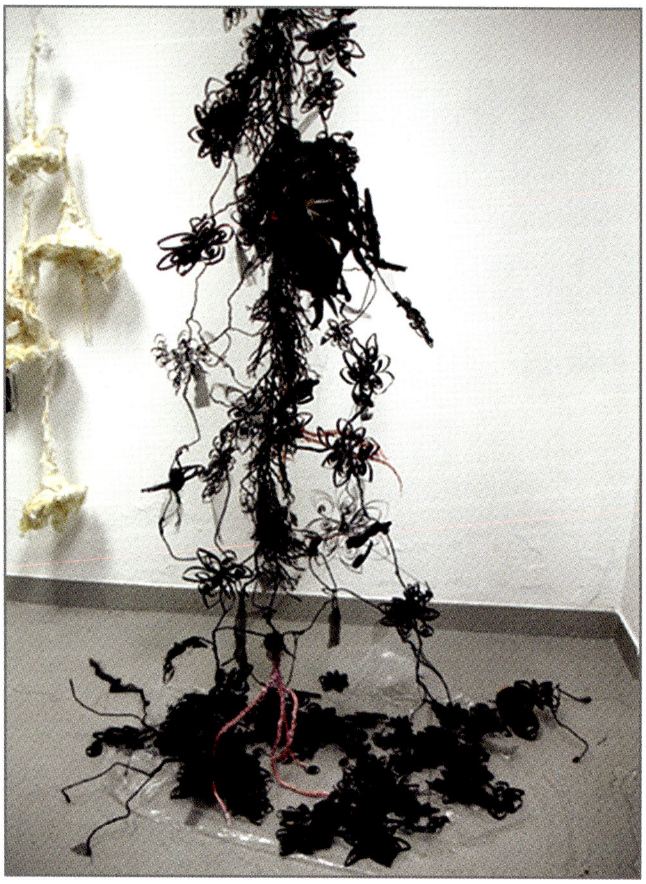

From the series "Altered States of Flora and Fauna", 2006.
Installation in progress, mixed media, variable dimensions.

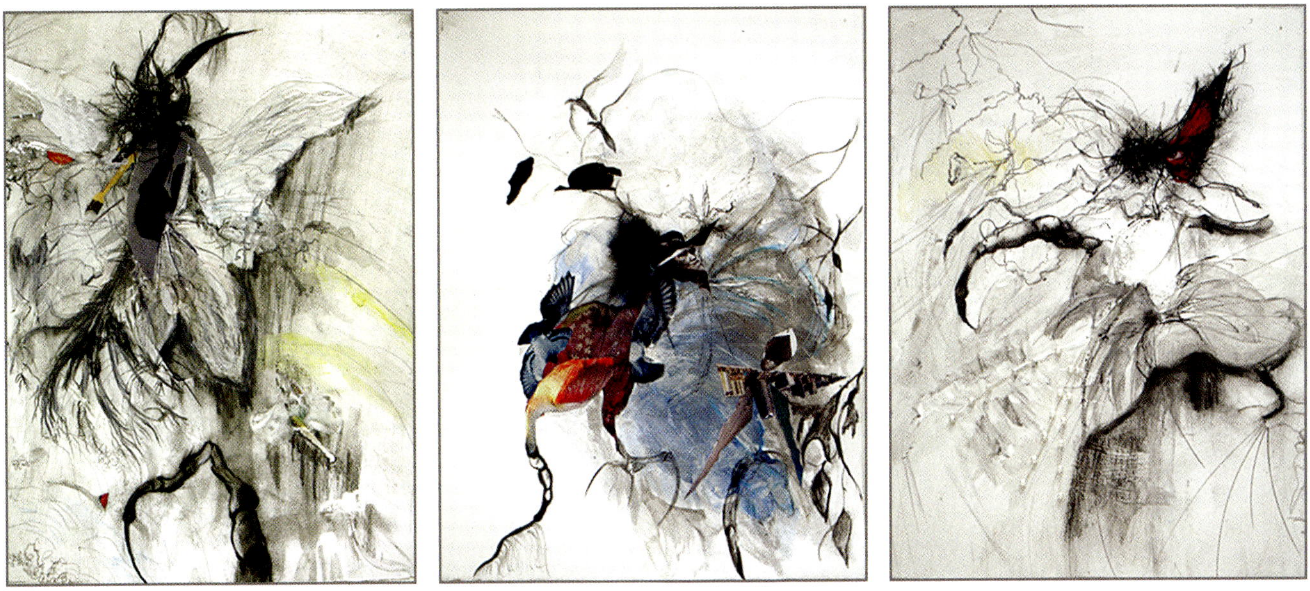

Untitled, from the series "Down by the Water," 2006. Collage, thread, beads, drawing on paper, 8" x 11".

CARLOS BETANCOURT

"How wonderful yellow is. It stands for the sun."
Vincent Van Gogh

A cocktail with my dearest friends anywhere; the crisp light; the huge blues; Morris Lapidus; pink flamingos on a Cypress tree in the Everglades; the Bacardi Building; it is not New York, it is what it is; a monumental Bahamian Starfish on a sand bar off Government Cut; Fire and Ice club; the everlasting sky; its multi-people-cultura viva; two and a half hours from Puerto Rico; Hiakutaki comet in a starry night in the Keys; awareness of the present; freedom *y alegria por la vida*; Keith Haring Pop Shop in Miami Beach; somewhere in Biscayne Bay reading a book in the morning on my boat, encircled by *delfines* swimming in clear emerald seas and a modern skyline beyond; *un pescaito frito con tostones*; the kitsch; Lincoln Road and Wynwood – now and then; the old rehab asylum on Española Way; Christo "Surrounded Islands"; the best drag queens; the Raleigh Hotel pool, or any pool; the Ceiba tree *en la pequeña Habana*; the Miami Circle; Miami Beach in the 80's and early 90's, (the 00's ain't that bad either); in a swamp behind Clyde Butcher's place; the artists and the artworks, the collectors and, (wow), the collections; tracking a hurricane; full moon nights at Fairchild's; the old lady in Miami Beach forever coordinated in fuchsia or chartreuse, (and a glittered hat); fishing off Stiltsville; *los poetas*; el mar, el mar, el mar.

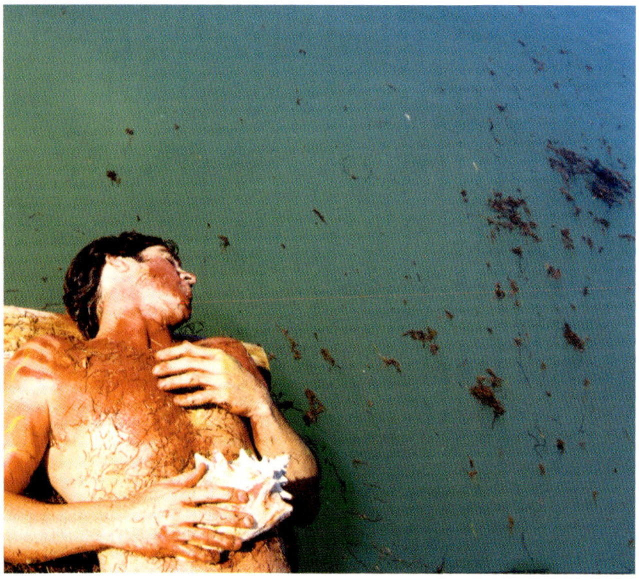

Tropical Cottage I – Muchas Manos and Conch, 2001. Metallic lambda print, 40" x 46". *Private collection*

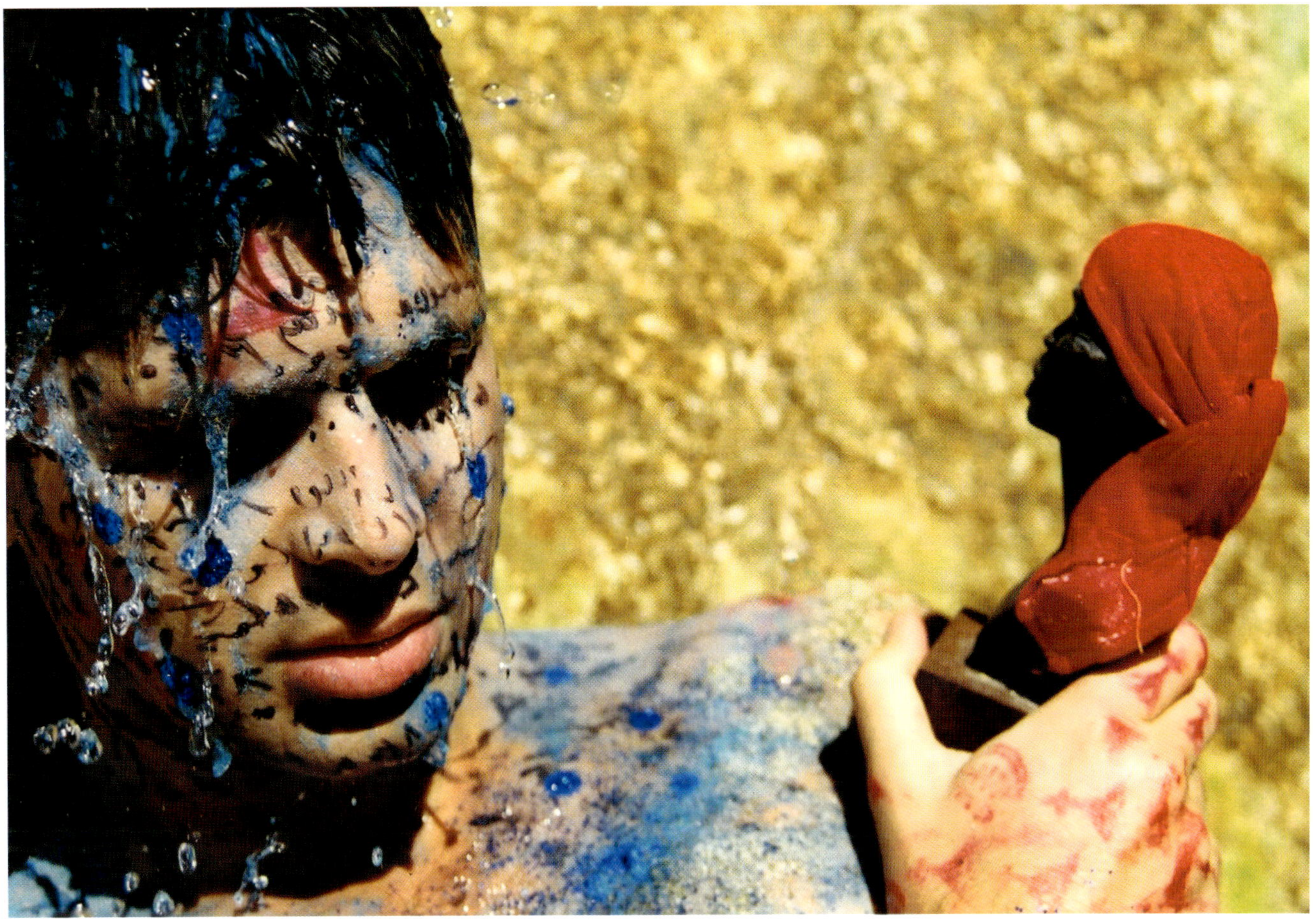

Interventions in California – Photo Performance with Deity, Luis and Modern Day Semi, 2005. Metallic lambda print.

FRANCIE **BISHOP-GOOD**

At the age of seven I was thrilled to have enough green stamps to get my first camera. That year was 1957; since that time my art has evolved and changed, but photography has been a constant anchor. My niece Carly has been the subject of my work for the last nine years. There are many sub-series in my work with Carly. *"Carly TV," "Carly, Wax Museum," "Carly, Fairs and Flea Markets," "Carly Suburbia," and Carly as Everywoman*." The first series, "Carly TV" happened nine years ago when I was taking family photographs in my brother's home in Allentown, Pennsylvania. The television set was booming in the background. Carly's initial innocence contrasted with the brashness of the TV was a jumping ground for my ideas. Carly reminds me of me. Perhaps she is my alter ego. Her intensity and chameleon like personality manifests itself directly in the camera and right at me. This intensity inspires me. Perhaps our familial relationship has just the perfect distancing for my work. I have the fortunate opportunity to observe her mature and change, sometimes changing slowly by staying in the little girl mode, and sometimes maturing drastically, taking on various roles that she emulates from the media.

I moved to South Florida in 1980. As a painter and photographer my first impact was the ever changing, enchanting sky and the color and feel of the water, juxtaposed with the really tacky, grungy streets, like State Road 441. These contrasts became part of the appeal of this area and a focus of my work. Strangers and family members lounging in the sun, with long shadows were ripe for my camera and paintbrush. Odd compositions, kitschy details, abundances of products and unusual people at flea markets were an important part of my new vision. Being an artist is the ability to close the door to the beauty and grime, know it; internalize it, and then be able to find one's own voice. I have used my niece Carly, as my model. She has become a canvas for my work. She can be an active participant or a stand in for my feelings and my fantasy life. Miami is the perfect backdrop for our photographic adventures. This area has blossomed into a major art arena, unique in its character. I have been fortunate to be part of this area with opportunities from collectors, museums, galleries, curators, alternative spaces, studio spaces, fellow artists, tours, audiences, great shows, Art Basel, public art, and grants.

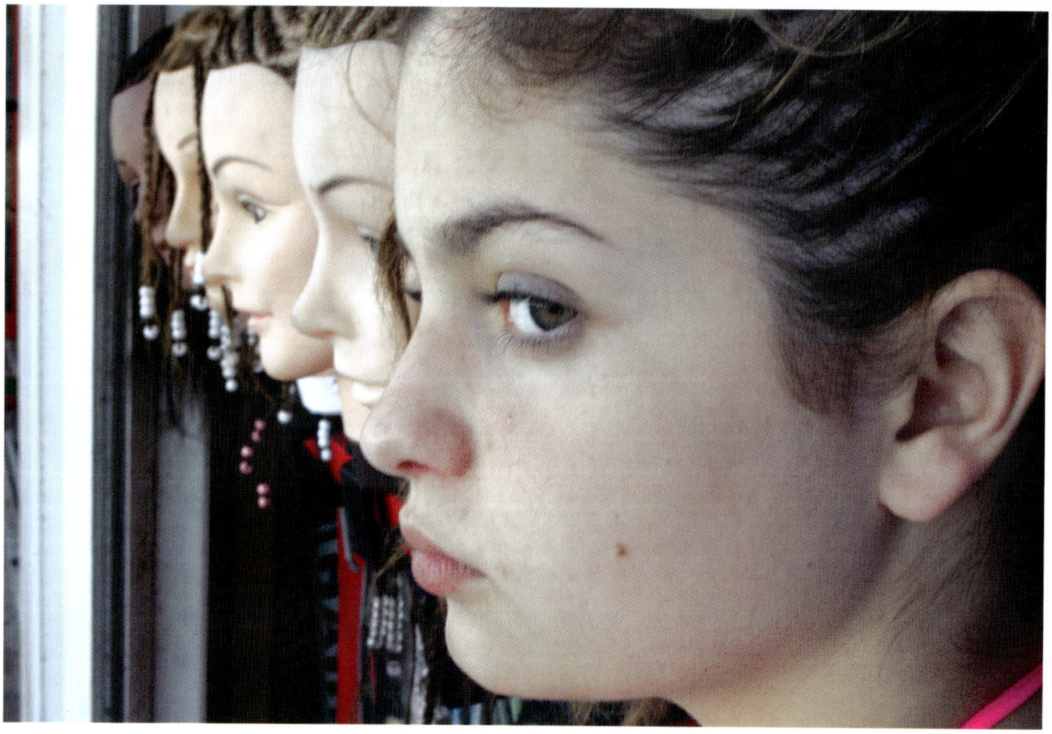

Carly Fair with Braids, 2005. Chromogenic Print, 20"x 30".

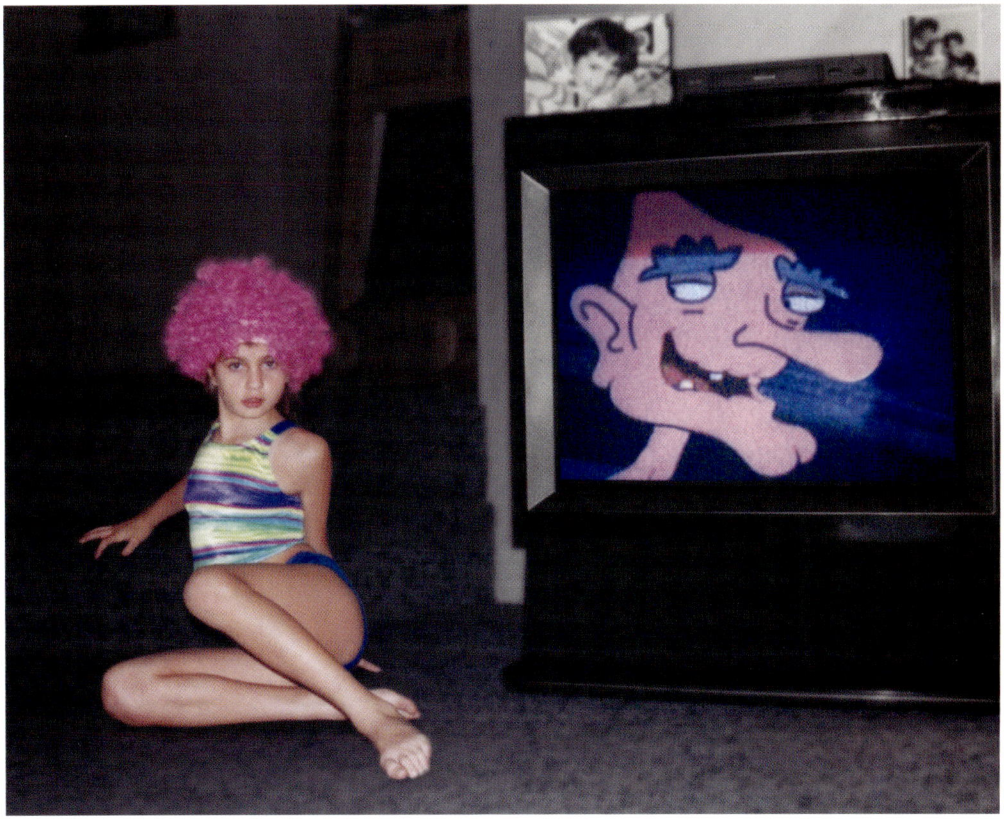

Carly TV, Pink cartoon, 2000. Chromogenic print, 40" x 50".

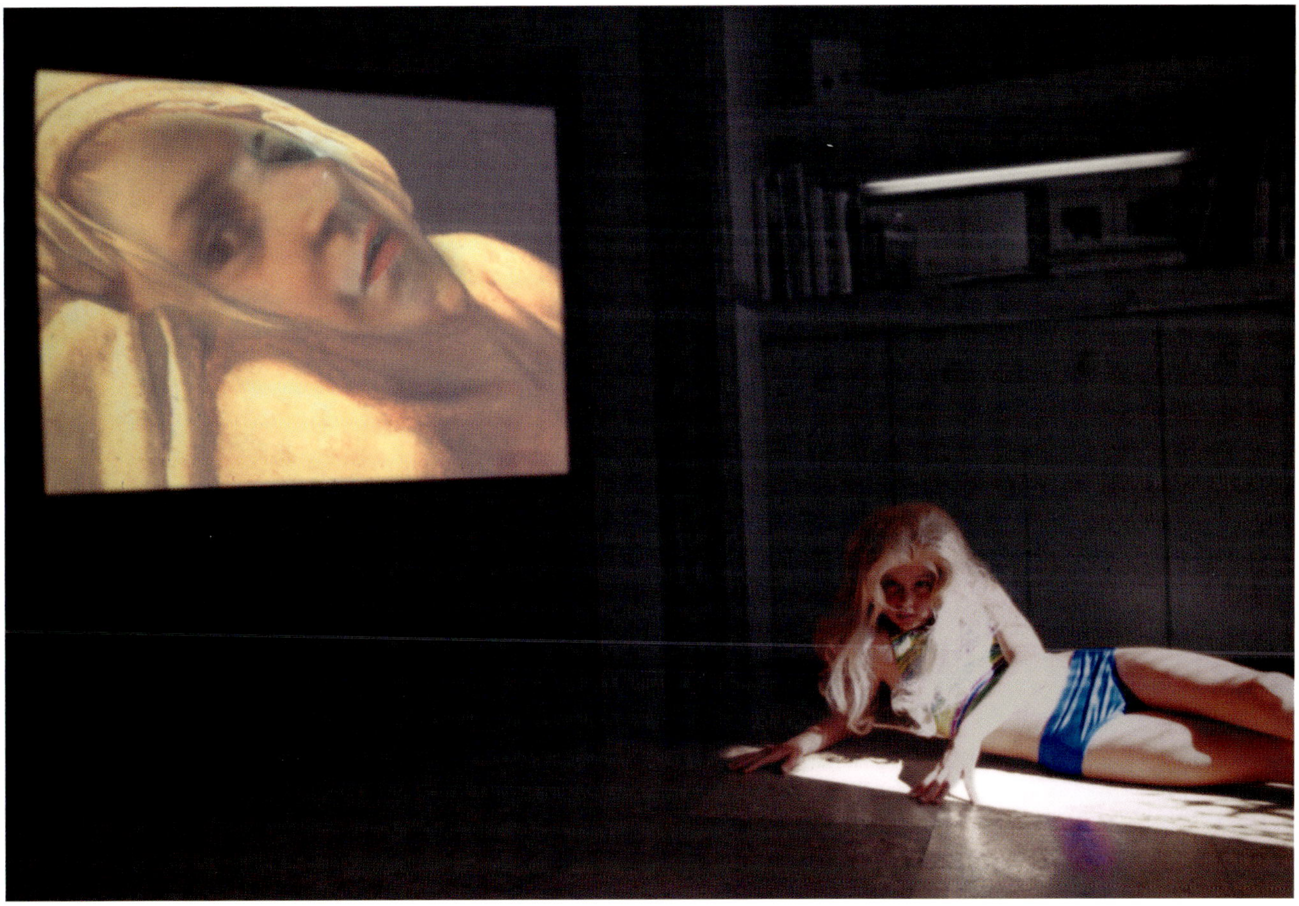

Carly TV, Marat, 2000. Chromogenic print, 40"x 60".

PIP BRANT

This work re-contextualizes news reports and morality debates concerning topics such as abuse of authority and economic strategies as possible sources for terrorism. The juxtaposition of nostalgic and sentimentality loaded tablecloths and dyed appropriated imagery counters the original purpose of a blanket or a decorative tablecloth that once covered a festive table surrounded by a well-behaved, tightly defined, American family. The depiction of public tragedy on these domestic pieces of cloth, once used to shelter a piece of furniture used to feed a basic human clan, is converted into a narrative that seeks to relocate states of social disarray. These tablecloths can resume their original postures and once again cover tables, but instead of providing somnambulist visual muzak for the dinner guest; they will be invited to consider the social implications of issues normally swept under the table. Potential dinner guests will be left to question as to what will be served.

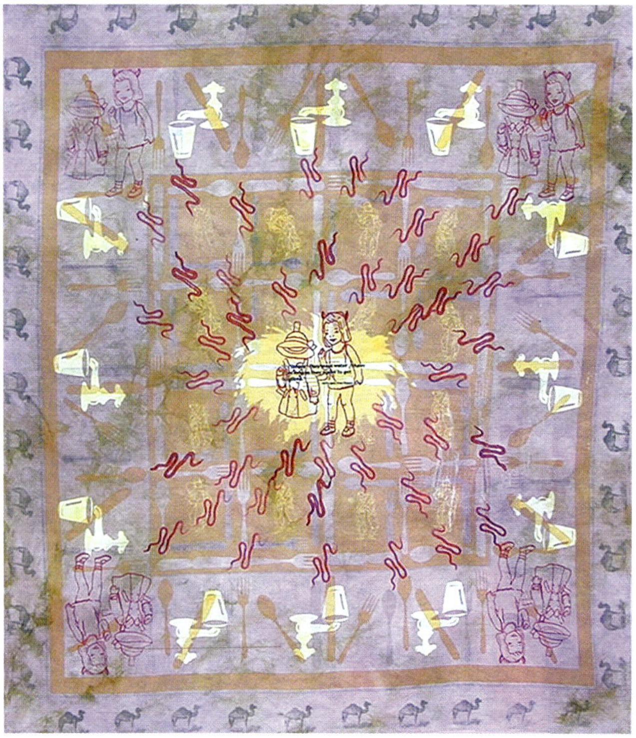

Chaplain's Baptism Deal, 2003. Found cloth, dyes, embroidery, 48"x 48".

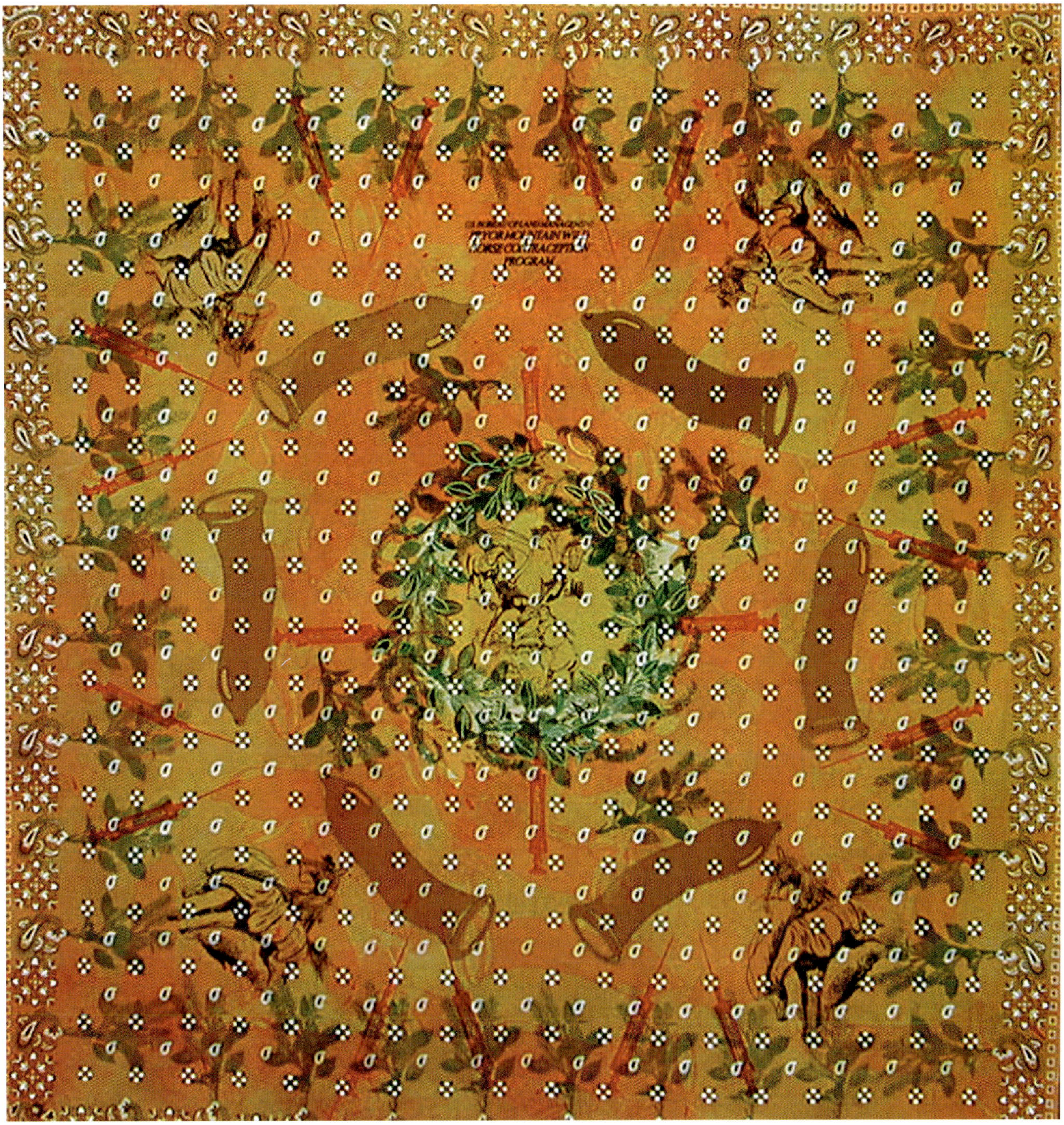

Pryor Mountain Wild Horse Contraception Program, 2004. Found cloth, dyes, embroidery, 48" x 48".

JENNY **BRILLHART**

My paintings are about light, structure, and my surroundings. I am drawn to objects that offer a formal approach to painting and composition making. The clarity and controlled specificity of the paint's value, color, and placement is critical. I aspire to make pictures that are considered and honest to subject and craft.

Place is important to my work and since I have been painting, the recreation of an environment is often a starting point for me. Originally from New Hampshire, by way of New York, Miami offered quite a different landscape. In the beginning, I couldn't get over the light and heat – the massive amount of light and how it absorbs the city, flattening the buildings and practically eliminating color. The low, outstretched uniformity of the entire environment – land, buildings, bay and ocean – is different from where I am from and brought to the forefront ideas only suggested at in previous work. I found the light and architecture provided many opportunities to make compositions concerned with geometry. While I strive for a particular realism, the choice of placement, value, size, and color of objects, within the picture is what I believe creates the artwork, as opposed to a literal description. I found reference to these formal ideas almost everywhere when I began to look at Miami. These visual ideas compiled with Miami's specific sense of light, heat, lowness, and flatness have provided the inspiration and motivation to make the work of the past few years.

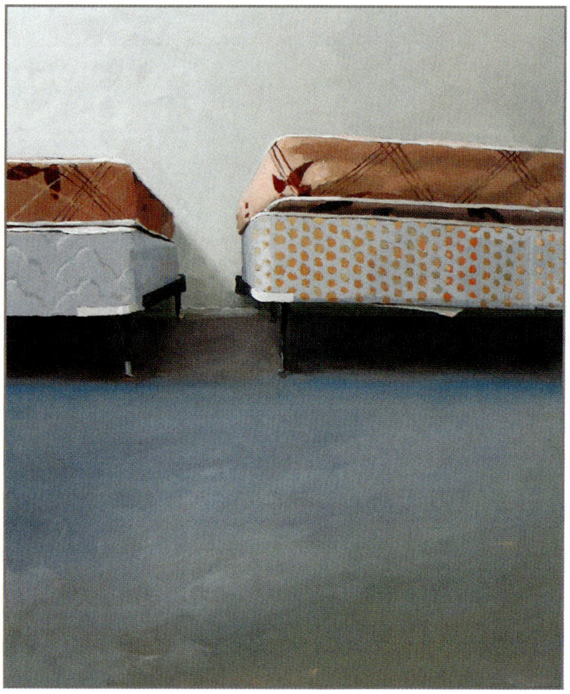

Saxony Hotel Interior #2, 2006. Oil on panel, 25" x 30".

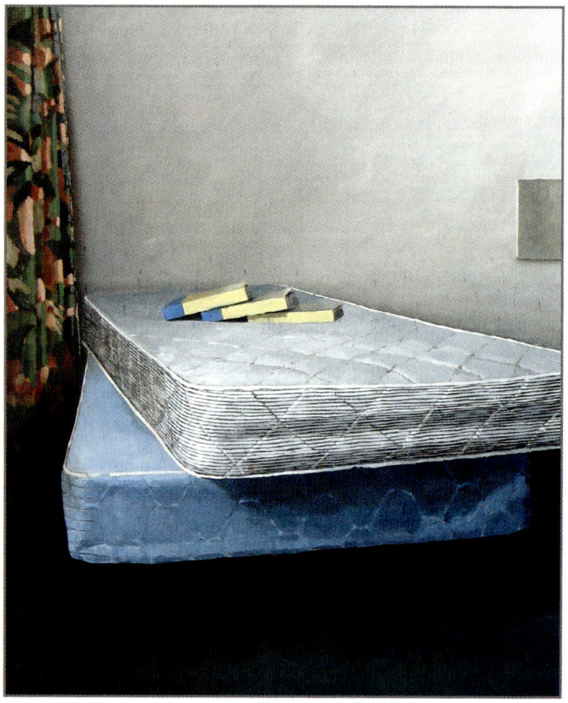

Saxony Hotel Interior #7, 2006. Oil on panel, 11" x 13".

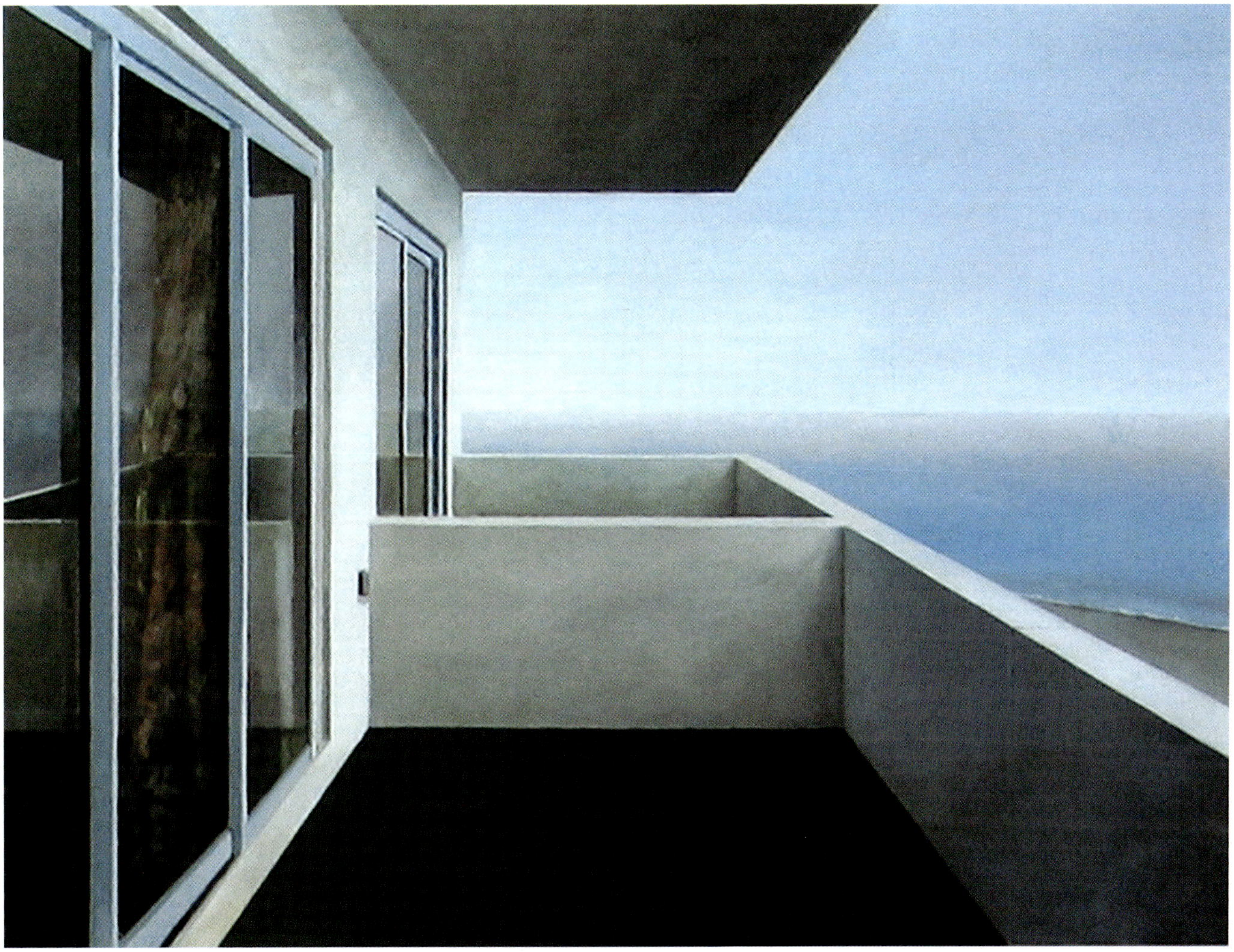

Saxony Hotel – North View, 2006. Oil on panel, 30" x 40".

CAROL K. BROWN

"Pe-des-tri-an n. 1. a person who goes or travels on foot. –adj. 2. going or performed on foot. 3. of or intended for walking. 4. lacking in vitality, imagination or distinction; commonplace; prosaic."

As I wander streets I am often amazed at the delicious array of visuals amongst the "prosaic." The angle of the observed and the observer is constantly shifting. By isolating, duplicating and changing scale of my subject, I am setting up hypothetical relationships, both physical and psychological. My anonymous subjects lie squarely within the realm of the public, but in their isolation, underscored by the intense shadows and ambiguous spaces, they give off very personal, private vibrations. The painterly quality of the images, redefines the original source material which are the photographs I take. There is a certain voyeuristic quality because the subjects rarely know they are being photographed.

Being an artist in Miami in the winter is a much better deal than slogging through the snow and slush as most New York artists must. However, summer is a different story, when I want to pack up my camera and paints and head north. At least in the winter, this multi-cultural city teems with excitement and has a constant flow of artists and collectors eager to exchange ideas. In many ways, Miami is a small city with a big city's energy and sophistication. I could never afford to duplicate my terrific working space in New York. This is a great place to get a lot done.

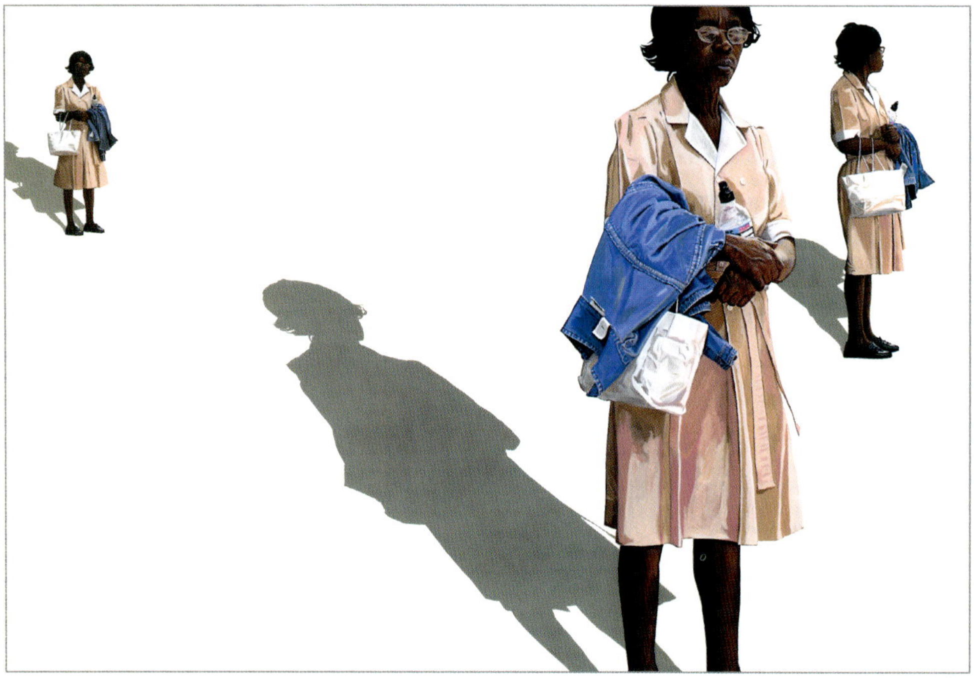

Pedestrian (Maid), 2005. Acrylic on paper, 12" x 18".

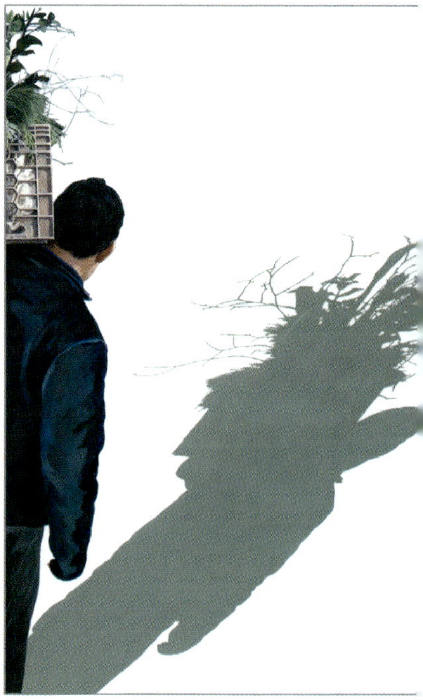

Pedestrian (Plants), 2005. Acrylic on p

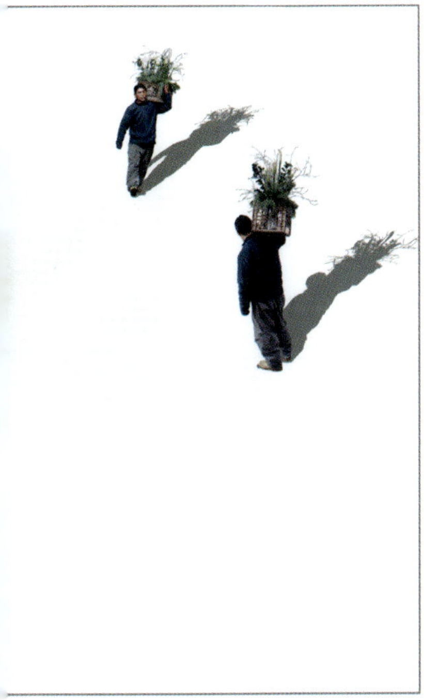

x 18".

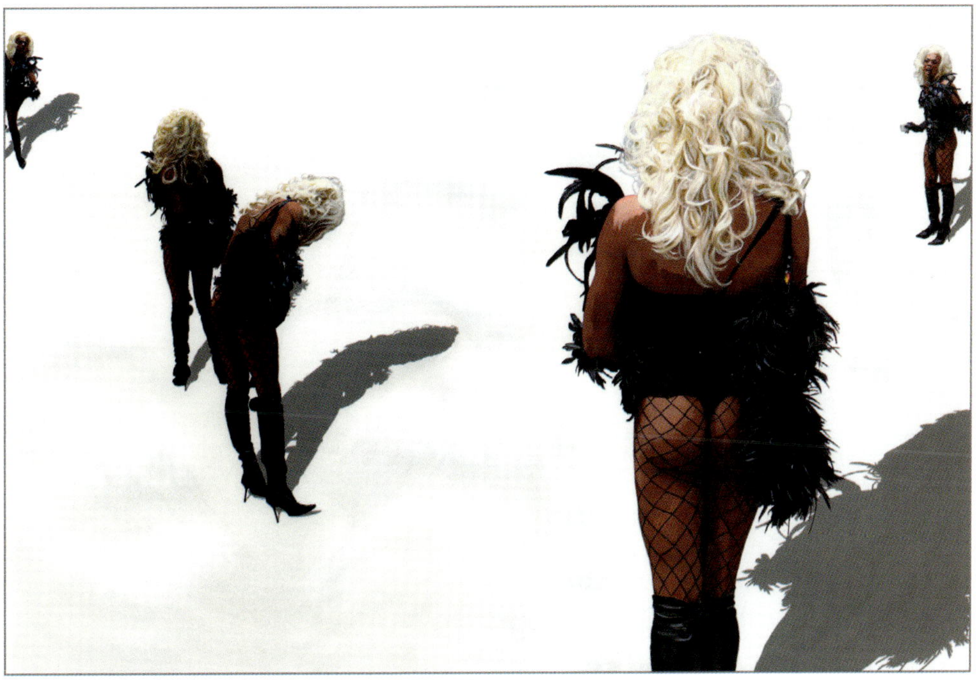

Pedestrian (Blonde), 2006. Acrylic on paper, 17" x 24".

ERNESTO **BURGOS**

In my work I investigate the encounters of different languages such as patterning, color, and texture. The visual information within my work is extracted from different places such as magazines, fabrics, cardboard, and paint in a way that when combined with each other begin to take on new meanings. I push the combination and construction of these materials to as many extremes as possible to understand how these languages and reduced vocabularies can take on different meanings within a work. There are issues of space and painting that are of great interest to me as well. I take the work off the two dimensional surface and construct within a space incorporating the ground and walls to see how space and perspective can also become a formal aspect of painting. These works now become installations where the encounter of languages along with the visual is interacting with the physical space to enhance the experience.

It has been very interesting and beneficial to spend a period of time in Miami and witness the changes occurring within the city's physical structure, and how this affects the arrival of artists from other areas, and the growth of those native to Miami. Miami is in a transitional phase which is allowing exploration with an endless array of possibilities. Still at a very young stage, slowly and steadily it is beginning to take bolder and bolder steps. These new directions are influencing the growth of the city as well as its people. One of the qualities that make Miami unique is the collision of cultures and customs from all the people that arrive to Miami from different parts of the world. The same could be said for the artists that are here, and the dialogue created amongst them and the city. I am very curious to see what Miami will become in the future with the collision of Miami's development and the constant arrival of artists from other places joining those who are native to the area. So far, in the short period of time here, I have seen amazing things happen and I believe they will continue to happen elevating Miami to be on par with other major art centers of the world.

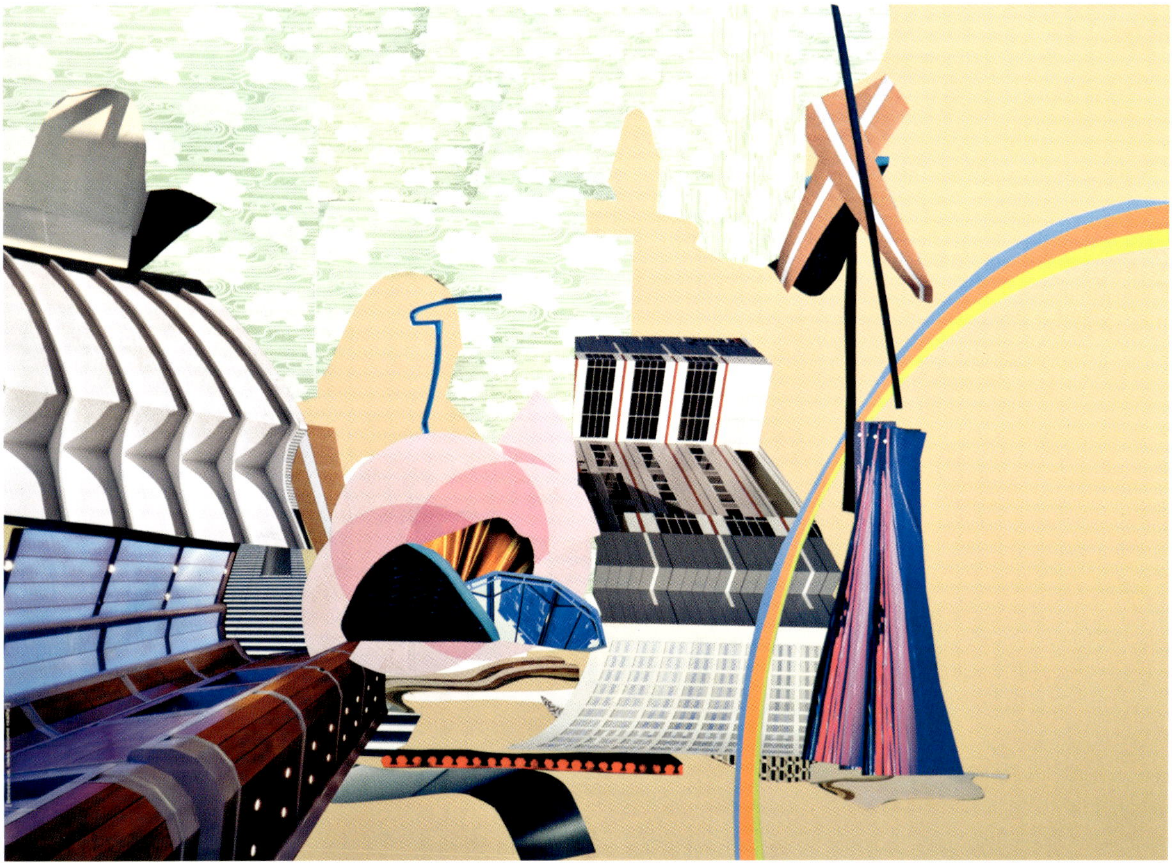

Untitled, 2006. Mixed media on paper, 22″ x 30″.

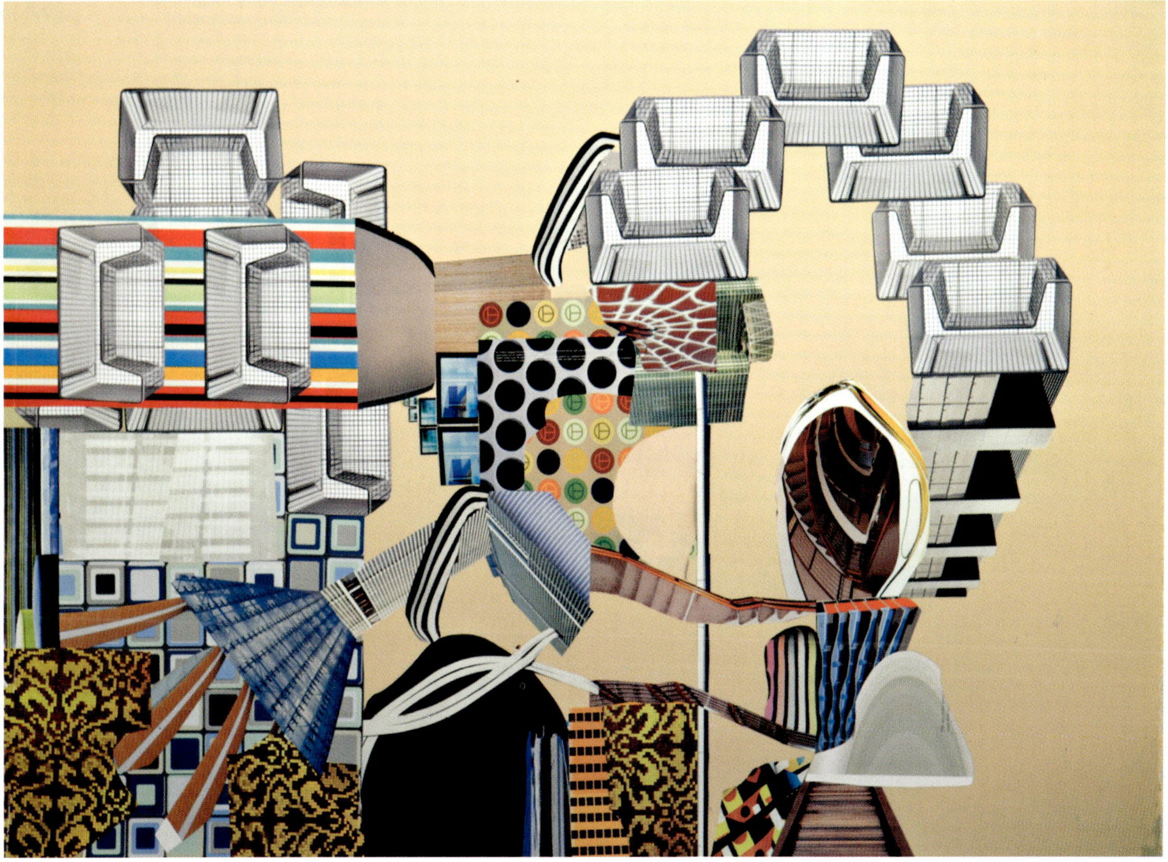

Untitled, 2006. Mixed media on paper, 30″ x 44″.

PABLO CANO

Born in Havana, Cuba in 1961, Pablo Cano was on the last flight out of the country before the Cuban Missile Crisis of 1962. Now a resident of Miami's Little Havana, Cano is regarded by art patrons and critics alike as one of Florida's premiere fine artists. Since childhood, marionettes have fascinated him. His primary work today continues to center around the marionettes that he fashions from found objects, and the performance pieces he composes to showcase these protagonists. Cano reveals *"I create a dream world where inanimate objects come to life – springing from my imagination in the Surrealist tradition. But my work is founded in Dada ideals. The Dadaists used chance, spontaneity and childlike innocence in order to create their statement. Their intention, as is mine, was to break with tradition and painting technique and to return to elemental basics of art, to start from scratch."* Influences from the color palette of Russian Constructivist Alexander Exter, who assembled marionettes in the early 1920's, and the mechanics of the pieces of Alexander Calder's *Circus* can be seen in Pablo's work. By incorporating carefully selected discarded debris from the urban streets he frequents, as well as detritus delivered to his studio by friends from all over the world, Cano has ultimately developed his own charming and inventive palette that has been described by many as unlike any other artist's today. Bonnie Clearwater, Director and Chief Curator, MOCA North Miami observes, *"Each marionette is a complete sculpture in its own right that is exhibited in the museum in its inanimate state; but when their creator and grand puppeteer Cano performs them, the figures take on a life force that causes the audience to suspend their disbelief."* She continues, *"It was clear right from the Cano's first productions (at MOCA) that a truly original artist, who marched to his own drummer, was in our midst. In the 1990's, at a time when conceptual art dominated the international art world, Cano followed his heart and passion, seeing treasures in garbage and bringing unforgettable characters into existence."* Cano widely employs numerous other art forms in his work including painting, fine drawing, and ceramic sculpture, and is accomplished in each of these areas. He earned an MFA from Queens College of the City University of New York in 1985. He has studied and worked in New York, Baltimore, Paris, and Miami. The Museum of Contemporary Art (MOCA) in North Miami has commissioned his work annually since 1997.

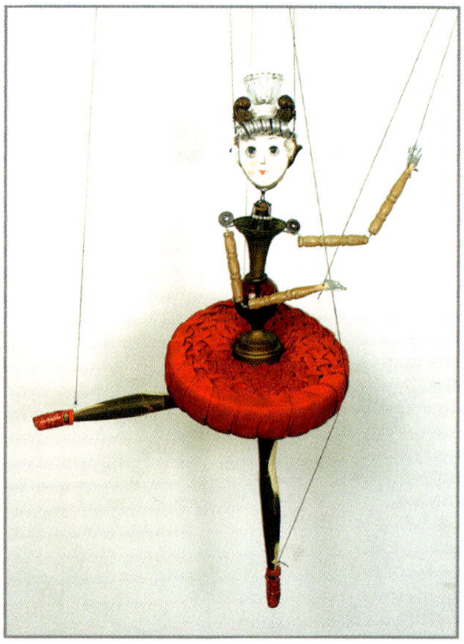

The Ballerina, from "Pablo Cano: The Toy Box" Marionette Production, 2004. Marionette, mixed media, variable dimensions. *MOCA Commission.*

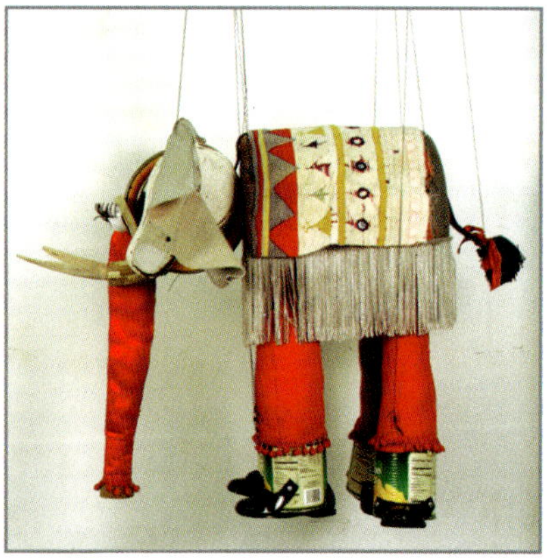

Peaches the Elephant, from "Pablo Cano: The Toy Box" Marionette Production, 2004. Marionette, mixed media, variable dimensions. *MOCA Commission.*

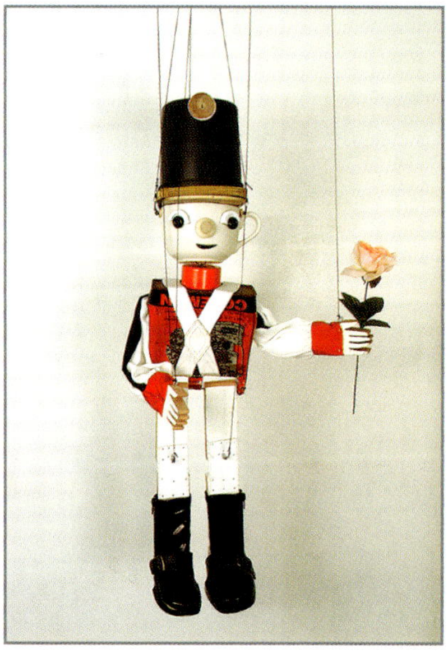

The Toy Soldier, from "Pablo Cano: The Toy Box" Marionette Production, 2004. Marionette, mixed media. *MOCA Commission.*

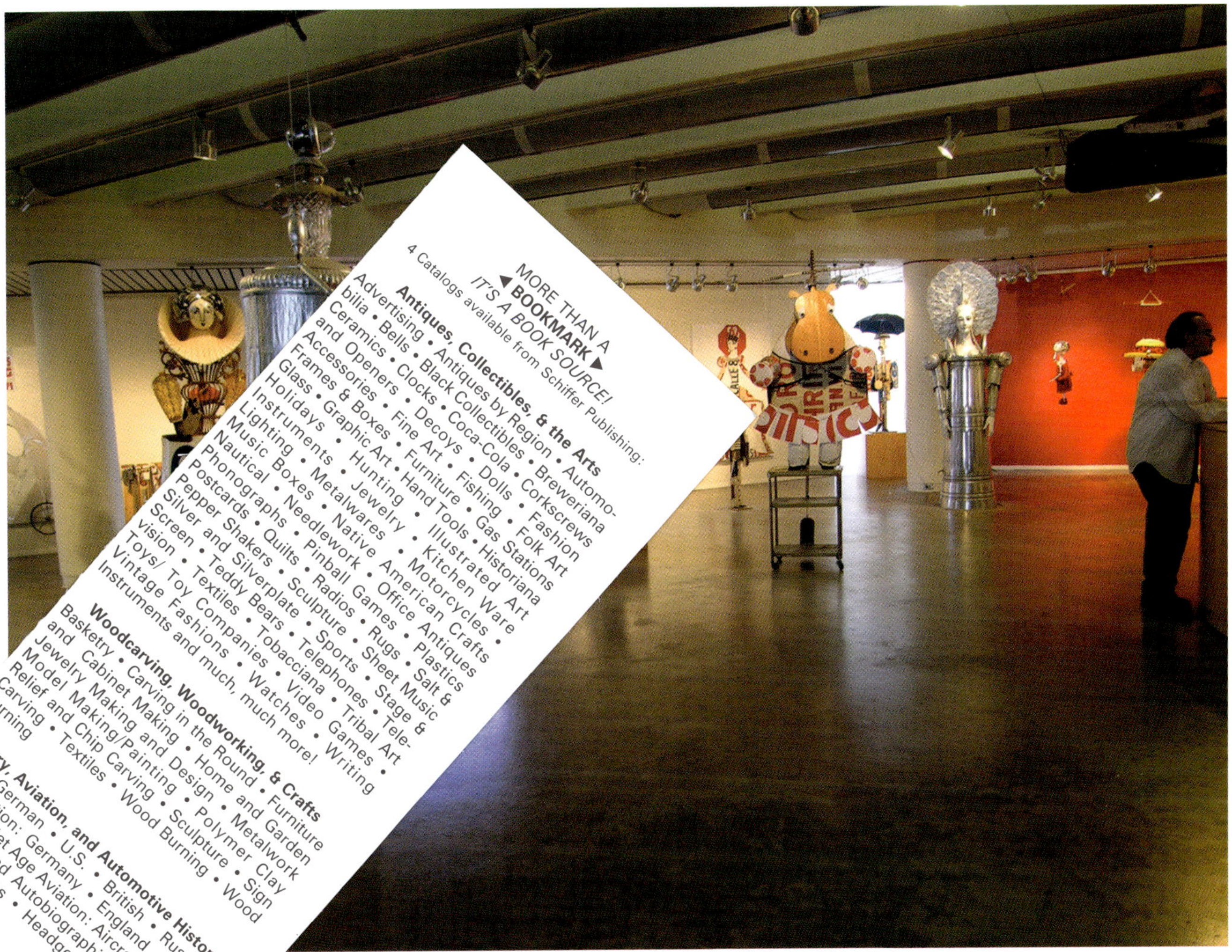

...o Home Base, Discarded Debris to Constructed Art."* Installation view at Miami International ... , FL.

ELIZABETH **CEREJIDO**

Re-constructing a Family Portrait pieces together fragments of my personal history that emerged while moving my mother from the apartment she shared with my father for several years. This era came to an end with his passing and with her diagnosis of Alzheimer's. The photographs of the apartment serve as a record of that domestic space through its various transformations. Going through my parent's possessions, I came across a black purse full of letters that my father had written my mother during a 10 year period of separation, from 1970 when she came to the United States, to 1980 when my father came over through the Mariel boatlift. The letters document a correspondence that narrates a story of love and romance, while the stacks of envelopes serve as a visual timeline. The contrast then between the images of the apartment and those of the letters represent two opposing elements: the former speak of closure and finality while the latter look to the future – hopeful and full of promise. The black and white video projection portrays my mother seated by a window, in a repetitive act of combing her hair. Shot in 8mm and transferred to video, the work plays with the idea of time and memory. Is this old footage or is it current? This ambivalence, and the video's faded look, references the malleability of her own memory between the past and the present.

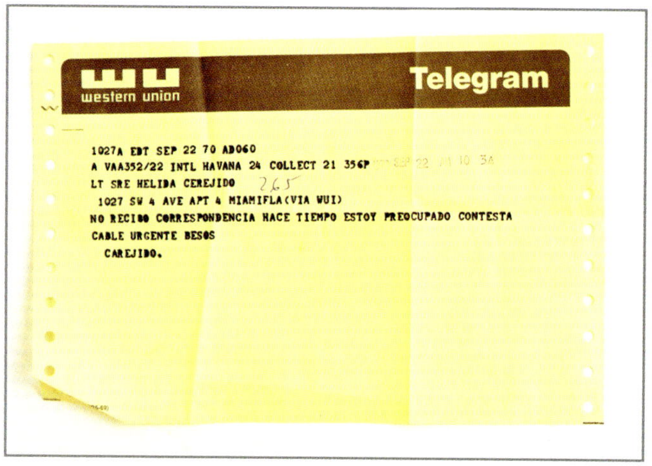
western union Telegram

1027A EDT SEP 22 70 AD060
A VAA352/22 INTL HAVANA 24 COLLECT 21 356P
LT SRE HELIDA CEREJIDO 265
1027 SW 4 AVE APT 4 MIAMIFLA(VIA WUI)
NO RECIBO CORRESPONDENCIA HACE TIEMPO ESTOY PREOCUPADO CONTESTA
CABLE URGENTE BESOS
CAREJIDO.

Preocupado (from Re-constructing a Family series), 2004. Digital color prints from 4 x 5 negatives, 20" x 24".

Miami holds a unique place in the lives of many. For a Cuban-American like me, it is the place that formed my identity as a bi-cultural, bi-lingual individual and continues to inform who I am in a more universal context, both personally and professionally. Being Cuban-American in Miami, means that everything one learns about Cuba is through others' eyes, so that a "virtual" Cuba has been created through a myriad of projections from our parents, the media, generations that came before us, after us, and continue to emigrate here, adding to the complex and often contradictory tapestry that is the Cuban Diaspora narrative in Miami. Since 2001, I have turned to my own story as a source for creating my photographic work. Turning to personal events that shaped my recent adult life, I discovered how intrinsically connected my creative life was to this place. A renewed sense of place and a more poignant realization of myself as an artist in the local and universal context emerged as a result, and continues to be the driving factor in my artistic and professional life. Miami has given a more profound and complex relevance to the projects I choose to be involved in, stemming from a need and a sense of generational responsibility to document, explore, and interpret what transpires here. As Miami continues to grow, unfold and re-define itself, I do, as well, both as an artist and curator.

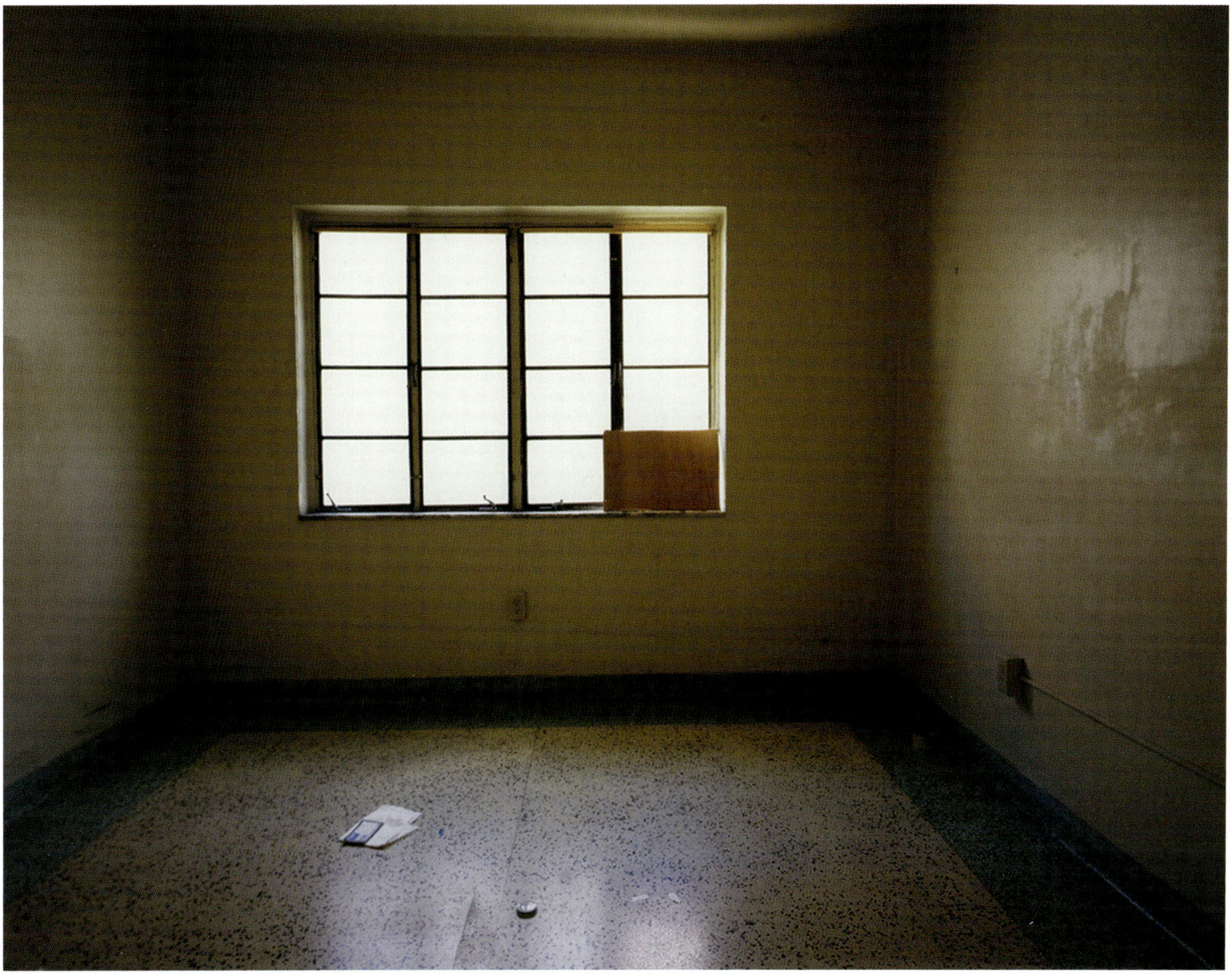

Empty Bedroom (from Re-constructing a Family series), 2004. Digital color prints from 4 x 5 negatives, 20" x 24".

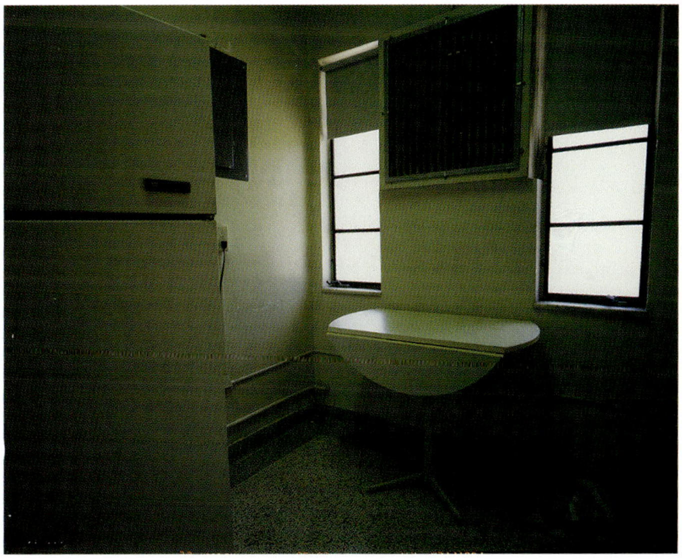

Kitchen with Table (from Re-constructing a Family series), 2004. Digital color prints from 4 x 5 negatives, 20" x 24".

ROBERT CHAMBERS

Edward L. Chambers, my father, raised me to be a scientist. He, like his father, spent most of his life as a cell biologist and researcher. I spent much of my childhood in his laboratories. Eleanora, my mother, is an artist, and from an early age, she taught me the world of art, from its most practical to historical aspects. Somewhere, between the laboratories and studios of my parents, I transformed into an artist who interprets the world through the lens of science.
Ironically, the place of my NYU graduate masters show, at 80 Washington Square Gallery, had been my father and grandfather's laboratory years before. My part of the show resembled a lab of machines, including a mechanical sidewalk. It seemed like I was taking their path in a new direction. The idea of combining contemporary sculpture and modern science with non-traditional materials has kept me busy. I remembered as a child in chemistry class, fantasizing about the molecular formula by associating the structure with example, alcohol (ethanol) looks like a dog with the 4 hydrogen's as feet, a head of oxygen, nose of hydrogen, body of two carbons and a tail of hydrogen. This is how I arrived at "Sugabus" a seminal bronze sculpture of sucrose completed for the Laumeier Sculpture Park in 2004. With time and reflection, the cosmology of science may intersect with contemporary art in dynamic new ways.

Being born and raised in Miami, I am thrilled at the development of the Arts scene in the past decade. When I departed to NYC in the mid 80's for graduate school, I felt an energy present in Miami, but the structure to utilize the energy had somehow not materialized yet. Rich ideas were brewing, alternative happenings were happening. There were great shows, and artists were appearing from all over the globe. What was missing was a little focus and organization. That changed with the arrival of Art Basel in 2002. It has always been my feeling that artists, on the whole, depend on each other for sustenance. I have learned in life that one must teach, as well as do. I have spent my life as a teacher as well as sculptor, including stints at NYU as an Adjunct Professor, and University of Miami as an Assistant Professor. Lately, I have seen myself as an alternative mentor for young artists in Miami, and enjoy seeing their success gained with integrity and vision.

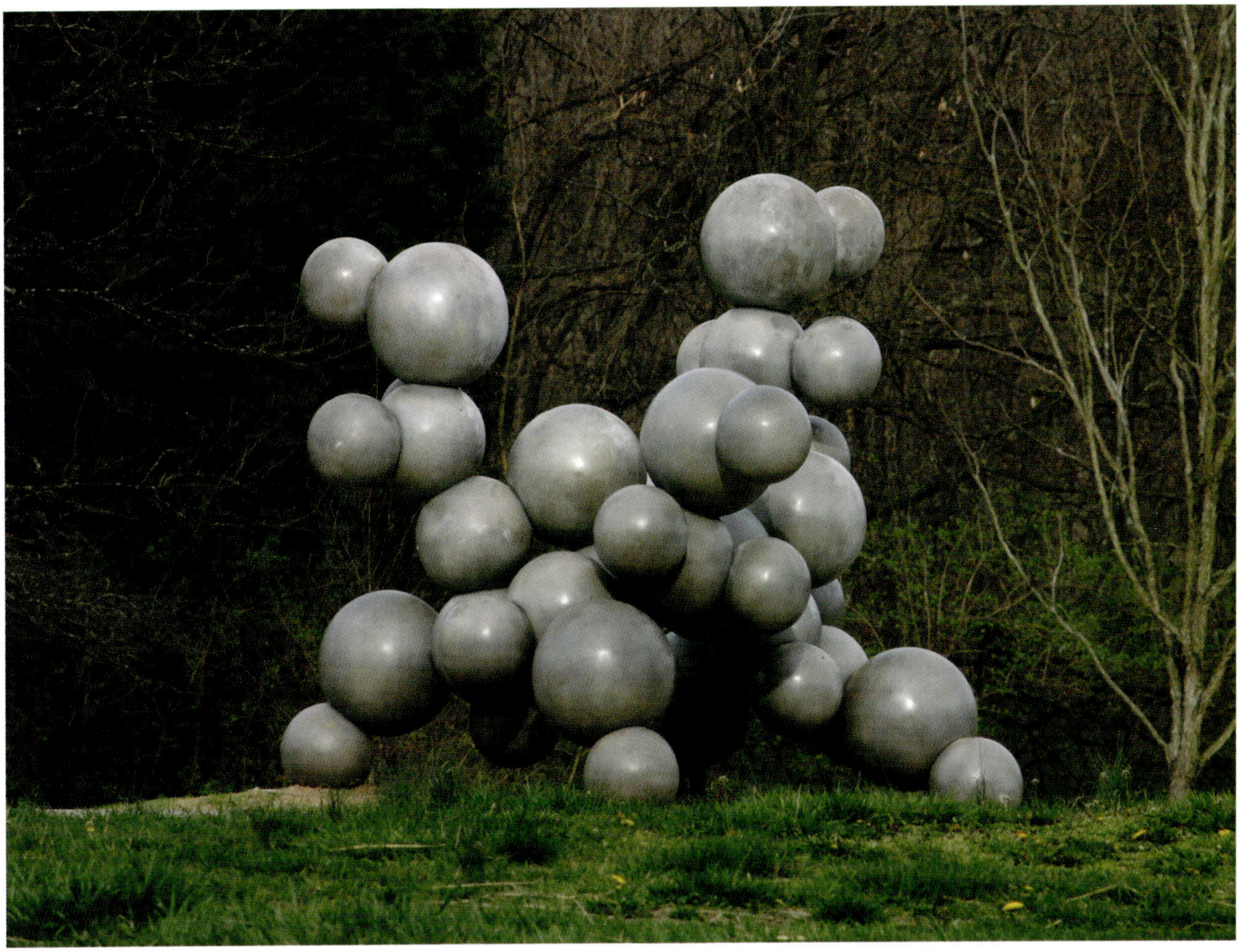

Sugabus, 2004. Bronze, 14′ x 12′ x 12″. Collection Laumeier Sculpture Park, St. Lous, MO.

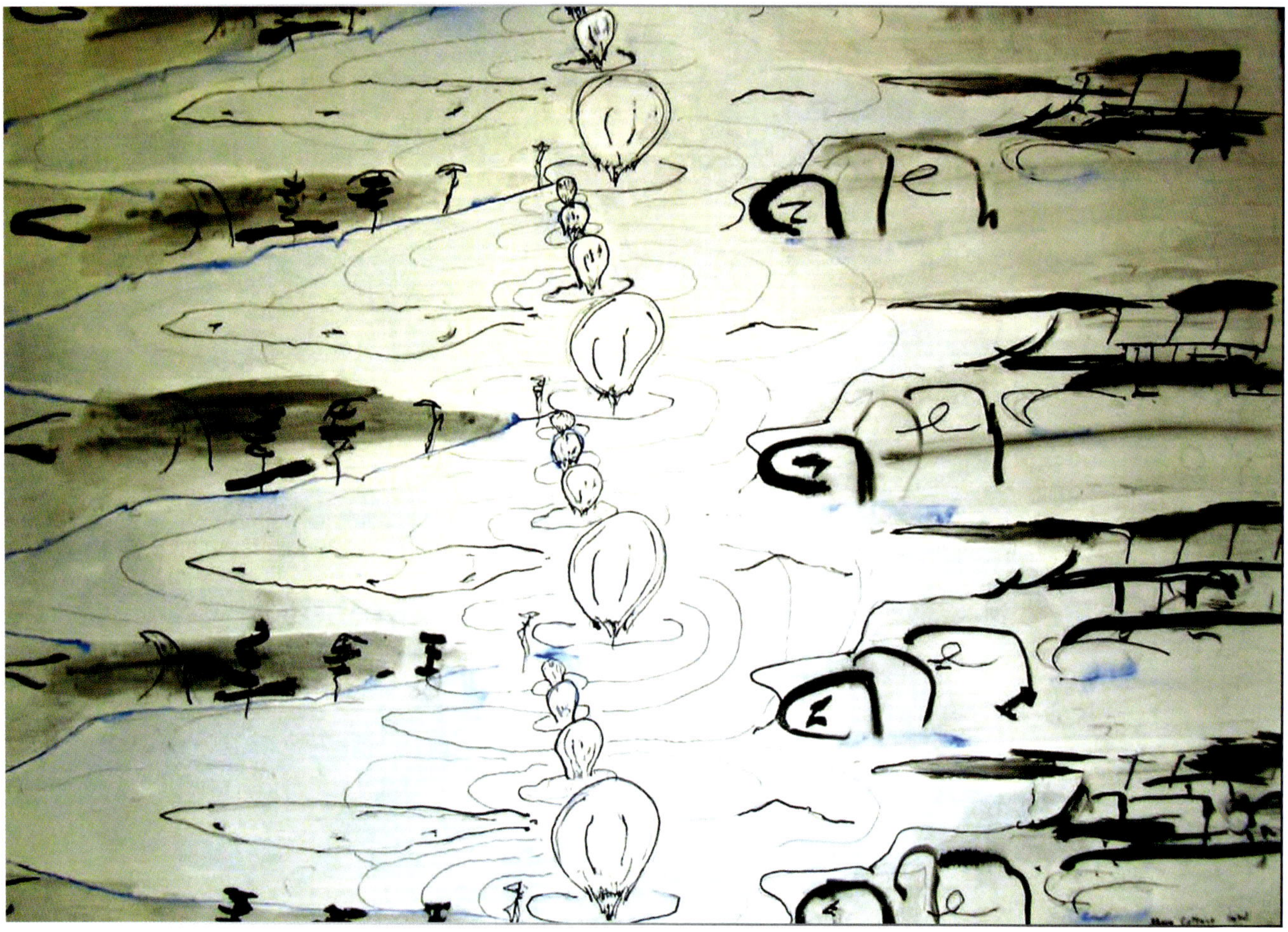

Shore Cottage 8 Bubbles, 2004. Drawing. Karesansui Garden Series, ink, graphite, and mixed media, 30" x 42".

Facing page:
Shore Cottage 8 Bubbles, 2004. Installation photograph, Karesansui Garden Series. Latex, silk, helium, rope, LED lights, electrical components, 20 x 1000 yds, Mount Desert Island, Maine.

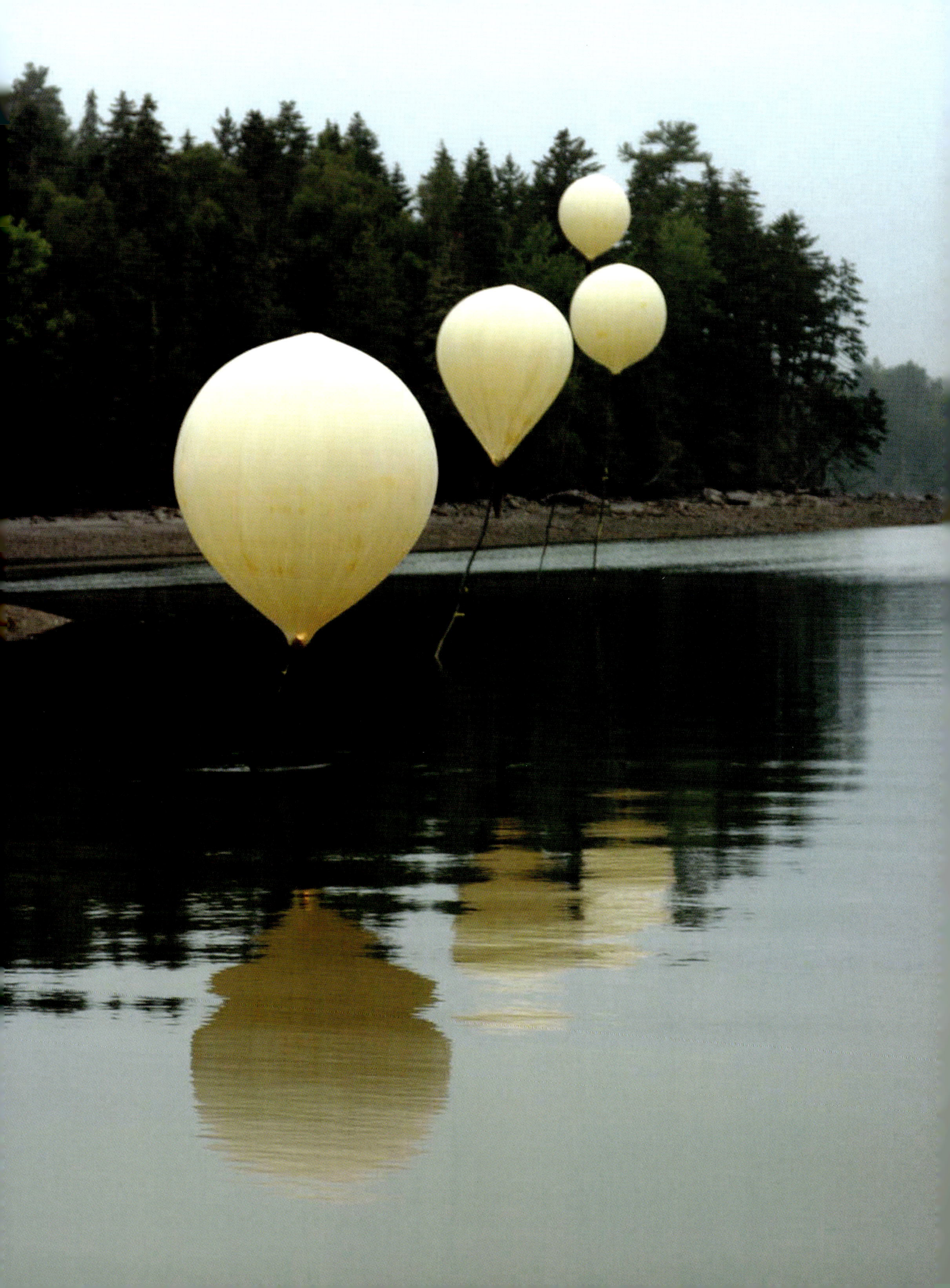

WESTEN CHARLES

Westen Charles is a Miami-based artist who creates multi-layered, subtly psychological work. His elaborate installations are unsettling and unforgettable. Characterized by a truly unique sensibility, Charles has worked with various materials such as bowling balls, stuffed animals, coconuts and laundry lint. He is adept at creating conceptual twists with sophisticated economy. An example of this can be seen in his signature piece entitled "*Bagged Cheetah*" where Charles has adorned decorative living room statuary with am improvised camouflage mask. Associative potential is paramount in Charles' work. The elements that he uses regularly inform and inspire his projects. Other inanimate objects that have graced his installations include trophy figurines, parquet flooring, rugs, and G-string underwear. Charles delivers a quirky, visually riveting allure through manipulating form and function with razor sharp ingenuity.

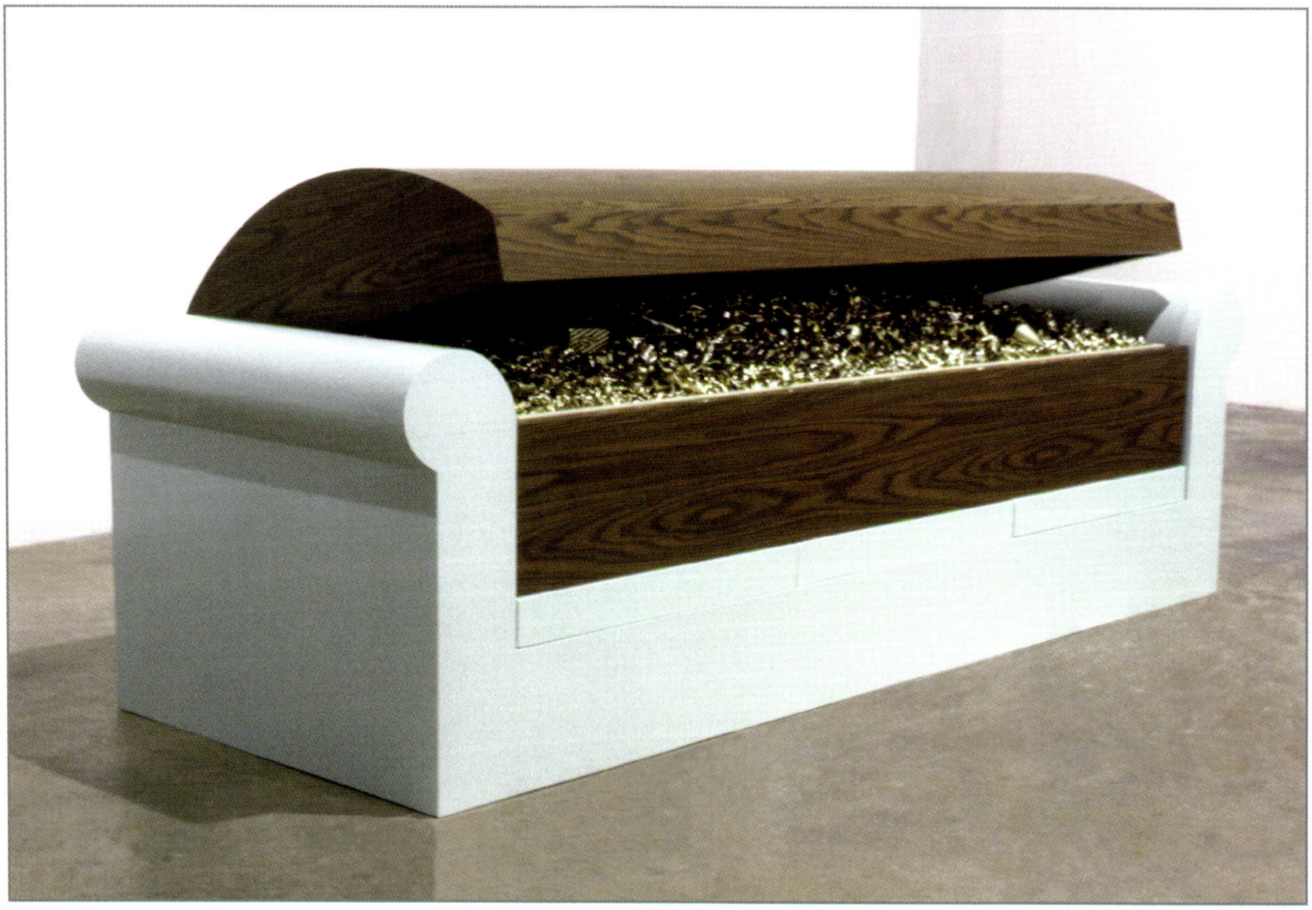

Fool's Gold, 2000. Mixed media, 48" x 120" x 42". Collection Miami Art Museum.

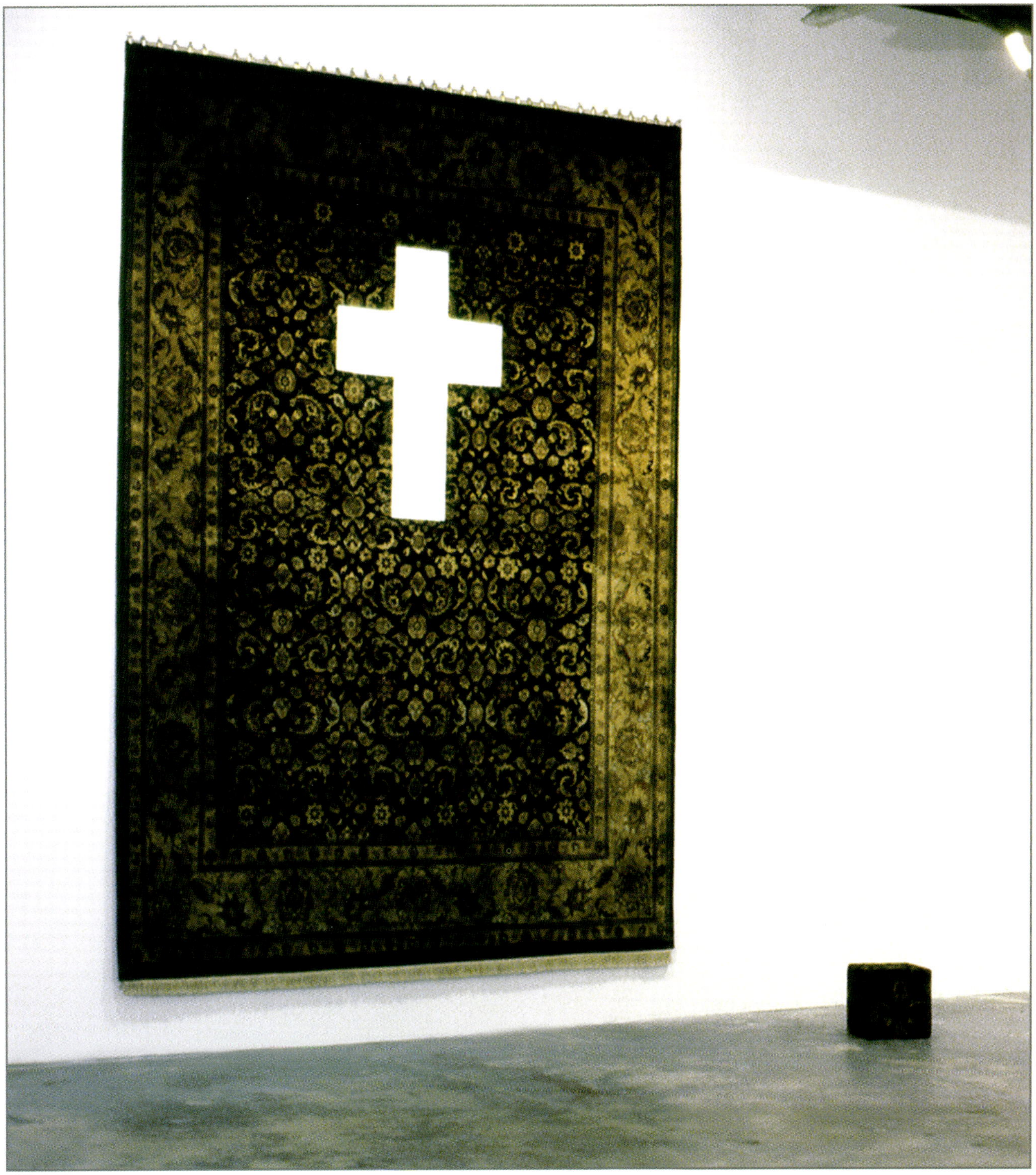

Cross cut Carpet, 2003. Indian rug and 12" covered cube.

CLIFTON **CHILDREE**

My work comes from inner exploration of childhood fears, nightmares, fever hallucinations, and personal history reconstructed under the guise of resurrected and dusted off silent film. Photos from my grandmother's early years dancing in Vaudeville, a grandfather who dabbled in whaling and told tall tales, and a host of other colorful characters are part of the history pool I fish from. Curious as to what happens in the gaps of the stories, what isn't caught on film and what isn't openly discussed; I create my own fill-in scenarios. These fabricated tales tend to stray quite far from any semblance of reality as I get further into the process. But, I feel a real gut level connection with my family's past and enjoy wielding a bit of control over it. I add to it, and shape it a bit, creating if not a harmless fib, then a past with a new, reinvigorated voice.

I am fixing up my house within Miami's Little Haiti. The neighborhood lawn man offered to edge my yard at no cost, "Happy to see someone bringing the house back to life." After I planted a thorny Kapok tree near the entrance he yelled, "What happened? When you plant that tree, means you into Voodoo!" He also mentioned that the tree would light up at midnight. I asked about zombies. "WHAT! Zombies will be walking by that tree at night!" Around midnight, I keep one eye on my front lawn for any sign of movement. Occasional drumming in the distance adds a jungle, voodoo type flair to the nights. Zombies wander along the road towards the hole in the fence where two dead chickens lay for months. One morning I even found my leftover lunch devoured inside my truck, corn littered the floor mats. I join the zombies sometimes, sneaking outside in my ripped clothes with my eyes open wide and my arms stretched forward, slowly I work my way closer to where they are. I groan "foooood" in a deep voice then turn and run back inside. Although I know I would be a great zombie extra in Hollywood, there's nothing like the real thing in Little Haiti.

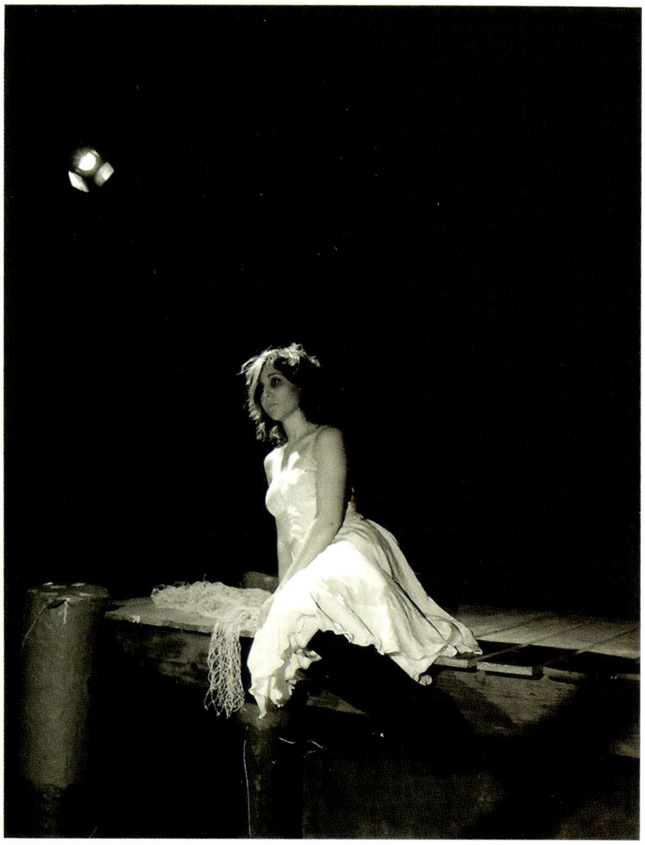

Dances on Pier , 2005. Still image from *She Sank on Shallow Bank.*

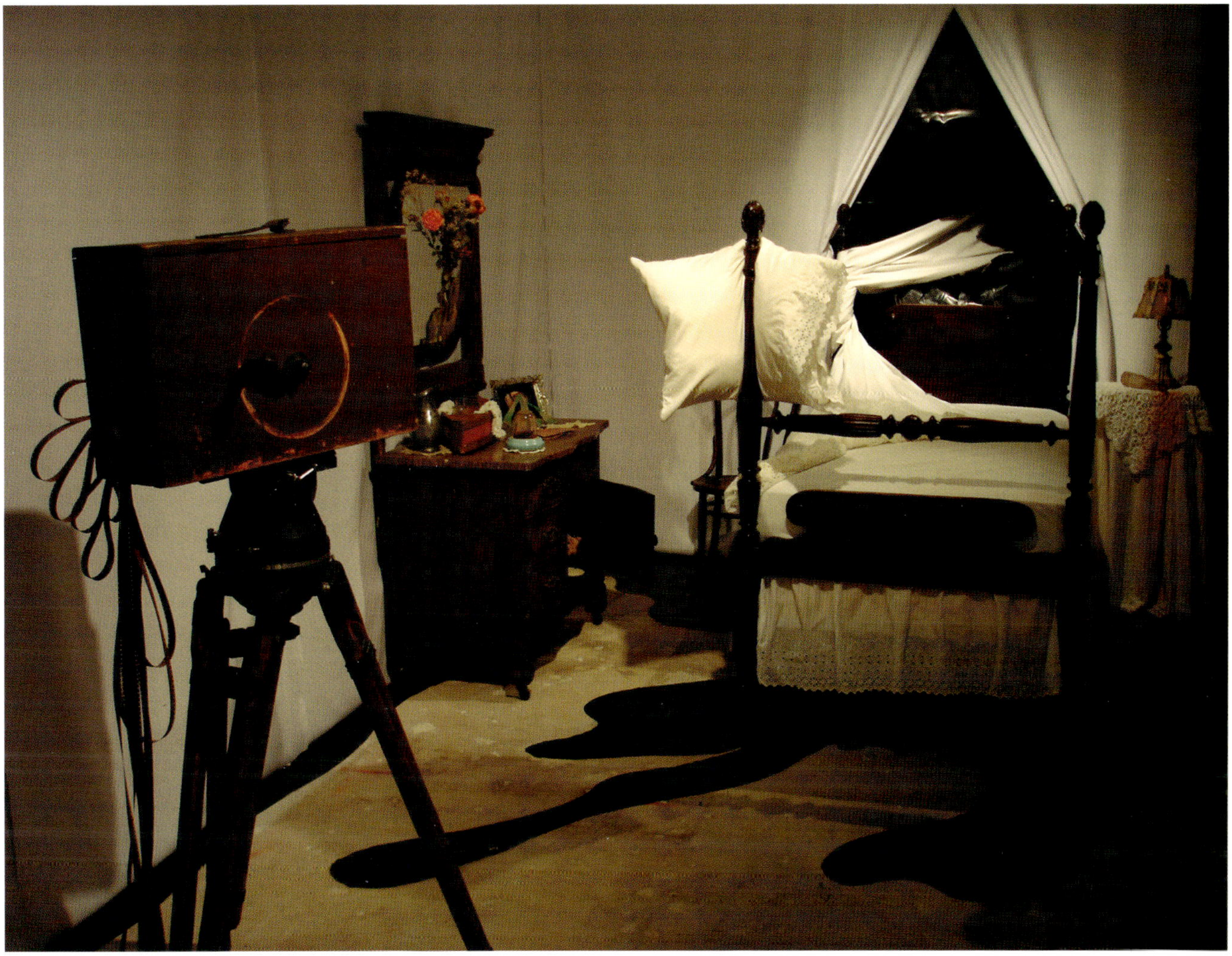

She Sank on Shallow Bank, 2005. Installation view at the Bas Fisher Invitational, Miami, by Nikki Rollason and Clifton Childree.

LOU ANNE COLODNY

My experiences in dance, theater, and museum administration have greatly informed my work. One can find a sense of space, drama, and focused ideas within my video and photographic images. Many of my videos are performative and are incorporated within large scale installations. The "video stills "enable the viewer to react to the single image which links to underlying ideas. These stills are created to mesmerize, tantalize and make thought imperative...I want people to react to my art. The sound, editing, filming, scripting and acting are by my own hand. I consider myself as a found object...used to explore emotional, physical and social pressures in our society. The videos are not autobiographical but rather tightly cropped or altered in an attempt to represent everyman/woman as universal. My current body of work explores the eternal quest for youth and beauty that is now, more than ever, a part of our popular culture. Our society's obsession with youth culture has spawned a multimillion dollar cosmetic and cosmetic surgery industry. Advertising, nightly news and weekly TV shows such as "Nip/Tuck," "The Swan" attempt to morph our society into one that is homogenized, looking the same and wishing to be accepted for superficial reasons. Youthful, pretty individuals are employable, "hot" commodities and sought after in our society. By blurring the lines between reality and fiction, I have intertwined these issues within my work which continually seeks to be psychologically and emotionally provocative.

Miami's young, emerging artists have become a "phenomena" reported in magazines, newspapers, blogs and in the national, and international art scene. I am an *emerging* artist and *young* to the art scene BUT not *chronologically young*. It presents a fascinating situation. Most of my friends are established artists who were the backbone of the Miami arts scene in the 60s through the 90s. They are the ones I hang with....they were the ones taking "risks," commenting on society and the world in which they lived. Now they are also the teachers in our colleges and universities...influencing the "recognized" artists of the day. I have often observed that to get recognition here, I should create a new persona...one that is in her 20s, better yet, I should not be identified as male or female, and in the tradition of Maurizio Cattelan, never be seen by anyone. I should change my voice...deal with cars, boom boxes, stolen images and music, and be self taught. My work should suddenly appear ...many times in many unprecedented places. 'It should be "cutting edge" which garners extensive news coverage, is collected by the consensus art makers, and accepted into a gallery. Sounds like a good art project. Yes? No! I am having a great time emerging and exploring the art scene as an artist. It is full of expectation, disappointment, growth and enthusiasm. I am like that 20 year old....finding my way into a mystical, often confusing world full of hierarchies, egos, and wonderful, gleeful art making.

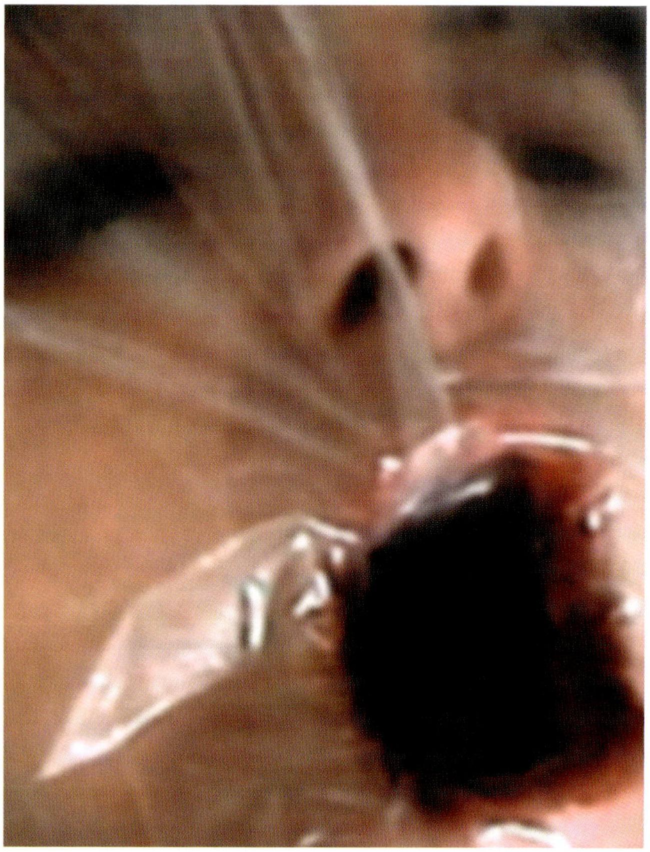

Untitled (breath 7), 2002. Lambda print mounted on gatorboard, 36" x 28", edition of 5 + 1 AP, Video still from *Breath.*

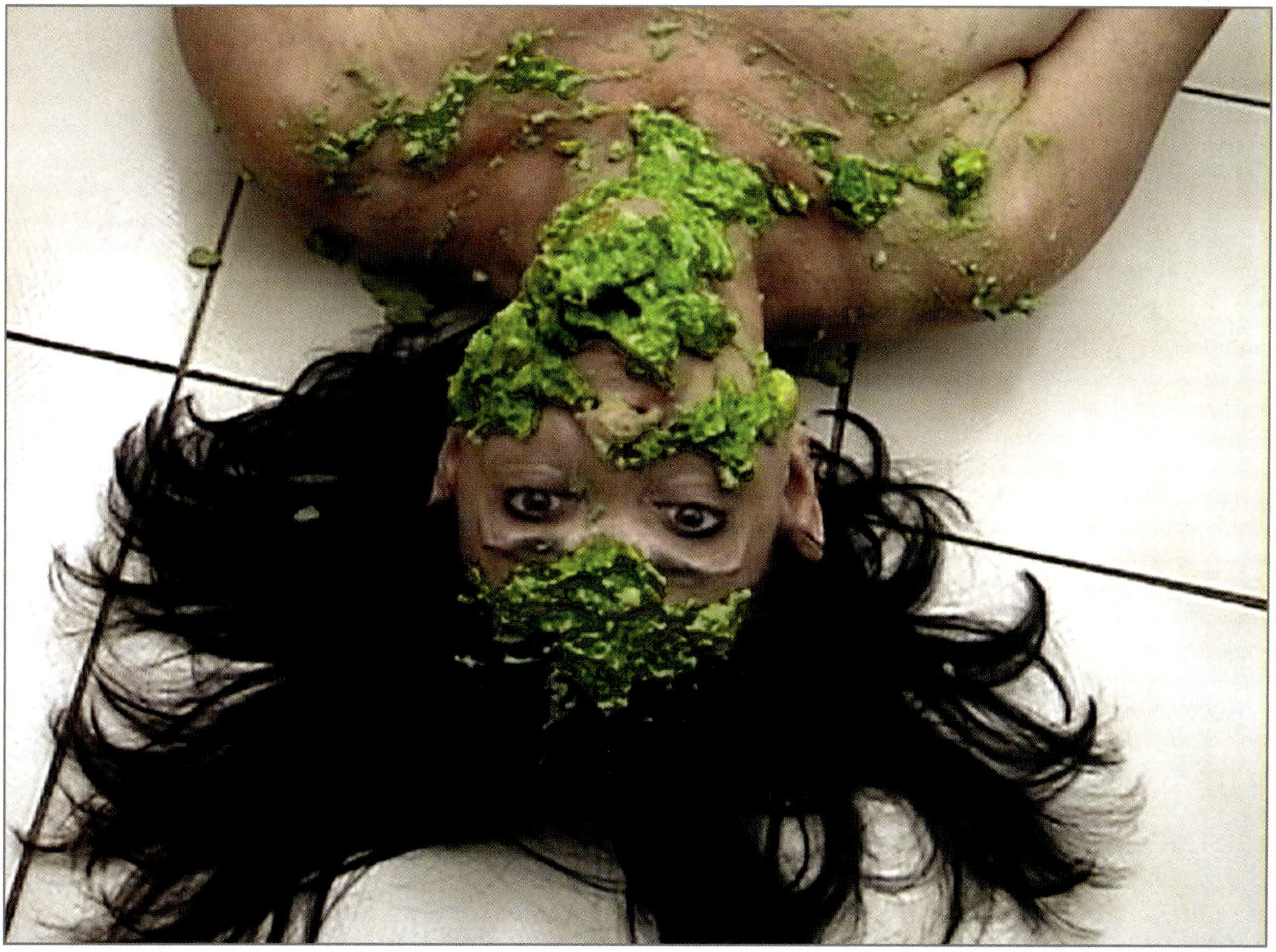

Untitled (green face), 2005. Archival inks on paper mounted on sintra, 16″ x 24″, edition of 5 + 1 AP, video still from *SATURATION.*

COOPER

Same as the last time except this time nobody was watching.
Are you afraid of the unknown? Its being afraid of the known or sometimes imagining the unknown based on the information you do have, that's where the real fear lies, it is in that place where you take your real experiences and mix them up with darkness beyond your sight. And sometimes you have to hide in that place, become that thing behind the obscured. Be the absence of ego or self and peer out until you can really see what is left of you. Are you a monster inside if you become one with your facade? Summon the image of the *Unknown Comic* (The Gong Show, syndicated television, 1976-1980), was he the same act when he was just Murray Langston unmasked? The character took on a new persona when masked, with entirely new attitudes and comedic routines. Was he ashamed or reborn? Consider John Merrick, *The Elephant Man*, does his mask instill more or less fear than his "natural" appearance. Does the persona outweigh the costume, or vice versa? What of *Michael Jackson's* surgical masks? *"We often look away when confronted with imagery of the sick, the deformed, the dead and dying, but in the nineteenth century there was a brisk trade in such photographs of "the other"; the circus freak, the bearded lady, Siamese twins, and so forth were popular subjects to be collected and traded. To the extent that we worry about exploitation of bodies which do not conform to the norm or suffer from some affliction, our reticence is humane; but to the extent that we refuse to confront the human condition, it is pathological." – William A. Ewing "The Body: Photoworks of the Human Form" "We all need our fright-wig period, but only the most fearful artists feel such a heavy, pounding need to express adolescent, in-your-face ideas about life, death, mortality and culture for the entirety of their careers. The artists I respect get more irreverent with age while, at the same time, they humanize; they lighten up, they drop the old mask, they actually start to care about things more and open up a little, laughing about things they used to take to heart as deathly serious. They evolve – for better or worse." – Centra Wilson "Salon: Brilliant Careers"*

Cooper's work employs dark and moody tableaus, presenting the viewer with fragmented elements from current and past society; piecing them together with peculiar methods that question social constructs and the assumptions of art-history and visual purity. These art works exist as minor monuments to both man's conquests and his/her subjugation. He is a founder of Locust Projects, an alternative art exhibition space in Miami.

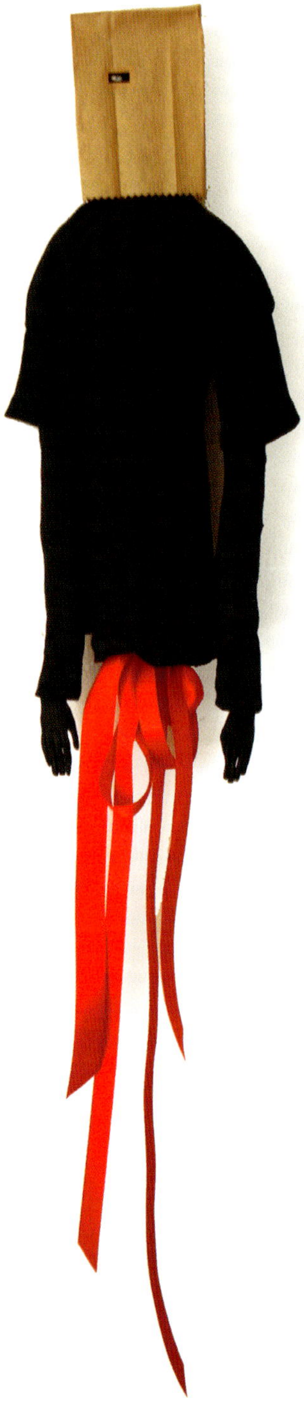

"Same as the last time, except this time, nobody was listening, and then one terrible night it all ended." (Subway dare version), 2004. Wood, oilseed blackboard paint, resin, cotton, acrylics, soil, foam, copper, paper, epoxy and various hardware, 1.5' x.5' x .5' (variable).

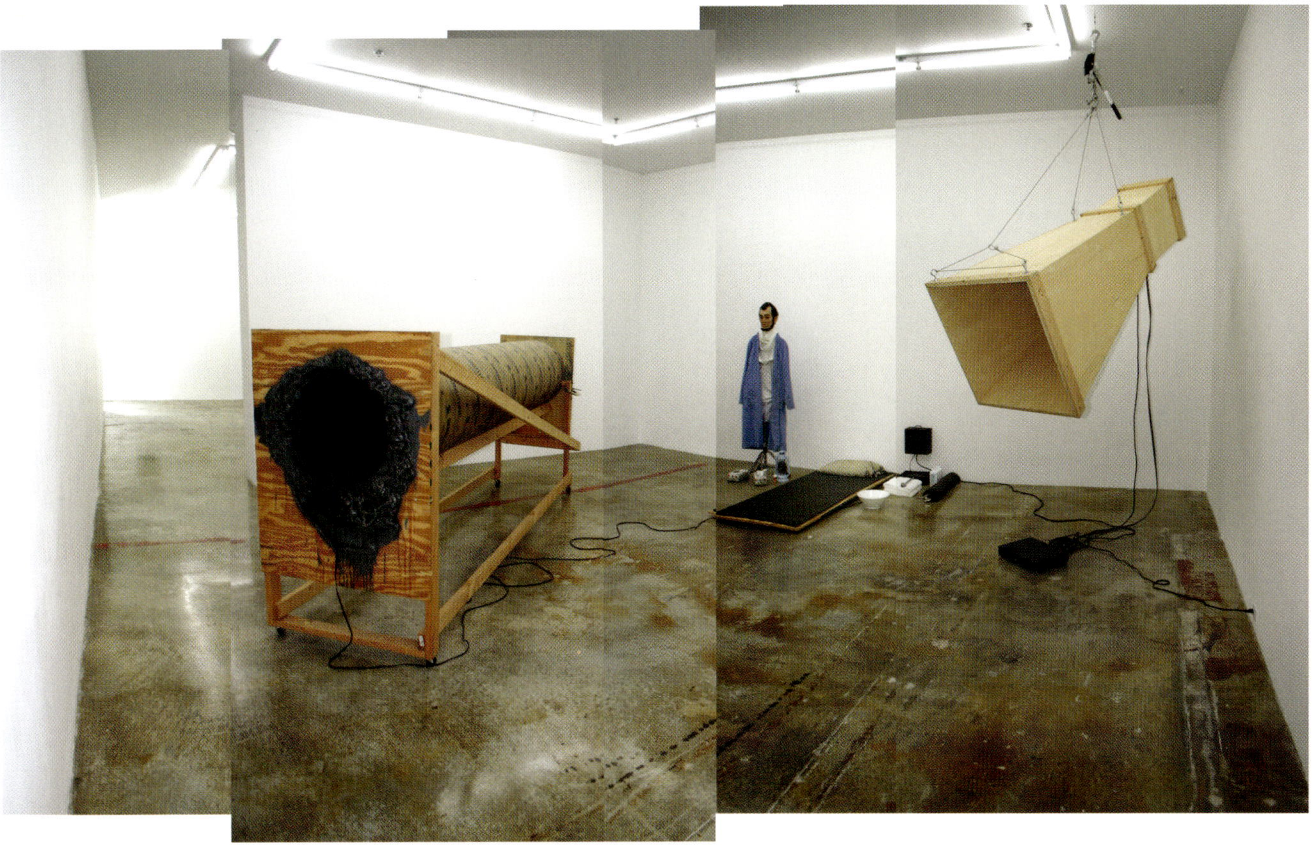

"Same as the last time, except this time, nobody is listening, because of the last time." (Minimalist artists die alone version), 2004. 12 minute audio loop, stereo equipment, wood, oilseed blackboard paint, concrete, resin, cotton, acrylics, soil, polymer foam, copper, paper, epoxy, and various hardware, 14' x 4.5' x 3.5'.

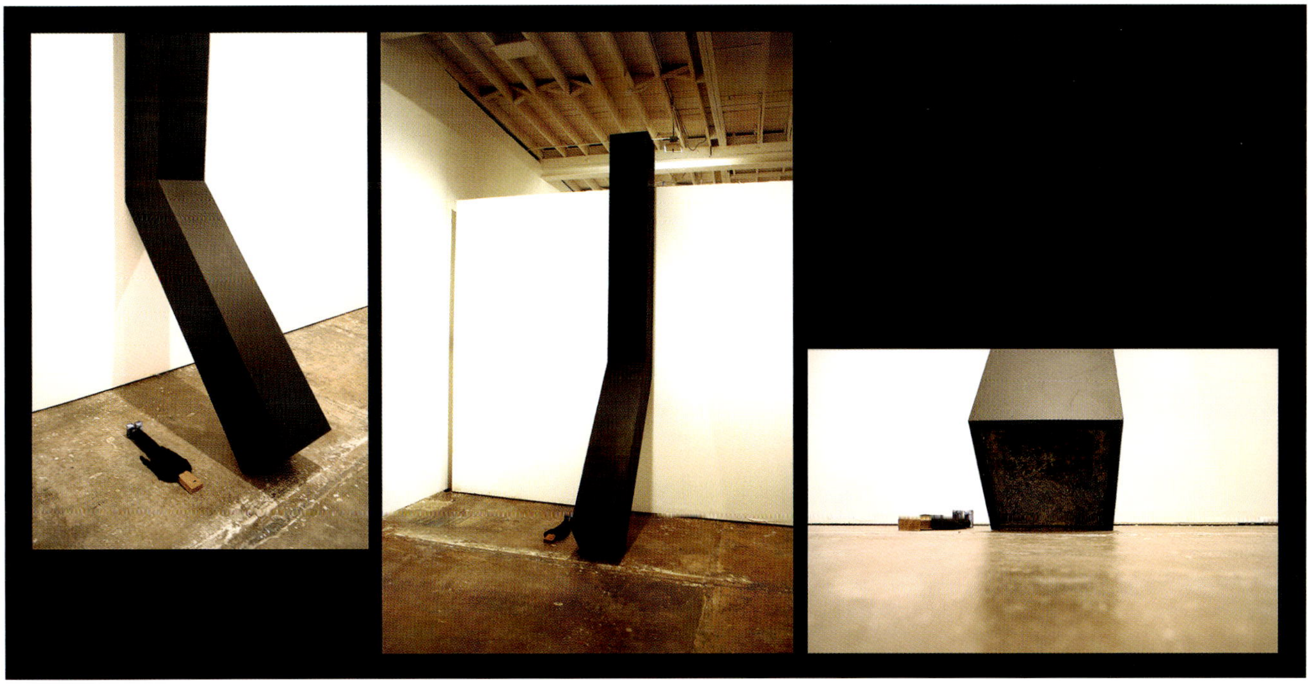

"Drainpipes and death myths, headrest bombs and dusty things in closets, rotten pastries and years of privation; but lets consider a moment in the past when we could have done things differently, or perhaps been someone else- 'locum temens' for the sake of change- through fences, across fields and out of windows with our American cousin," 2002/2005. Looped video on DVD, wood, paint, resin, cotton, wool, acrylics, soil, foam, copper, paper, electric audio devices, ink, steel cable, polymer foam, stainless steel, talcum powder, iodine, epoxy, and various hardware, 25' x 29' x13'.

CHRISTIAN **CURIEL**

The fragmented visual presence of memory from the age of innocence is disturbingly detached and familiar. Curiosity plays a colorful role in the events of childhood. The process of learning and constructing self-identity through the latent memories of youth serves as a catalyst for my creative world. History and figuration serve as natural ways to comment on the human condition. I often use allegory and symbolism to comment on current events and allow viewers to access, imagine and re-live childhood. Storytelling in my paintings works like memory functions: non-sequential and fragmented, constructed, and revealing time. Rather than linear narrative, I depict moments of activity or curiosity in which the viewer begins with what is given, questioning and developing different stories depending on personal experience. At first glance, images of the normal and everyday appear simple and innocent, yet upon looking closer, the tragic and anomalous begin to emerge.

Home-cooking, warmth, and abundant colors, of family and closest friends. Hand-painted spirit store signs. Cold mangoes at a warm beach. See through pink flotation devices, 90 miles closer. Humidity, air conditioning, and proud feelings of investment that helped create a vibrant artistic urgency. A place filled with artificial beautiful heat. Old men in guayaberas smoking fat cigars. Storytelling and folklore. Cuba. Platanos, y un cafecito with warm, tan sugar froth floating at the top. So many colors, drama, palm trees with Christmas lights, lost love, lessons learned. Where I tattooed my wing, and lost my father, and found my mother. The Bell Haven trailer park – a place I struggled hard – and overcame. Miami is filled with the memories of my rapid youth good and bad. Home no matter where for the moment I reside.

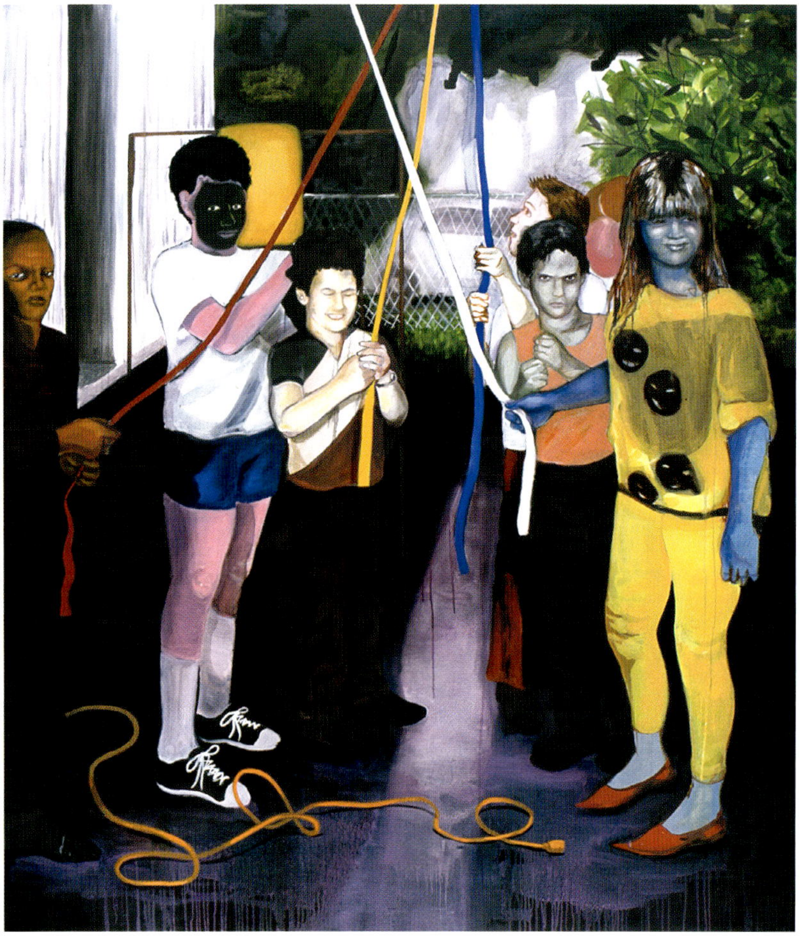

Pulling on Strings, 2004. Oil on canvas, 5′ x 6′. Collection of Rachel Lehmann.

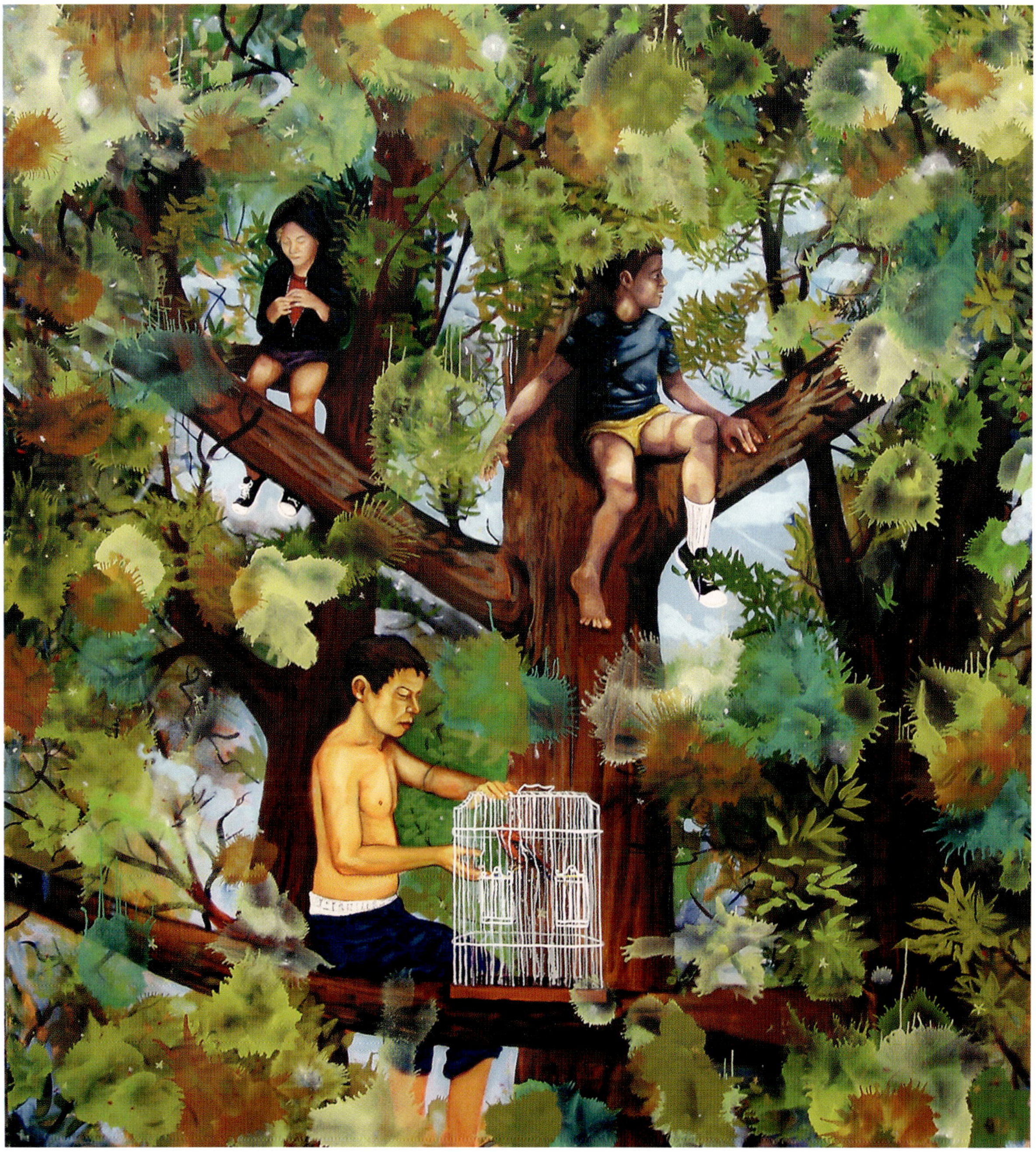

Treetop Barons, 2005. Oil on canvas, 6′ x 6′. Private Collection.

DASH N

Dash N. was born in Miami Beach, Florida in 1980. Living semi-nomadically, Dash has taken residence in various locations – Los Angeles, Oaxaca, Barcelona, Miami, Paris, and Abiquiiu – since leaving New York in 2003. She currently lives and works in New México. These images from the series *"Every Cell...."* derive their imagery from maps, imagined and real, and found images that evoke the uncertainty of the current and future political and environmental climate. These works were made after the completion of a six-month collaborative piece with artist Kol Solthon, which began and ended in Miami.

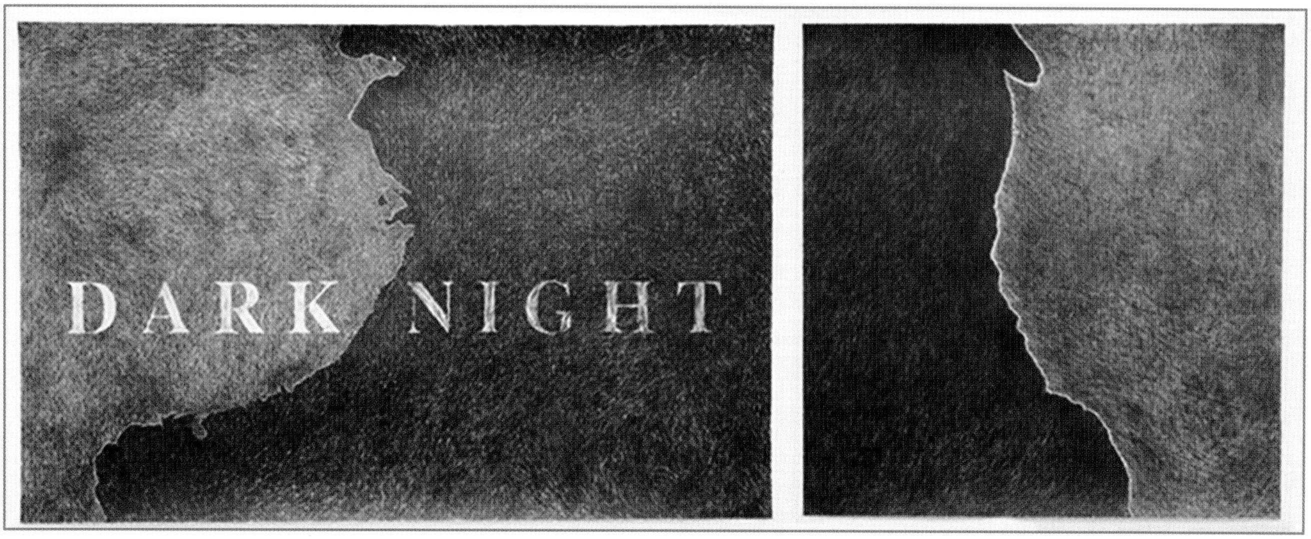

Untitled I (Dark Night), 2006 (diptych). Graphite on paper, L: 23.5" x 38.5", R: 23.5"x 23.5".

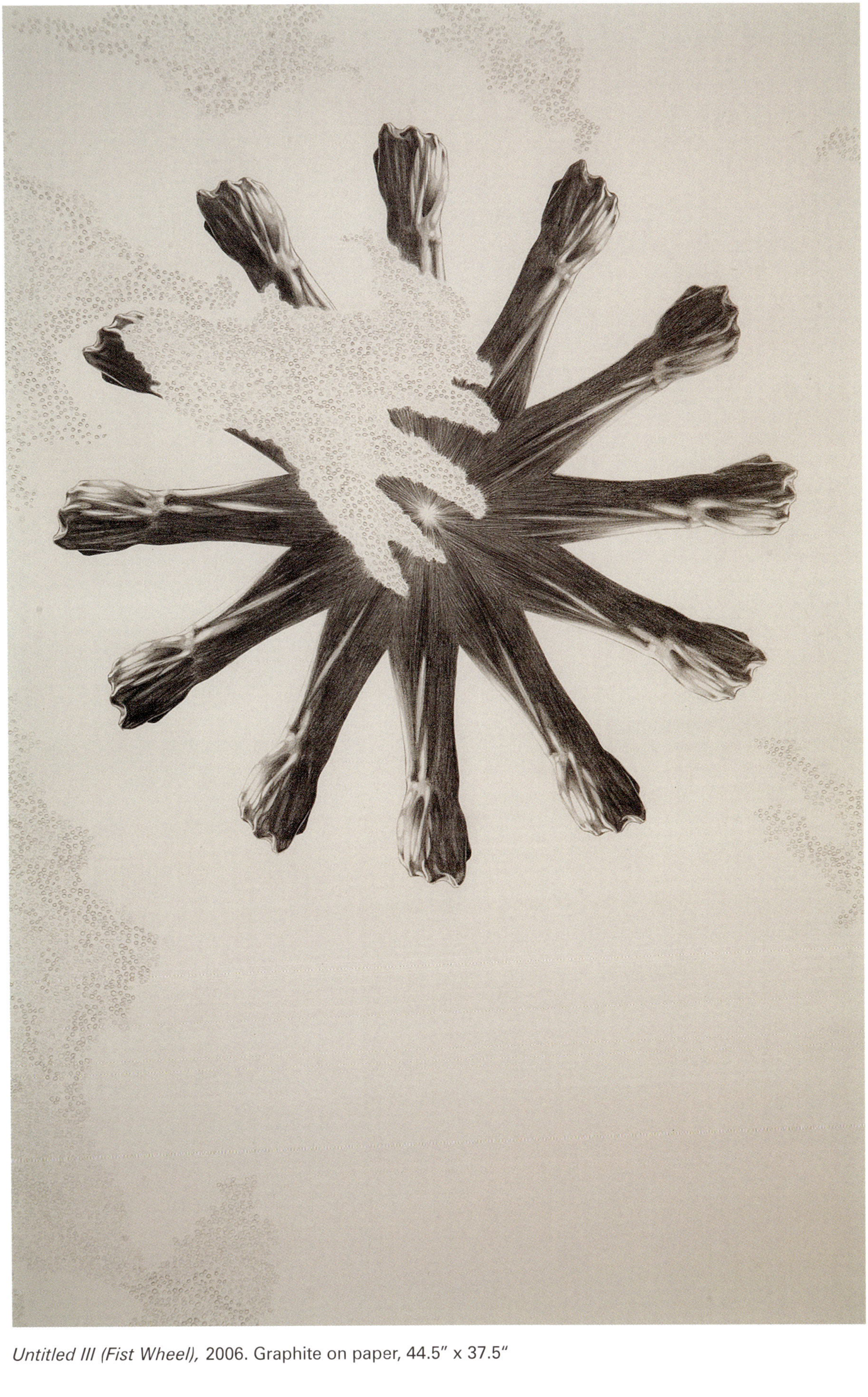

Untitled III (Fist Wheel), 2006. Graphite on paper, 44.5″ x 37.5″

IVAN TOTH DEPEÑA

Generally, my work attempts to dissect consciousness and perception, which in turn reveals the underlying complexity of the apparent and the mundane. It seeks to depict an honesty and present-ness found in journals and that most documentaries retain. The work and its processes mainly intend to document my thoughts and experiences and sometimes peek into collective gray areas. My work lies somewhere between the pacifying and the disturbing, between the psychological and the emotional and finally between commentary and muted fear. In my most recent work, I have begun to implement foreboding thoughts of our near future and some imagined "next steps" in the process of evolution. Thoughts of a world run by marketing executives, submerged in media and devoid of emotion. Thoughts of a world where financial status has started to leak its way in to human evolution. I have been having and creating images of animals, humans, extinction, mutation and how the world (and the life in it) will finally come to evolve. Wondering what would happen if certain technologies begin to morph our environment, creating a sort of magnetized cityscape where billboards, signage, nature, etc... have mutated in to a chaotic science fiction like reality. I have been thinking about how some or all of these things can somehow combine to create new life forms and interesting visual landscapes. My earlier work documented tenuous and obscure relationships and opposing subject matter in their natural state. The new work is starting to actually create these relationships and present them within a fictional and interactive environment.

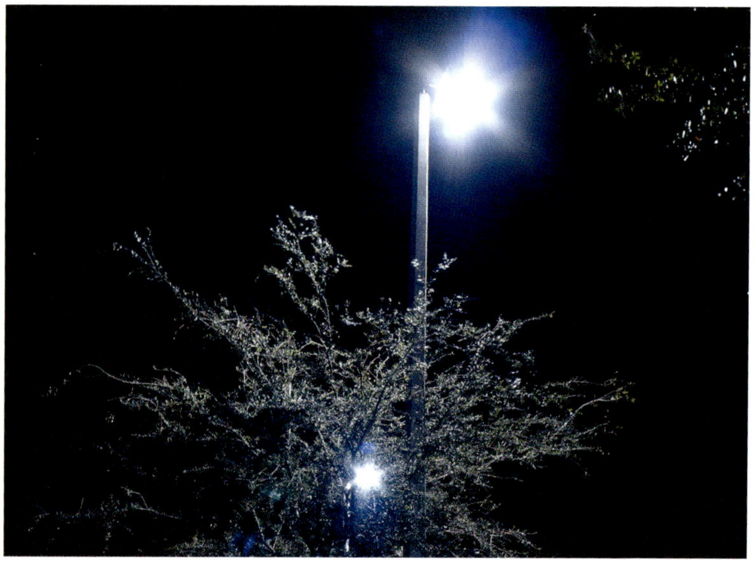

"Untitled" from the series *"Incidental Antinomies: The Portraits,"* 2004. Fuji light jet photographic print, 35" x 45".

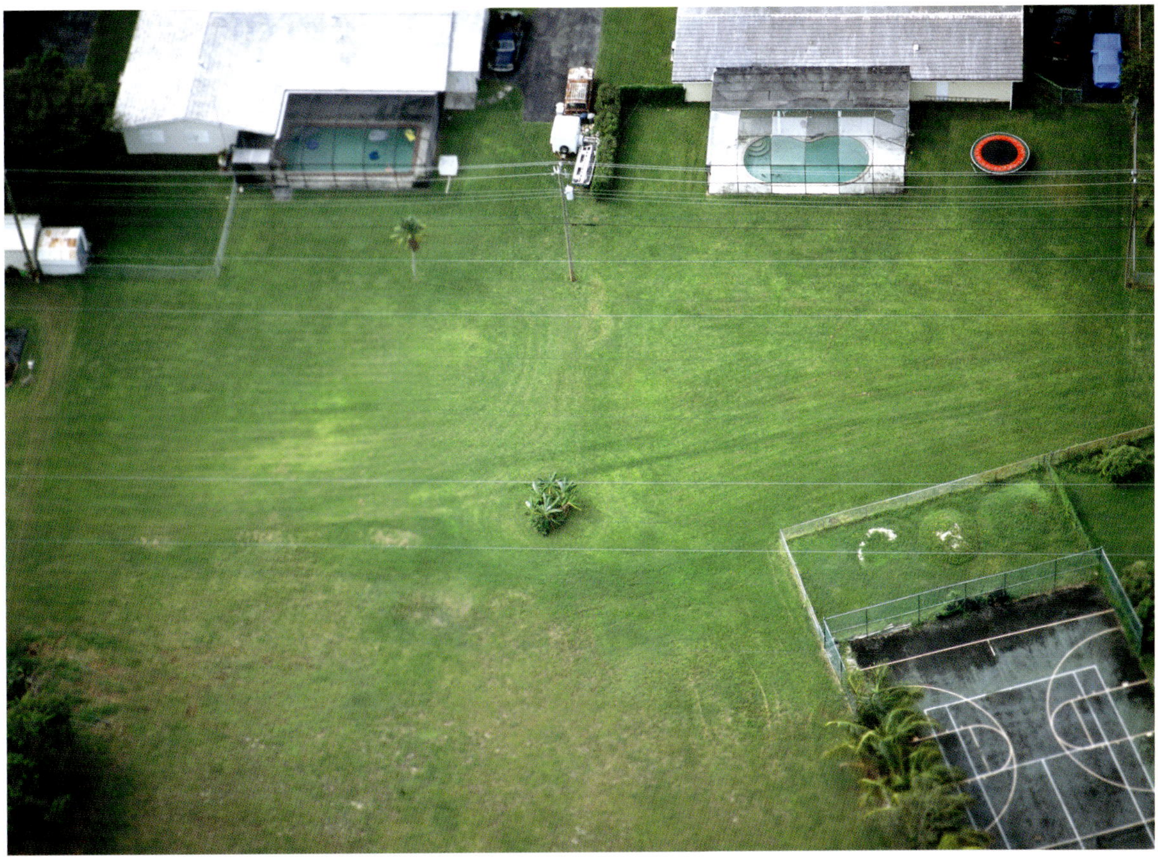

Untitled (Yards/Trees) from the series *"Hereafter,"* 2005. Fuji light jet photographic print, 30" x 40".

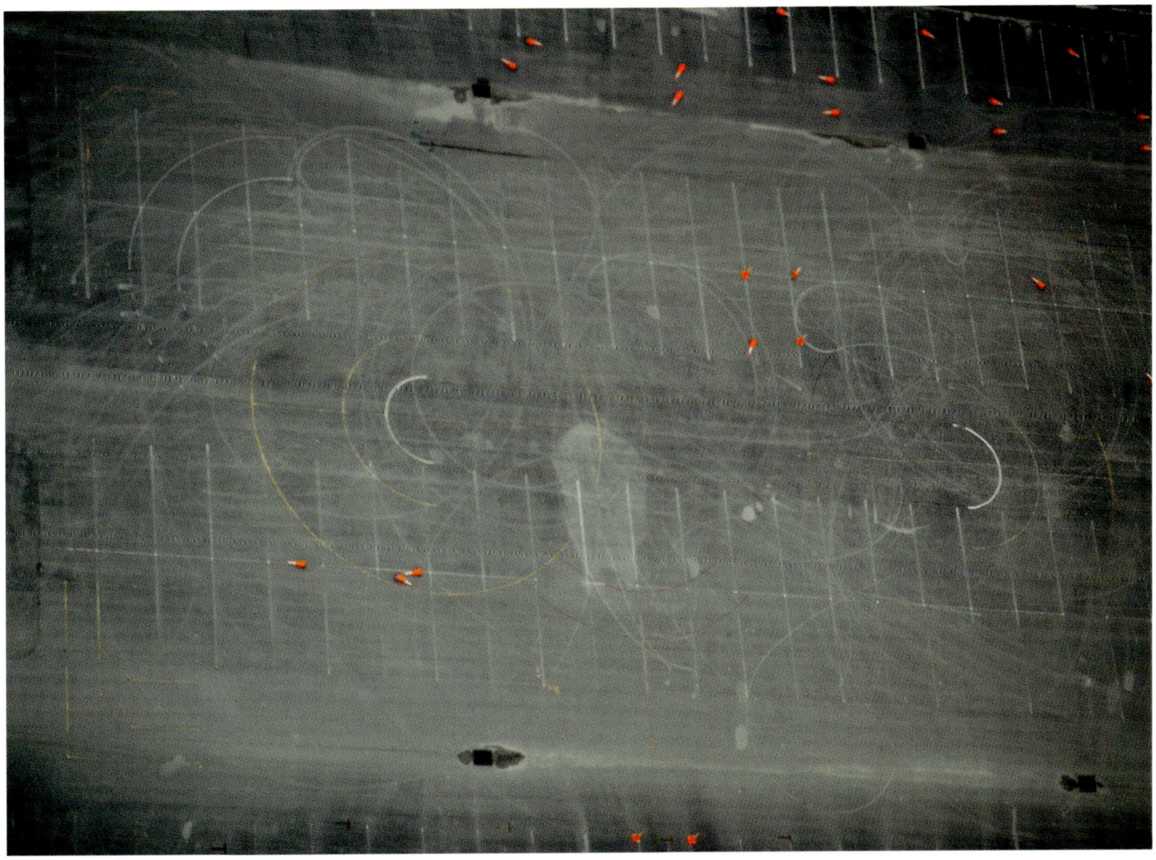

Untitled (Cones/ Lot) from the series *"Hereafter",* 2005, Fuji light jet photographic print, 30" x 40".

CHRISTIAN **DURAN**

In my art I wish to convey the idea that one does not need to search at great length to observe and experience spirituality. People and nature are in themselves astonishing phenomena that are linked through a common vigor. This occurrence is most readily observed through similar structures and their physiology, such as veins and arteries, as they may relate to roots and branches. All of these forms function towards the sustaining and maintaining of life within that organism; one with blood and the other with water. I perceive these similarities to be non-coincidental and universal by nature, as well as exist as symbols of life. I use these elements in my work as metaphors of the union between people and nature. In my new work, I present the human body and nature as connected, interactive, and interchangeable. Through my work; I aspire to find my own poetry and beauty concerning the intangible self, as well as bring to mind a broader and truer perception of the human psyche.

Living and painting in Miami has been extremely motivational and influential in my life. This place has been a safe haven where I have been able to experiment and develop as an emerging artist. When I first returned to Miami from Kansas City in 1999 I was in need of an outlet, an environment where my work could grow and flourish. Because of Miami's art community I was able to befriend many great people such as artists, curators, and gallery owners which have in many ways contributed to my career today. I continue to live and work in South Florida because of the energy and potential herein. Undoubtedly, Miami is an invigorating and nurturing place for my art and life.

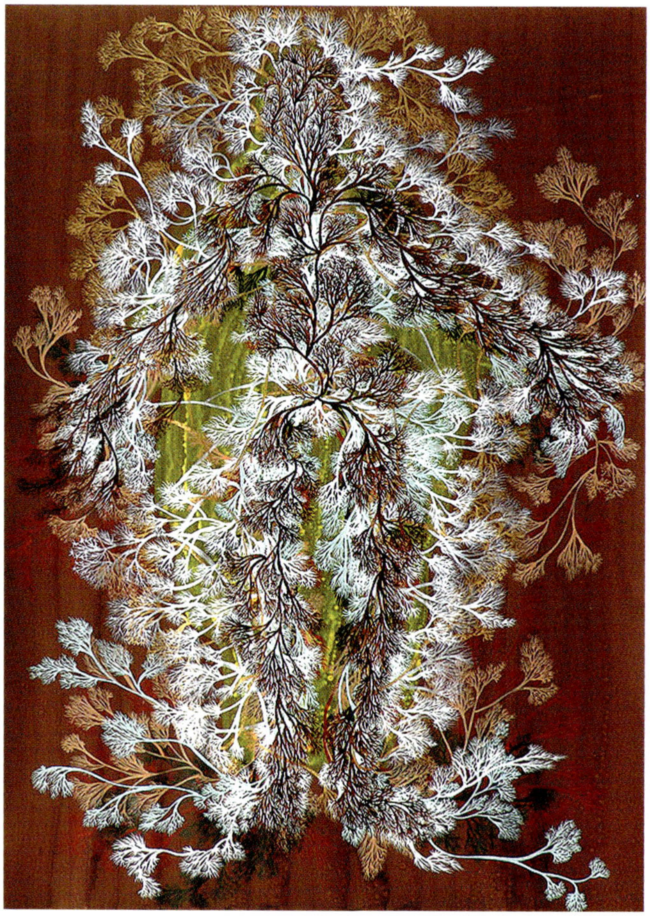

Mother, 2006. Acrylic, metallic powder on paper, 39" x 27.5".

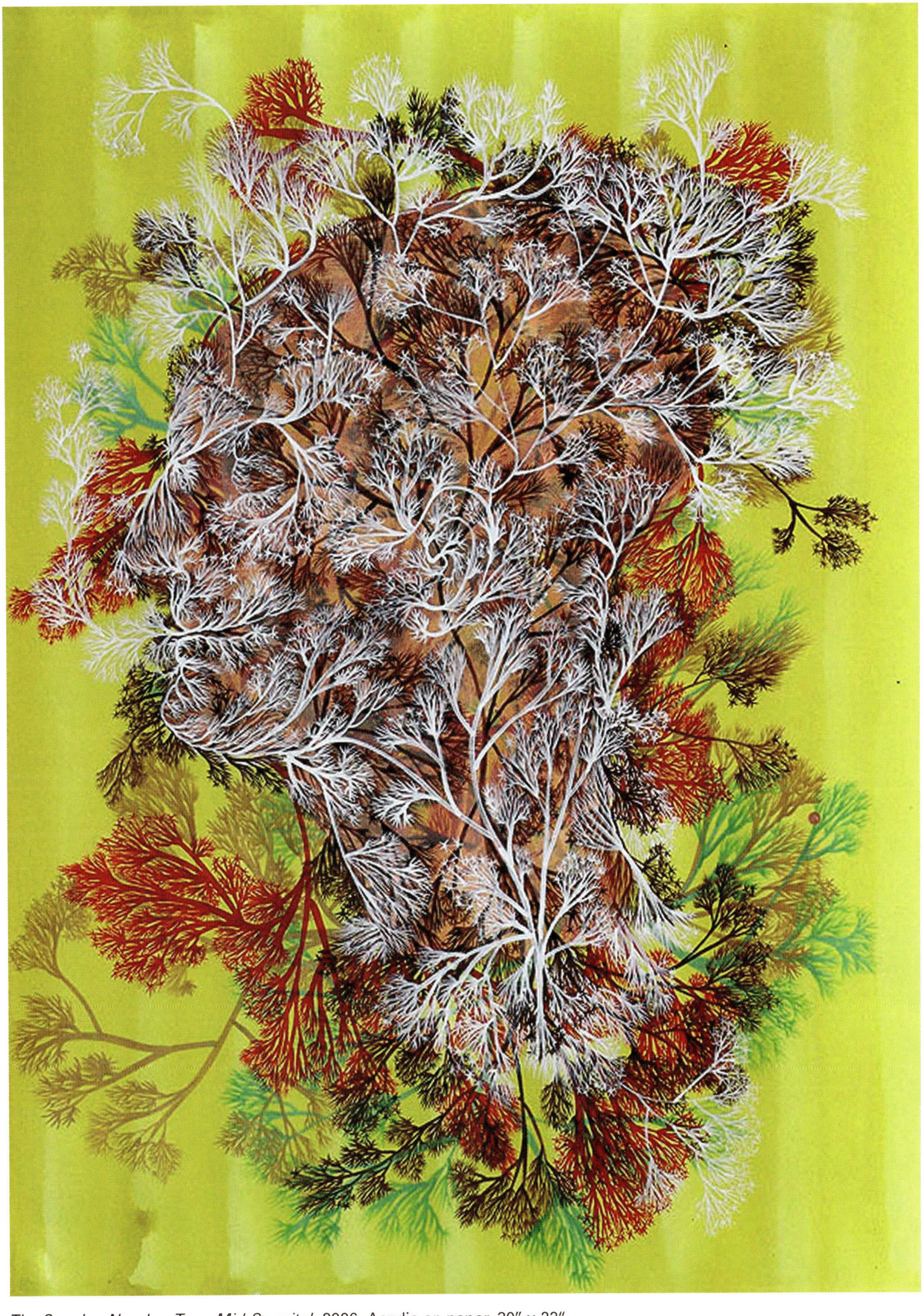

The Speaker Number Two: Mid-Saggital, 2006. Acrylic on paper, 30" x 22".

EDOUARD **DUVAL-CARRIÉ**

I personally believe that most artists are in one way or another, reflections of their immediate surroundings. What they are confronted with on a daily routine is bound to affect and influence their personal visions of the world. This general tendency would simplify my answers to inquiries on the relative importance of popular culture in the context of the contemporary art world. But with the advent of a rapid globalization and the proliferation of information at all levels, this permits everyone, and particularly artists, to take their ideas from a global well.

The city of Miami, and not forgetting its sister beach front, have been home to me for the last decade and a half. And I have yet to tire of life here! I always make the same comment to visitors to this area. Miami is like a chest full of drawers, each drawer filled with wonderful things that one has to plow through in order to have an inkling of the amazing complexity of the place. And I have not yet gone through the whole chest!!!

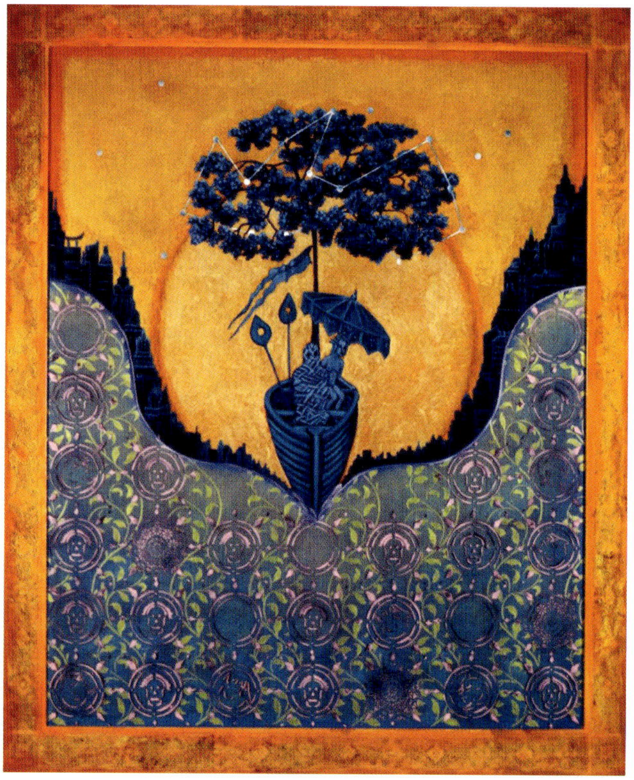

Le Monde Moderne, 2004. Oil on canvas in artist frame, 84" x 68".

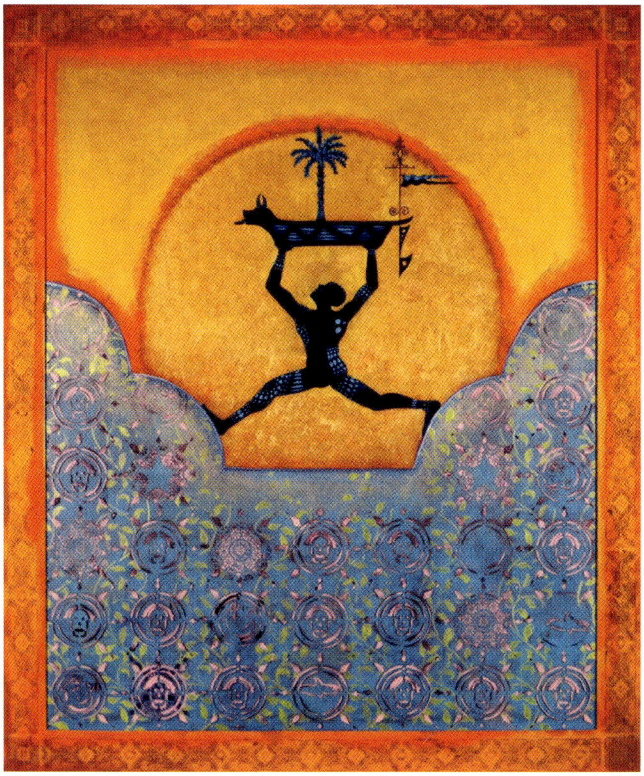

Dambalah le Passeur, 2004. Oil on canvas in artist frame, 84" x 68".

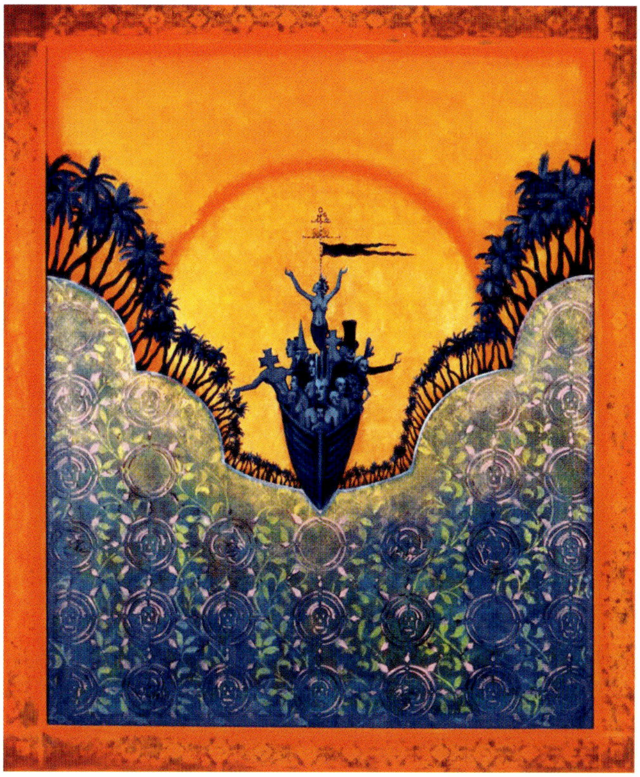

La Grande Ville, 2004. Oil on canvas in artist frame, 84" x 68".

Next page:
My Life as a Tree, 2006. Mixed media on aluminum with light backing, 144" x 96".

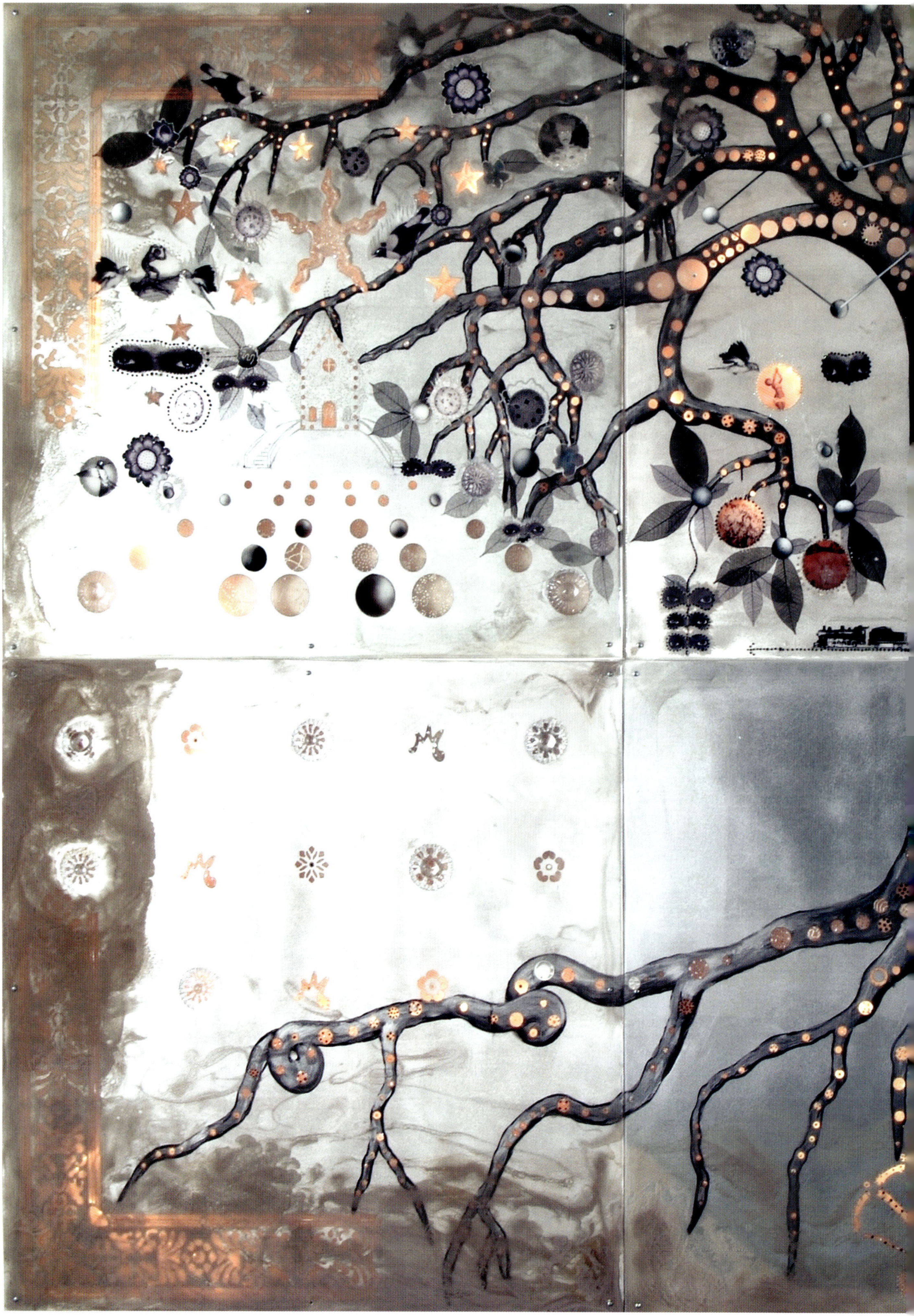

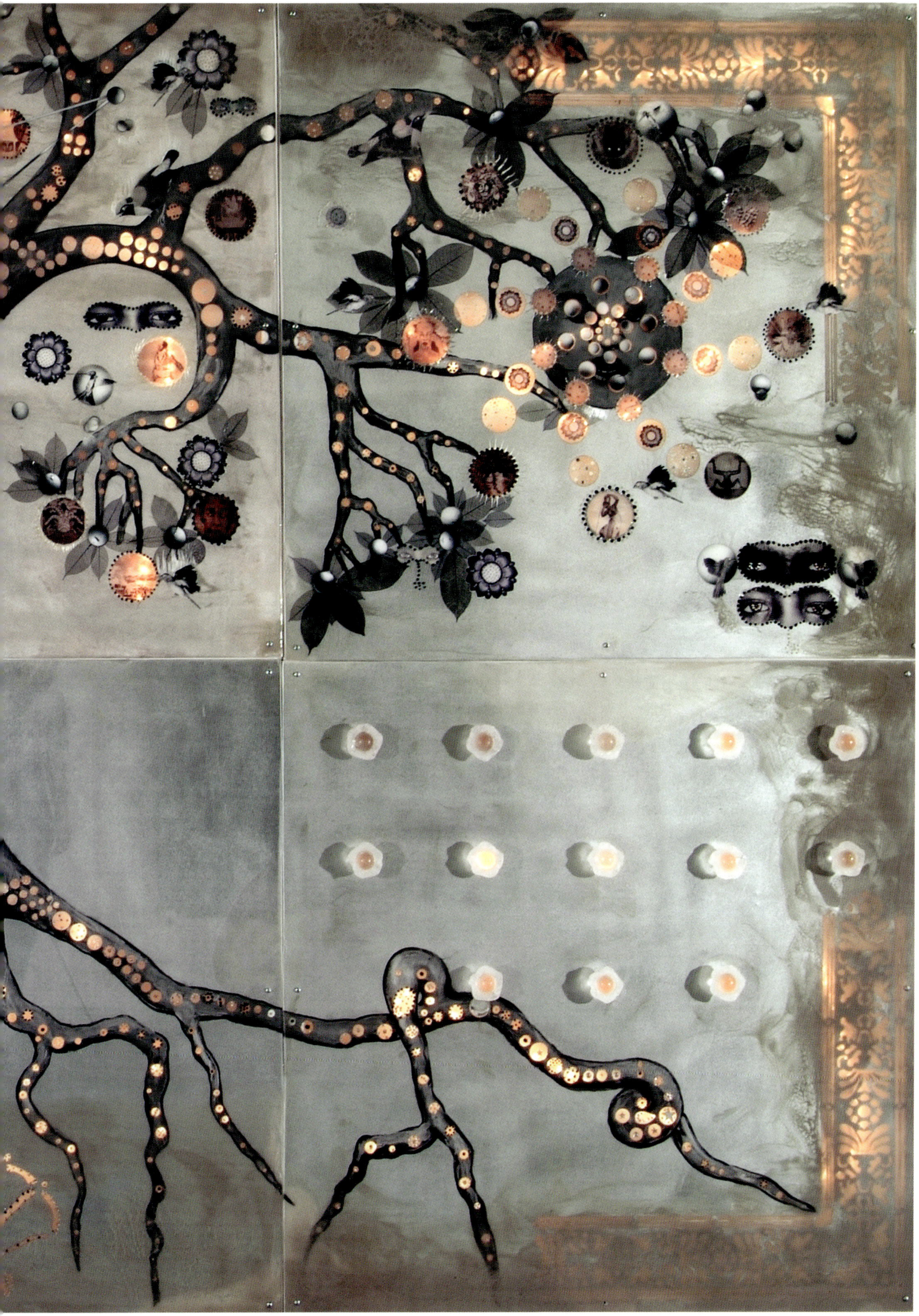

FRANKLIN **EINSPRUCH**

All of my paintings are done from life. My particular interest in painting is the response to the observed world and the translation of that response onto a surface, doing so with gestural energy. I place enormous faith in the Impressionist method, which promises that form can be conveyed through the concise use of observed color, thus providing the viewer with the pleasures of figuration and abstraction at the same time. I also sympathize with the goals of certain kinds of Asian art which value sincere imperfection and evidence of the artist's hand, especially what that hand reveals about the quality of the mind. I feel my work succeeds when I convey the sense of a person in a rough field of paint that would normally defeat a likeness. The person is important, and the rough field is important. I therefore believe in the inherent worth of the activity of painting: the confluence of materials and perceptions.

You can go all over the continental United States and not see light like the light in South Florida, a sharp, defining light that suffuses colors with rippling warmth. It got into my painting. Once I figured out how to control it, it seemed like every color in existence became permissible. I carry that light around with me, in a sense – a liberal attitude about color to which I compare other art, and other places, formed by three decades of life in Miami. Even as those other places call to me with charms of their own, something about my work remains persistently Miamian, a liveliness that refuses to calm down.

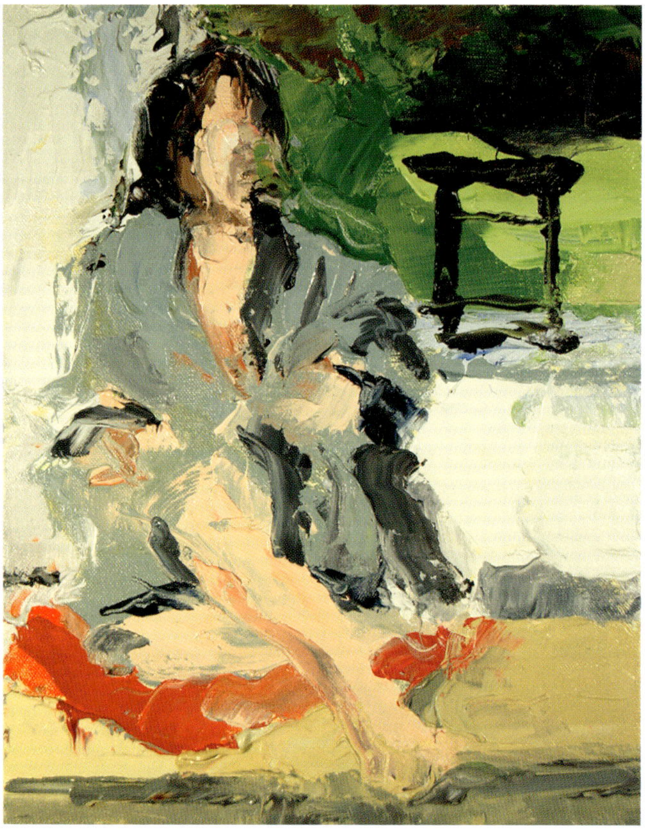

April: Blue Robe (N.S.), 2006. Oil on canvas, 14" x 11".

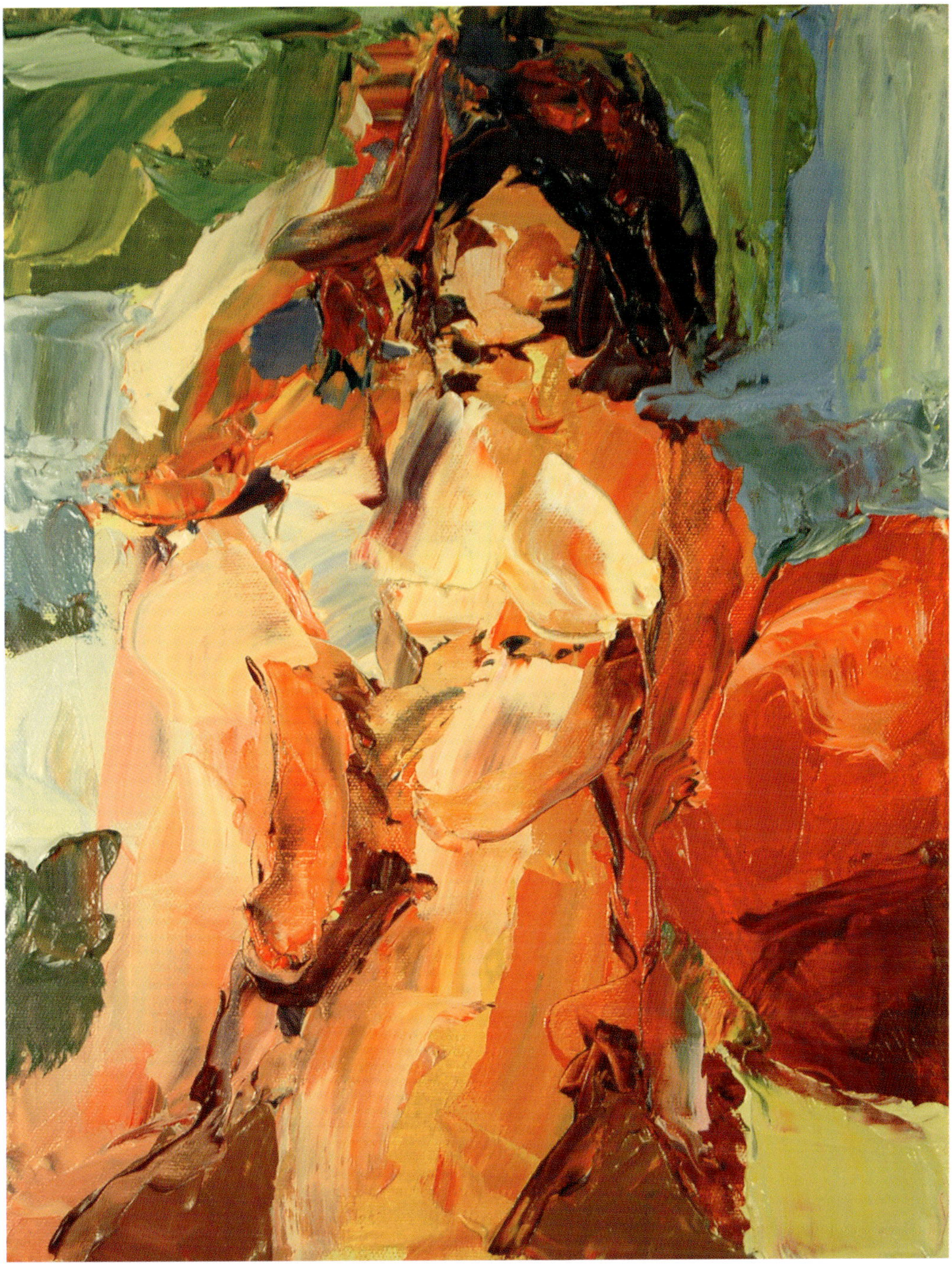

March: Nude (B.R), 2006. Oil on canvas, 14" x 11".

JOHN **ESPINOSA**

John Espinosa's work is set within a terrain where the known and the unknown collide. This is where humans come to terms with the finite limits of their own existence. It is the hyper fluctuating place where belief structures and scientific facts are forged. Espinosa's imagery is a concoction of cultural references that melds multiple classic and contemporary mythic narratives and grafts them onto diagrammatic physical structures. Often, the works appear as ritualistic instruments or quasi-scientific dioramas that pinpoint peak moments of collective epiphanic rapture or deluded mesmerization. These specific moments involve hypothetical physical transformations resulting from materials or beings reckoning with unfathomable energies or forces. For example, in *'Frozen upon Entry'* three fawns positioned in a triangulated pattern collectively gather an unknown external force. Through a retinal burst, the fawns translate that energy into a three dimensional symbol that alludes to electrical energy flows and to a telepathy or abstract cognition just beyond the reach of language. Thus, intangible perceptual data reconstitutes into solid matter. In many cases, diagrammatic symbols are embedded into the physical design of Espinosa's sculptures, so that the form functions metaphorically. For instance, the precarious equilibrium of *'Frozen upon Entry'* references a teetering state of mind, dangling precariously between revelation and delusion. Similarly, *'Standing Still While We Move across Land'* depicts a photosynthetic-like cycle where the flow of ultraviolet light sustains the system. The UV light activates the pigmentation of the birds, which consequently direct that energy toward a central structure that powers the device that generates the UV lamps which discharge the UV light and so forth. This cycle metaphorically references the feedback loop of information, seduction and consumption.

John Espinosa was born in Bogota, Colombia and raised in Orlando, Florida. He is a graduate of Miami's New World School of the Arts (BFA – 1998) and Yale University's School of Art – Sculpture Program (MFA – 2001). Espinosa currently lives and works in Los Angeles, California.

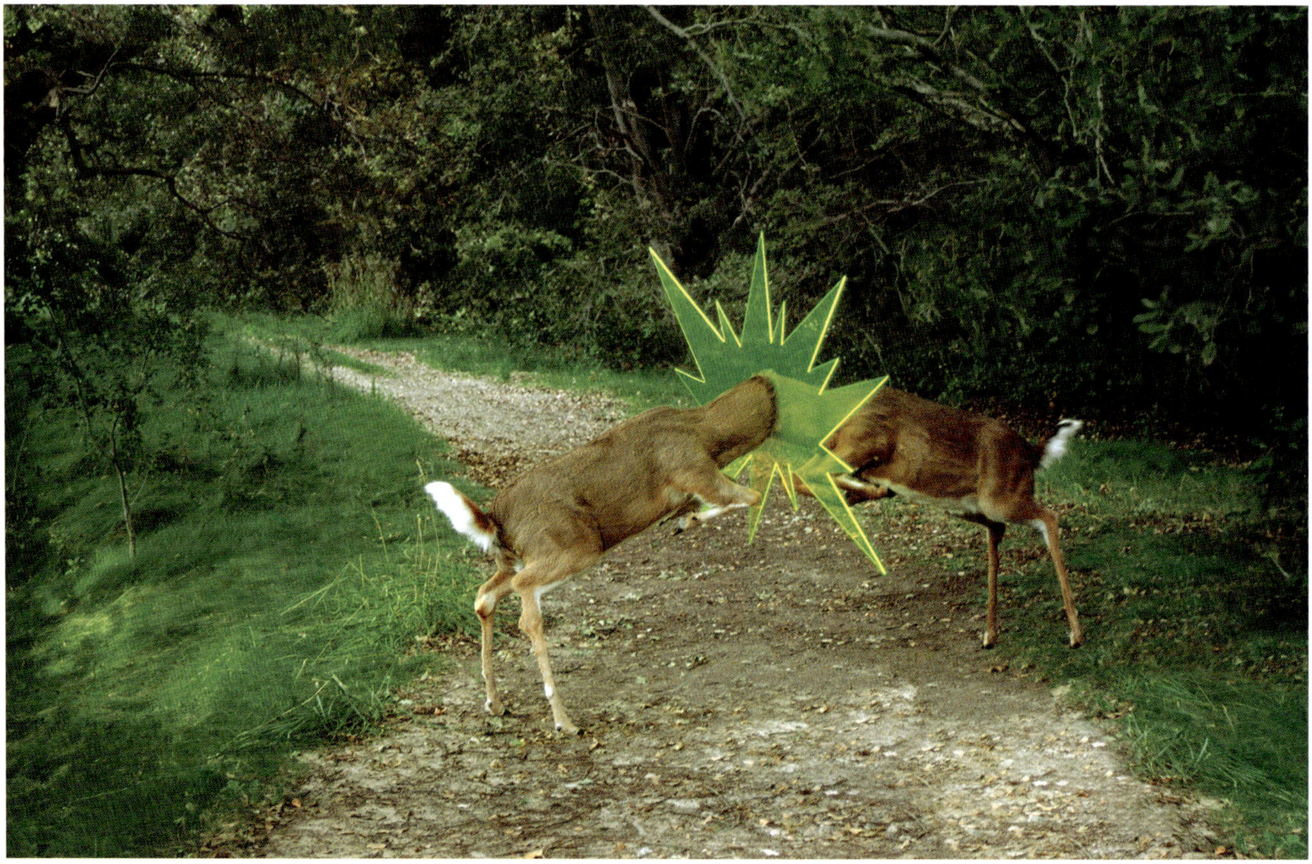

Things you can or can't learn from TV, 2001. Fluorescent acrylic laser cut from autoCAD file, deer capes, polyurethane foam, steel, 72" x 80" x 14'.

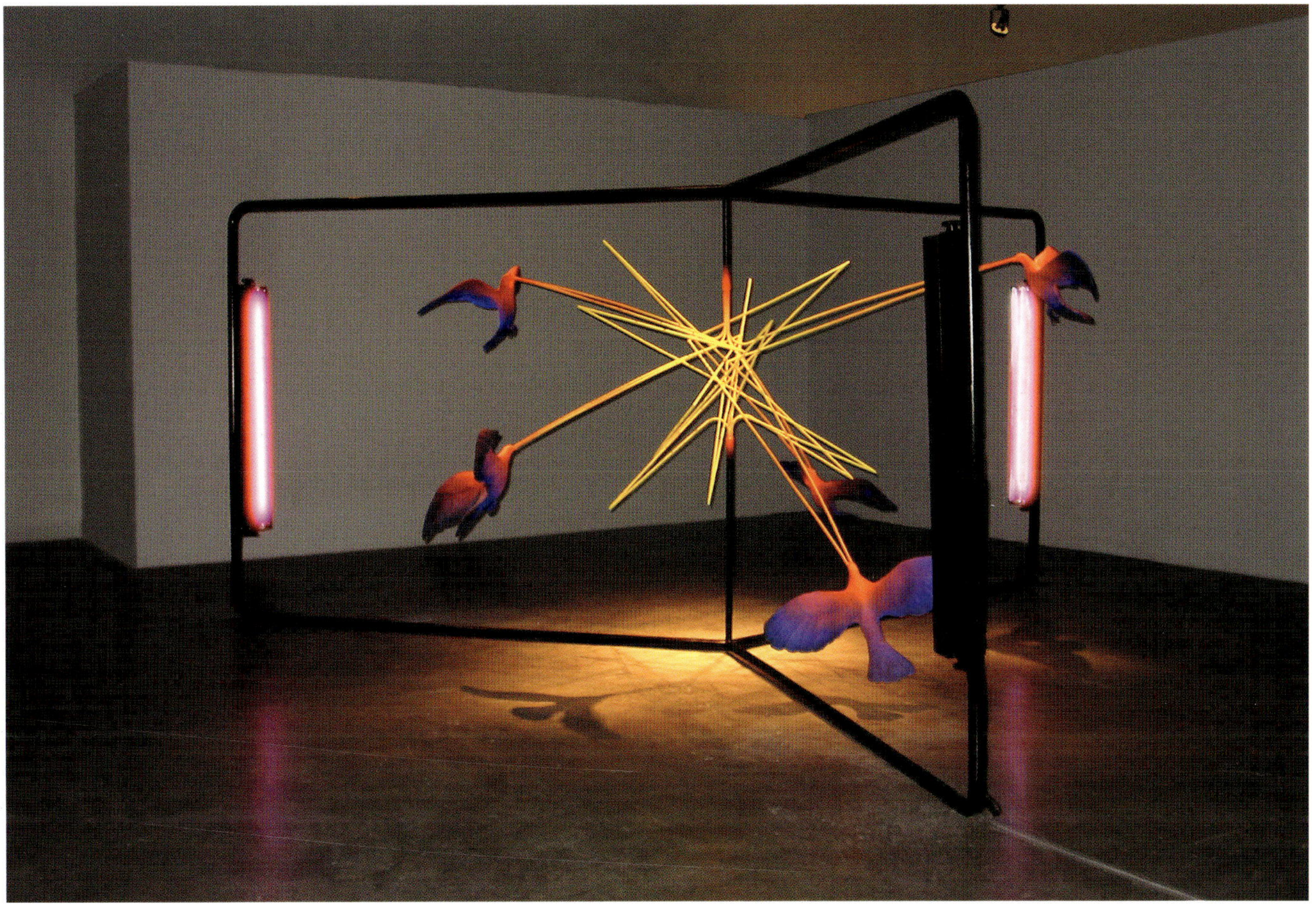

Standing still while we move across land, 2004. Ultraviolet light, 3 FX Master wf-uv lamps, resin, polyurethane foam, wire mesh, UV sensitive acrylics, stainless steel rods, steel tube, enamel, 7.5'(H) x 22' (D floor coverage).

CHARLES **FALARARA**

As a young child in Brazil, Charles Falarara would accompany his father to their asphalt company, where he would amuse himself sculpting figures out of tar. Soon after, he taught himself to draw, and by age seven was an apprentice to a group of ceramicists. He especially enjoyed the cyclical process of working with clay: creating figures, breaking them down, and then creating new forms. As a teenager he apprenticed with a sculptor, while also directing a ceramics atelier. His career as an artist led him to New York and later Miami, where he opened an art studio. Falarara enjoys the physicality of his work. Transforming raw materials into figurative or abstract forms inspires him. The shapes are organic and contemporary. He explores the elegance and proportion of the human form. He often juxtaposes materials in surprising ways: tar, bronze, concrete, and clay, stone, wood. An excellent craftsman, Charles is accomplished in creating murals and frescos. His oil paintings often include layering of other materials such as sawdust, gold leaf and paper from his stencil work.

Miami is a diversified community and to be a part of it is very important. Being an artist in Miami also means to be environmentally conscious. This process of modernism and progress is the future role of Miami in this new contemporary evolution. Little by little it feels like a metropolis, rather than a resort or tourist site. Where most of our blue skies were, giant concrete blocks have been erected. Being an artist in Miami is to be the community, it is to be the ambient, the colada at the Café, and the olla around the corner. Much more of that happens around us everyday. (David Whitman)

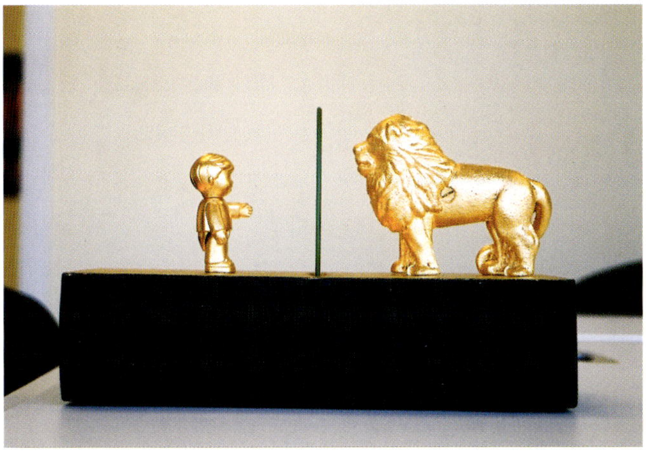

Plastic Boy and Metal Lion, 2004. Plastic, cast iron, glass, mahogany wood, latex paint, 24 carat gold leaf, 12" x 4" x 2.5".

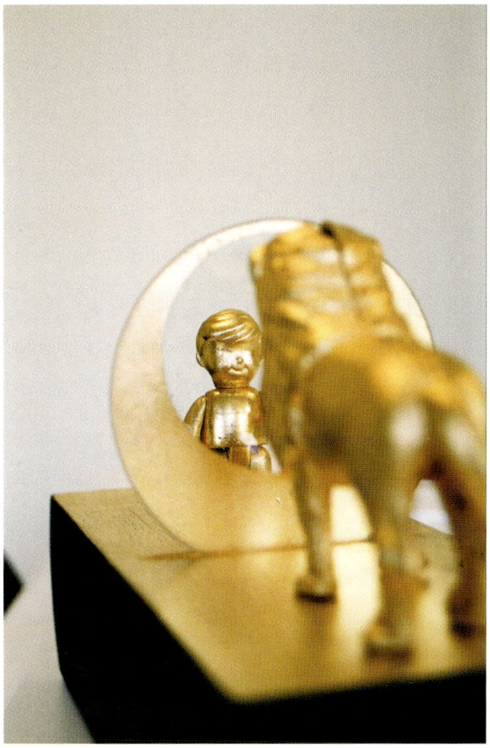

Plastic Boy and Metal Lion, alternate view.

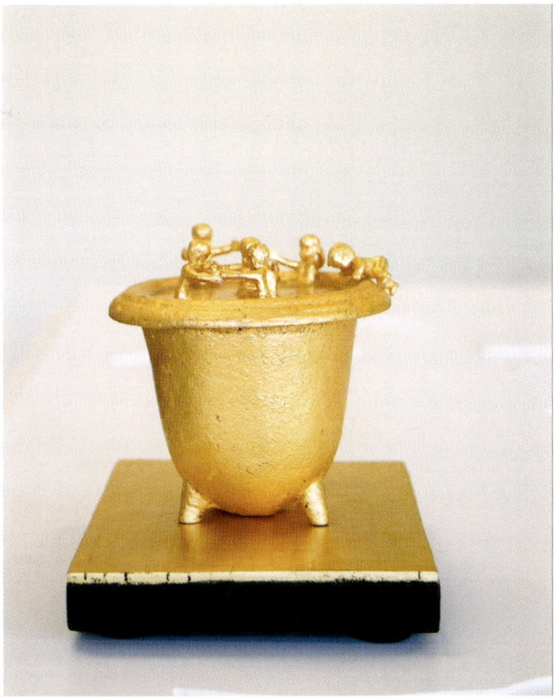

The Bathers, 2004. Cast iron, plastic, resin, fired clay, wood, latex paint, 24 carat gold leaf, 5.5 " x 12"d x 4".

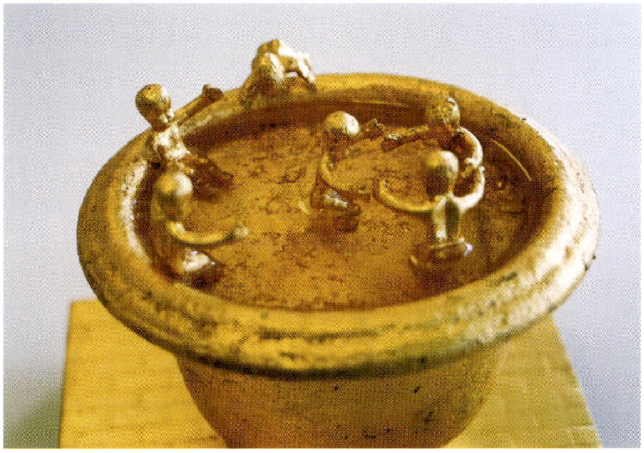

The Bathers, alternate view.

JASON FERGUSON

Born in Trinidad and Tobago in 1972, Jason Ferguson lives and works in Miami. His work consists of painting, drawing, installation and video. With a strong sense of formal design, he comments on social, political and personal experiences within each of the structures. Categorization, isolation and the subtle form of insight can be found all through the work. In addition, he is a member of FeC-uOp, a collaborative group of three artists that create work dealing with performance-based social interactions and experimentations

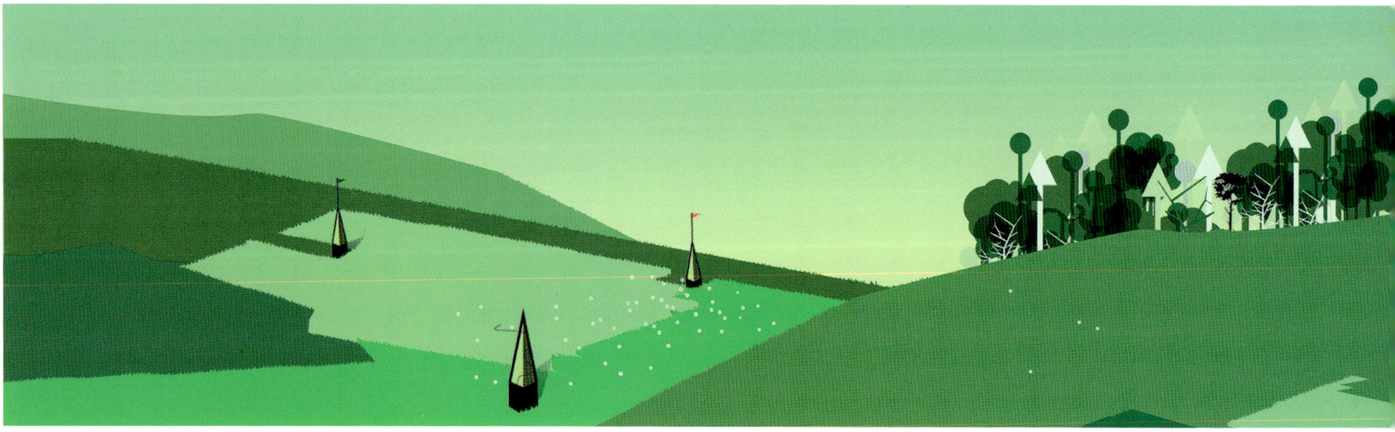

Tremendous landscape series, 2006. Digital print on PVC, 95.5" x 17".

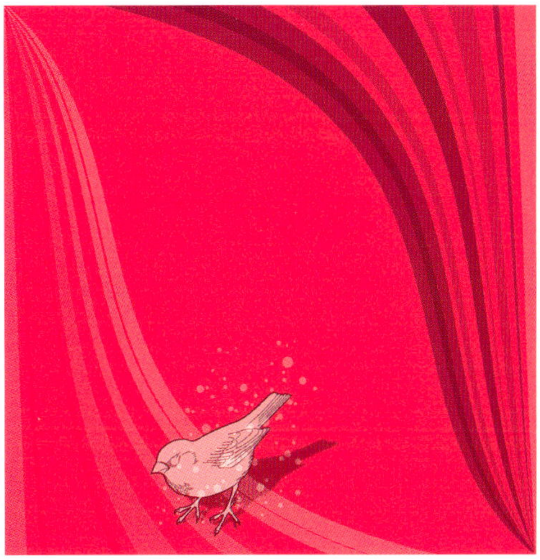

Sparrow, 2001. Digital print on PVC, 96" x 96".

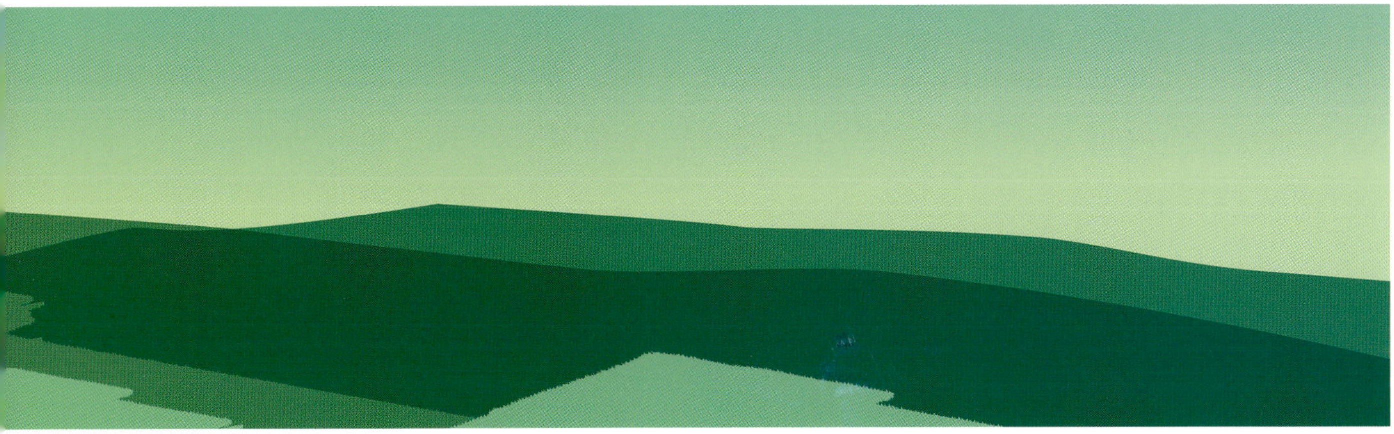

TERESITA **FERNÁNDEZ**

Teresita Fernández is a sculptor who integrates architecture and the optical effects of color and light to produce exquisitely constructed, contemplative spaces. In her sculptural environments, Fernández alters space to create illusions, subtly modifying the physical sensations of the viewer and dramatizing the role architecture plays in shaping our lives and perceptions. Her room-sized installations evoke quietude and mystery, reflecting such diverse aesthetic influences as Roman and Ottoman architecture and Japanese gardens. In other works, she creates large-scale, referential constructions, such as a pool, a waterfall, and a sand dune stripped of specific context. With these pared down pieces, she invites viewers to draw from their personal memories and observations. Employing common building materials to startling effect – tiny plastic cubes form a shimmering rainbow and acrylic rods suggest the flexible strength of bamboo – she inspires viewers to see a new relationship between built environments and the natural world. With lyrical and immaculately executed indoor and outdoor works, Fernández is pushing boundaries of sculpture and installation art into the fields of architecture and landscape architecture.

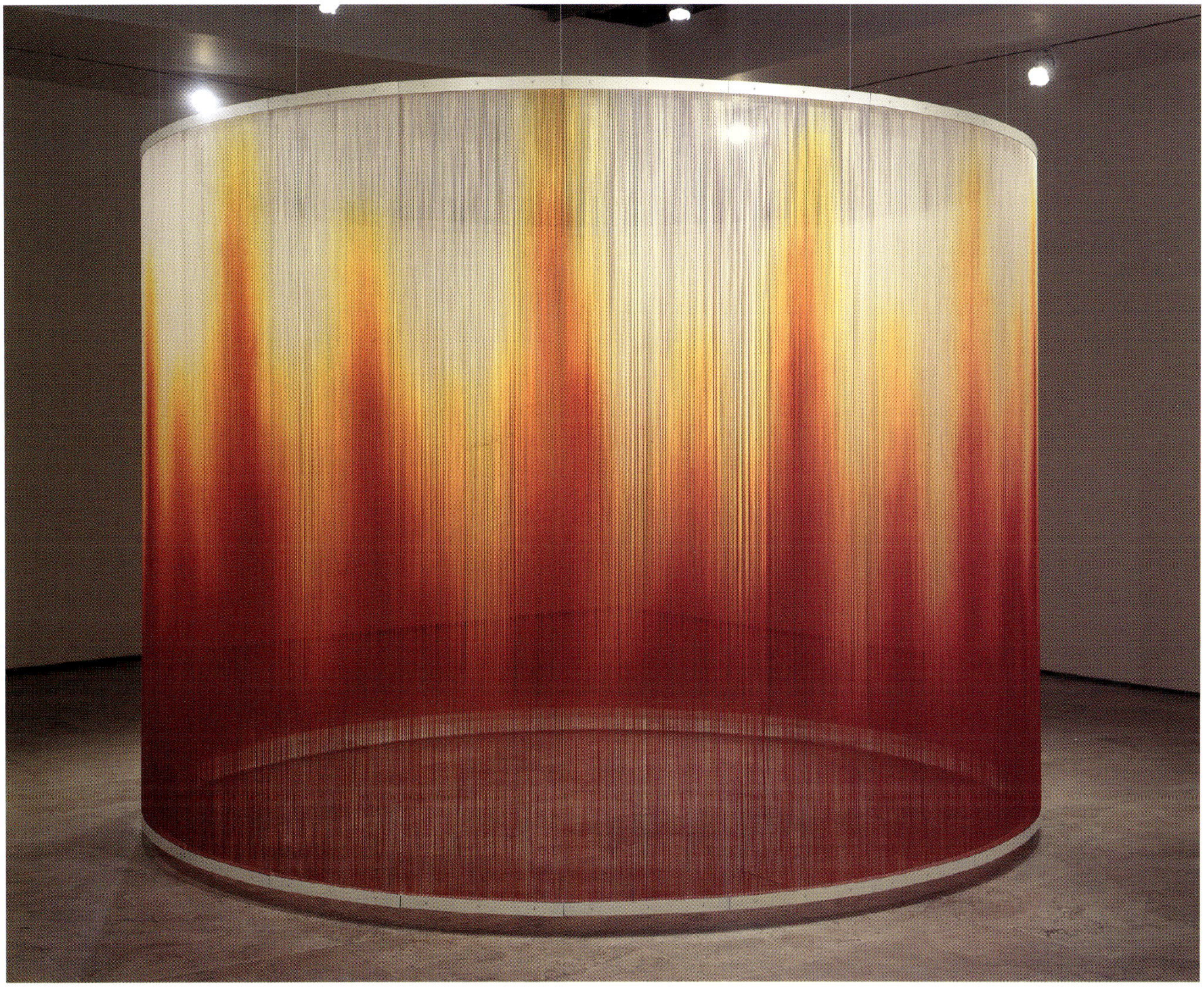

Fire, 2005. Silk yarn, steel armature, epoxy, 96" x 144" (D)

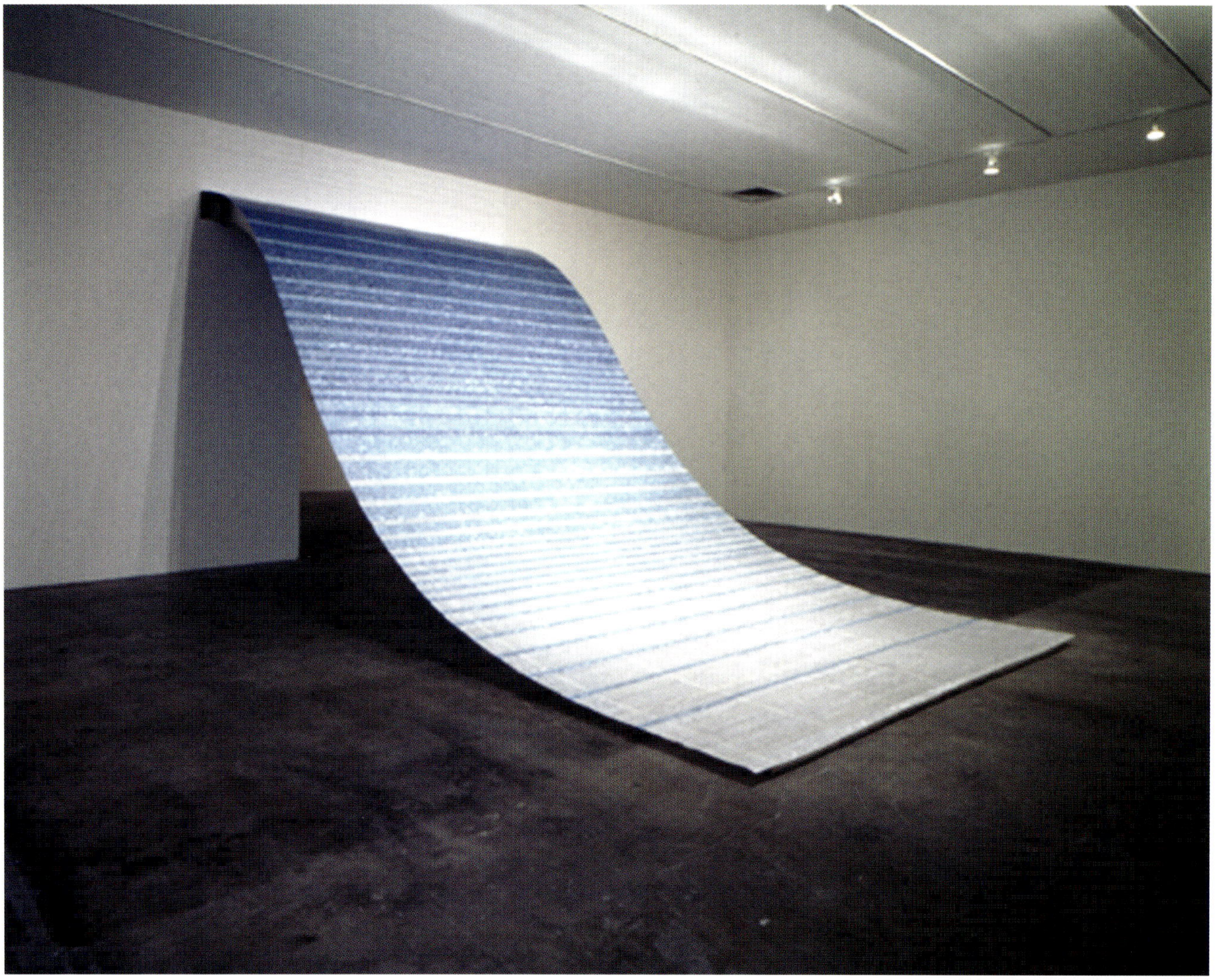

Waterfall, 2000. Aluminum, plastic, 144.09" x 144.09" x 335.83".

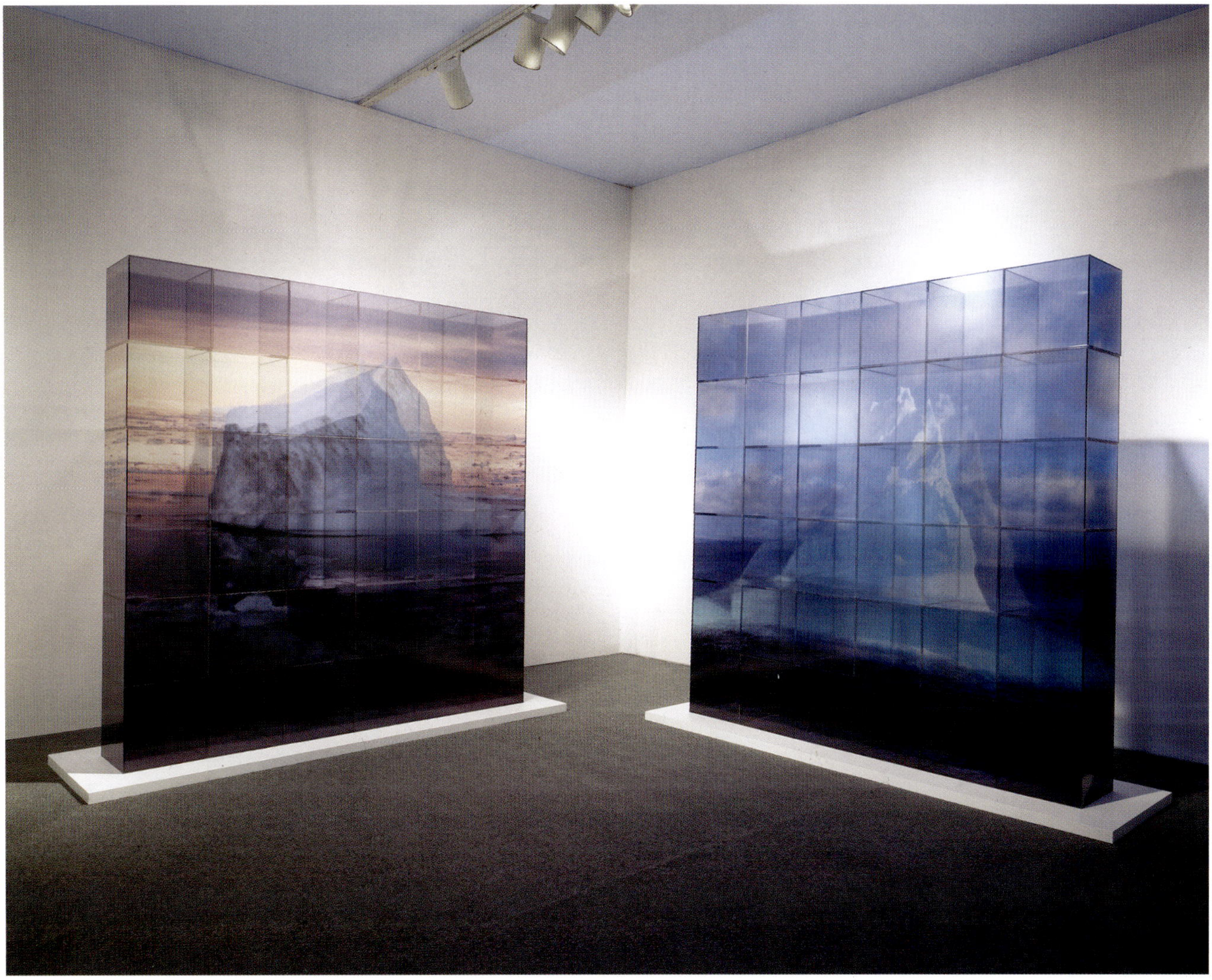

Quiet Ice (Gray) and (Blue), 2006. Plexiglas cubes with photographic image overlay, approx 72″ x 72″ x 12″ each. (Edition of 2).

NAOMI **FISHER**

"Fisher's distinctive work confounds us with its mixture of beauty and terror, with its unsettling, coyly feminist imagery of women. In Fisher's drawings, improbable vegetation 'invades' some feminine figures in casually erotic poses, with branches of hibiscus and tufts of grass springing from their bodies. Others are instead entangled in the 'arms' of humanoid trees. Nature reveals her predatory and invasive character even more explicitly in her photographs, in which bodies appear physically imprisoned within the tropical flora. Naomi Fisher explores the complex and unresolved relationship between man and nature through her photographs and drawings, suggesting a 'mother-stepmother' type of nature that, despite being the victim of man – who wants to transform her – dominates the tropical landscape and flatters her prey with an explosion of forms and colors...The striking beauty of the work alludes to Japanese aesthetics and to Kurosawa's films, as it addresses the affinities between beauty and violence; pleasure and torture."
M. Giovannotti, art critic

School of the Arts and received her BFA from the Maryland Institute College of Art. Fredric Snitzer Gallery has represented Fisher since 1999. Since then, she has exhibited extensively including the inaugural exhibition at Palais de Tokyo, Paris, France; Deitch Projects, New York; The Contemporary, Baltimore; Miami Art Museum; Brooklyn Museum of Art, New York; Institute of Visual Arts, University of Wisconsin, Milwaukee; Museum of Contemporary Art, North Miami; Tel-Aviv Museum of Art, Israel; Weatherspoon Art Gallery, University of North Carolina, Greensboro; and the National Museum of Trinidad, West Indies.

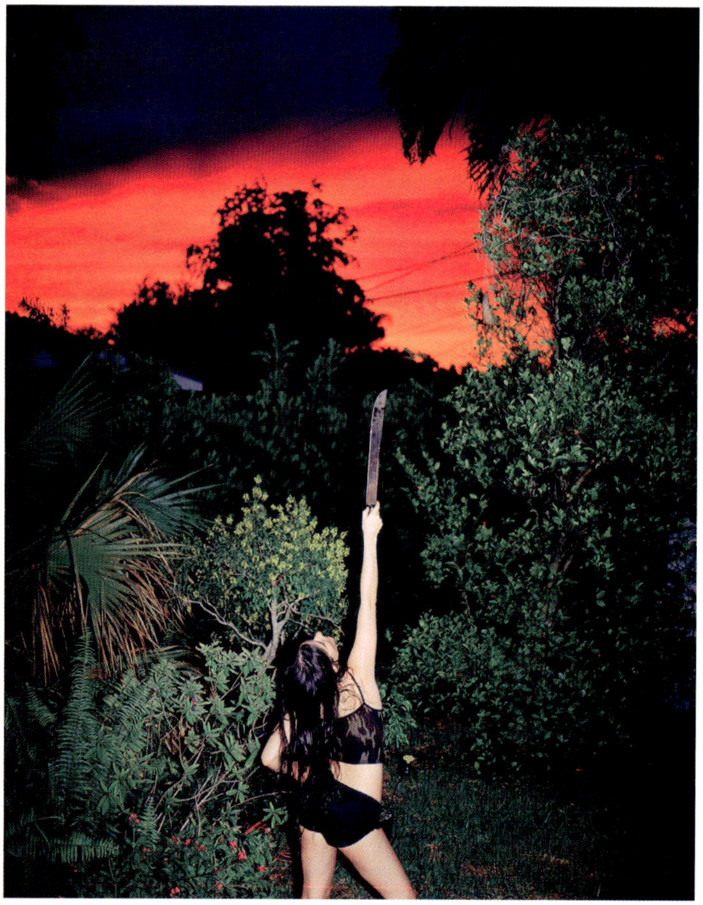

You Know that it's Real if You Feel that it's Real, 2003. Cibachrome, 60" x 50 ".

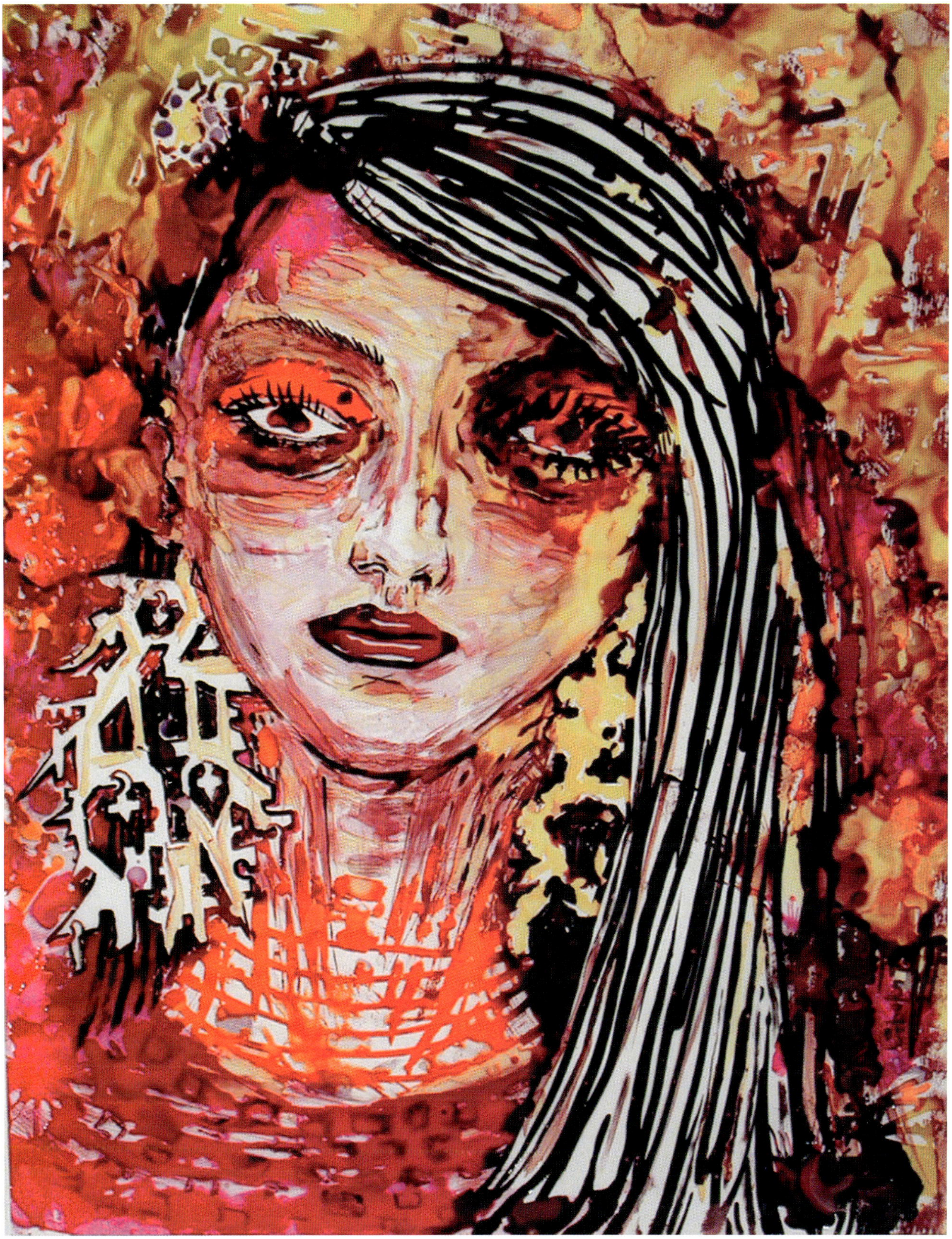

Ladies 5/9/05, 2005. Ink on vellum, 24"x19".

ROBERT **FLYNN**

My experience is my production. As a recent homeowner and dedicated do-it-yourselfer, I have been teaching myself yard work. Watering, mowing and weeding and countless other chores devoted to the garden have become my plight, or rather inspiration for subject matter. Vast stretches of dirt have been made green again. Very little of this has to do with nature. Friends and neighbors alike vie for the trophy lawn, participating in a turf war over curb appeal. Nature has become objectified; the backyard a modern day fetish.

I came to Miami by happenstance. What I found was a close-knit community of artists and creative people with endless energy and enthusiasm. I chose to stay.

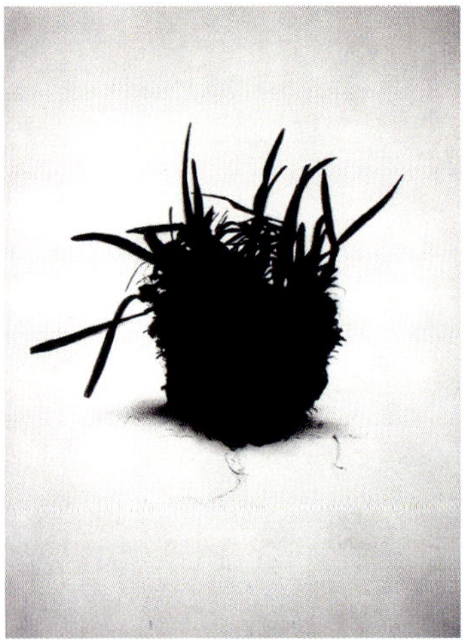

Plug #4 , 2005. Graphite and charcoal on paper, 30" x 22".

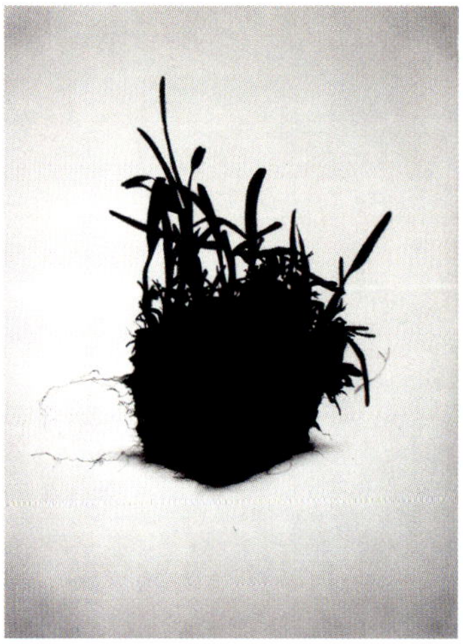

Plug #5, 2005. Graphite and charcoal on paper, 30" x 22".

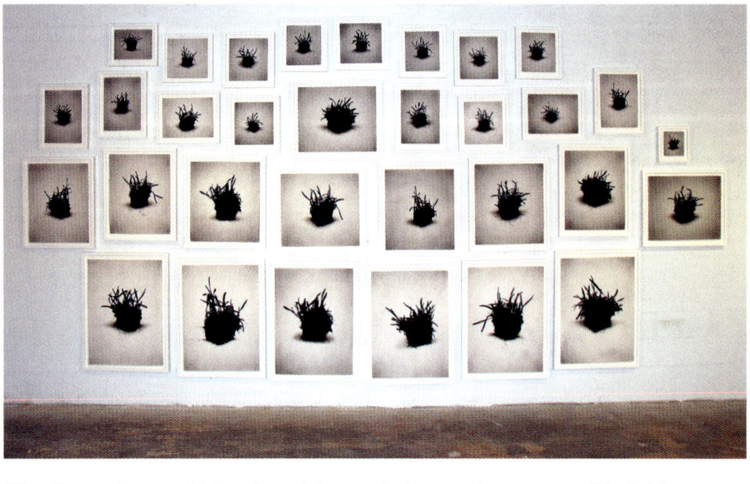

The Great Lawn, 2005. Graphite and charcoal on paper, Variable dimensions, 11' x 18' shown.

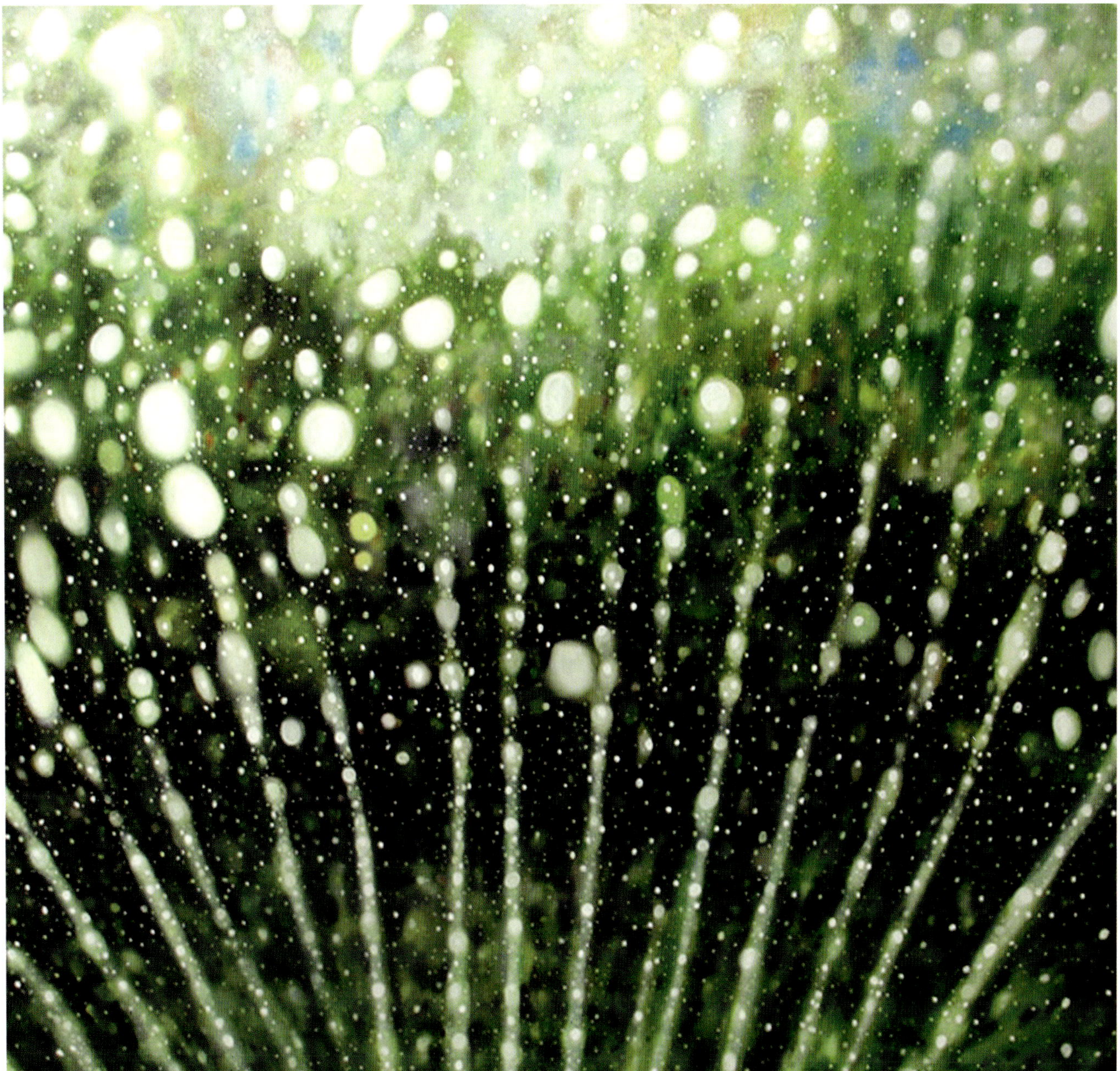

Sprinkles (Oct), 2006. Oil on canvas, 85" x 85".

LYNNE GOLOB GELFMAN

I am curious about handwriting and using nontraditional tools to make marks. My marks, sometimes layered and erased, refer to baskets, textiles, lichen and architectural structures. I am curious about illusion. From a distance, my paintings appear to be thickly painted. Close-up they are often smooth and sanded fine. My new work adds another layer embodying the element of chance. The top level shows a chemical resist that pulls apart the paint. I play with the reaction of the resist to create movement across the image. Patterns of small spheres evoke associations with foam, spindrift, bubbles and hover over the sub-painting that suggests animal-like skins.

My favorite Miami experience is walking in the sea at low tide, through ripples of sand, water and light. I love tropical foliage, interlacing fronds of palms, bananas and heliconias. There is a special quality of bleached light that appeals to me as well as living in an almost Latin American city.

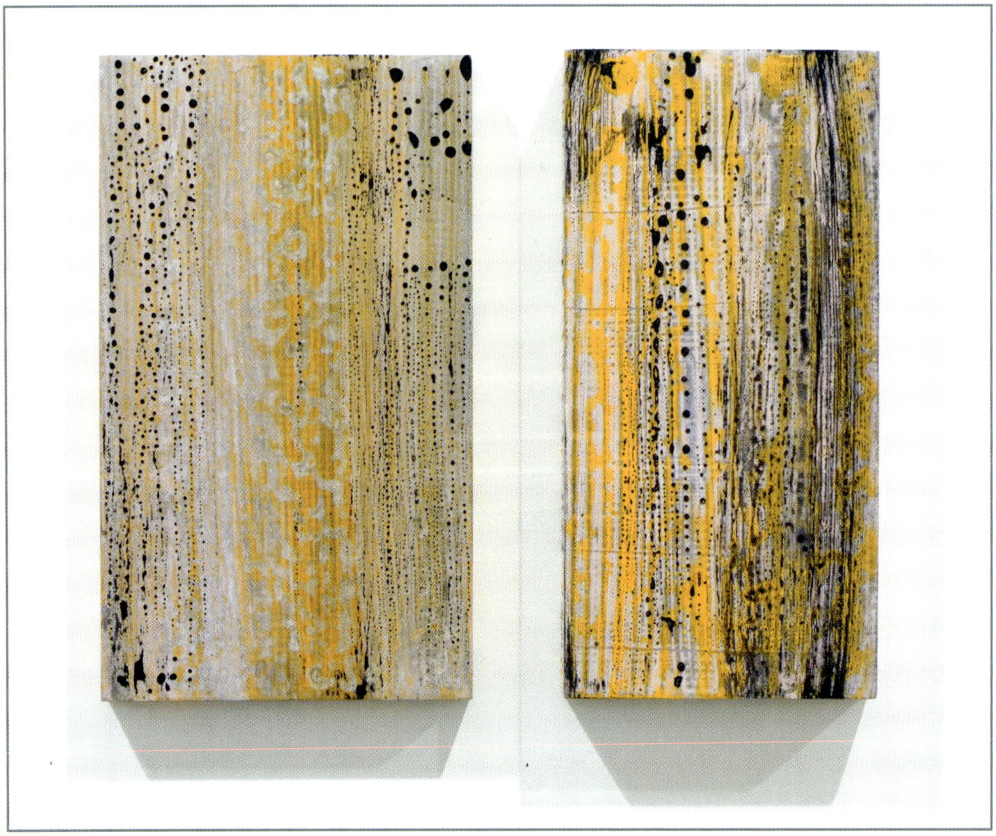

React #910 and # 911, 2005. Acrylic on panel, 20" x 12" and 20" x 10".

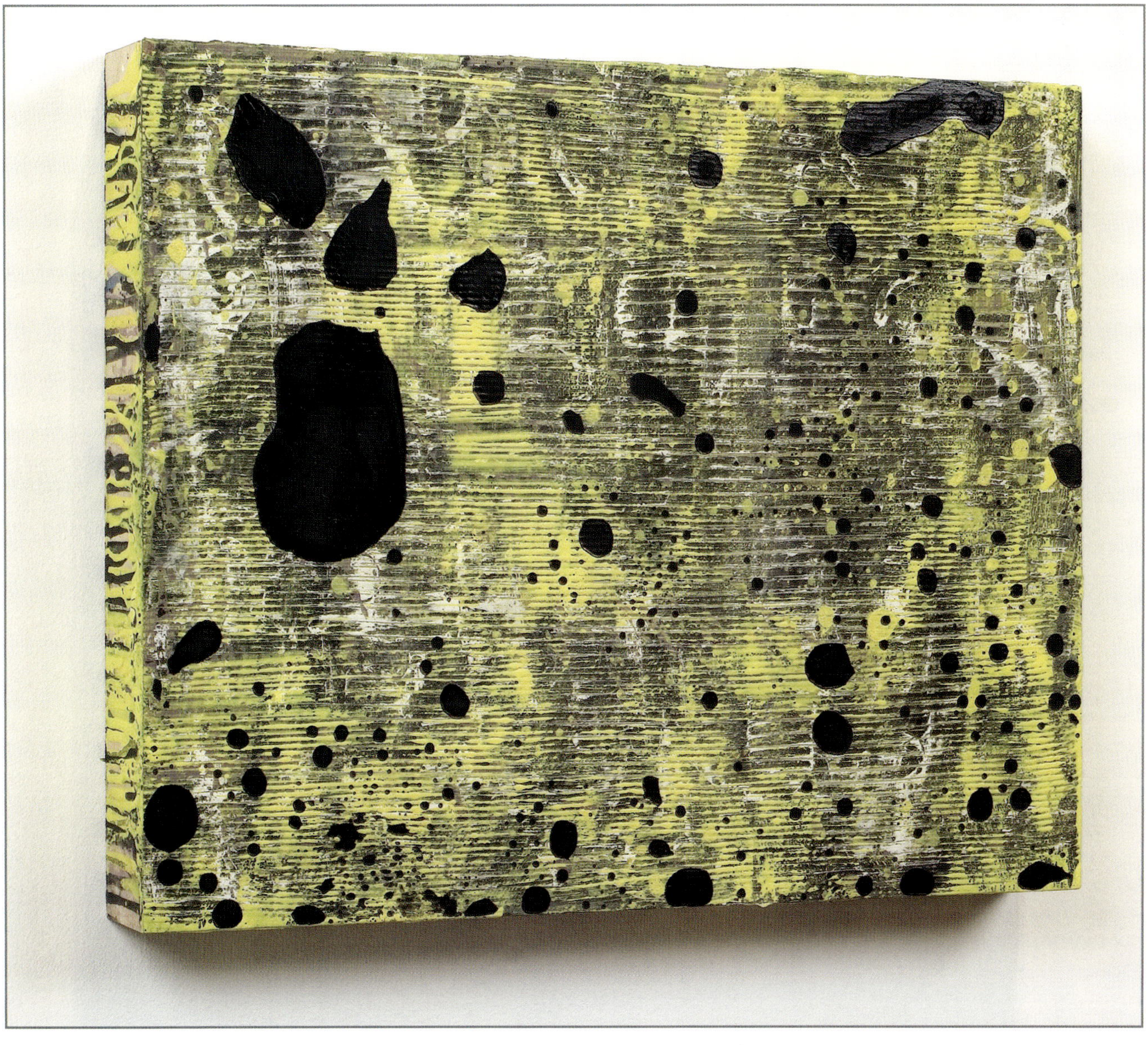

React #903, 2005. Acrylic on panol, 16" x 20".

JACIN GIORDANO

I find it difficult to make a painting without considering the romantic mythology surrounding art history. My process begins with the intent of dispelling these myths. My paintings are intensely labored and constructed. I think of them as crafted rather than executed. They are crafted with the same soft sentiment found in a stitched quilt and pieced together with a similar sort of ferocity found in Frankenstein's Monster. I use yarn, glitter, glue and fragments of paint to create an assembled collage. The segmented stripes within the works originate as long, straight lines of acrylic paint poured on glass. Once dry, the paint is peeled from its bed of glass, cut into fragments and finally adhered to canvas or wood. In this way, I am dissecting and antagonizing the romanticism of painting by slicing paint into manageable, tangible pieces. In my paintings color becomes metaphor. I am drawn to juxtapositions of color versus black and white. For example John Keats' reaction to Isaac Newton's scientific breakdown of rainbows seems to epitomize the opposition between romance and science. Keats could no longer celebrate the rainbow as a muse because he believed that Newton had reduced its color and fantastic charm to a mere black and white scientific fact. In the movie *The Wizard of Oz*, Dorothy lives a dull and monochromatic existence on a Kansas farm; contrasted by Oz, which she experiences in fully heightened color. Both of these examples share the idea that life is black and white while fantasy can contain any color imaginable. My recent body of work is entitled *The Rainbow's End and All of the Plastic in Between*. This title simultaneously refers to two opposing "ends" of the rainbow. On one end is the fabled pot of gold. A symbol of childhood, it's the kind of happy end only found in fairy tales. The other "end," however, is the very end of this fairy tale fantasy. It is the realization that no matter how far we travel toward the rainbow we will never get closer to its treasure; it's the realization that the rainbow is nothing more than a transitory illusion. Our childhood idealism disintegrates, gradually replaced by the hard truths of a plastic, black and white reality. In my paintings the black and white stripes are meant to represent (among other things): adulthood, callousness, science and logic, masculinity, certainty and coolness—but most notably it is the disintegration of color. In turn, the colored segments are childhood, poetry, rainbows, warmth, femininity and romanticism. I also use textiles and embroider yarn into my paintings to heighten the efficacy and warmth of the colored stripes. The yarn and embroidery is lifted from the world of craft typically associated with feminine practice as opposed to the painted pours which are lifted from a male dominated world of high art. Within these works, though, I try not to choose one side over the other, but instead draw attention to a time when their conflict is most present.

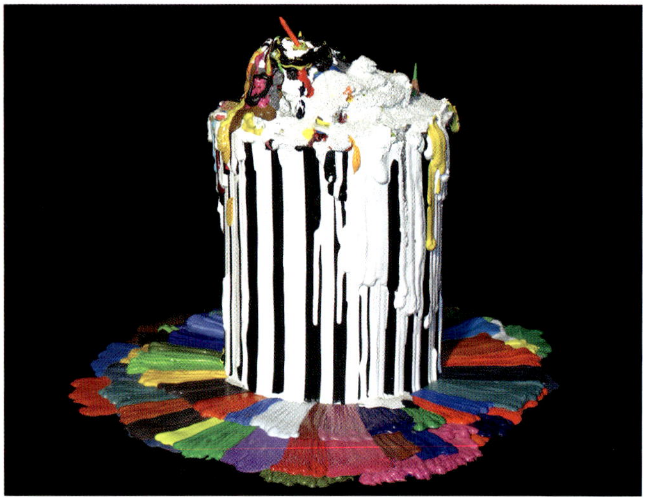

A Pot of Gold, 2005. Acrylic, yarn, glitter, colored pencils and paint can, 12" x 12" x 12".

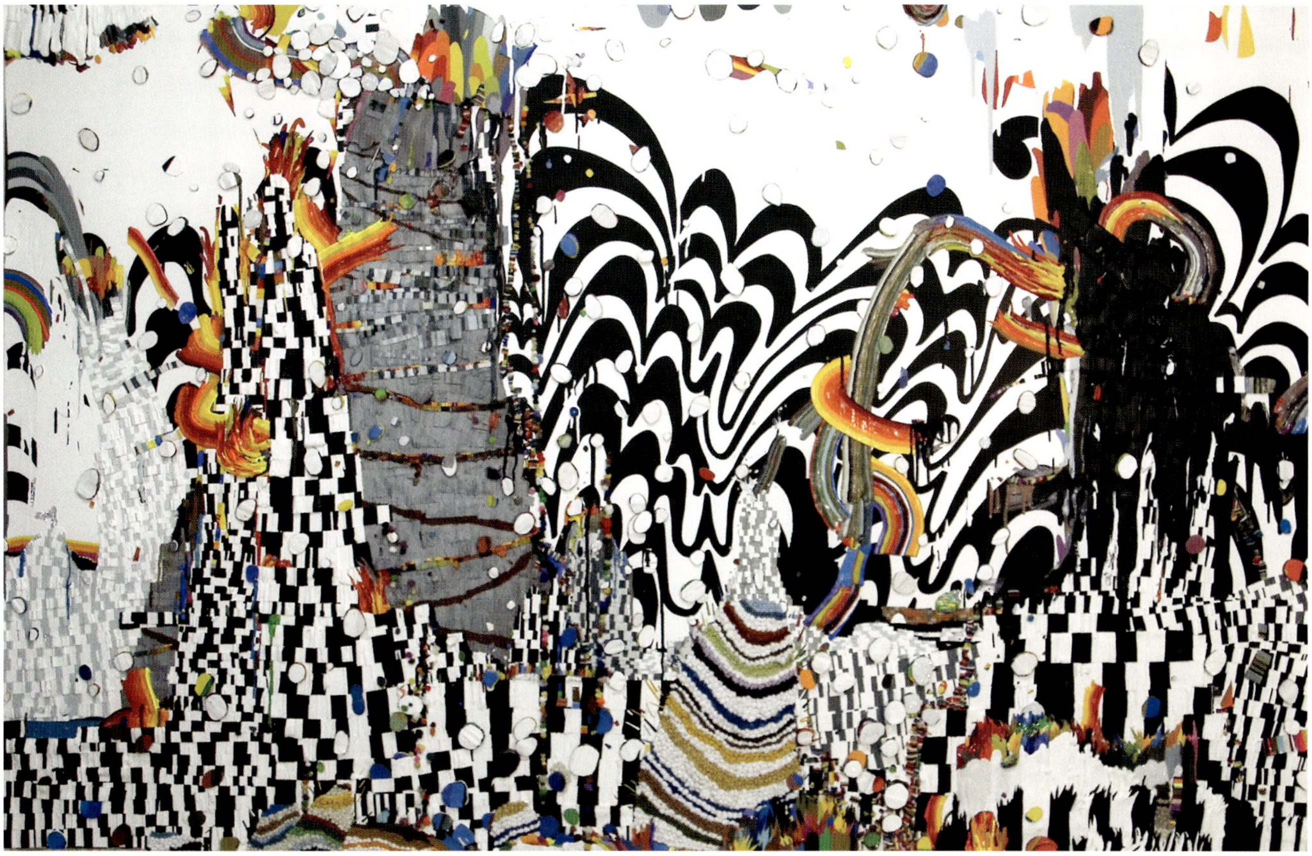

The Day Was Born of Fire and Smoke, 2005. Acrylic, yarn, and colored pencil on wood, 60″x 84″.

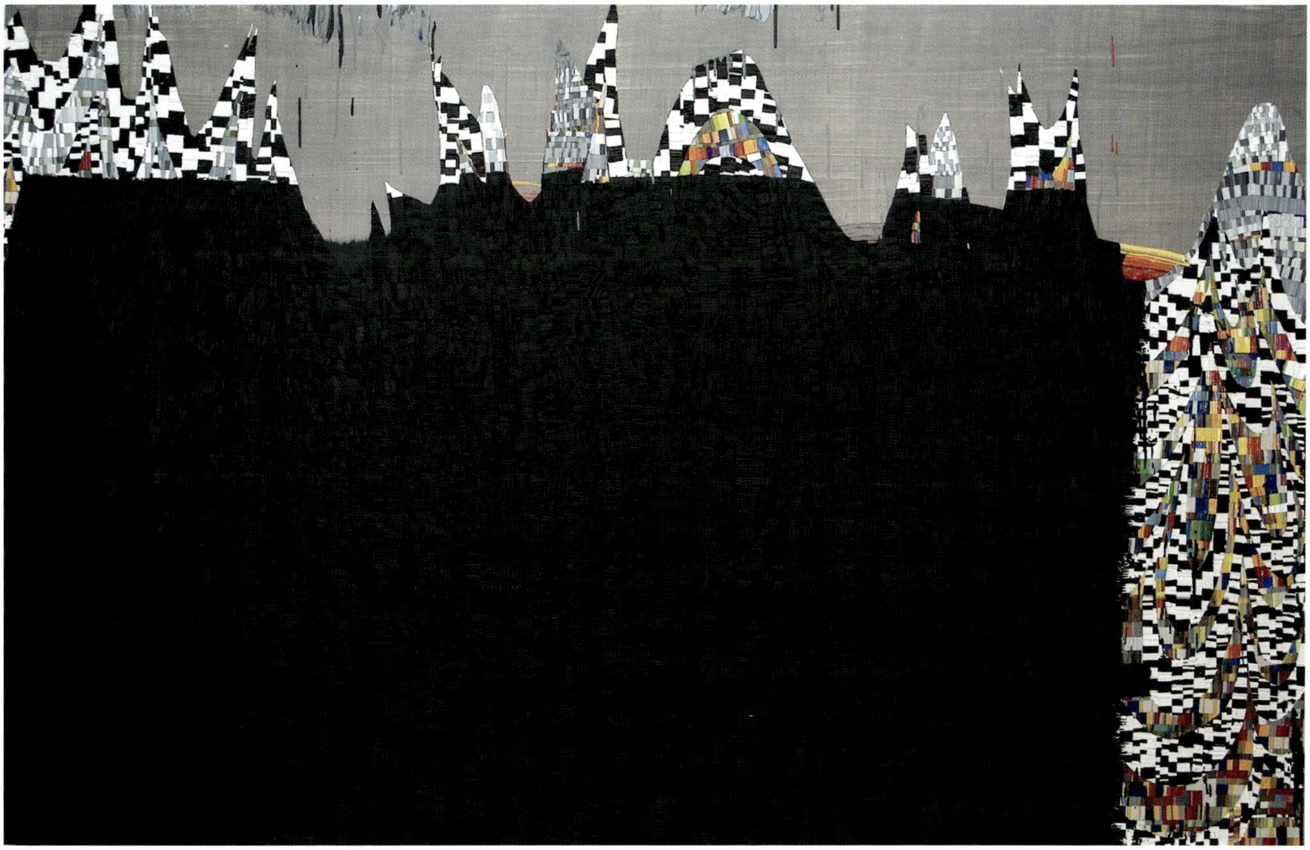

Night Rise/Sunset, 2005. Acrylic on wood, 60″x 84″.

LUIS GISPERT

"Luis Gispert is a young contemporary artist born in Jersey City, New Jersey, and raised primarily in Miami. He trained first at Miami-Dade Community College and then at the Art Institute of Chicago and Yale University. Today Gispert lives and works in Brooklyn. His earliest creative recognition was tied to his participation in a group of young South Florida-based artists who challenged the reigning paradigms of Latino/a representation in that region. Gispert's vividly colored photographs and booming sound sculptures have since been shown widely throughout the United States as well as Europe, South America, and the Middle East. The multimedia installation he created for the 2002 Whitney Biennial was one of the most critically acclaimed elements of that exhibition, and his work has become a virtual mainstay in recent surveys of contemporary art practices. Gispert's work cannily explores and confronts familiar aspects of youth culture, art history, hip-hop music, and, most recently, the artist's own Cuban American background. His large-scale photographs mounted on their glossy supports, feature ethnically diverse groups of cheerleaders enacting poses that are variously derived form canonical art history – for example, the Renaissance period (Antonio Pollaiuolo) or the Conceptual art movement (Bruce Nauman) – global religions, or popular culture."
Roberto J. Tejada, critic curator University of San Diego, from UPNE Hood Museum

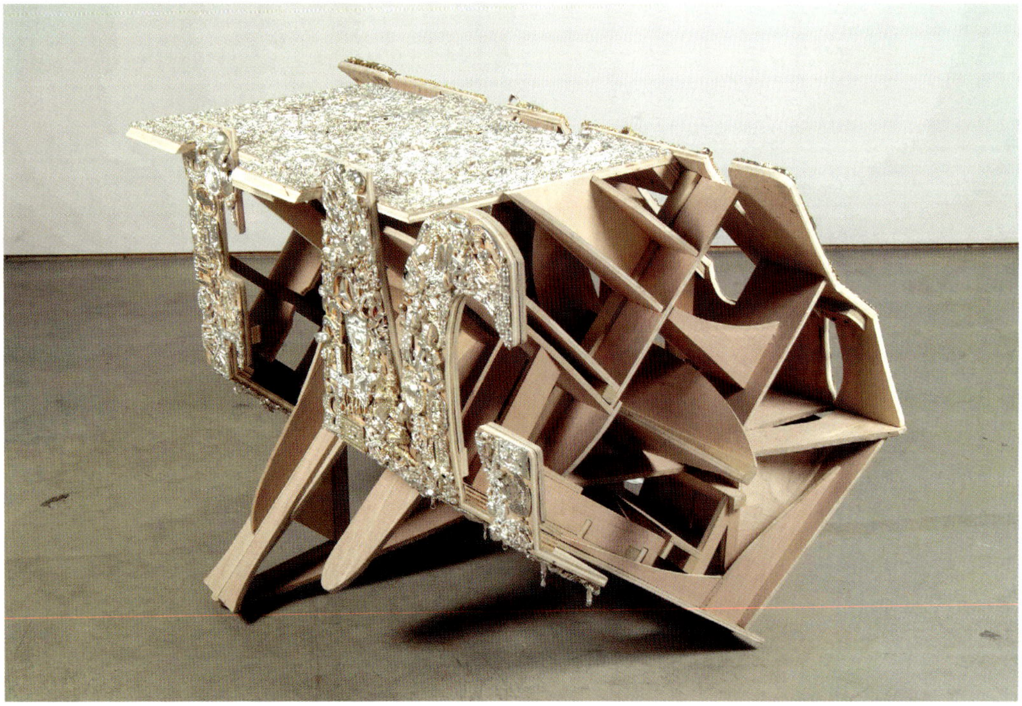

Fucking Fake Flondes, 2006. Wood and mixed media, variable dimensions.

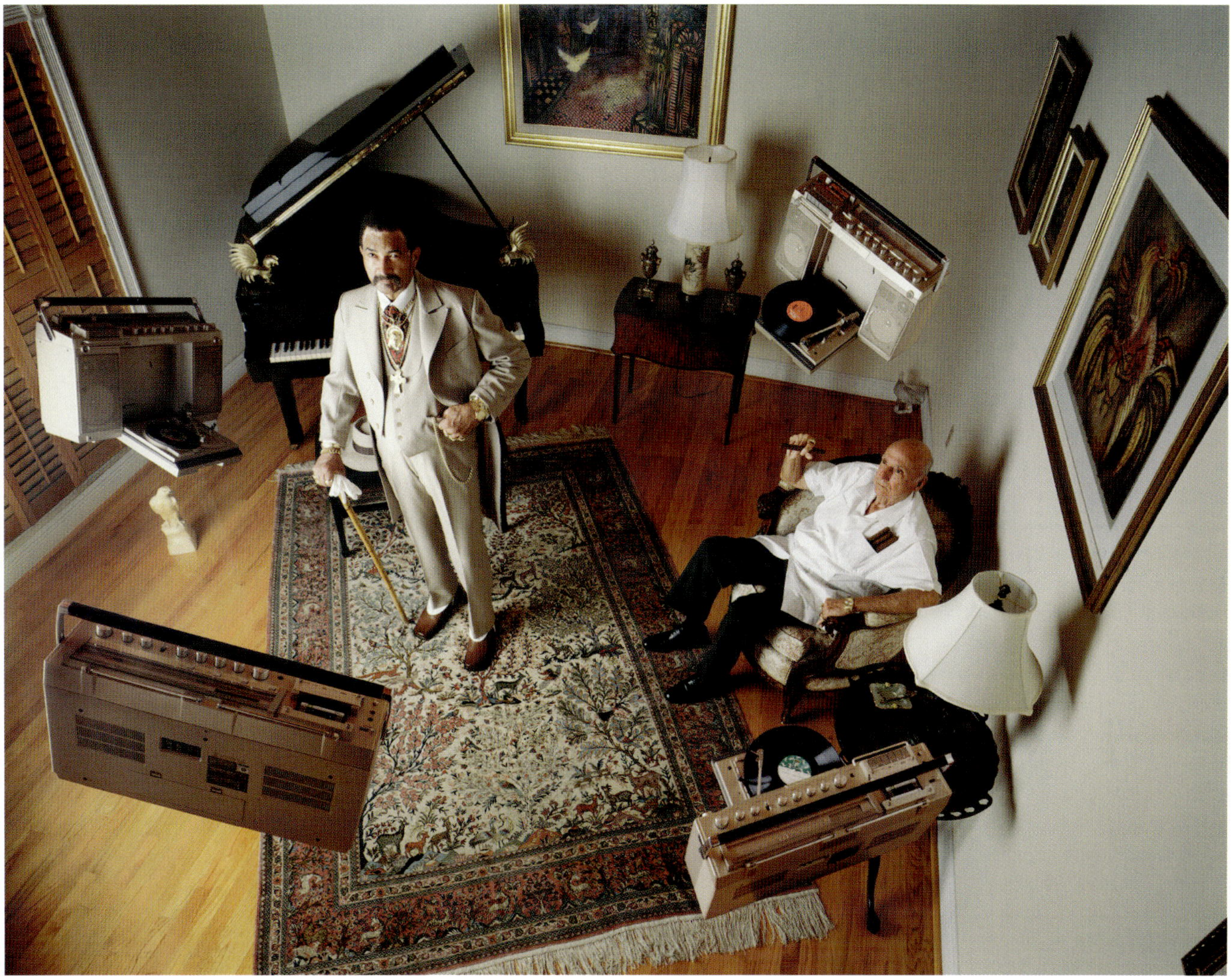

Untitled (*Turntables),* 2003. Cibachrome, 50" x 64".

GUERRA DE LA PAZ

Guerra de la Paz is the composite name which represents the creative team efforts of Alain Guerra and Neraldo de la Paz. Since 1996, when we began collaborating out of our studio in Miami's Little Haiti, our work has evolved through the constant experimentation with the usage of found objects and has manifested into various ongoing series in a variety of mediums and formats. Currently we have focused our attention on unwanted garments. Collecting a wide range of items from piles of discarded clothes for their hues and prints, texture and sheen, acquiring a palette of vast quantities of unique pieces that when singled out can reveal the identity of our eclectic society while exposing evidence of an unseemly lifestyle of easy disposability and mass consumption. Through a similar aesthetic and a common knowledge of both painting and sculpture, we set out to explore and develop a variety of ways to reproduce the essence of the piles of clothes from which we collect our materials. From capturing their purity in abstractions which mimic their random compositions, to intimate pieces that are carefully placed and modeled in a figurative fashion, to simulating nature by creating elaborate three dimensional impressionistic landscapes in larger than life installations.

Miami has been both inspiring and instrumental to our work. Its natural and urban landscapes, cultural diversity, and the (sometimes severe) tropical weather are all main contributors to the rich source of visual information we have gathered and incorporated into our own sensibility. What is generally considered eyesores by the majority of the local population has been a driving force in our creative process. Torn and tattered billboards, naively painted murals faded by the sun, garments entangled in barbed wire fences, and dumpsters filled with unwanted clothing from local rag trade businesses have been stimulating preludes to the art we produce. Based on proximity, our work reflects the energy found within our immediate environment to conjure imagery that conveys universal messages.

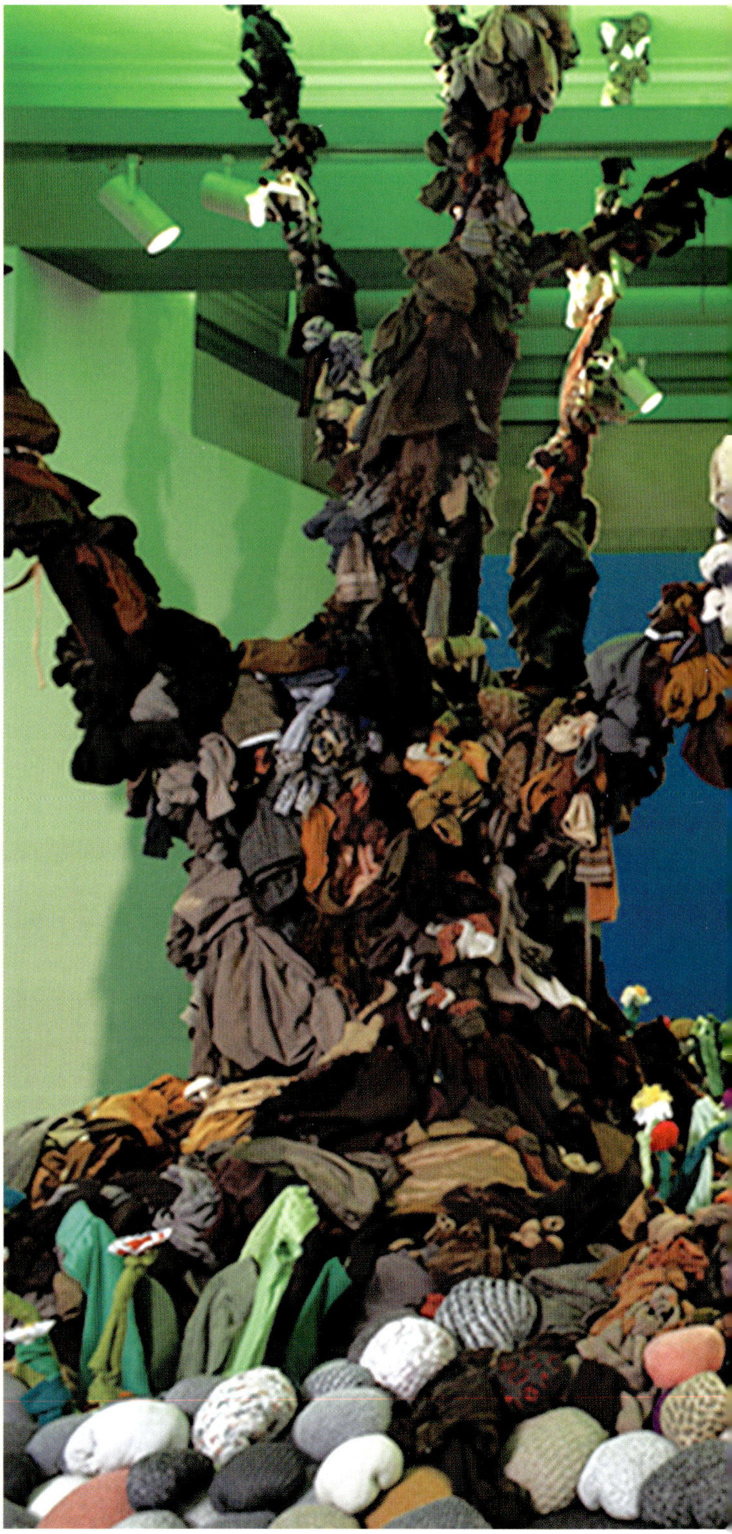

Oasis, 2005-2006. Site specific installation, recycled garments, wire, wood, ceiling brackets, interior latex paint, bird soundtrack. *Chicago Cultural Center.*

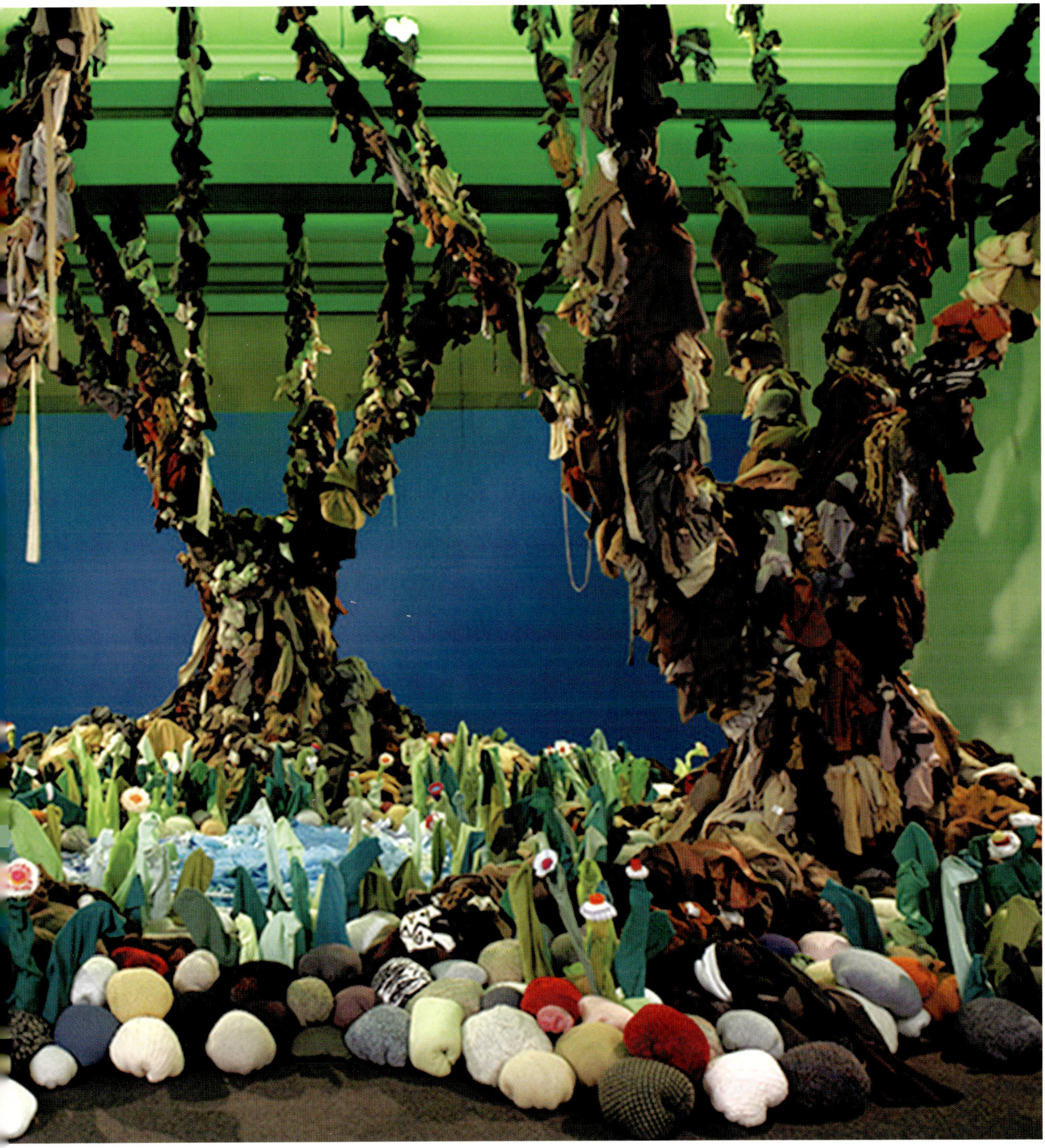

ADLER GUERRIER

I make artworks about urban spaces and small narratives primarily based on my experience of the complexity of the city through walks and drives.
Miami is often a subject in my works, and at times, functions as a place holder for an urban space. I am interested in the study of Miami's history, urban plan and its perpetual evolution and re-manifestation as a city and place where people live, act out, and project their narratives.

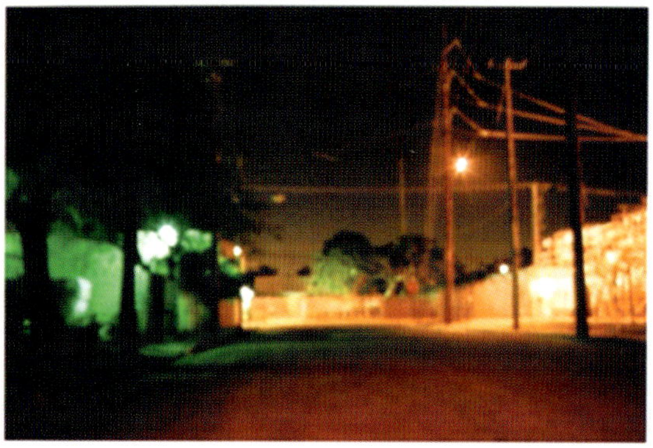

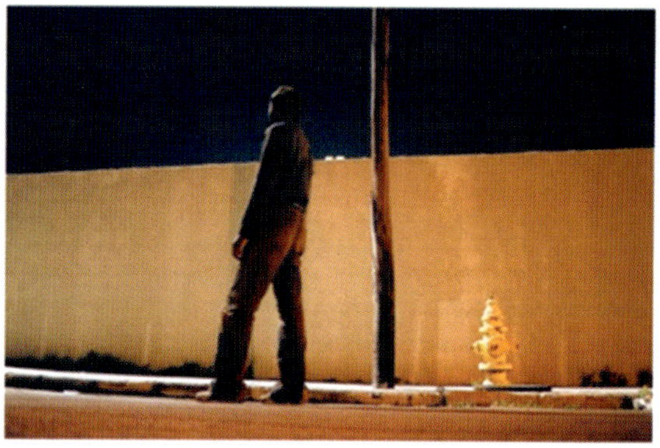

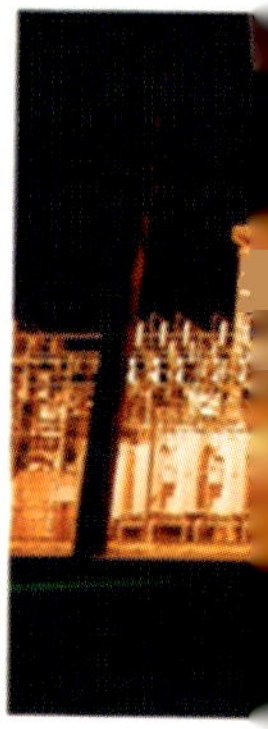

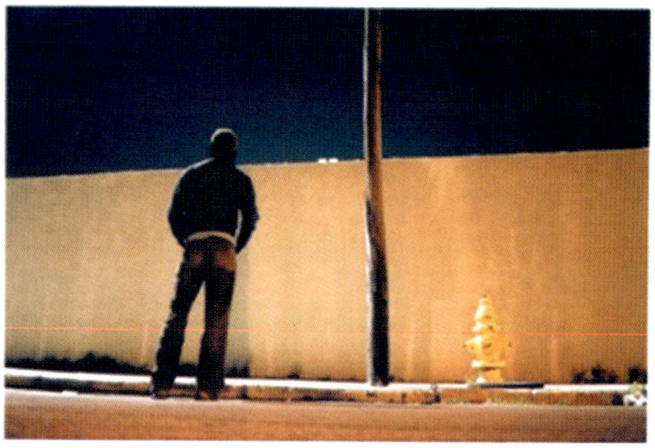

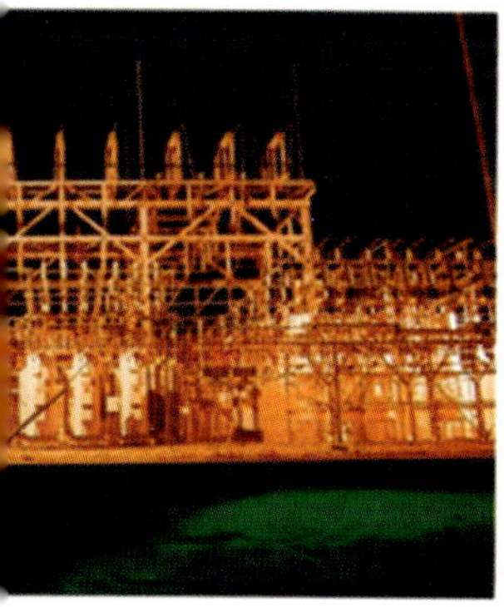

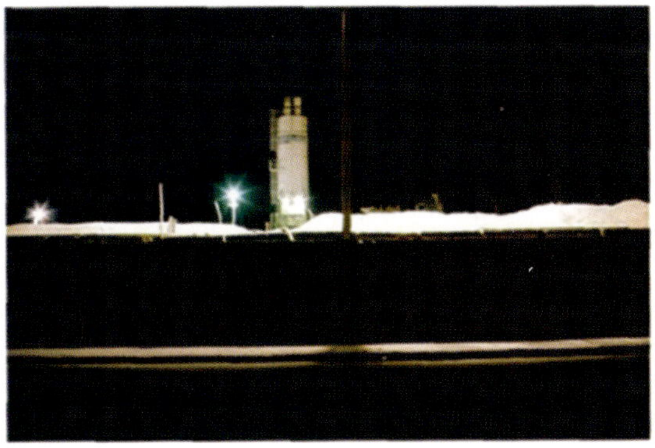

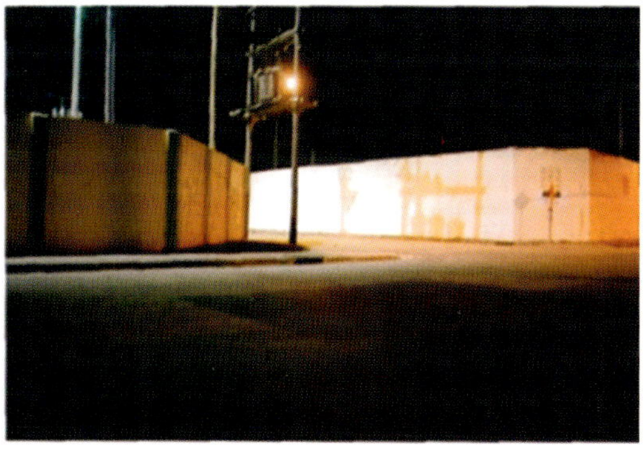

Untitled (Overtown north), 2006. Color photograph, seven each, 11" x 14".

JASON HEDGES

I feel the greatest commonality we share as humans is our interaction with food and drink because no one is exempt from a need of them. I find myself drawing lines connecting us with what we cultivate, produce, and inevitably consume. I strive to capture and distill down relevant icons from food stuffs into a palatable format to engage in a self critiquing dialogue of art and contemporary society while maintaining the inherent beauty of the one. However, there are several aesthetic and symbolic liberties taken throughout the process to direct the viewer along a specific conceptual narrative about what the said theme has to do with the viewer. In my view, what we cultivate and produce is a pure extension of us in the same way art is an extension of the artist, no matter how adorned or refined it becomes it is the keystone of existence.

Being a young artist in a young city has been a motivating set of experiences for both involved parties. Beginning my interactions with the city long before I had any desire or physical aptitude to create makes me quite excited for what has and will be happening here. I find myself surrounded by great artists, friends, various individuals and institutions who on a daily basis "Make it happen" for all involved parties. I look forward to the years beyond our adolescents as a community and city.

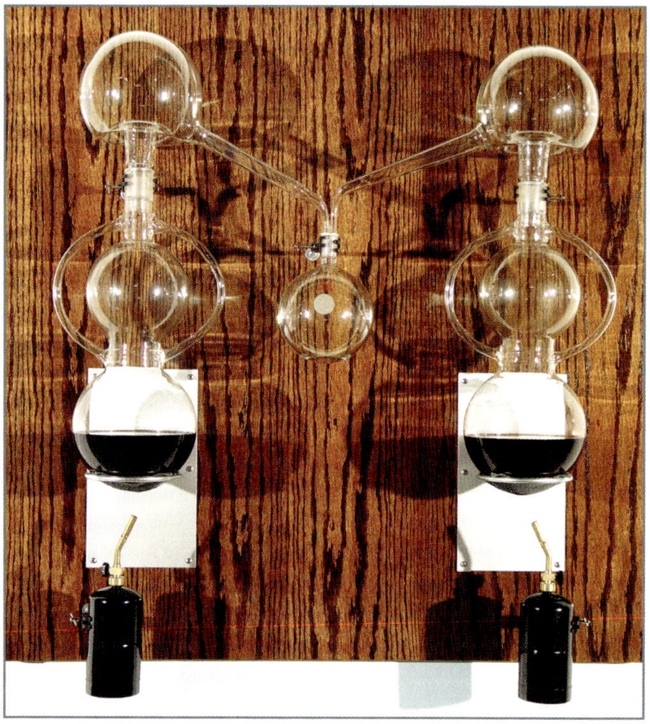

Double Pelican, 2004. Glass wine, aluminum, propane burners, oak. 48" x 48" x 12".

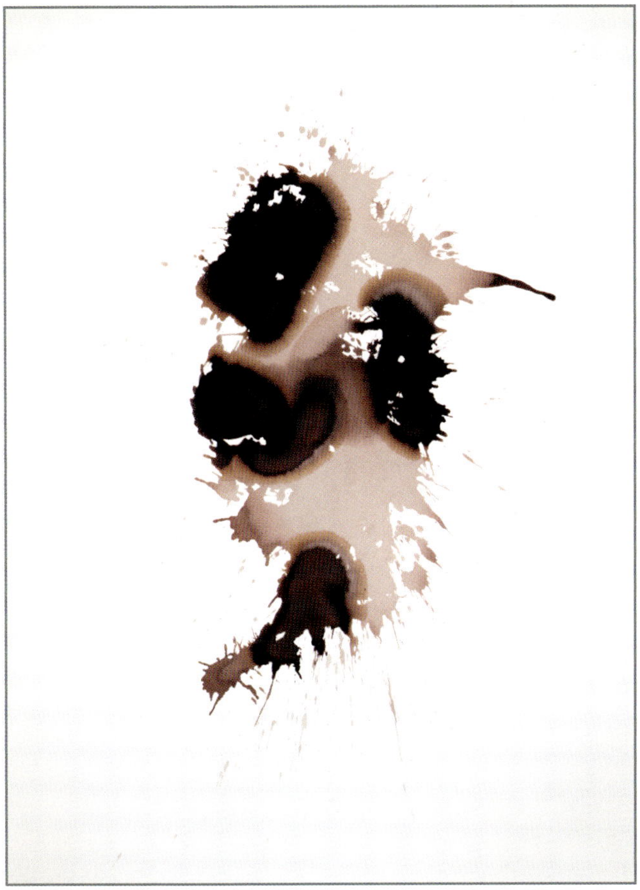

1985 Burg, 2006. Joseph Drouhin, Beaune Clos des Mouches, 1985. Wine on paper, 40" x 60".

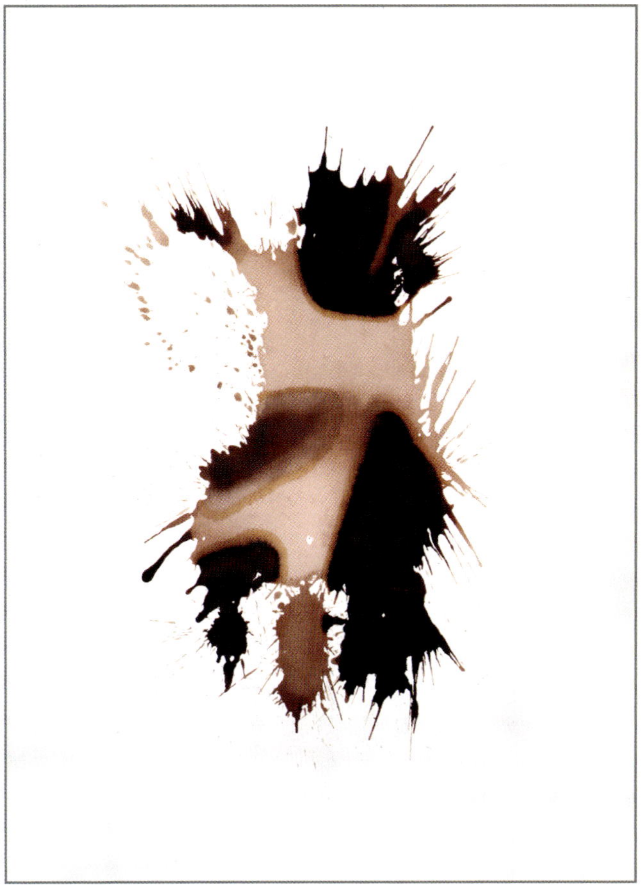

2001 Zin, 2006. Chiarello Family Vineyard, Felicia old Vine Zinfandel 1002. Wine on paper, 40" x 60".

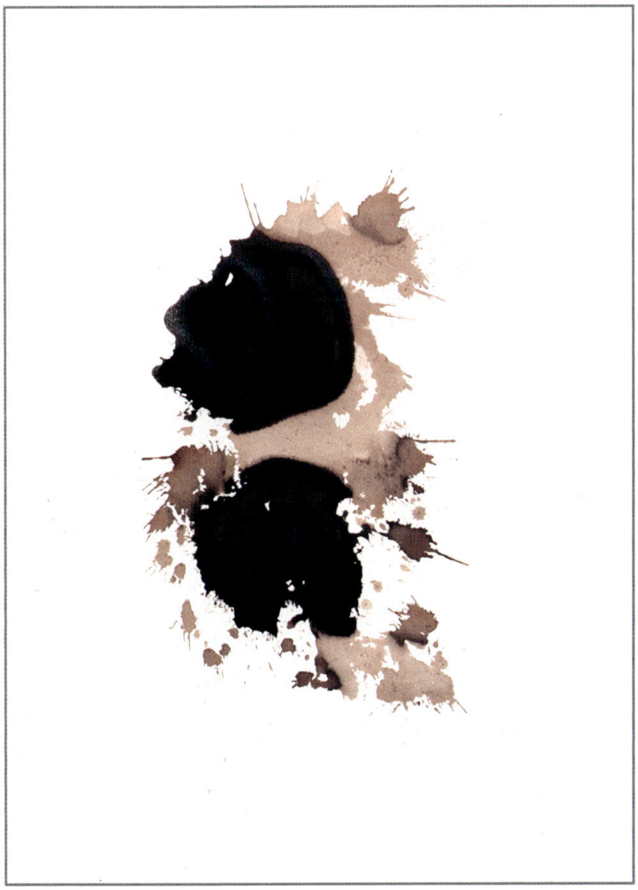

Gaja Barbaresco 2001 #1, 2006. Wine on paper, 40" x 60".

2003 Burg, 2006. Maison Chanson, Gevry-Chambertain, 2003. Wine on paper, 40" x 60".

QUISQUEYA **HENRÍQUEZ**

During the last few years, my work has focused on and developed two areas of research. One is the subject of cultural stereotypes related to the social and cultural characteristics of the Caribbean on account of its insular and peripheral condition. Aspects such as climate, geography, preconceived notions and certain dynamics of perception related to the customs of this region are reflected in the series titled "*Mockeries*." The series *"Mockeries"* also deals with differences and characteristics of "otherness" as a package of specificities considered exotic and, thus, attractive and repulsive. The other area of research is the relationship between public and private. Based mainly on the city and its public spaces, urban life and its residues, these works reflect the behavior of an individual in such spaces, and the manner in which the individual consumes, transforms, and intervenes in such spaces. These works comprise a broad registry of the motives, cultural and political, behind such actions. Beyond the thematic inclinations of my recent pieces, my work has developed in multiple mediums ranging from photography and video to sound art and installation.

I arrived in Miami in the summer of 1993, after 3 years of living in Mexico. At that time, very few artists living in Miami used contemporary art mediums to develop their ideas, which made me believe my work would not be easily accepted. I felt I was in the wrong space at the wrong time. Rather quickly, I realized the contrary. Only 2 months later, I had my first individual show and, less than a year later, I became a part of the local art community. Miami is a porous city, full of small and great concavities that attract one in order to nourish and be nourished. During the nineties, all the pillars of art simultaneously strengthened. Some galleries redefined their focus according to new art practices, and areas such as the contemporary art collecting, emerged and developed. Even museums redesigned their spaces to reflect the new aesthetic and functional demands of the contemporary productive methods of the visual arts. As an artist, it was extremely important to witness such changes and be part of the process that transformed the art context of Miami of the early XXI century into an international one. At the moment, my work is much more present in the museums of Miami than in the city in which I currently reside. With more than two exhibits a year in Miami, I have the impression that I have never left this city. Miami still harbors the spirit of a city open to all, in particular members of the art world, who wish to broaden their professional experience.

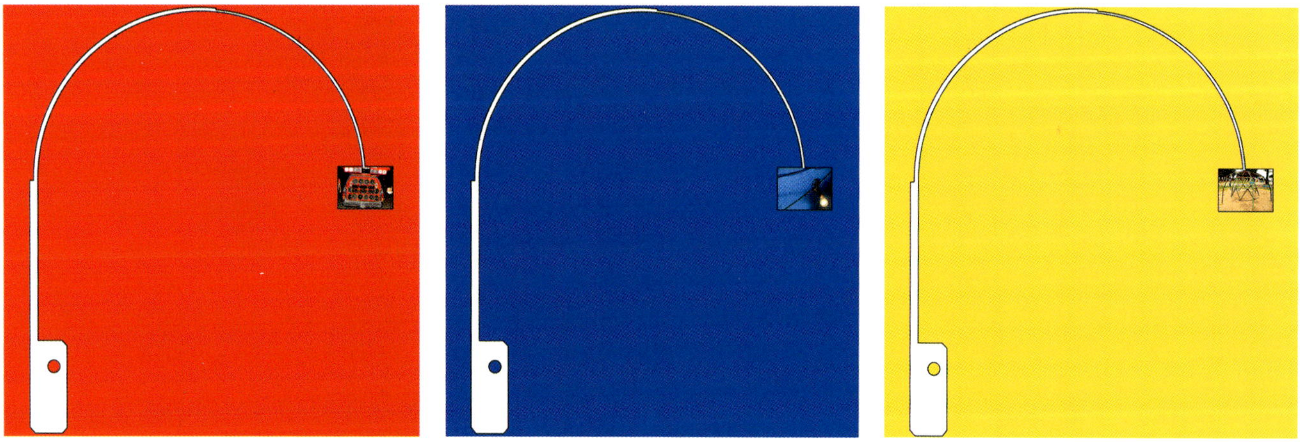

Arco Lamp, 2006. Wall papers (red, yellow, blue), graphic and digital image, ink jet print, 60" X60" each.

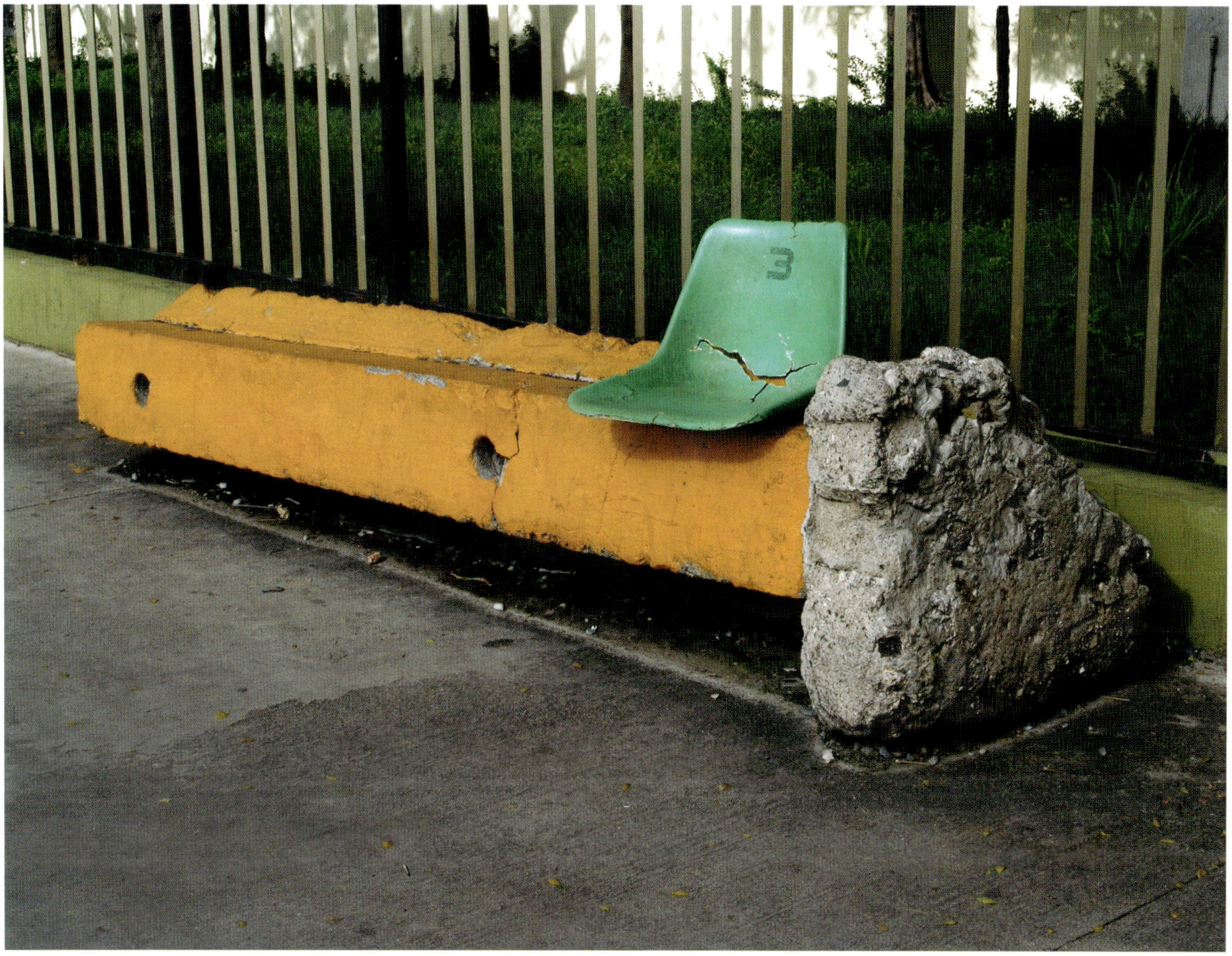

Mobiliario Urbano (from the Series: Public Space), 2004. Digital image, 24" X 32".

ALEXANDER **HERIA**

The *Family Series* resulted from a personal revelation about the relationships and living arrangements of gay men. Having understood these relationships in a different context, I discovered an overwhelming number of gay men living in utter domesticity. The daily lives and partnerships of these men are no different from any other family: the dividing of household responsibilities, housecleaning, cooking meals, entertaining friends, watching TV, lounging around with each other and with pets. Similar to images of couples depicted in advertisements in home and design magazines, the *Family Series* documents these gay men with a universal, emotional quality, illustrating that we are all the same in our home environments and in our quiet, daily living amongst our families.

Miami is light.
Miami is color.
Miami is wishing.
Miami is Gomorrah.
Miami is fluid and changing, always.
Miami is being *Cubichi.*
Miami is living through hurricanes.
Miami is my first car, a Chevy Chevette.
Miami is where I grew up, over and over again.
Miami is the ugly and the beautiful.
Miami is of the flesh.
Miami is *un chancletaso por ser insoportable.*
Miami is tripping at the Copa at 16.
Miami is *mi mami.*
Miami is the most amazing skies.
Miami is so totally dichotomous.
Miami is all highways and interchanges.
Miami is growing out of control.
Miami is a blessing and a curse.
Miami is my home.

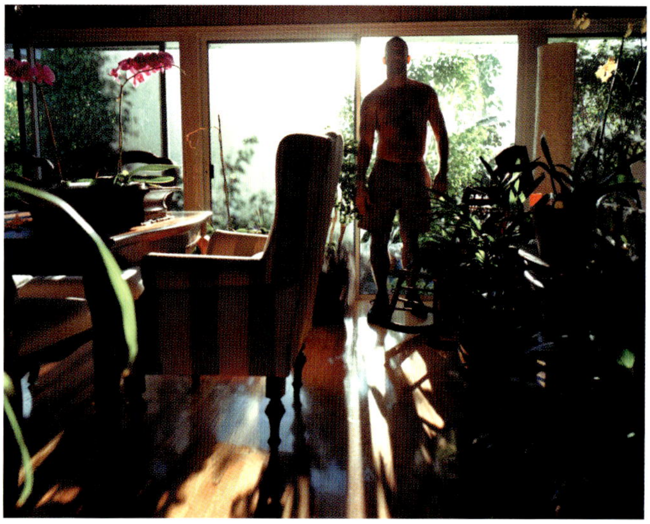

Family – Alex, 2005. C-print, 24" x 20".

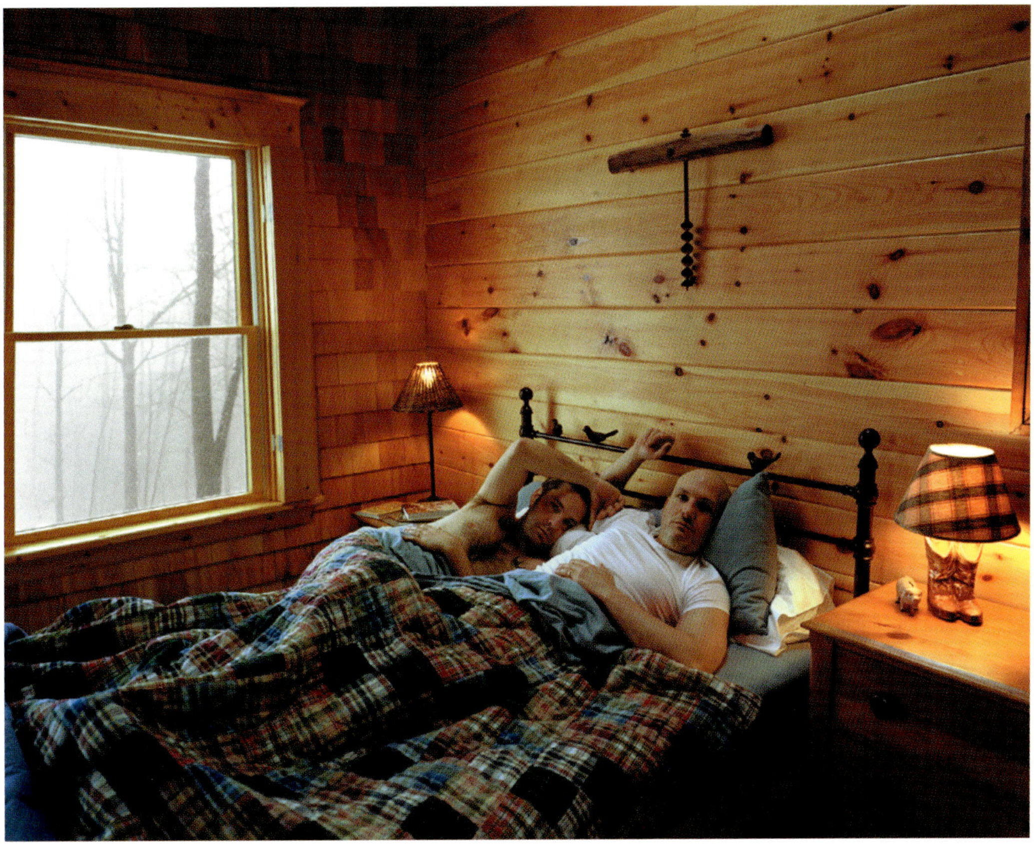

Family – David and Mario, 2005. C-print, 24" x 20".

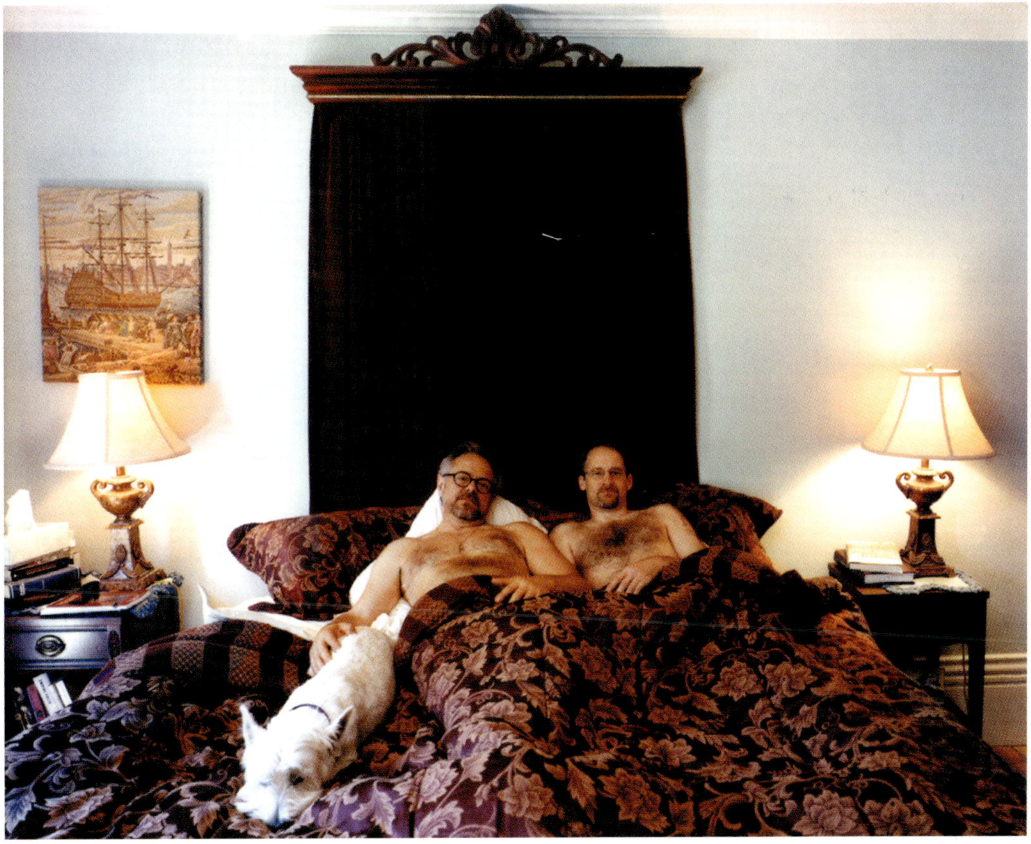

Family – Henry and Marty, 2005, C-print, 24" x 20".

ROBERT **HUFF**

Architectural form is often perceived as an imposition on the natural landscape. My work has concentrated on the relationship between the man-made architectural form and the natural free flowing forms found in the environment, especially the studio environment. The integration and disintegration of these relationships becomes the starting point for many of my pieces. Through the manipulation of various materials I explore the qualities in our environment that imply human presence. A presence that is beautifying and destructive, violent and serene; yet filled with visual stimulation. The vast majority of our dwellings are fabricated from mass produced materials, which have a predictable appearance, they are in essence a product of a manufacturing society. A society based on ease of fabrication, established modular systems for construction and delivery. These concepts have always held a particular fascination for me and become a part of the driving force in my work.

Miami has always been an interesting place to be an artist. The light is unparallel, it is bright and clear with a definite influence on the way we see things. Miami's reputation as a mecca for the sun and sand was always a major contention, for it was difficult for outsiders to see the environmental influences on the work being produced, let alone take it seriously. I don't believe that I could have prospered as an artist without these challenges. The influx of immigrants begun in the 1960's drastically changed the sociology of the area and had a profound influence on the visual attributes of place. I have always considered myself a landscape artist and these changes produced an interesting marriage with my midwestern concepts. My work not only concentrated on the light and natural landscape but also became involved in the architectural impositions on that landscape. Some of these architectural impositions took foreign shapes, contrary to the more traditional "white bread" architecture created after World War II. This atmosphere has provided an extremely rich source of information for my work.

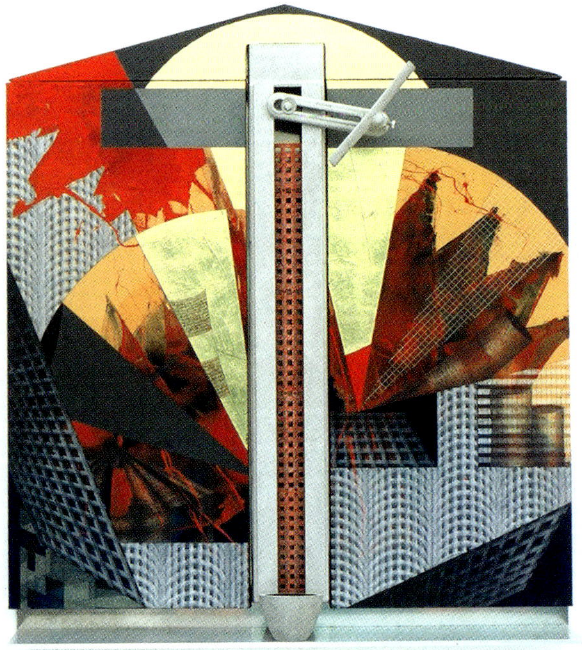

Station #11, 1998. Acrylic, pencil, gold leaf & aluminum, 51" x 46.25" x 7.50".

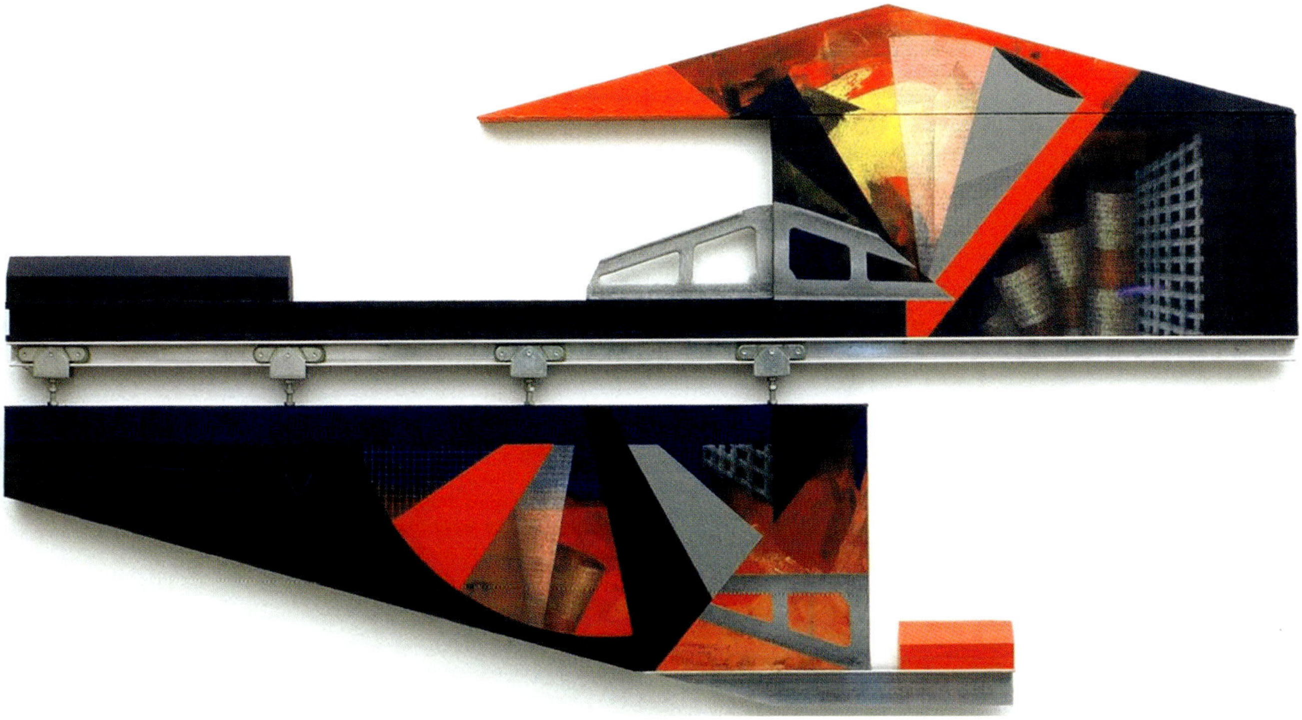

Slider #1, 1998. Acrylic, pencil, wood & aluminum, 38″ x 72″ x 1.5″.

JIAE **HWANG**

Scientists send shuttles into space for a greater perception of our planet and in a search for the extraordinary. I have a similar desire in my artwork, however; my interest in exploration is specific to the internal landscape of human consciousness and experience. Wordless thoughts, sensations of light and emotions are all seemingly intangible, yet these are the components which define us as unique human beings, and inside of us they compose small planets of their own. The multimedia projects *I am the Smallest Planet of my Own* and *Take my Hand to the Farthest Star* are my ongoing investigations of self metamorphic memoirs. They consist of diverse experiments ranging from video sculpture to sight specific installations, as well as collaborative audio projects and video narratives. Through these mediums I seek to bring various emotional states to the surface. My work is an attempt to enlighten the viewer's mind from the limitations of observation. In my animations, elements appropriated from my surroundings are carefully orchestrated and placed in foreign contexts. These re-contextualized objects cease to serve their traditional functions, rather; they are used as vocabulary to stimulate our senses in unforeseen ways and to subvert the pre-existing encodings in our mind.

Miami is a young magical beanstalk burgeoning in the sun, and I am a small caterpillar just happy to be here...

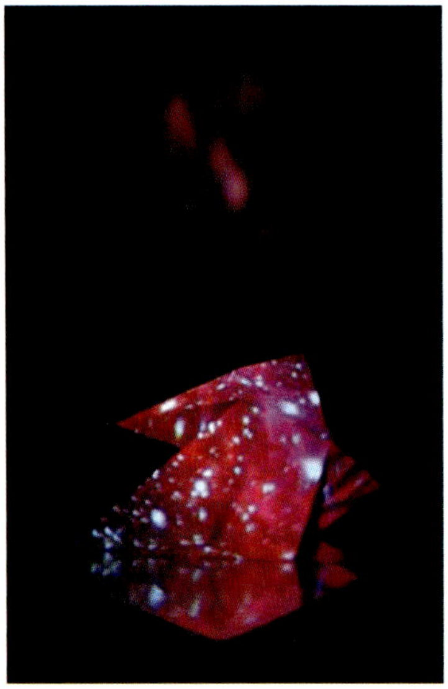
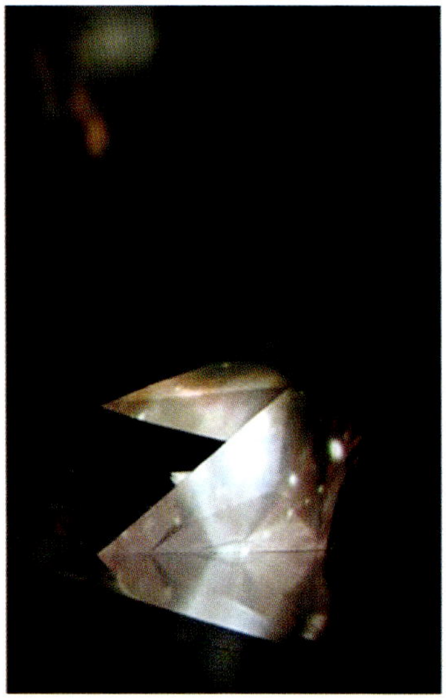
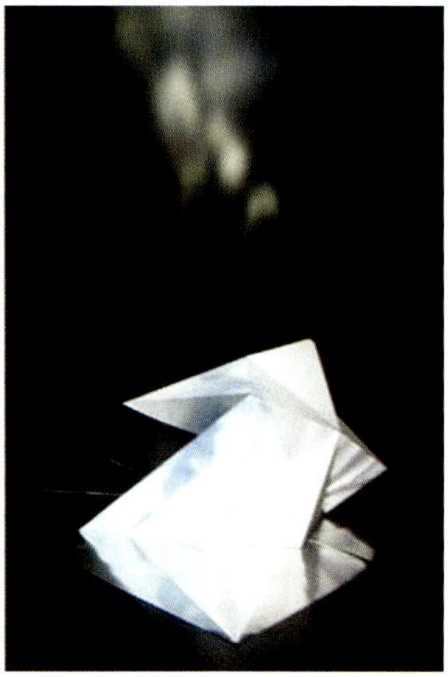

I am the smallest planet of my own (space ship) installation view, at MDCC Centre Gallery, 2004. Video projection on paper sculpture, 5' x 5' x 5'.

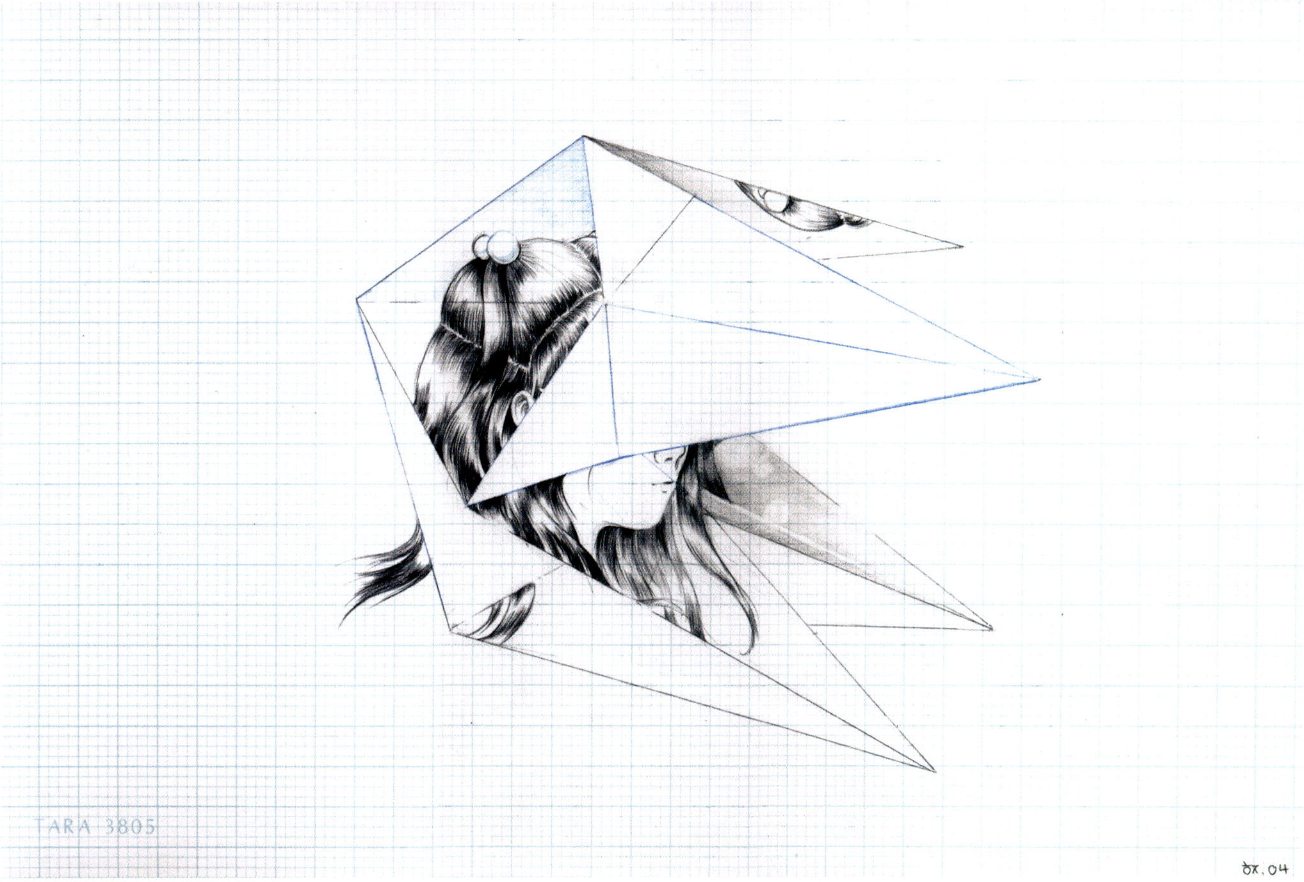

Inter-dimensional space fold, 2004. Graphite and colored pencil on graphed paper, 16" x11".

JULIE LARA **KAHN**

I create interdisciplinary artworks that cross and re-cross boundaries among visual art, performance, social engineering, and mass marketing. My elaborate productions involve covert and overt audience interaction which not only create extended portraits of people and places but also nurture community through participation. Although there are invariably artifacts and aesthetic ephemera resulting from each project, the heart of my work is interpersonal dynamics, social criticism and examination of the extraordinary side of ordinary life. My projects often involve meticulous planning and execution, and I believe my artwork is as much about this process as it is either the intricate participatory events that accompany each work or the objects that remain after the opening. Because I am interested in examining the artistic process while simultaneously making work about broader contemporary issues, my projects also invariably layer some aspect of the art world into the discussion and increasingly incorporate an unexpected encounter between the art world and the larger world. For example, in 2001 at Dorsch Gallery in Miami, I created *Got Milk?,* which involved a cereal tasting at the gallery, interviews with gallery visitors about childhood breakfast table memories, and a 12′ organic multi-grained mandala that I constructed on the gallery floor. The following year I invited 100 Miami art world personalities to provide me with personal information for a deck of art world trading cards, titled *OPEN SEASON Miami*, which I packaged and traded by way of cigarette girls during that year's Art Basel Miami Beach. I recently launched the second set, *OPEN SEASON Havana,* during the IX Havana Bienal. For the past several years, I immersed myself in the life of Florida Crackers in order to understand and create a portrait of this important rural subculture – people with increasingly rare, generations-long ties to the land. The resulting exhibition, *Swamp Cabbage,* entailed a show of large-scale color photographs, sound, video projections, and a panel discussion with scholars at Locust Projects Gallery accompanied by a wild game tasting at the nearby Food Culture Museum, where crowds from all corners of Miami sampled dishes such as: swamp cabbage, quail in wine sauce, venison & wild hog sausage chili, fried catfish and alligator tail, and soft-shell turtle stew, all harvested from the wilderness and prepared by Cracker families. My largest purpose is to break down the traditional barrier between artwork and onlooker by inviting the viewer into the creative process. I have accomplished this not only by working with the usual windows into the unknown – photographs, videos, and sound installations – but also by offering a taste of a childhood food, an opportunity to break bread with strangers, an environment conducive to unexpected interactions, and a chance to exchange opinions with scholars and people from diverse walks of life. In this way I hope to make discoveries on my own about what distinguishes us and what binds us together, and to share these discoveries by way of community, the land, and the food chain.

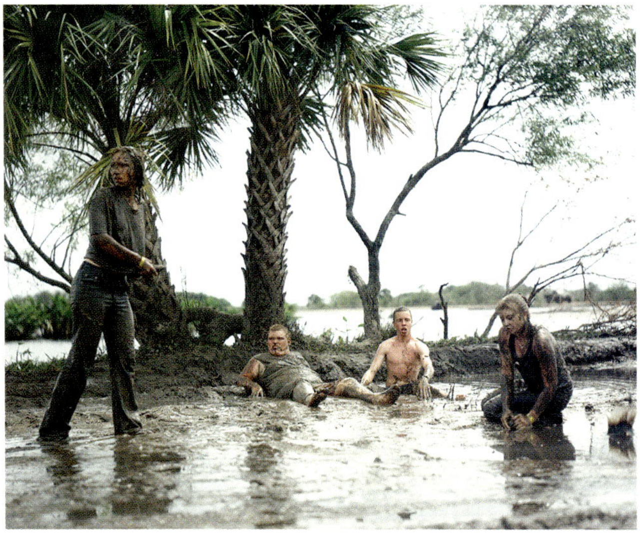

Mudhole (from Swamp Cabbage), 2005. C-print, 27″ x 33.75″.

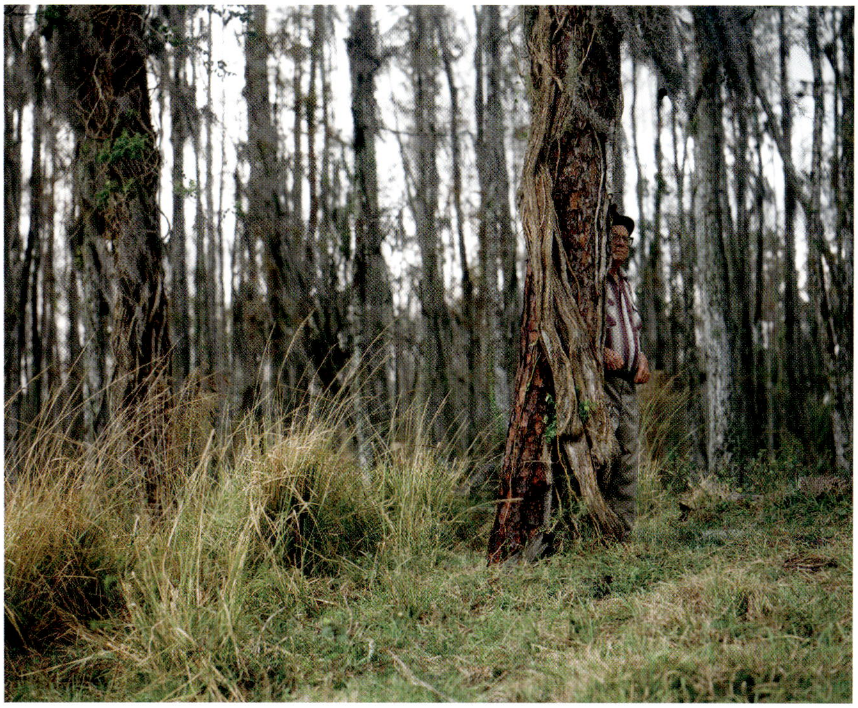

Moonshiner (from Swamp Cabbage), 2005. C-print, 27" x 33.75".

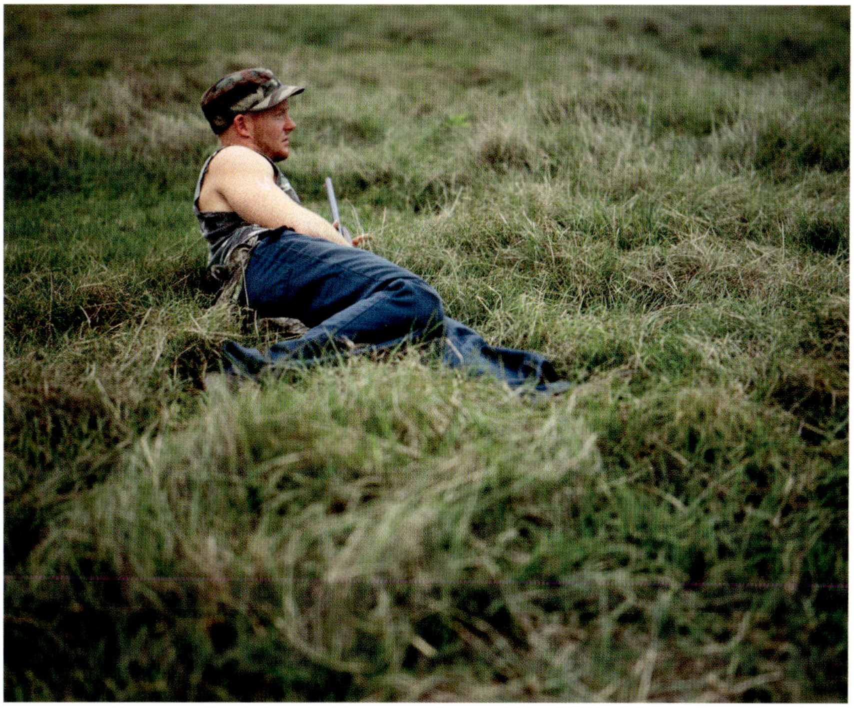

Dovehunt (from Swamp Cabbage), 2005. C-print, 27" x 33.75".

BAYUNGA NSIMBA **KIALEUKA**

My paintings deliver for me a purpose when there is nothing else to hang on to. As an artist, I see fit to more than preserve the ideals of cultural identity. I find it far more significant to confront the representation of social self via testimonials of isolationism, affection, mischief, status, and kinship. The challenge of personal truth and happiness is central in my expression.

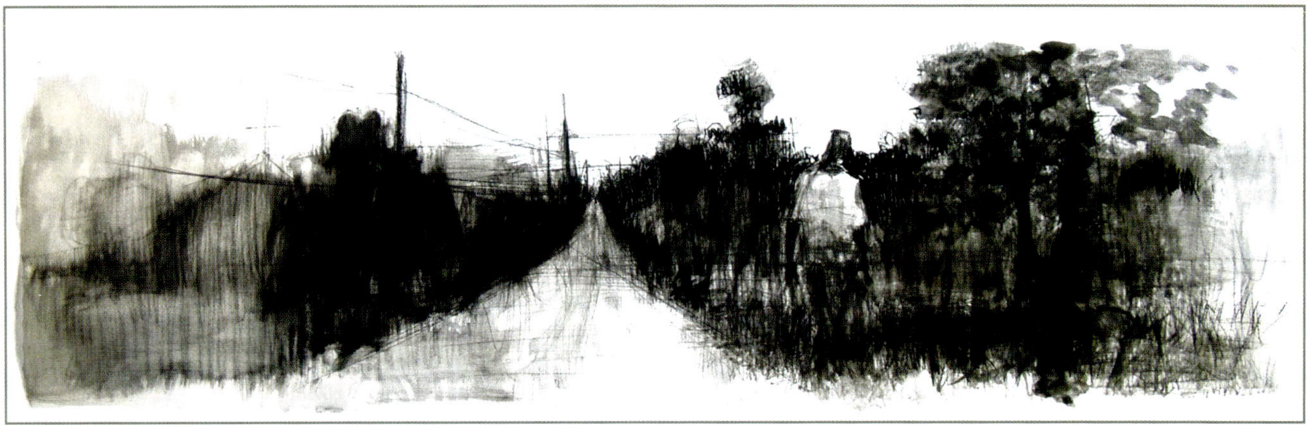

Old Cutler, 2004. Charcoal on canvas, 12" x 40".

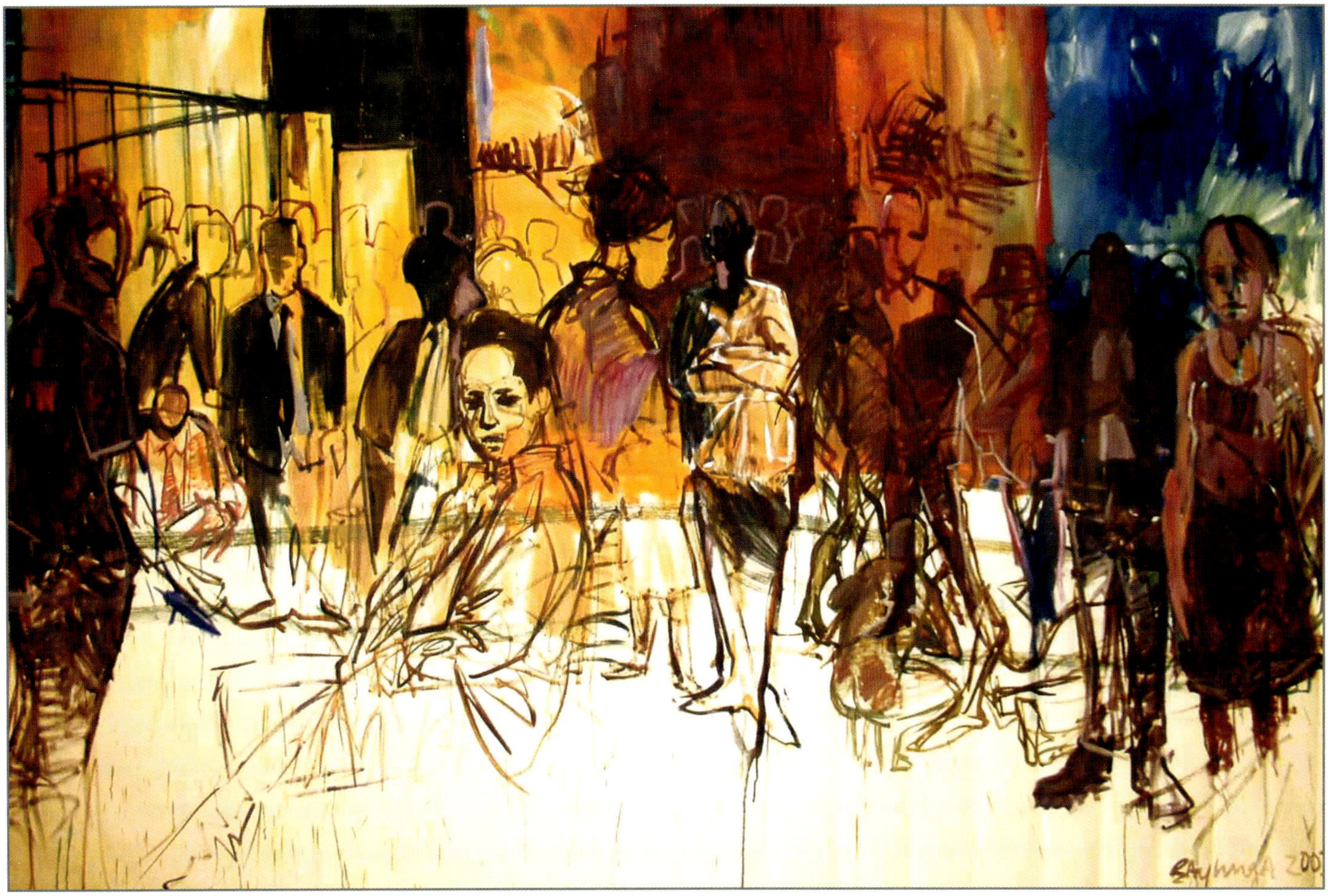

Concentration, 2001. Oil on canvas, 72" x 120".

SUSAN LEE-CHUN

Camouflage is a method that allows an otherwise visible organism or object to remain indiscernible from the surrounding environment. The ability to blend into an environment provides an element of protection, given that the ultimate goal is to hide or go undetected. Although animals have acquired this ability by an evolutionary process, I have taken it upon myself to camouflage my racial identity. Installations, such as *The Camouflage Series* (2005), *Incognito* (2005), and *The Unrecognizable Other* (2006) present fabricated spaces that I construct with patterned textiles as wallpaper and soft sculptural objects. These installations often function as a stage or platform that I perform within and photograph myself. I also wear a garment or protective wear that I have specifically designed out of the same fabric as the installation, which serves to conceal my presence in the space. However, it is apparent that I am unable to blend in perfectly, which is symbolic of my inability to conceal my identity. In all the performances, my intention is to conceal and reveal my presence to the viewer. Here, the interaction between the viewer and myself paraphrases the focus on race and gender in our culture.

As a non-native of Miami, my perspective is borne of the comparisons I draw between Miami and the cities with which I am more familiar. Miami is a city that appears to be in constant flux, much like the life of an artist. The city is undergoing mass development and rapid growth, and most all of the inhabitants are in some way intricately tied to the growth of this city. Here, the initiative to take risks is high because of the numbers of people invested in putting Miami on the map. The numbers and commonality create a collective fervor to succeed by pushing limits and redefining boundaries. This is visible in the burgeoning art community. In fact it's difficult not to notice the potential and energy in the art scene. As an artist it's encouraging to see those in the arts community-artists, curators, collectors, galleries, and museums – work to ensure that art remains a vital component in the growth of Miami. I find myself benefiting from this environment as it challenges me to examine my work objectively and to take the risks that shape my work.

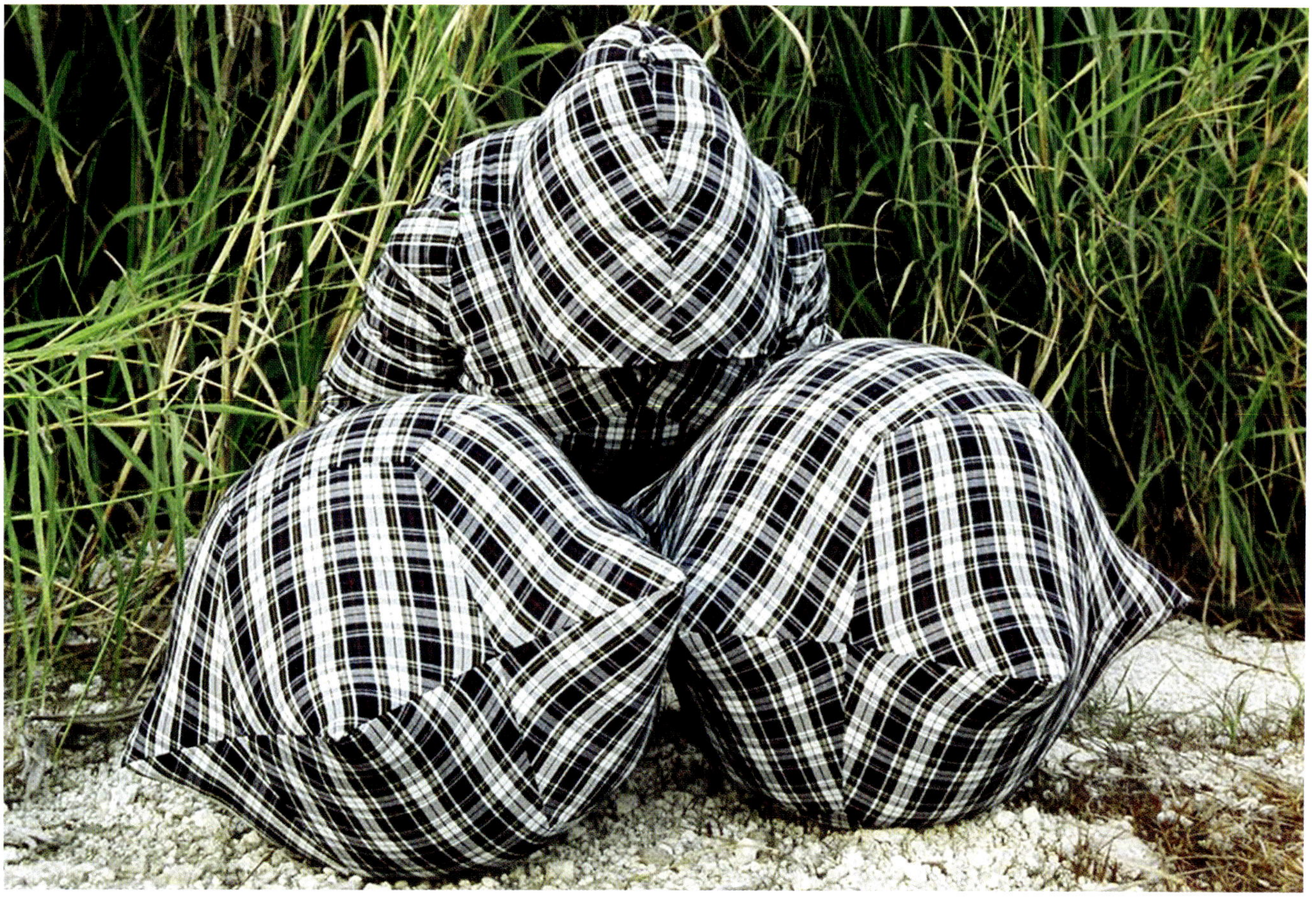

The Unrecognizable Other: Still #1, 4/2006. C-print, 20" x 24".

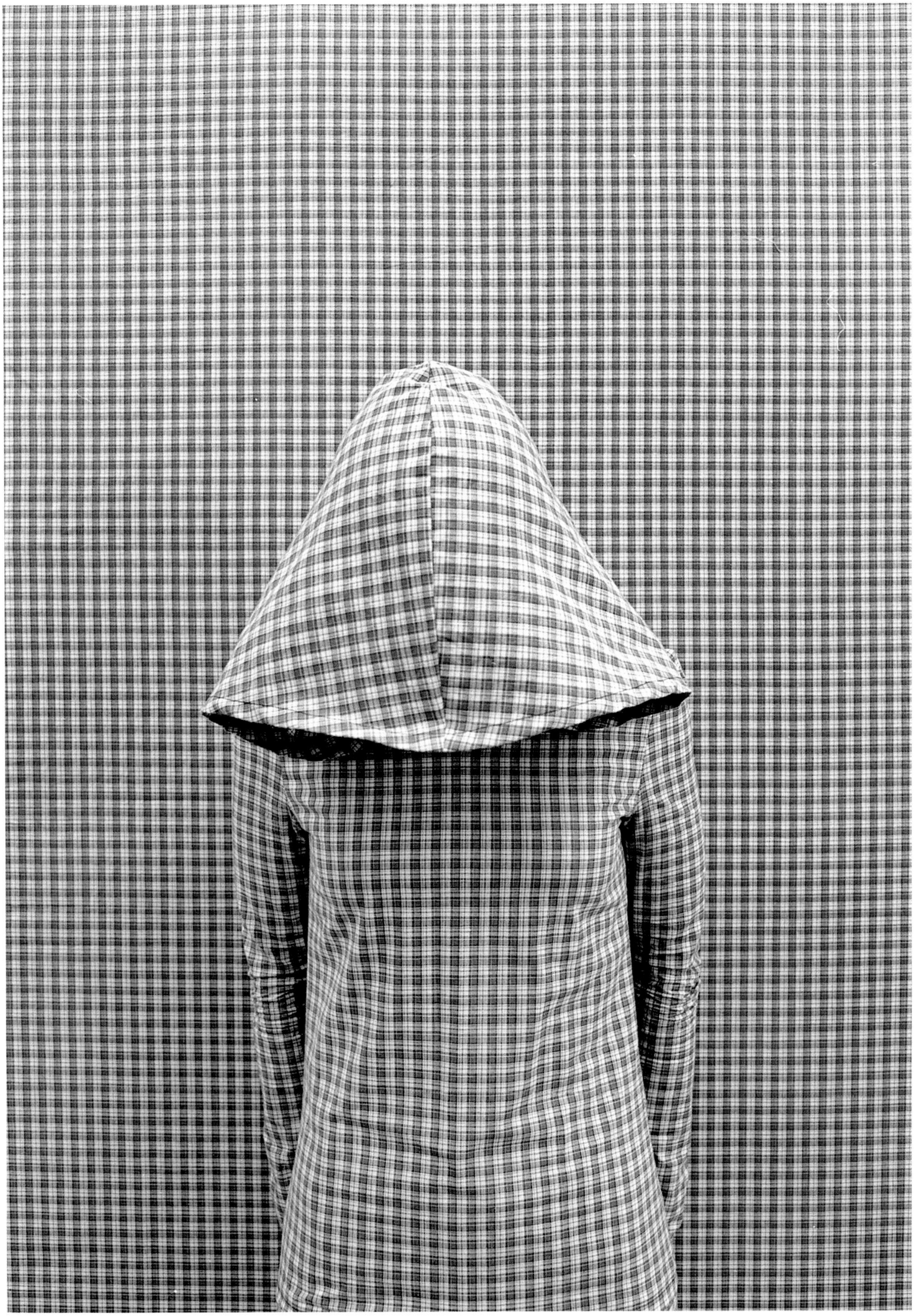

Incognito: Still #1, 3/2006. C-print, 16″ x 20″.

MIRA LEHR

To observe nature and to reorganize its complexity into a higher order is my passion. This new universe I create becomes more powerful than the reality that inspired it. The process is the result of paring down, peeling back layers of Japanese paper and moving the paint around until I arrive at a place that is both magical and filled with light. At some point I allow the accidental and chance to come into play. It's as if I suspended thinking and another part of my brain takes over. I can say it's "complete" but it never comes to an end because the search is eternal. It's like playing God, there is always more to discover.

I moved to Miami Beach as a young child and aside from some years spent in New York at boarding school and college at Vassar, I have always lived here. When I returned from New York, it was 1960 and the "art scene" in Miami was extremely quiet. After a frustrating search for artistic stimulation I co-founded The Continuum, a center in which artists could work and exhibit. Workshops were provided with visiting scholars. This offered what Miami did not have, a vital space for the exchange of ideas and the development of a visual arts community. Some of our visiting artists and scholars were Jack Flam, Matisse expert, Robert Motherwell, John Chamberlain, Hans Hofmann, and his long time students, Nieves and James Billmyer. In addition, we also held concerts, poetry readings, dance recitals, and conferences relating to the interaction between art and science. Thomas Banchoff from Brown University lectured about fourth dimensional graphics. Though no longer in existence, The Continuum, was the first cooperative group of women artists in the southeastern US, and is now archived in the National Museum for Women in the Arts in Washington DC. Miami is now a different place filled with galleries, artists and, for a brief time each year, Art Basel. It has changed us; the "art world" now takes us seriously. In addition, the natural beauty and ease of living are all positives for artists here. A new cutting edge city is developing. I enjoy being part of it. What was once a vacation paradise is now becoming a rapidly evolving city whose future in the arts is a promising one.

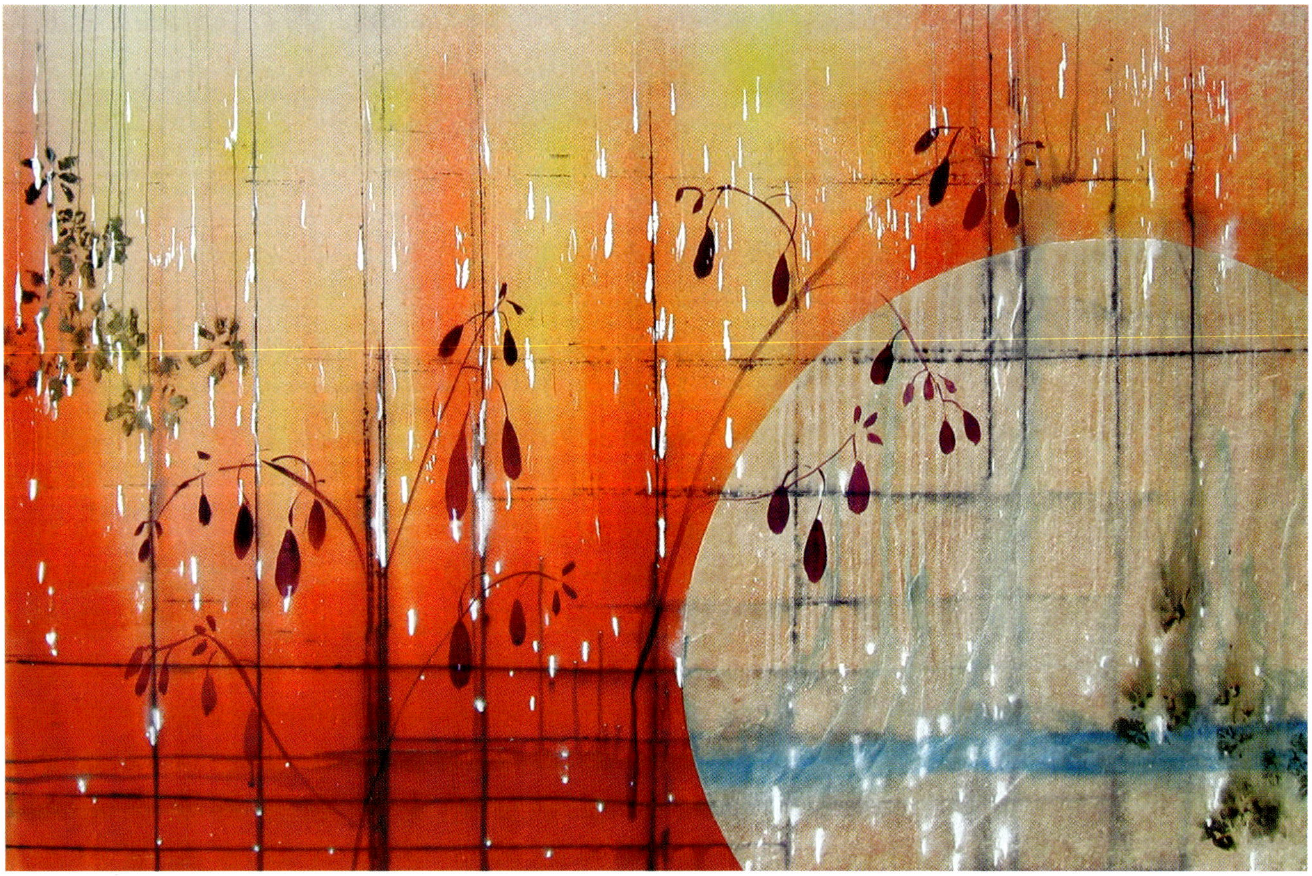

Macau, 2005. Mixed media on canvas, 40" x 60".

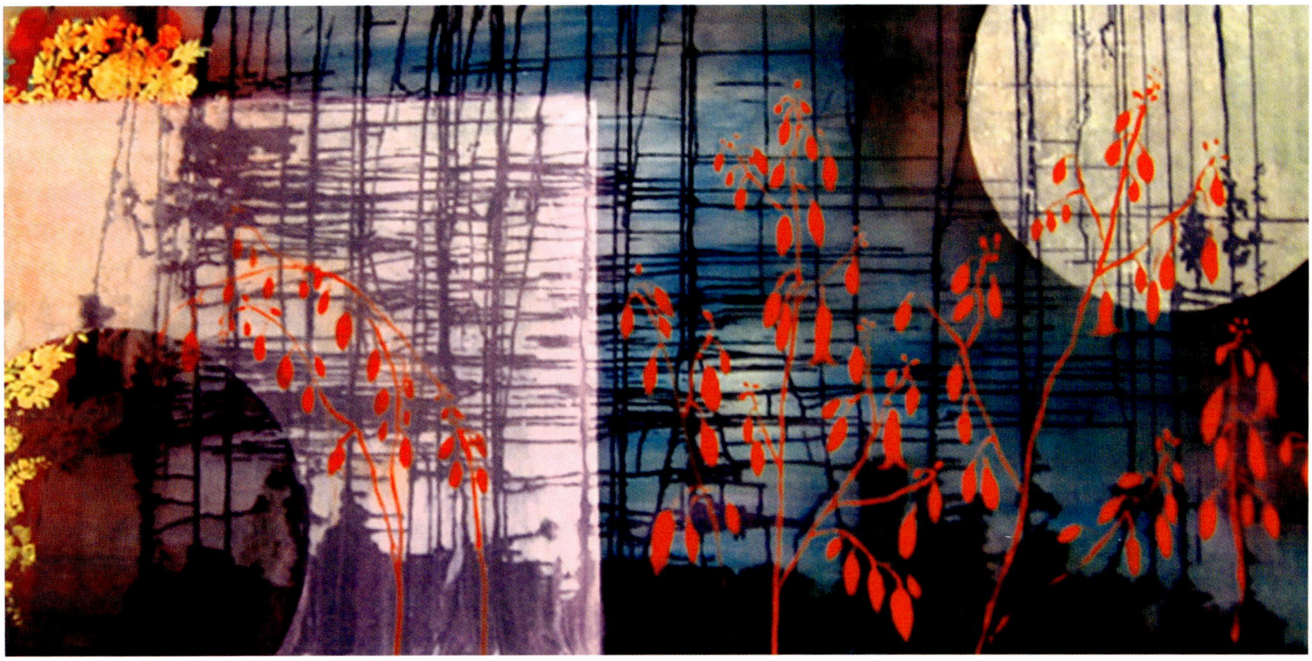

Jersey, 2005. Mixed media and Japanese paper on canvas, 60" x 120".

JOSHUA **LEVINE**

Darwin,
Evolution, revolution.
Survival of the fittest.
Natural Selection vs. Genetic Manipulation
Biotech, cloning, Dolly.
Creating our pets.
New Species, unique breeds.
Intensified features and traits.
Better living through science.
Bio-pharms.
Corporate branding.
The Human Genome Project.
Breeding tomorrow's medicine.
Cracking the code, patenting the drugs.
Basic building blocks of life,
a child's Tinker-Toys:
A,G,T,C.
Genetic flaws, disease,
Biodiversity eliminated.
DNA.
Your identity. Who owns it?
What are you? Who are you?
Who is watching you?
Blending of biology and technology.
Patenting genetic organisms.
Nano technology, self-replicating machines.
Artificial intelligence, limbs and organs.
Smart animals, smart skin,
Synthetic Biology.
Killing for Conservation,
Exhibitions for the future.
Harvesting foods of the future.
Feeding the world.
Bigger fish, riper bananas.
How do they taste?
Are they safe?

Miami is not just a physical, geographical place on a map for me, but more a state of mind. Having relocated to New York over 8 years ago, Miami is no longer the place I call home, but rather a place that my mind goes to escape. I search through my memories of growing up on Miami Beach in the late 70's and 80's. I see crumbling Deco Facades transformed into the slick neon beacons of change and re-birth. I see an area where one can go to transform themselves into something else, something new. I see bright pastel colors passing by me as I feel the sunlight drenching my body and the wind whipping on my face. I retreat there mentally when I need to think of all the future possibilities. I know that even though the names and the interior spaces change, the facades will always remain the same. Miami is the anchor in my ever changing life. I may not be a *native*, but I will always be a *local.*

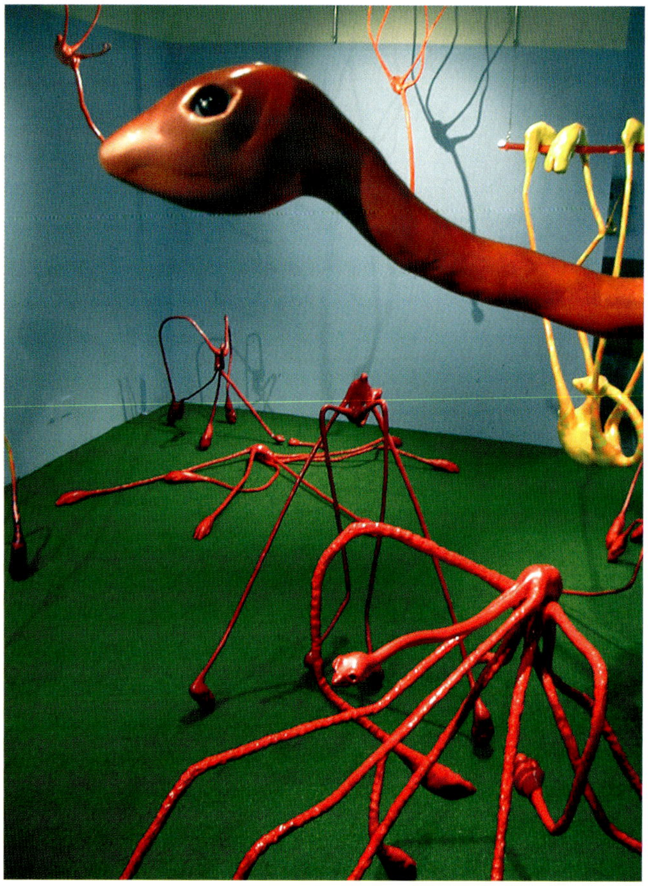

Trans•gen•ics (installation view), 2003. Mixed media, dimensions vary; installed at LUXE Gallery, NYC.

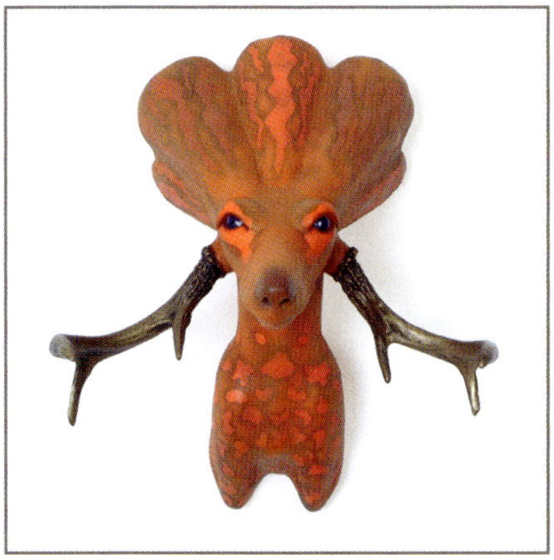

Trophy Head (Orange Horned), 2006. Mixed media, 13" x 11" x 10."

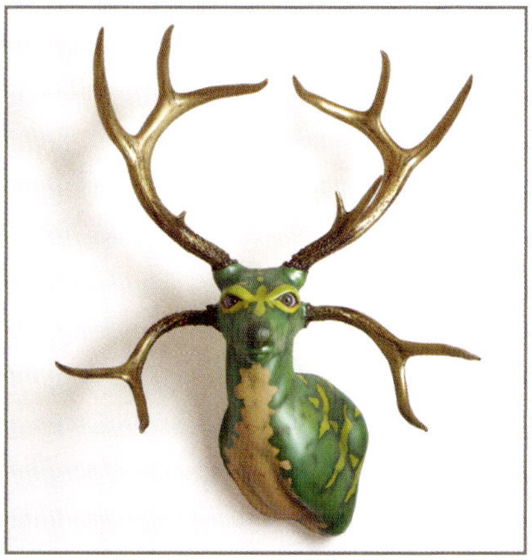

Trophy Head (Green4Horns), 2006. Mixed media, 26" x 22" x 15.25".

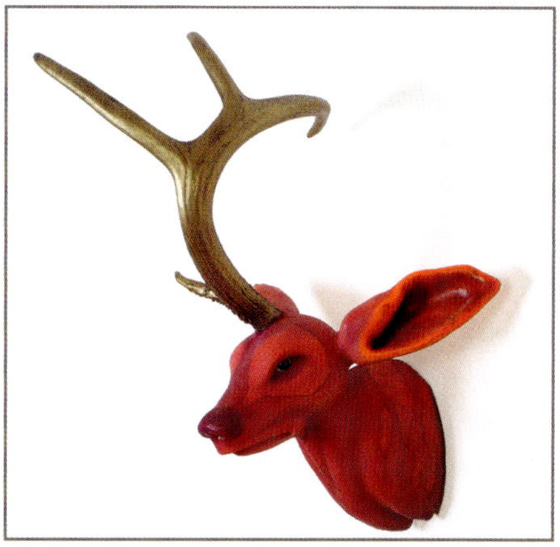

Trophy Head (Magenta Uni Horn), 2006. Mixed media, 17" x 12" x 11".

PETRA LIEBL-OSBORNE

Petra Liebl-Osborne focuses on site-specific art works. Depending on the subject she chooses from a variety of traditional and new media, painting, three-dimensional works, fabric, photography, video and digital imaging to create objects that represent specific sites. As an artist and architect, her view is concentrated on the tectonic context of the visual environment, and most projects show a direct dialogue with the architecture –it is the artistic interpretation of architectural landmarks. Since 1996 Liebl-Osborne has been exploring the space beneath the water's surface with underwater camera and video. The images represent the perception of the specific architectural space, and mirror experiences with the color BLUE as the surrounding element. The *Acqua Pietra Luce Projects* focus on a historic architectural landmark. For the *Castello Maniace* work, Petra Liebl-Osborne used a photo series she had taken of the inside and the outside of the building itself. The photos were mounted in light boxes and re-installed inside the antique structure; so the images of the thousand year old castle itself, as the only source of light, illuminate the bare and somber interior. The images of the *Villa Vizcaya Project* that is still in process, show photo series that mirror the building on the surface of its own pool. The strict and geometric lines of the architecture loosen up into abstract amorphous forms. Water as the defining element of Vizcaya's site, becomes a tool for Liebl-Osborne's artistic compositions. *(Nicola Borgmann)*

From my very first stay in Miami in 1988, I was taken by the atmosphere of this international metropolis in the tropic hemisphere with its very open spirit. Coming from Europe, I was fascinated by the unbelievable mix of professional world and Southern joy of life; by the abundance of nature with its jungle flair, and everywhere, the ocean with its bays and creeks and canals infiltrating the city. I watched the art scene grow with an enormous energy. I saw new galleries, museums and collections coming up. In this vivid, young and open Art World I felt very much at home, and got a lot of inspiration. In the academic realm at University of Miami and Florida International University, I was warmly welcomed, and I feel wonderfully integrated into Miami's artistic and scientific world. For my personal path as an artist, Miami plays a major role. Miami's architecture, its stunning colors and its specific culture of the swimming pool are influencing my work ever since arriving, and have become a topic by itself. The Blues, the Turquoises, the Pinks are overwhelming still today. The underwater views in swimming pools, the color experiences in combination with a weightless floating generate an irresistible change of perception. And when in certain moments the rectangular architectural space of a pool starts to dissolve and the elements of water and sky seem to melt together, a certain cosmic effect is evolving. A rational concave box turns into a dazzling irrational figure. These images of ever changing reflective lines and forms develop infinite shades of Blue and are to me a symbol of Miami's great attractions: Architecture, Art and Nature.

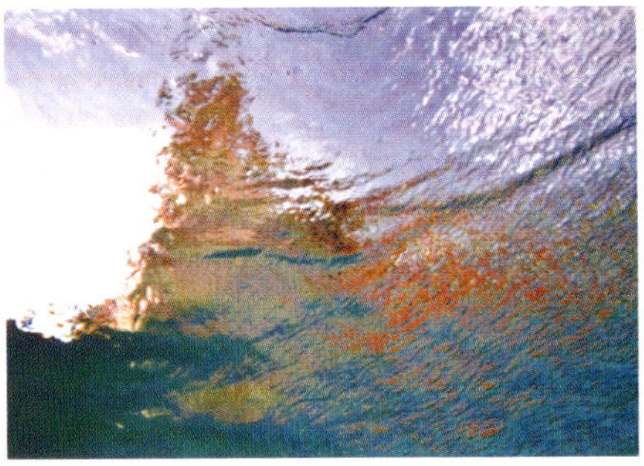
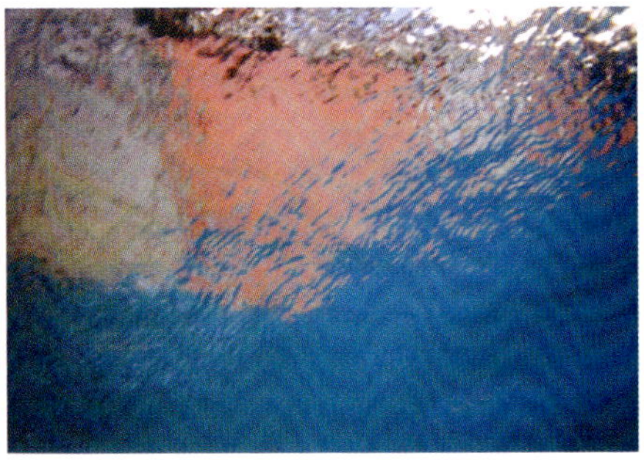
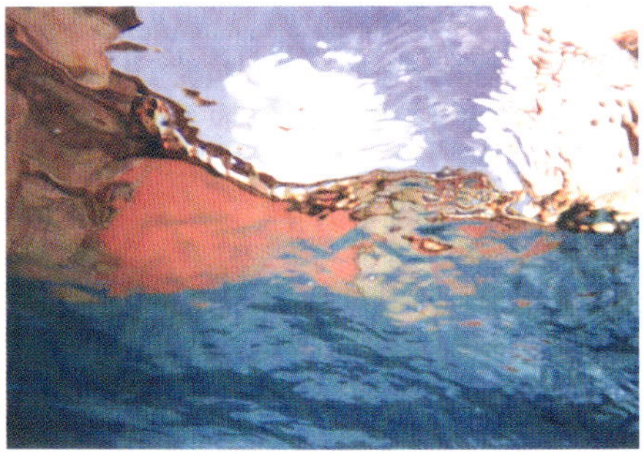

Acqua Pietra Luce II – Villa Vizcaya/Miami, 2006. Photo series, 24" x 36".

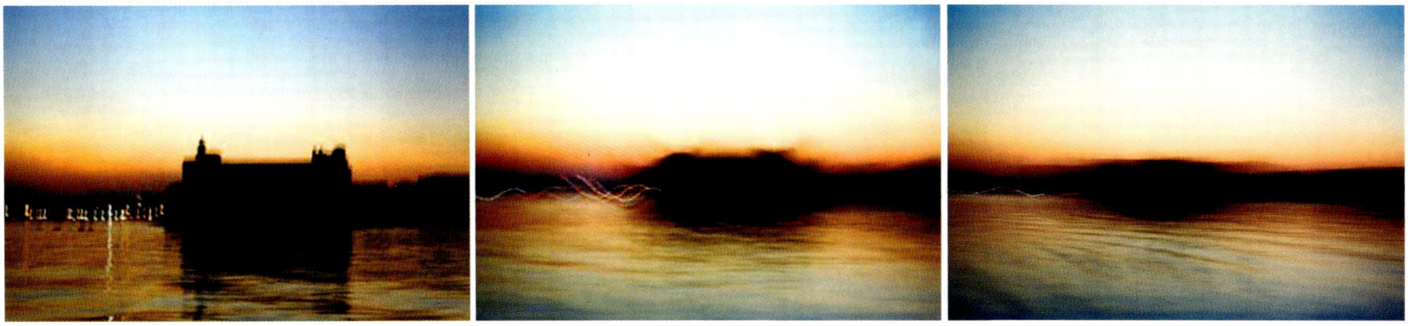

Acqua Pietra Luce I (at night) Castello Maniace/Siracusa, Sicily/Italy, 2003. Photo series in light boxes, 25 " x 17" x 4".

FRANCESCO LOCASTRO

My paintings are inspired by pop culture iconography and cartoon imagery as well as the work of masters of varied genres and periods, such as Frank Frazetta, Chuck Close, Joel-Peter Witkin, Sebastian Krueger, Richard Estes, Grant Wood, Edward Hopper, Gustav Klimt, Albrecht Duerer and Hieronymus Bosch. I mostly work in oils and acrylics on canvas or wood, but occasionally use resin on varied surfaces. By juxtaposing cartoon images with realism, I try to frequently address the opposing aspects of social and political issues: In today's westernized world, the line between reality and fiction is increasingly blurred. Escapism is the new religion of a society destined to overdose on mind-numbing consumption. We stay indoors to view "reality programming." Maxed-out credit cards temporarily fulfill the American dream that is not quite within our reach. Movie star idolatry rules the dogma of mediocrity and the government structure dictates the politics of greed and hegemony as basic characteristics of survival of the fittest. My art leaves little room for interpretation. What you see is what you get. Some artists aim to appeal to the "higher' part of our nature – i.e. – the head. My work aims for the gut. In Freudian terms, it is work of the id as opposed to the superego. It is work that takes human need and desire not as something to transcend but as something to fully indulge in.

I have been fortunate enough to bear witness to the cultural (re)-birth of the city of Miami, and within that microcosm, had the chance to be a driving force in introducing a new art movement, more akin to markets such as Los Angeles and New York. At the moment, the movement I represent (currently known as "pop-surrealism") is still perceived with skepticism, but is, at the same time, rapidly gaining momentum in South Florida. Within Miami's art market, my work and the artists' work I represent exists inside a vacuum between disinterested and indoctrinated local galleries and a young, avant-garde support audience, backed by savvy collectors ready to invest while the work is still affordable. Still, general support for this emerging movement is growing fast and major institutions, such as the Museum of Contemporary Art North Miami, and the Art Center/ South Florida, are leading the way in quickly adjusting to the changing art climate. Working as an artist and curator in Miami is something I have certainly been able to use to my advantage, not only am I able to take an active part in forging an emerging, and still flexible art market open to new voices and fresh ideas, but also, being an artist resident in Miami, I am able to distinguish myself on a national level among my peers who are competing in more "culturally saturated" areas such as Los Angeles and New York City. The opportunity to exhibit work in the growing art center that Miami is shaping up to be, is an offer many artists from all around the world are increasingly welcoming with open arms. It is an incentive, which, for a curator like me, translates into the ability to bring a higher level of quality art and culture to the city.

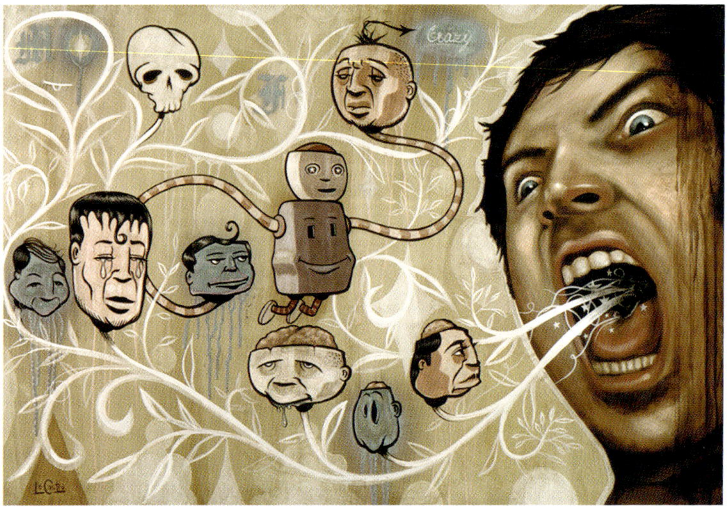

Crazy MF, 2004. Acrylic and spray-paint on Masonite board, 30" x 40".

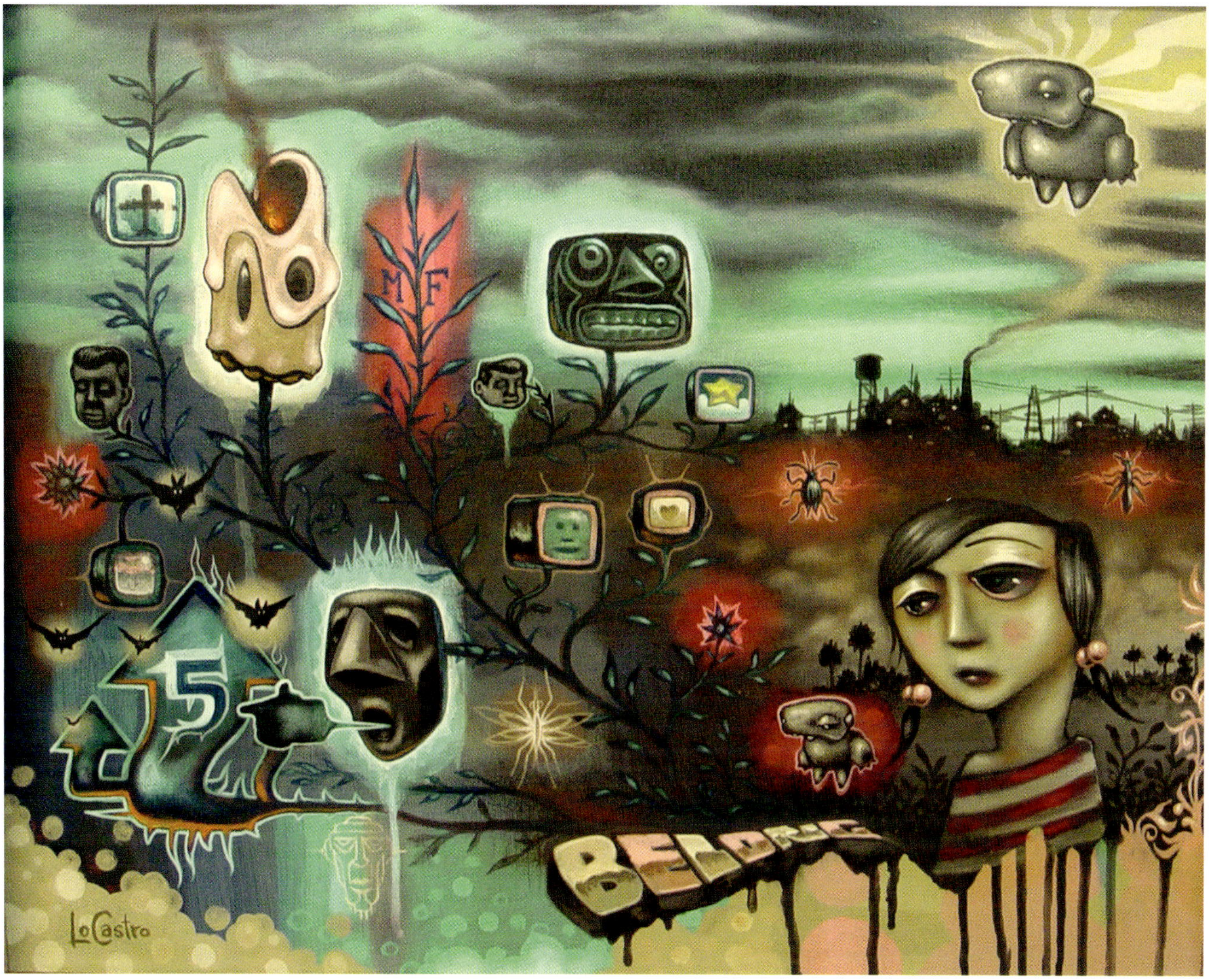

Small town Dream, 2005. Oil and acrylic on canvas, 16″ x 20″.

MICHAEL **LOVELAND**

This new series is about interpreting the world around me, it discusses how I translate the materials I find and how I employ them. In our present state of the world, media bombardment is more apparent and growing larger. I find it is necessary to filter my surroundings to produce pure construction. My newest inspiration has arrived from the man-made compositions of tractor trailer skins and delivery truck doors. Their crude repairs and painting out of graffiti with mismatched colors allows for a developing propensity of dimension and layering within my work. There is a complete chance operation that occurs in everyday life; like marks left behind on a wall. That's what I find so approachable and familiar, what most people pass, disregard, or see as common.

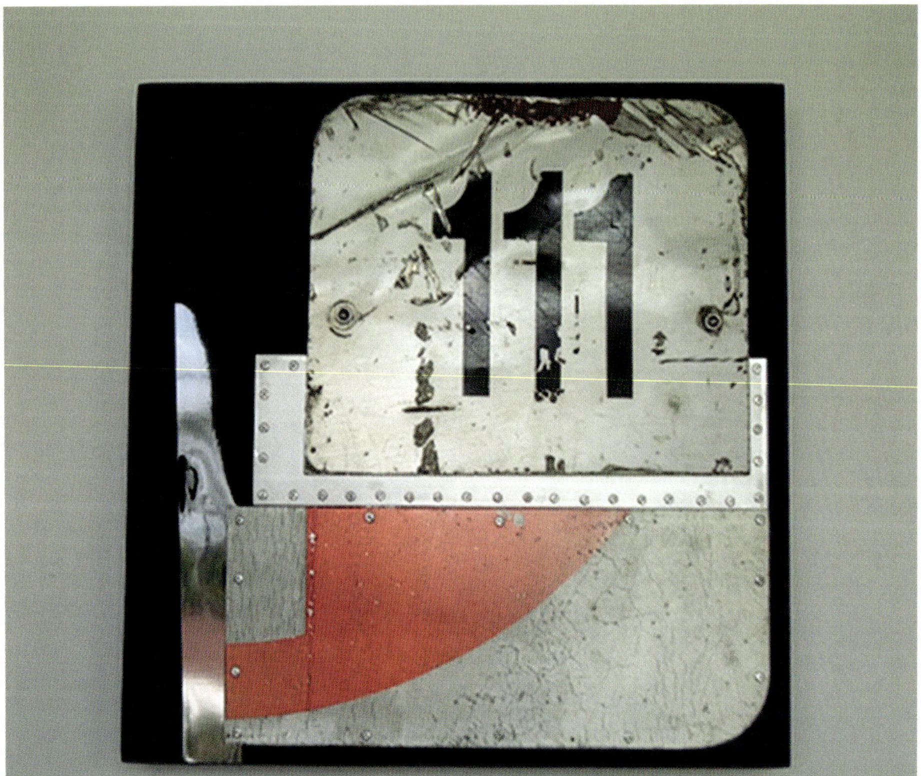

Triple 1, 2006. Aluminum, fabric, and steel, 20" x 20".

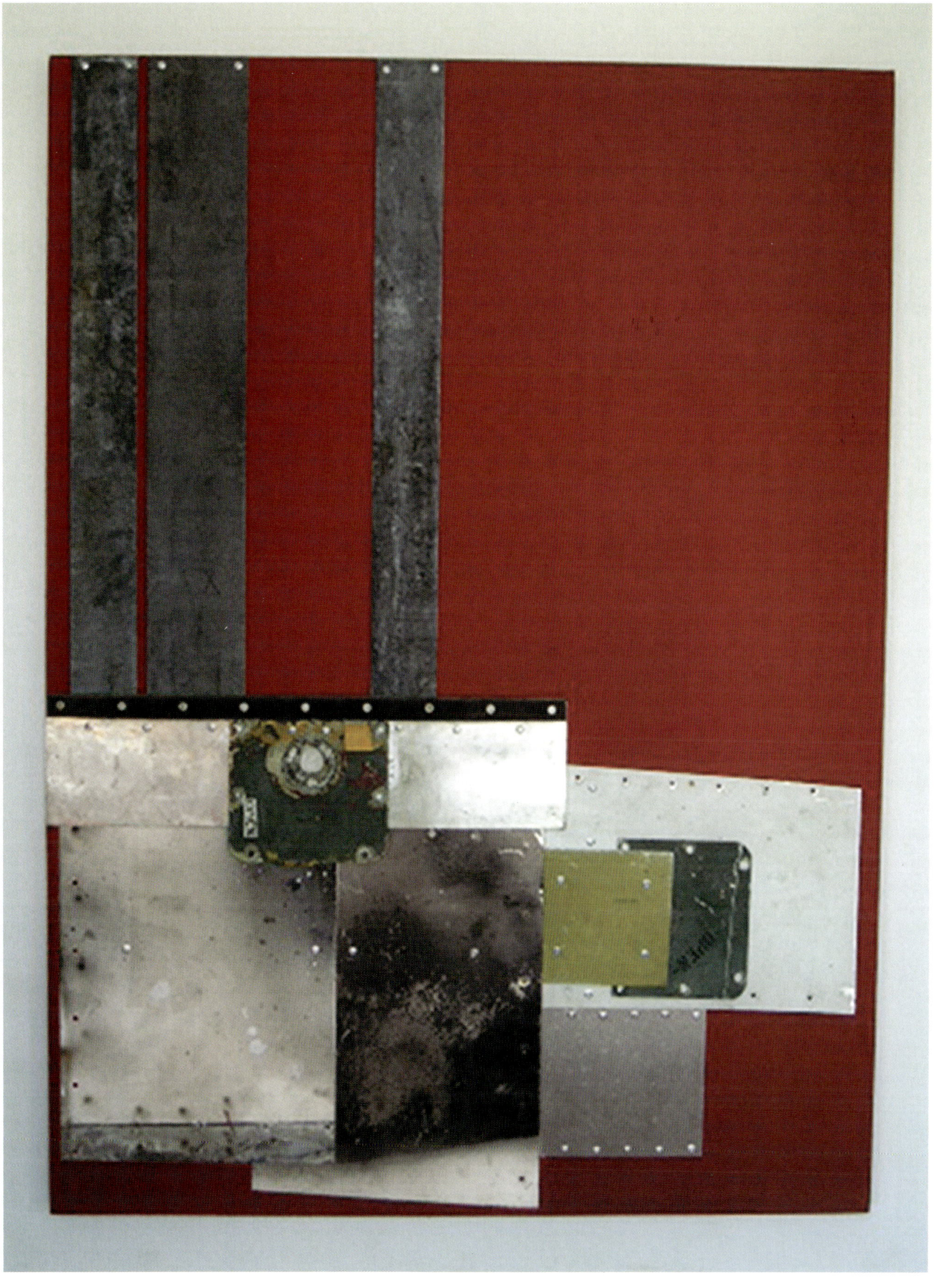

Open, 2005. Aluminum, fabric, and steel, 26″ x 35″.

PEPE MAR

My work departs from a background in painting, which has evolved and combined with my collage sculptures. The collage sculptures are heavily informed by consumer culture, as their individual parts mainly consist of found and purchased objects. Camp and violent at the same time, I seek to explore the possibilities of mutation in color and form in these almost human yet monstrous creations. My work gives visual reference to a "profound artifice." Each of my collage sculptures is in a way, a self-portrait, exploring aspects of my own personality, such as escapism, music, and the artificial highs and lows that come with life itself.

I came to Miami at a time when I wasn't really sure what to expect and when the "arts" scene had just begun to take off officially. I found a community of artists, from an initial residency at an artists' space, to projects and installations at an artist's non-profit space. I found Miami helped to nurture my inspiration to continue making art here; it became in the six years I have lived here, a city of options, collaborations, and possibilities for creating art.

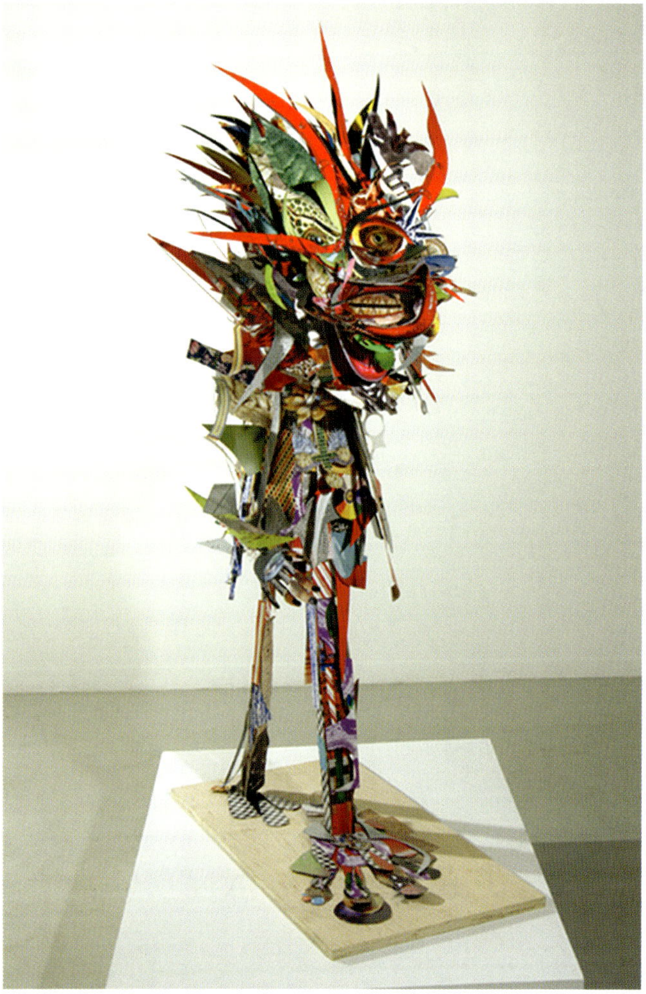

On to You, 2006. Collage sculpture, dimensions variable.

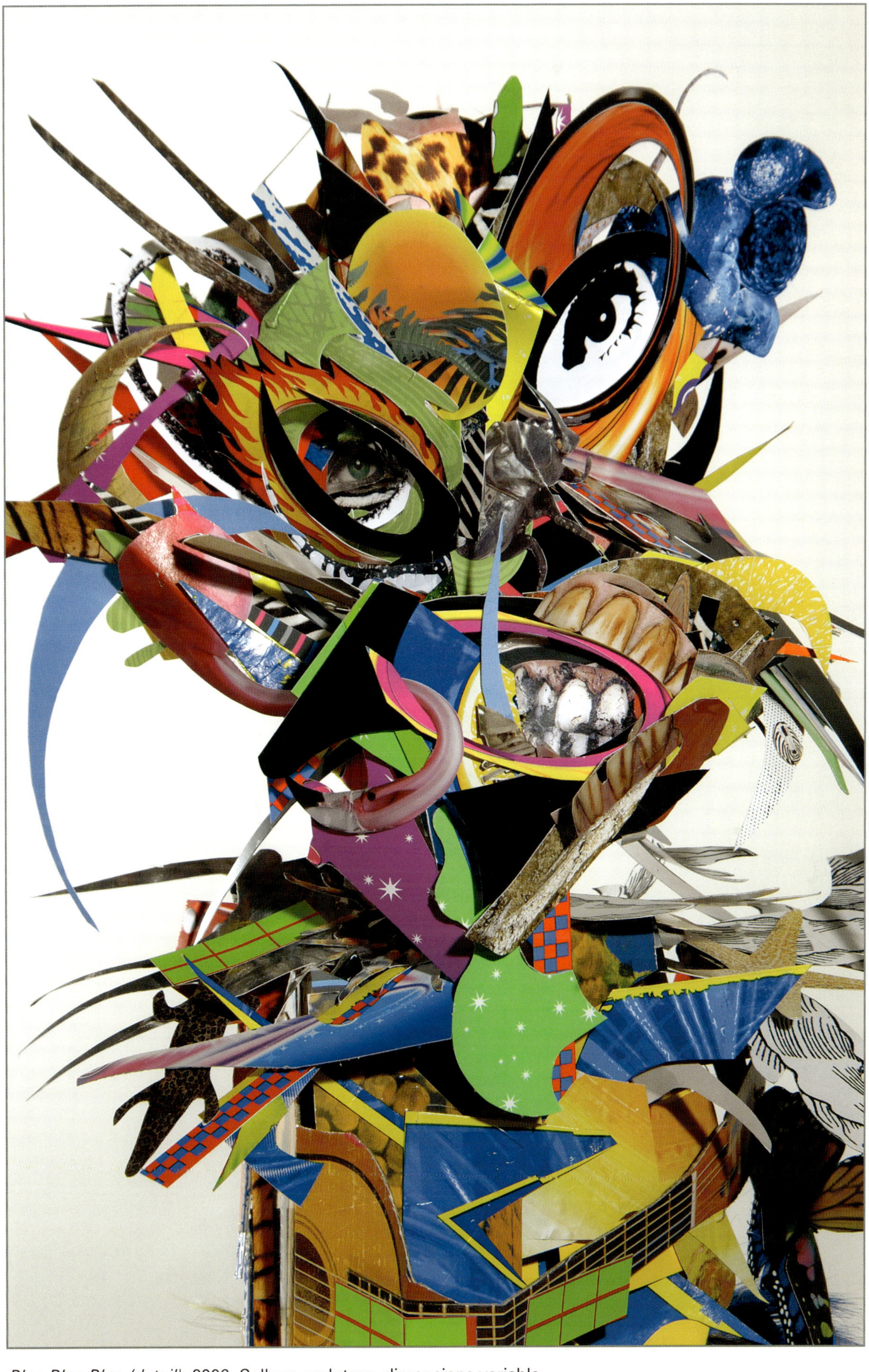

Blue Blue Blue (detail), 2006. Collage sculpture, dimensions variable.

JORDAN **MASSENGALE**

While utilizing visual sources from movies, the internet, periodicals, and the physical world, my paintings and drawings embody a questioning of what it means to work from and reflect upon observation, memory, and imagination. Recently, I've drawn and painted "horror vacuii" compositions as metaphors for life's multiplicity, celebration and disarray. I build pictures through selective decisions while considering a chimerical outcome or appearance. My method of working involves designing a composition with various imaginative forms and selected images, while allowing the work to develop its gestalt and meaning over time. Each picture is addressed, left and revisited over days and weeks, allowing for new discoveries and feelings to in-generate pictorial solutions that were vague at an earlier developmental stage. Moreover, these pictures are never predetermined, and remain amorphous until a visually appealing, and viscerally recognizable scenario begins to cohere. As opposed to practicing a *signature style* as a trademark device, I address picture making from an inquisitive standpoint, while accepting that I possess no conclusive answers worthy of redundant stylization. I do not however, regard this as a creative attenuation of sorts, but rather a matter involving pictorial problem solving as an empirical practice and a precursor to abstraction.

I have lived in Miami for about 12 years. After visiting Miami Beach a few times in the early 90's, I decided to attend the University of Miami to pursue an MFA in painting. The U.M. painting studios were located in old clapboard army barracks in the schools arboretum surrounded by flowers, fruit trees, and birds. Although I did not paint these forms as subjects, I was affected by their presence. Miami's landscape is atmospheric as opposed to topographical or physical, as intense light permeates and dissolves forms into colored fragments. People, cars, buildings etc. appear to be flickers of color rather than solid forms. These observations I've had while living and working in Miami have profoundly affected my paintings. Culturally, Miami embodies an unrivaled celebratory aura as well. Our vast cultural mixture ensures that the city is always vibrating with energy. In the past four years I have been given the opportunity to curate and co-organize art exhibitions involving both professional and student artists alike in various Wynwood warehouse spaces. Thus, Miami artists have had an opportunity to experience exposure outside of the local gallery and museum venues.

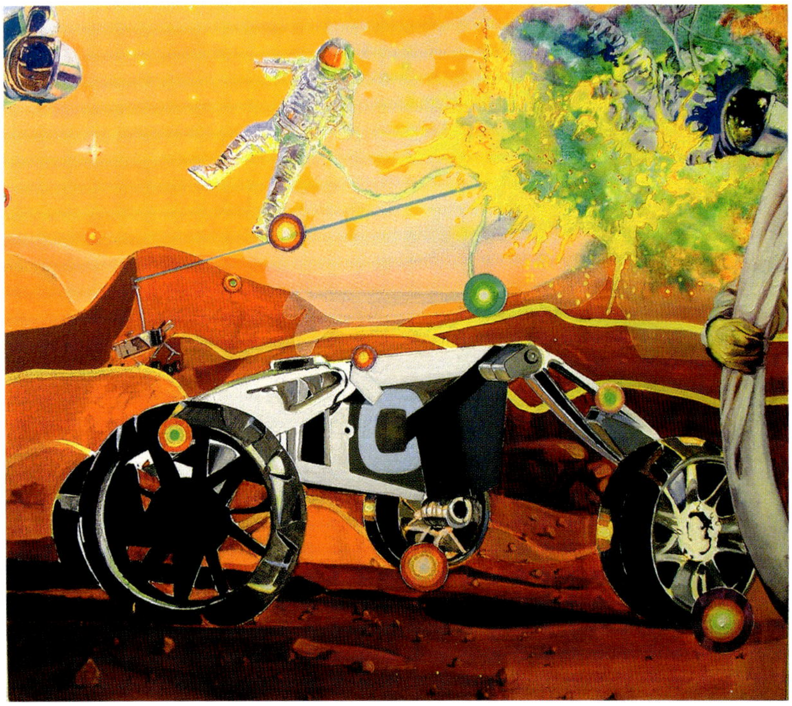

Pulsar (Marz), 2005-06. Oil on canvas, 34" x 40".

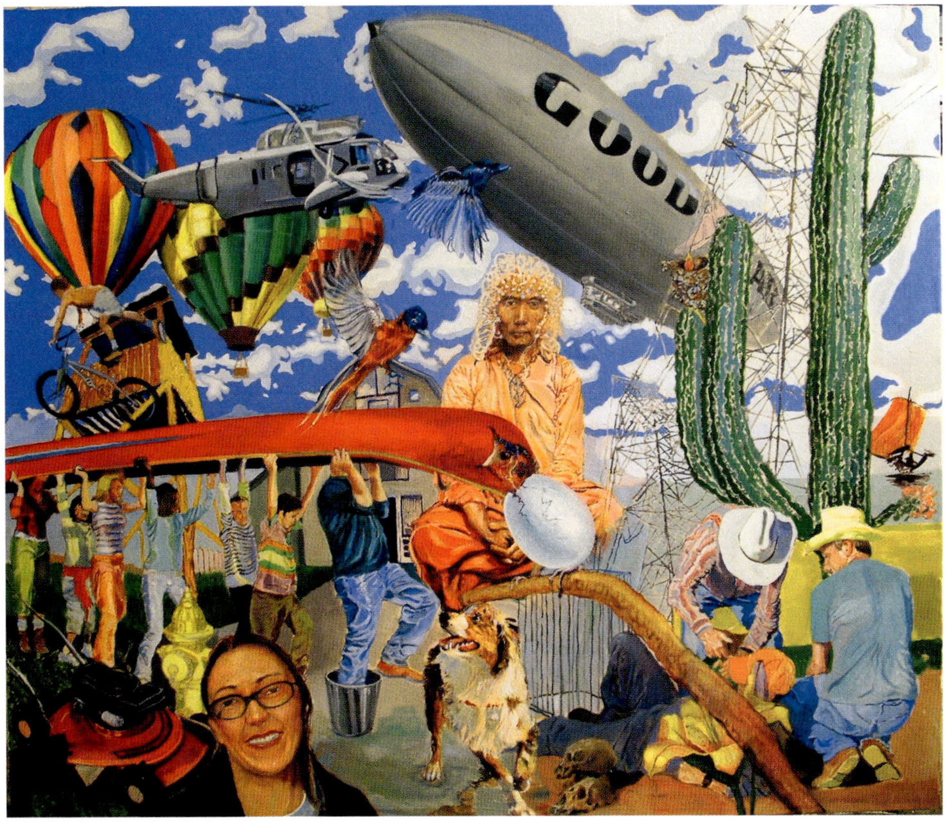

Good Thoughts, 2005-06. Oil on canvas, 54" x 66". Private Collection.

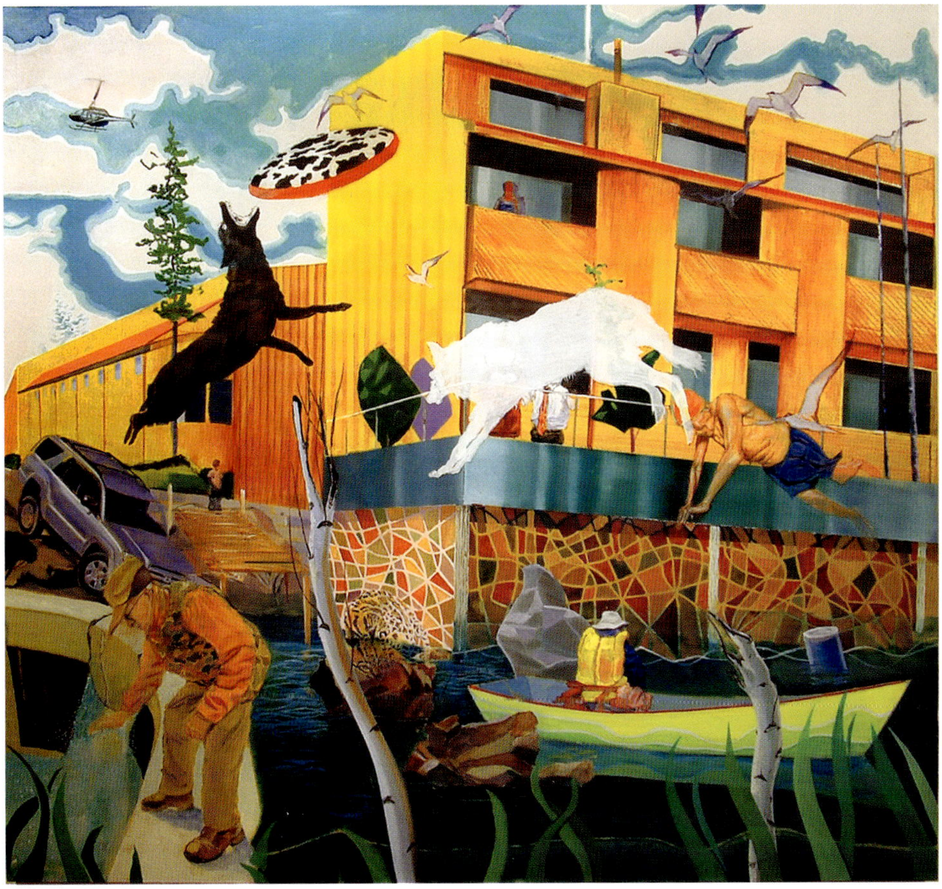

Getaway, 2005-06. Oil on canvas, 54" x 62".

MARITZA MOLINA

Maritza Molina, a young artist born in La Habana, Cuba to a classical guitarist father and an opera singer mother, emigrated to the US with her family at age nine. She first trained at Miami-Dade College, and later received a full-tuition scholarship and BFA from Rhode Island School of Design, with multiple-year scholarships and honors from World Studio Foundation, NY, and the National Dean's List. Molina's work has appeared in numerous solo and group exhibits, such as The Armory Show and Exit Art in New York; Museum of Art Fort Lauderdale, FL; Polk Museum of Art, Lakeland, FL; Bass Museum of Art, Miami, FL; Yale University Art Gallery, CT; Studio Soto Gallery, Boston; Chicago Latin Film Festival; Sagamore Hotel, Miami Beach; Art Basel Miami, Design District, and Art Miami. Most recently, Molina was a Cintas Foundation Fellowship Award Finalist. Molina works in photography, performance, installation, video and drawing. Her themes are re-current with her own existence and experiences, extracting from what is closest to her, in a primordial, intuitive, philosophical, conceptual, and emotional manner. Using familiar objects symbolic from her life, she stages herself in her work, composing scenarios in her still-images resembling a moment in time. Throughout her artwork, Maritza tackles universal issues of human identity, the role of women and religion, freedom and our relationship with nature, and the quest for truth and meaning. She confronts stereotypes and expectations, visually and aurally, in a lyrical fashion.

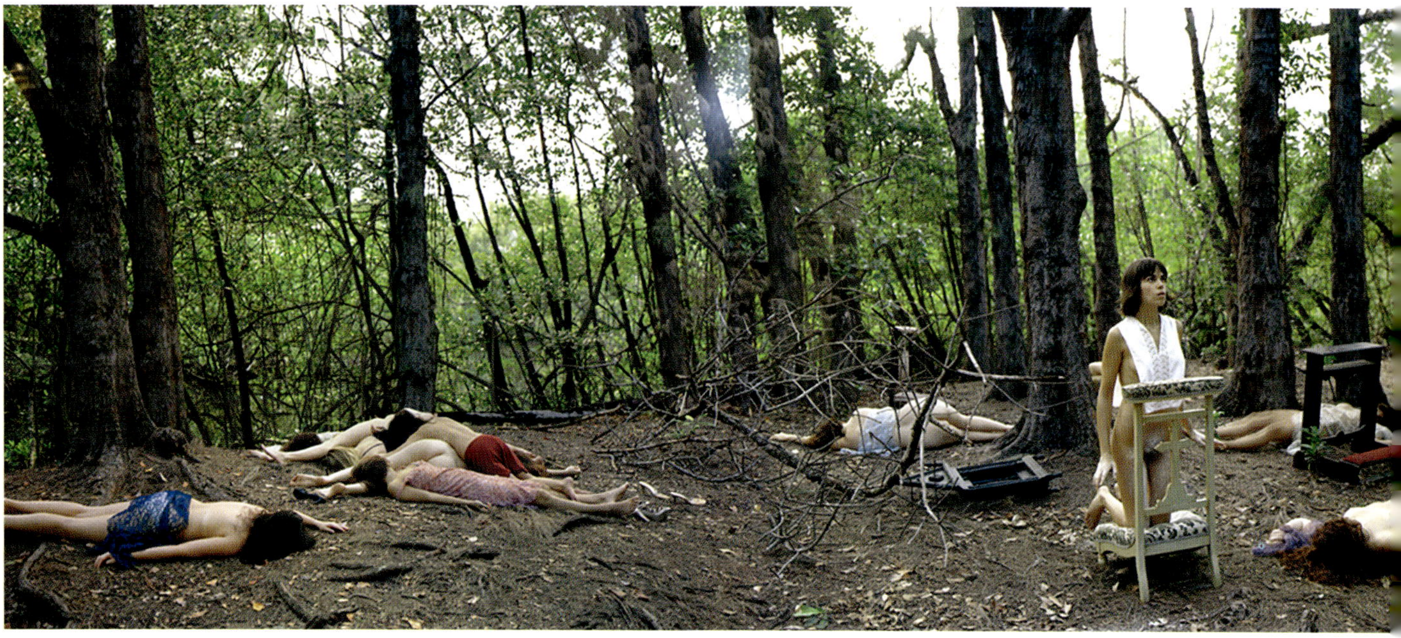

The Test Of Purity (And The Wasted Women), 2005. C-print, 20" x 77".

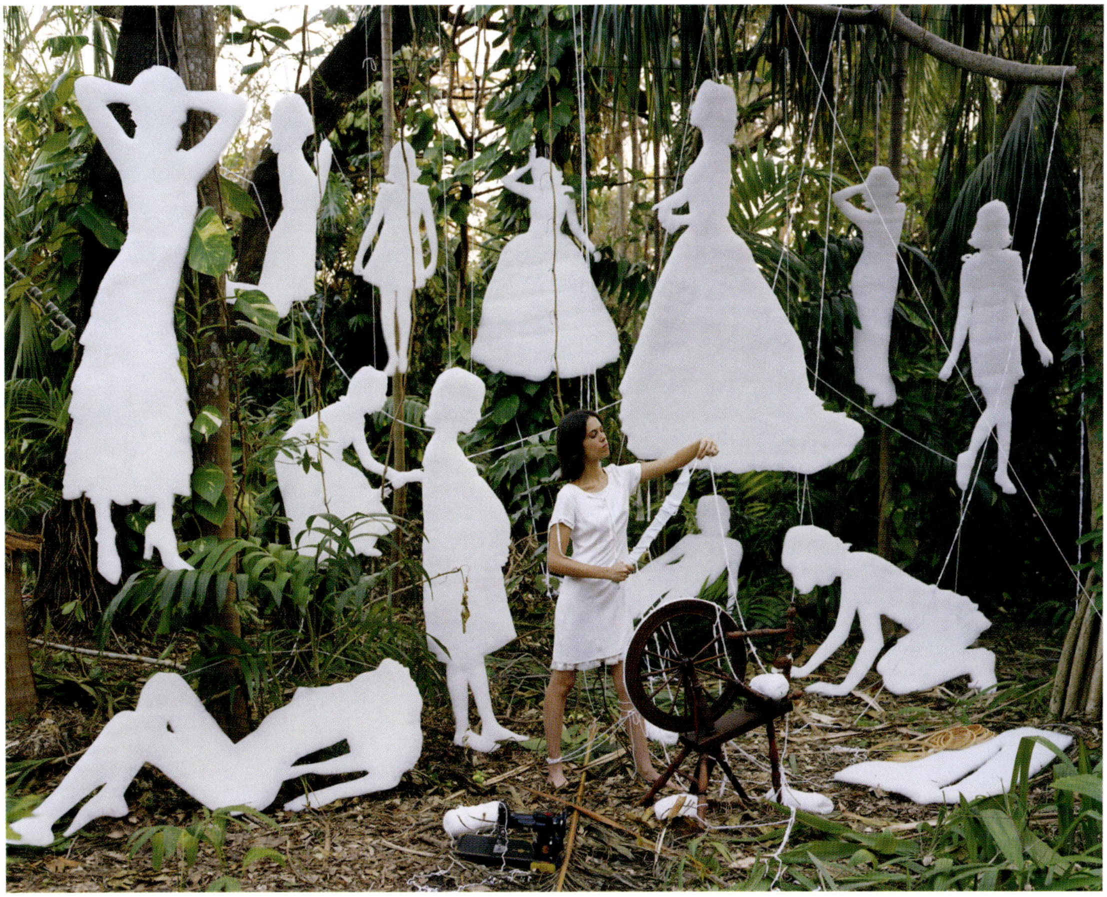

Cutting The Pattern, 2005. C-print, 40" x 50".

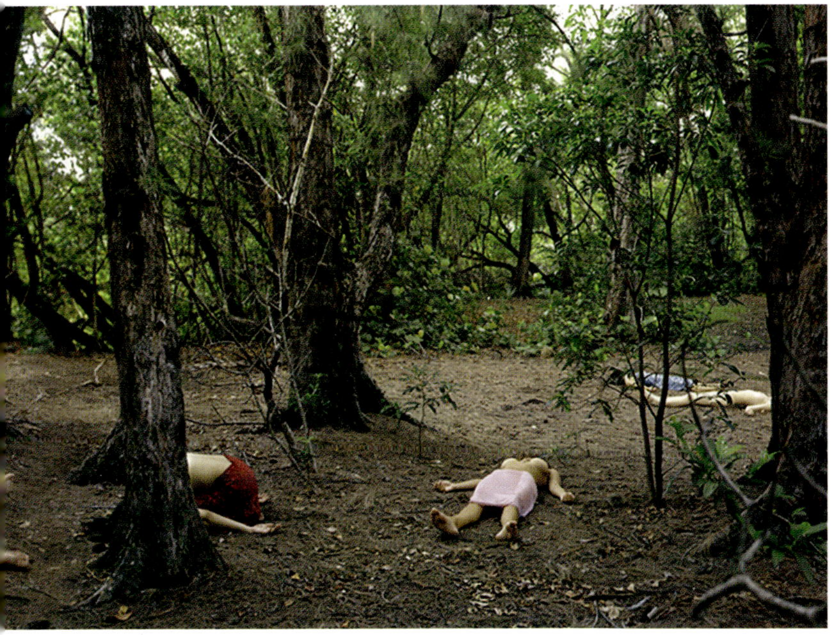

BEATRIZ **MONTEAVARO**

Beatriz Monteavaro is a Cuban born artist whose work is influenced by British new wave music, science fiction, horror movies, and Disney World. The combination of these inspirations results in dynamic, colorful drawings of fantasy landscapes that illustrate her wild imagination. She combines detailed work in pen and loose acrylic brushstrokes to create bizarre worlds composed of smaller scenes that read like the pages of a comic book. Her most recent works detail the exploits of 80's rock stars Adam Ant, Gary Numan, and the Go-Go's in a narrative of her own creation. Adam and Gary's adventure so far has included being turned into apes while retrieving black eyeliner from the evil Souxsie Sioux, securing a getaway on Pablo Picasso's spaceship, and being restored to their proper selves by Bela Lugosi. In the process of turning them back, Bela set off a malfunction at Walt Disney World's Space Mountain that caused the dead to rise in Paris. Adam, Gary, and Bela end up hiding out in Notre Dame after separating from Pablo, who has become a zombie. Marie Curie sets off an eruption in an Adventureland / Polynesian volcano to call on the Go-Go's, enchanted aquamaids, who Curie has resurrected using alchemy and science, to stop surfing and come to their rescue.

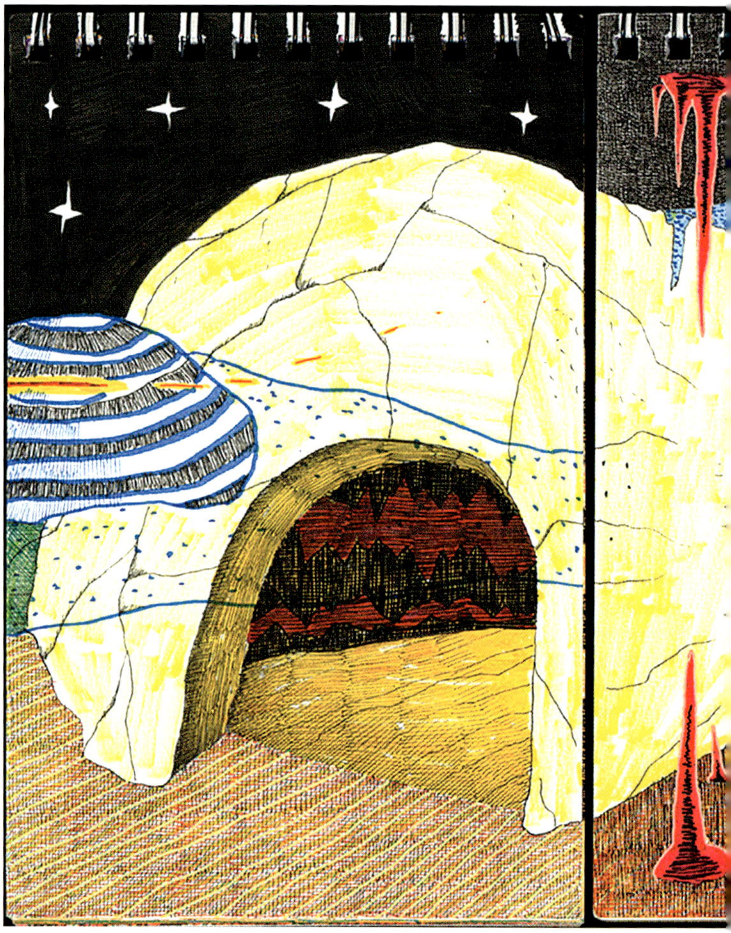

Dust to Dust (detail), 2004. Ink and gel pen on paper, 9" x 216". Collection of Diane and Robert Moss

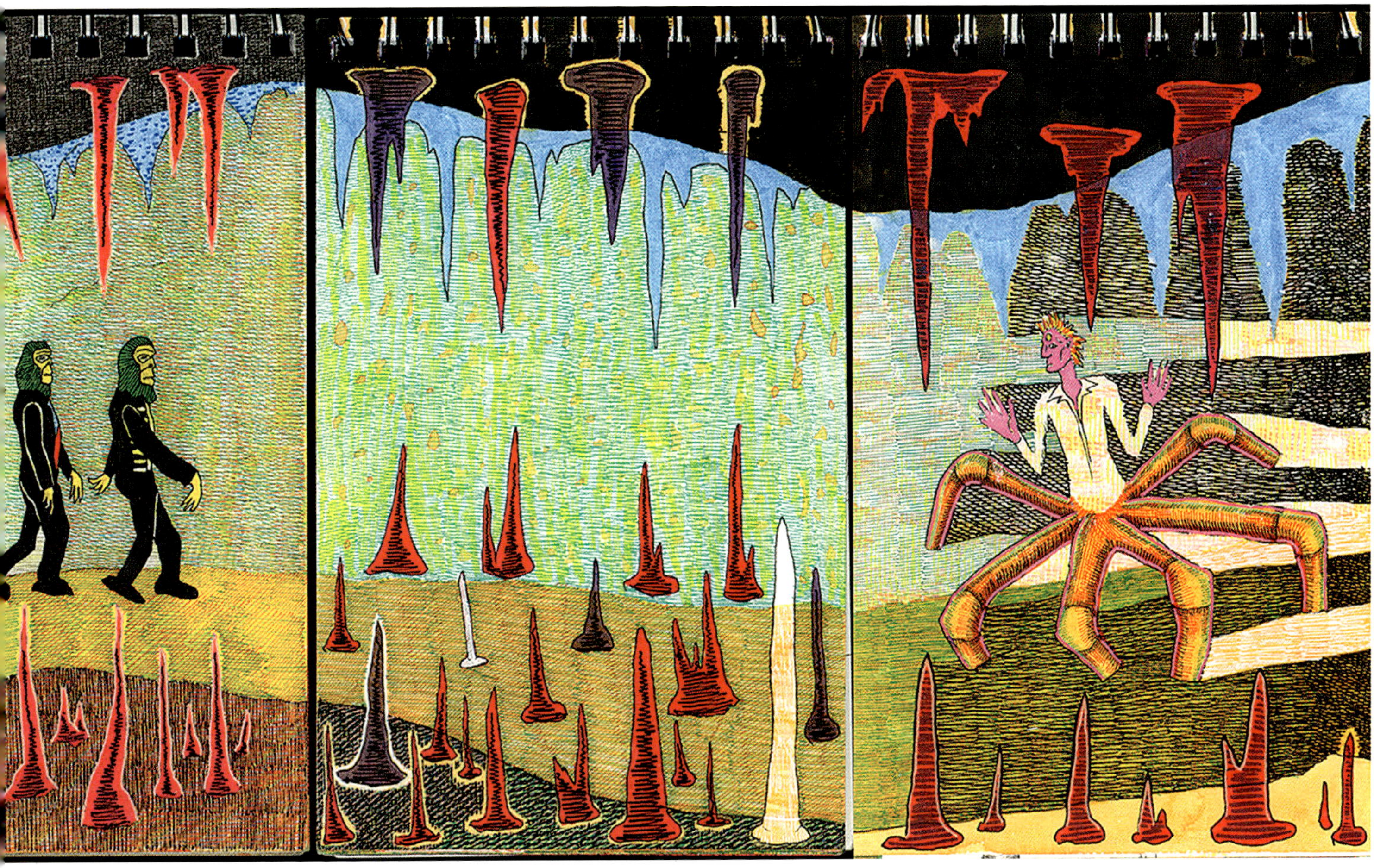

GEAN **MORENO**

The Adventures of Things
I don't know why but I sometimes think of this t-shirt my first girlfriend gave me. It wasn't fancy or anything; just one of those novelty rags that you find in every Florida tourist shop. This one had a perfect sunset emblazoned with the words *"New Smyrna Beach – You're Secret Spot!"* I can't remember when or how I lost possession of it, only that I haven't seen it for many years. Sitting in Gean Moreno's studio yesterday, I thought about that t-shirt once again. I imagined that my ratty old shirt might have somehow found its way here and was now buried deep in one of the many piles of assorted debris that litter his space. Not that he took it from me, but that through some odd, yet perfect chain of events, it ended up here. Somehow this is how I feel when I look at Gean's work. All these images and objects on top of more images and objects, all having traveled far and lived entire lives; and now they are parts of something else; ingredients of these weird accumulations placed in empty rooms and surrounded by all these strangers that just stare and attempt to decipher how and why they are here. And now that I think about it, isn't that the reality of everything?
John Espinosa, Sri Lanka, 2004

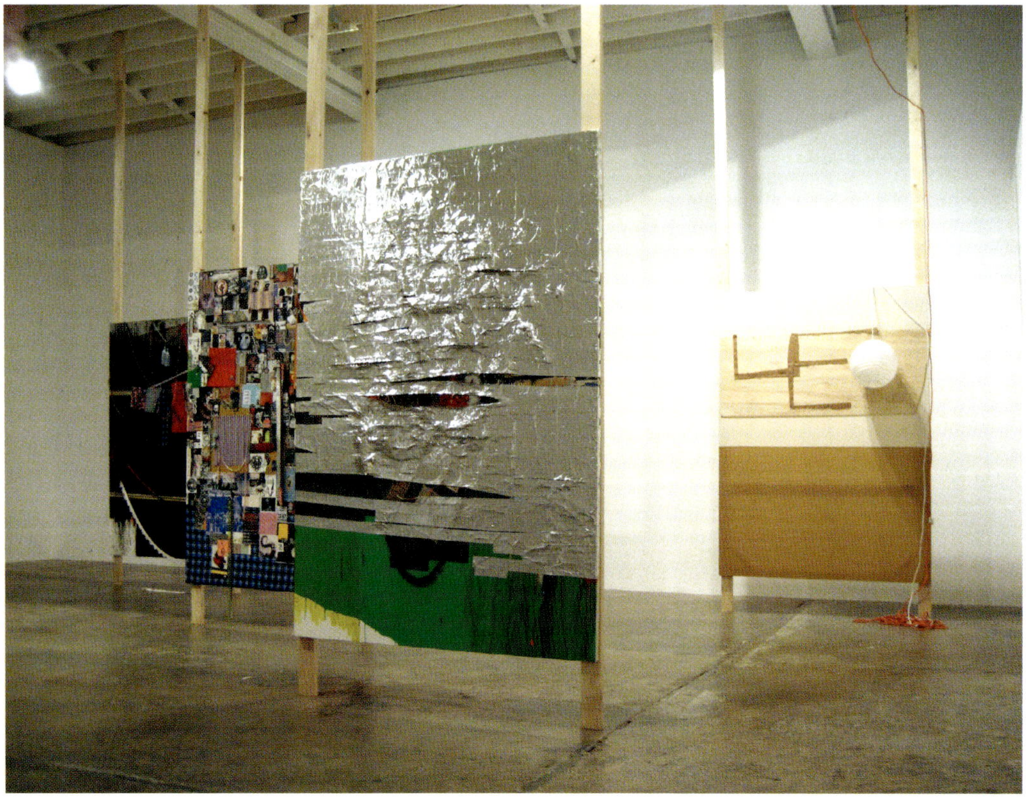

Installation view of *"Elephant"*, 2006. Mixed media on wood panels, variable dimensions.

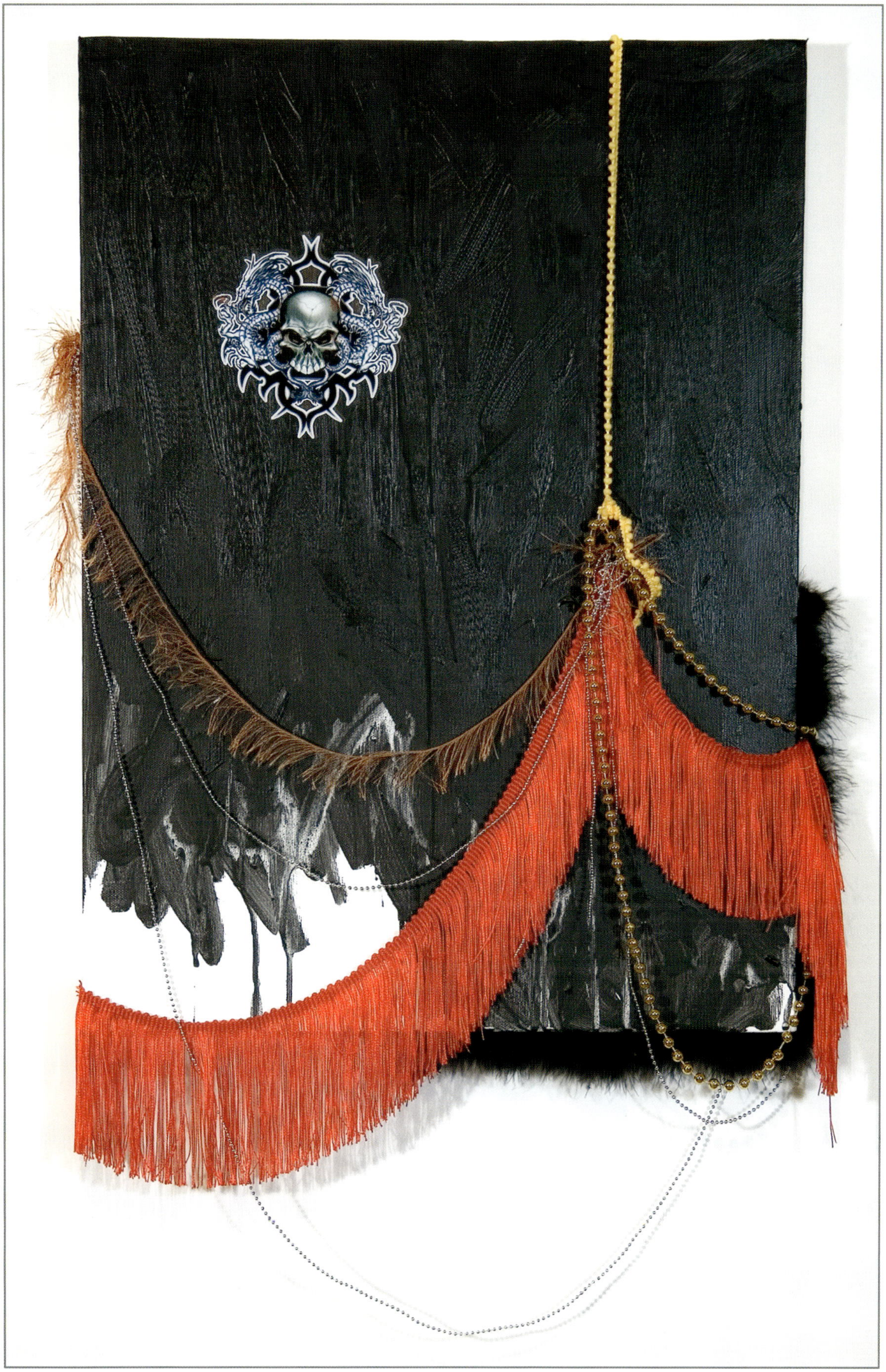

Untitled (skull painting), 2006. Acrylic, sticker, trims on canvas, 24" x 18".

VICTOR MUÑIZ

My work tells many tales, lies and confessions. Personal inspiration immersed into a conflict of identity. A journal.

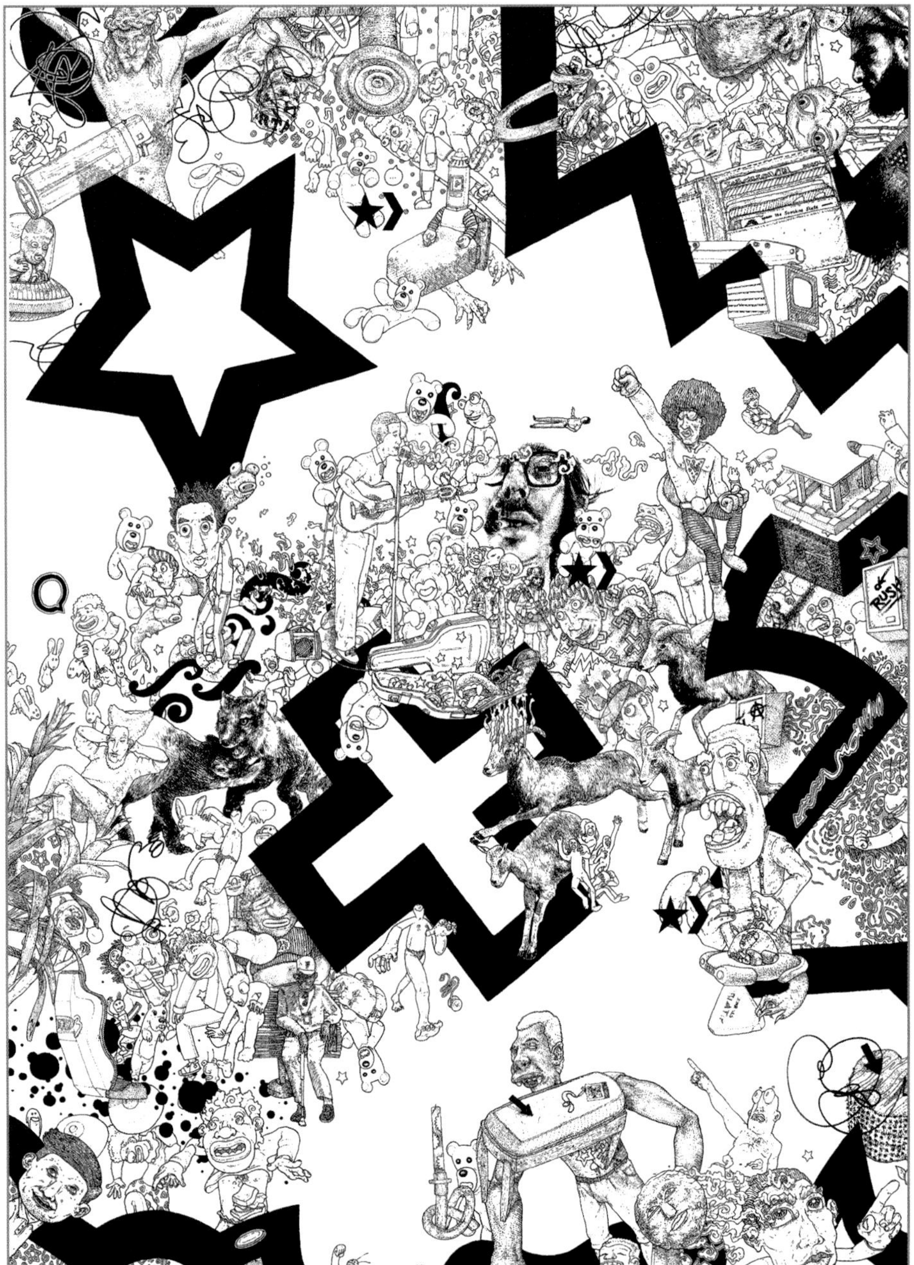

Convert, 2005. Ink on paper, 11″ x 17″. *Converse Billboard Commission.*

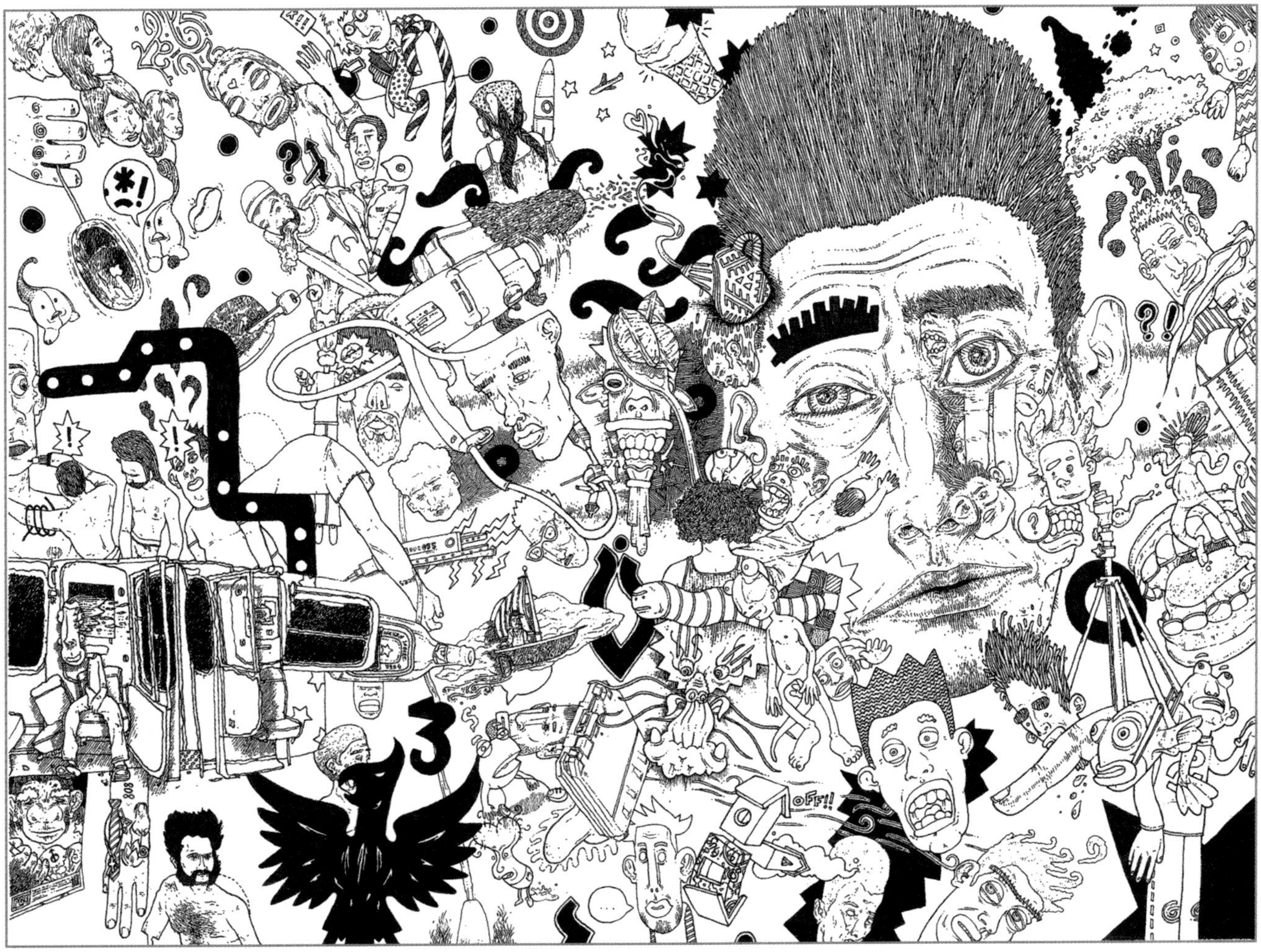

Miami³, 2004. Ink on paper, 9″ x 12″.

GLEXIS NOVOA

"See Novoa's Escher-like panoramas of futuristic hyper-reality, where triangle and cube is the core of imaginary constructions. From above the roofs we observe pointed towers and ring-shape forms, highlighting huge slabs of truncated solid mass. Absolutely empty of human presence, these cityscapes evoke a desolate abstraction in which life is transformed into concrete and marble. Drawing – not painting – these possible worlds is what interests Novoa, a perspective virtuoso who indulges a practice considered second to painting and passed along (since the Renaissance) to the architecture profession. His pulse is careful and precise and his fantastic images are realistic and obtained in extremely small detail. Glexis Novoa elaborates visions reminiscent of science fiction. I can recollect some of his futuristic ziggurats with converging stairs leading to needle-shape obelisks evoking the buildings of ancient sacrifice. This is where political – not just religious – rites take place. As Georges Bataille concluded, monumental architecture (buildings, statuary, and roads) is the stage for the ritual, but eventually it becomes sacred itself. Novoa's first work on marble was 'Inundaciones 2000', a permanent 84-foot long site-specific drawing at Centro de Cultura Contemporánea de Barcelona in Barcelona, Spain. I find something intractably romantic in Novoa's vision that after a tradition of 500 years of drawing on paper, he decides to draw on marble, an ideal medium for a messier art form, sculpture. Since 9/11 Novoa has started depicting marginal Expressionist perspectives of a ruinous global village; a mix of all the histories one can muster in one big spectacle. His pictorial foresight comes close to Paul Virilio. In his essay "The Overexposed City," Virilio leaves open the possibility that architecture will simply become another way of dominating the planet by destroying the urban environment. Novoa goes past this moment, when the planet has already been obliterated. An example is Europa, a work from 2003 at the Bernice Steinbaum Gallery. The piece showed a multicultural, postcolonial EU just before the forces of fundamentalism win over, the fulfilled prophecy of Al-Qaeda. A makeshift war campsite, the sky filled with huge eyeball surveillance machines, domes of all kinds, minarets, gothic towers, spires displaying thin flags, as if in some unlikely Christian/Islamic HQ. Who and where is the enemy? Inside itself, amorphous, plotting destruction. The end of history may not be the final synthesis of a great unfolding – neither utopia nor dystopia. Not a whimper, not a bang. What is there after the end? Another beginning? In "Approaches to Nothingness," Edgar Morin explores the idea that death does not mean the destruction of our bodies, because at some point our selves can end up in the equivalent of some supercomputer's hard drive. This is the awareness of one who has already disappeared. Perhaps Novoa hints at the oblivion of our collective memories; if we ever come back we will repeat the same mistake all over again – which, as we know, has already happened."

Alfredo Triff

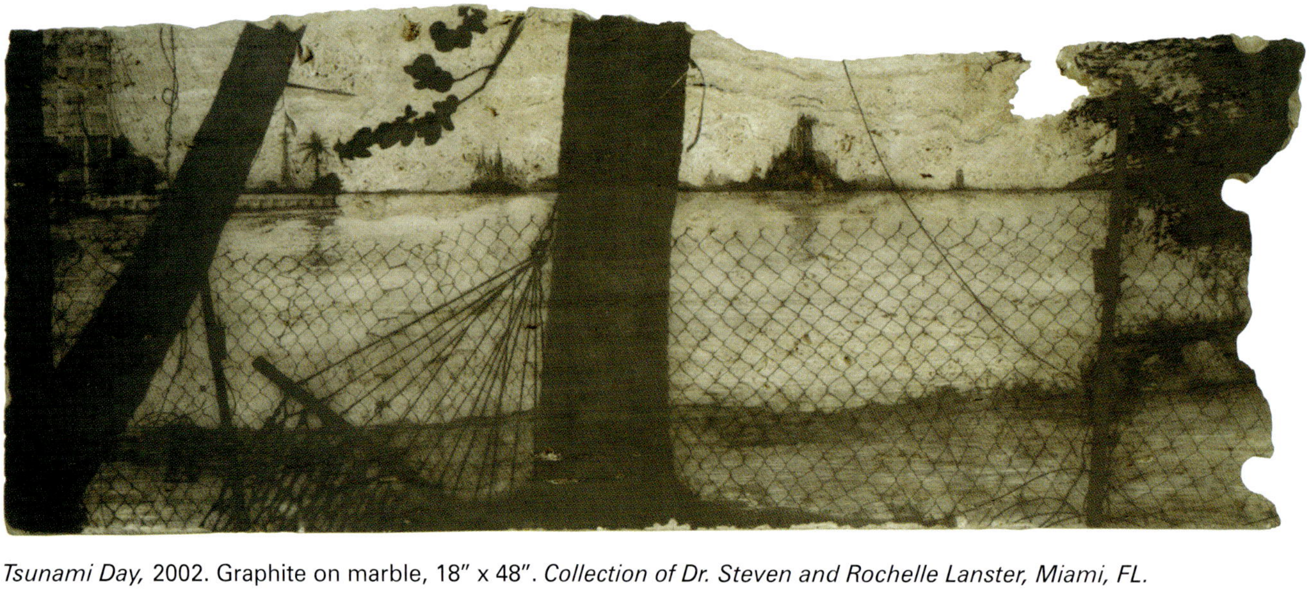

Tsunami Day, 2002. Graphite on marble, 18" x 48". *Collection of Dr. Steven and Rochelle Lanster, Miami, FL.*

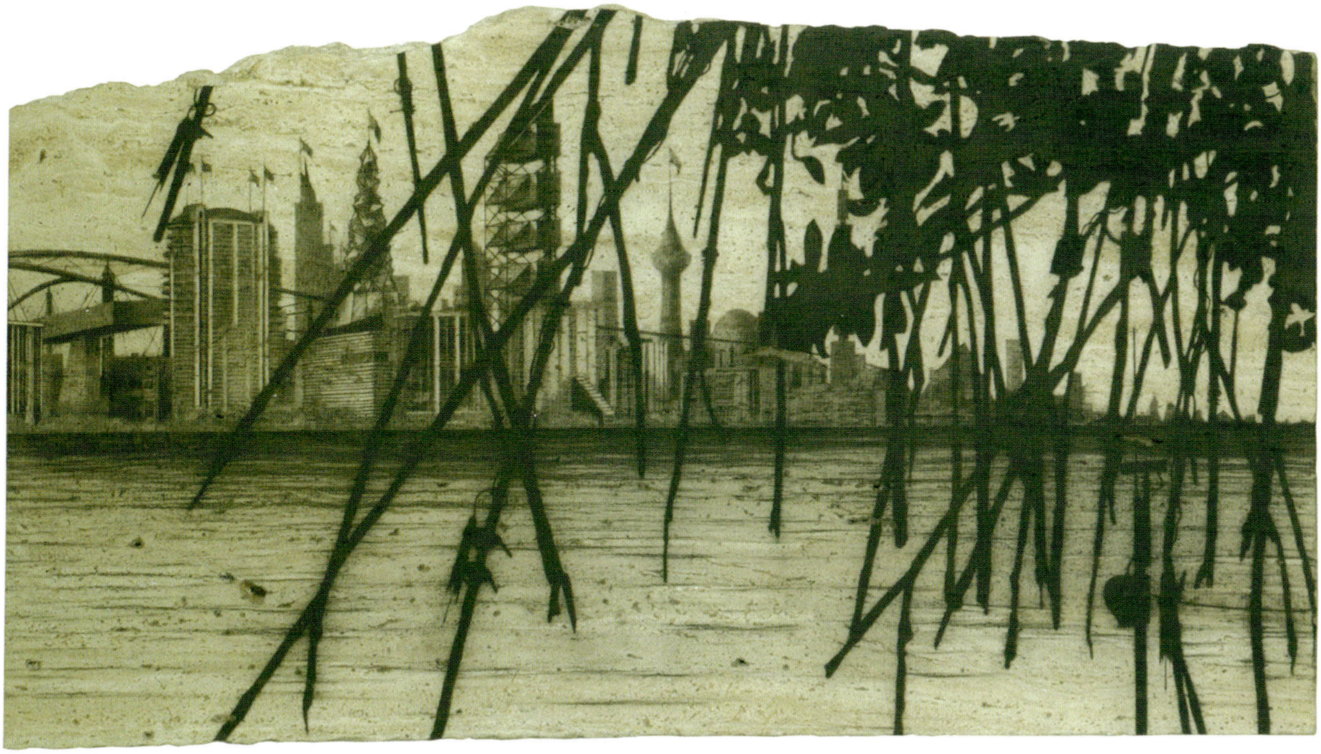

Illegal Zone, 2002. Graphite on marble, 12" x 21.5". *Collection of Dr. Martin and Jeri Zaiac.*

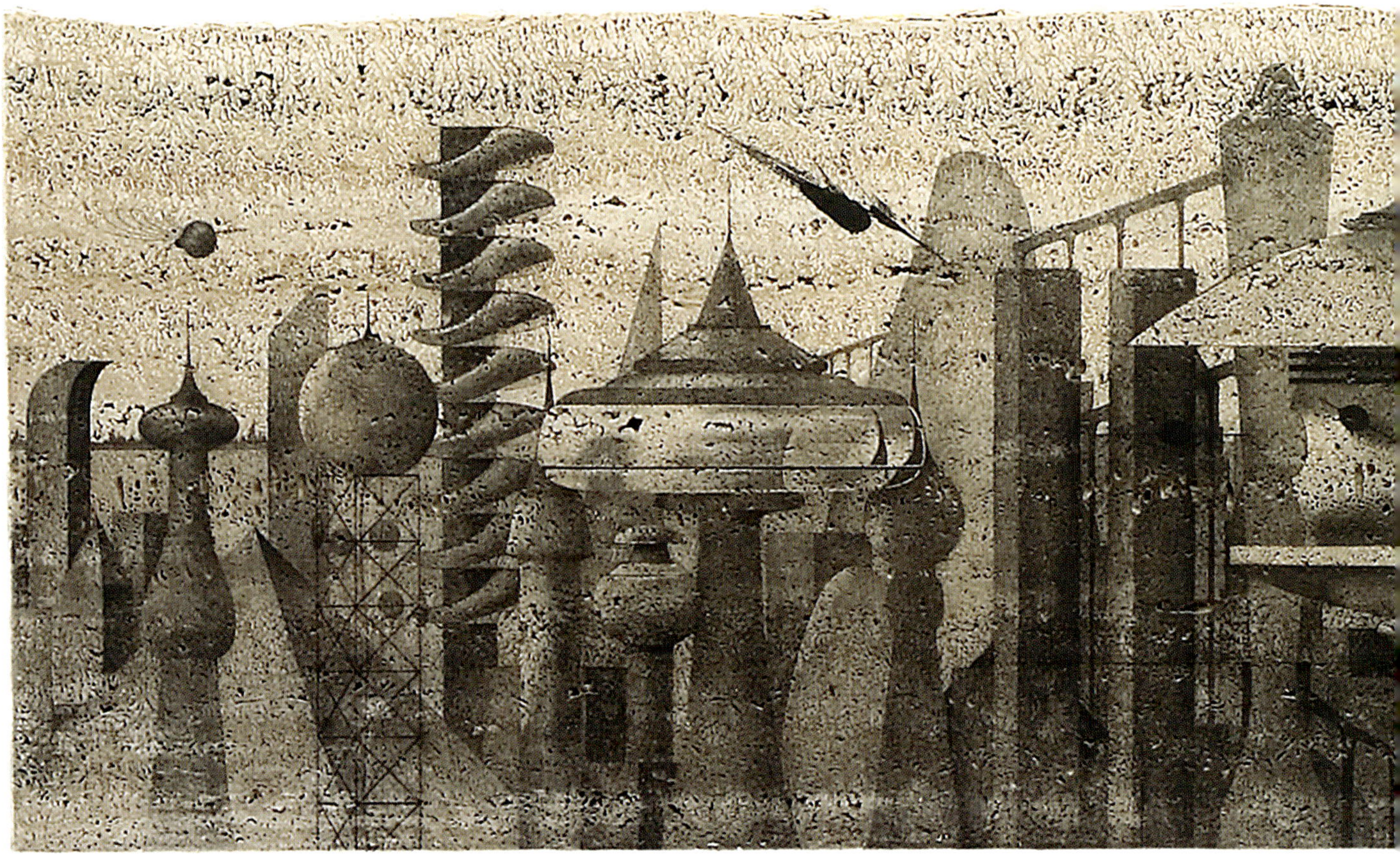

F.L.U.C. TOW (Flying Checkpoint Tower), 2004. Graphite on marble, 10.5" x 36" x .75".
Collection of the Lowe Art Museum, University of Miami.

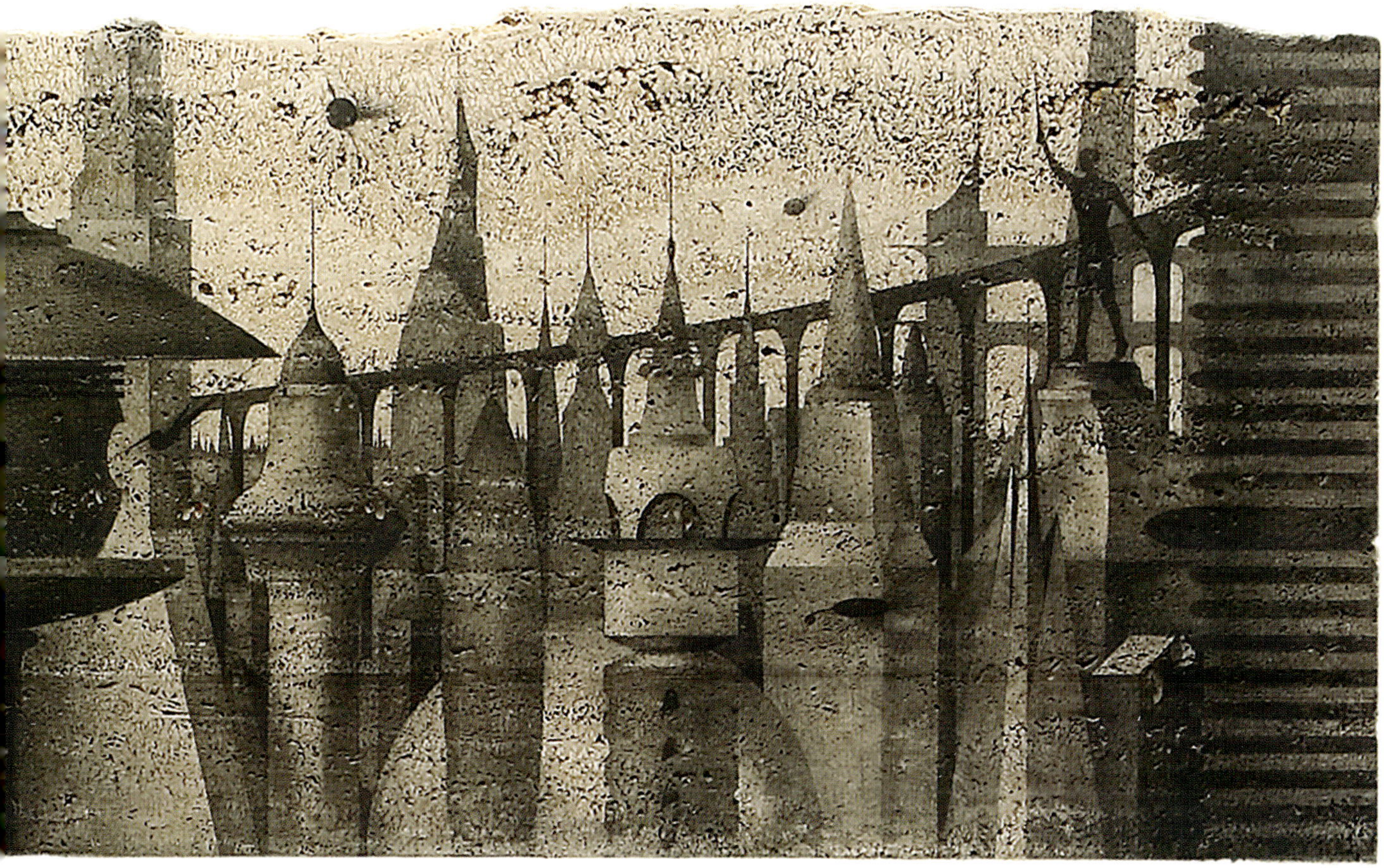

BRANDON **OPALKA**

Painting is a mix of cerebral meditation and a romantic desire to visualize beauty. What I find important in art are its fundamental elements such as form, color, light, composition, line, and space. They act as catalysts for many of the undulating forms and textures created in my work. The landscapes I paint are enigmatic worlds derived from both organic and synthetic forms and textures. The images for my paintings come from sculpted forms and photographs that create semi-personal compositions. Although the process involves drawing, model making, and photography, the final product is still oil on canvas. The intricate details and shades of colors reflect my beginnings in street art and an appreciation for landscape painting in a historical context. My background as a graffiti artist influences the bold, graphic shapes in my work, while traditional landscape paintings become a blueprint for movement and light. My goal as an artist is for the viewer to be won over by the fluidity of color and form, creating an illusion and the belief that they have seen a new, real place.

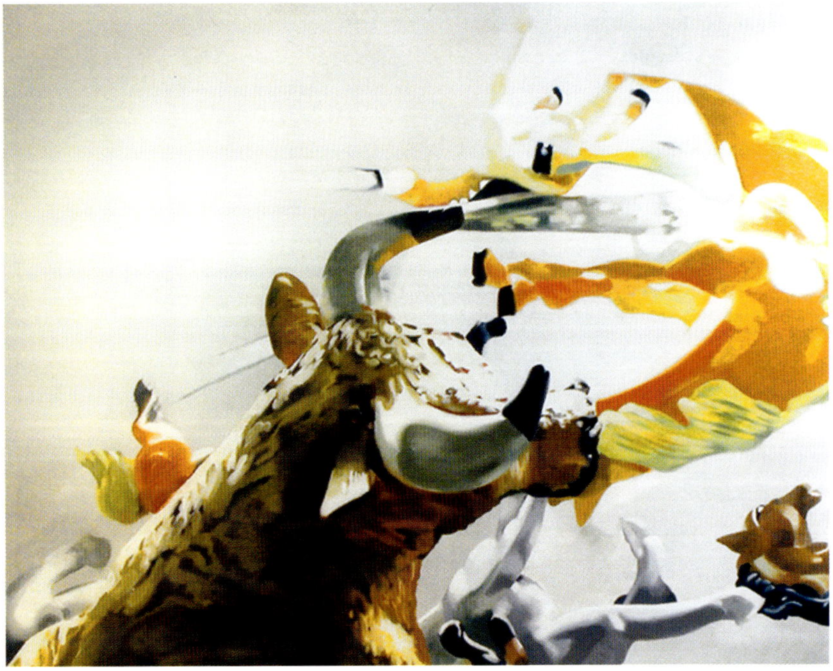

Silver bull, 2004. Oil on canvas, 40" x 50".

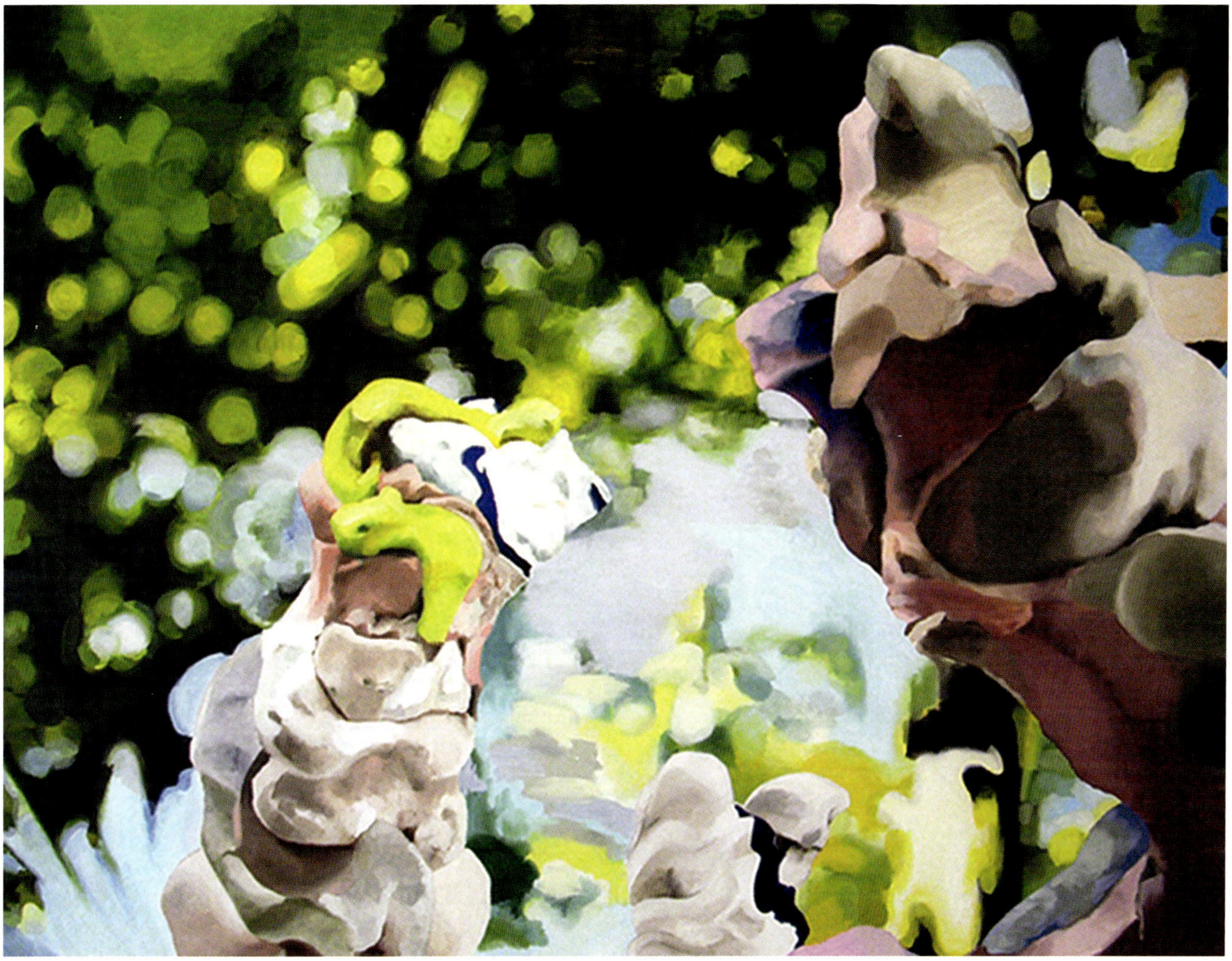

Brave New World, 2005. Oil on canvas, 36" x 46".

MARTIN **OPPEL**

"Archaeology is the art of digging the dirt. We place our spoons and combs against the ground and put on a face of surprise when the dirt yields to non-dirt. But in the work of Martin Oppel, there are no such surprises. There is the steadfast return to myths of transcendence, projections from the general to the specific, and the fascism of geometry. There is the beleaguered return to God, the mesmerization of nature, and humanity's attempts to reflect on the unknowable. The surprise of Oppel's work, however, is in the ground itself – which we continue to dig, to recycle, and to believe. Oppel reveals a world where the digging is never done, where symbols perpetuate new symbols but no new meanings, where the sophistication of our tools stands in stark contrast to the sameness of our findings. Through his work, Oppel pairs this existential sameness against the ennobling persistence of art (reflection, critique, and contemplation) itself."
Alexander Seth Cameron

As a major American city coming of age in the 21st century, Miami is the stage where one may witness the aggression of human progressive tendencies. Complicated by the importance of preservation, paradox revels in this construction littered landscape. The construction site exists at once as past and future. Natural landscapes fumble with the economy of current building practices, in an effort to decide whether to defend or invent history.

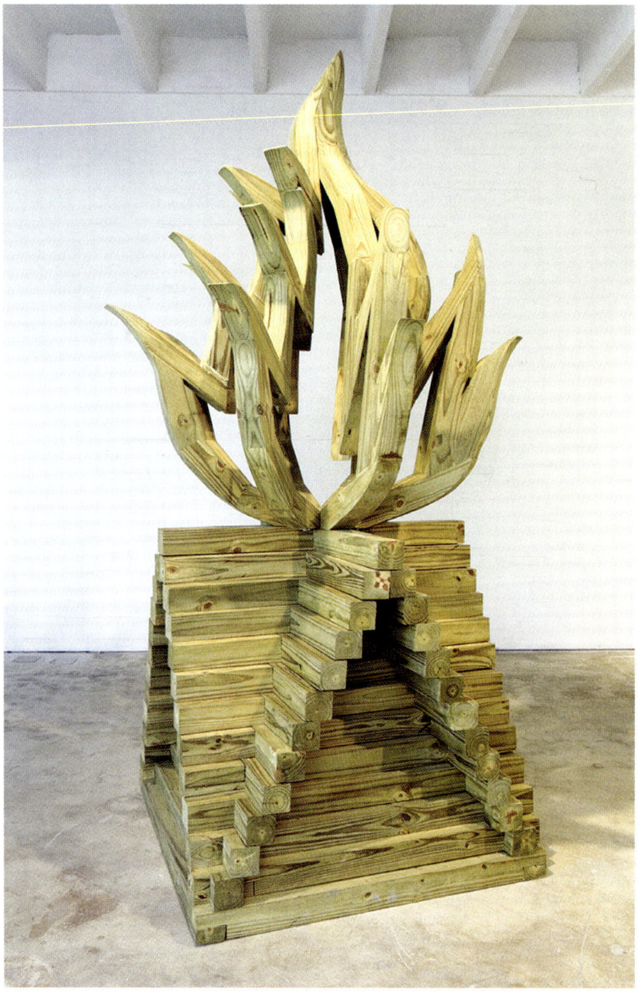

Soul Fire, 2005. Pressure treated pine, 48" x 48" x 93.5".

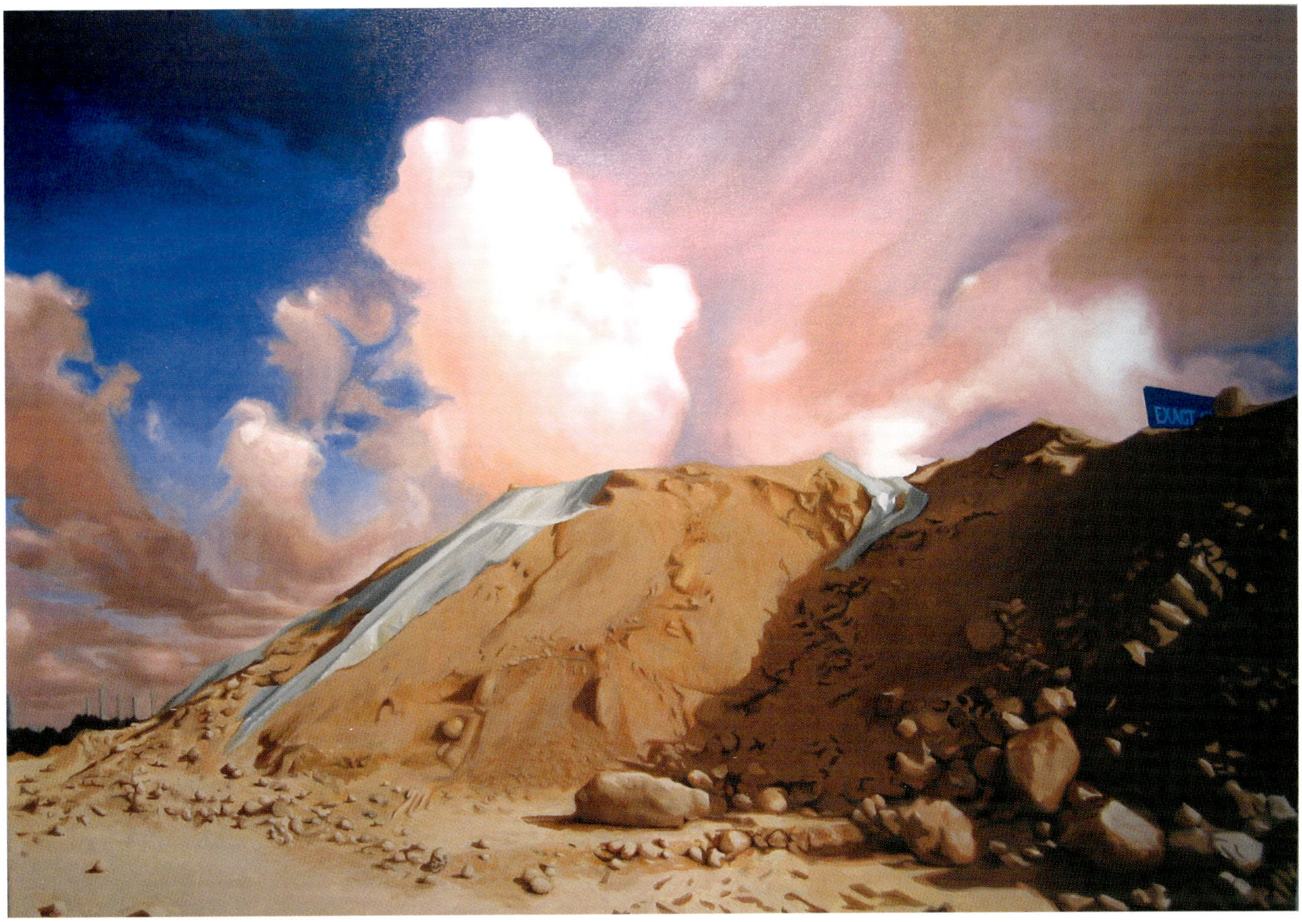

Miami Hills, 2004. Oil on canvas, 37" x 54".

CHARO OQUET

My work centers on the investigation of identity politics. Through my work I want to express existence, spirituality, a feeling of collectiveness, the unity of reality and the unity of all being in society. At the same time my work addresses the idea of excess and how we order and understand it, the transformation of materials, from the discards of our consumer society, to sacred objects in the third world. My sculptures join raw elements from nature and man-made objects. A curious blend of performance and object-making, the most important part of my installation projects is firstly what happens between me and the people I encounter every day; the conversations, the layers of negotiation, and the things that are constructed. My installations and projects aim to be a place for negotiating new methods and demanding a new set of positions intended towards the formation of a new way of understanding the possibilities that contemporary art has with other cultures, ancestral rituals, and myths, thus creating a place of investigation and process rather than a site for fixed arrangements.

I came to Miami in 1989 via Santo Domingo, where I had been living for a year. Miami was where my immediate family had moved to in the early 80's, and the place I visited on my trips to and from New Zealand and Europe. I never wanted to live here, but because I had a young child and family, it seemed the logical place to move to when I separated from my husband the first time. At first I thought Miami was a cultural wasteland. It wasn't until I started to know it, that I realized this was the exact place I needed to be in, the place I had left New Zealand for. I was looking to get closer to my culture but I didn't really want to live in the Dominican Republic again. Miami was ideal, it was the capital of the Caribbean and Latin America, it was close to the DR and you could get to know all the different Hispanic and Afro-Caribbean cultures without leaving the Peninsula. Here I got to learn more about Haitian culture than in the DR. I learned about the Afro-centric religions which are what I was researching at the time and could take trips to the Islands to study the culture firsthand. I moved to South Beach when everyone would tell you not to move there. I loved it. I am in love with Miami and everything it has to offer. As an artist I have been able to do everything I wanted to. I am still not bored. This city is a place for people who want to do things. It is new, there are many things more to be done, and if you have the spirit of creating new and great things, this city allows you to. In the 90's I was very involved with developing the Art Center/South Florida. I started their children's art camp, helped develop their print room, recruited many of the artists which changed the way people saw the Center, ran their children's program, and had a studio there for 3 years. Later I moved right in the middle of downtown in a large studio that used to be a bank. Myself and another artist had an entire floor to ourselves on Flagler and First. We had to battle the pigeons and clear out lots of junk to get to it, but it allowed me to start to do sculptures and installations. In 1996 to 2002 I founded the Miami Arts Collaborative under the auspices of the Rhythm Foundation. This non-profit organization's main purpose was to identify Dominican Artists in Miami and to propagate Dominican culture in South Florida through the Dominican Arts Series – a yearly festival of arts, student workshops, dance, history and music. In 2003, together with my partner David Vardi, we founded Edge Zones: a non profit arts organization dedicated to the research, conceptualization and execution of events that strengthen the contemporary art environment in Miami. We view our mission to create a place which would launch challenges against existing contaminated concepts. Conspiring with a group of local artists whose work is often under-represented, assisting in their production and disseminating their developments in national and international forums. In the broader view, our objective is to become a fundamental piece in the development of contemporary art, both locally and nationally.

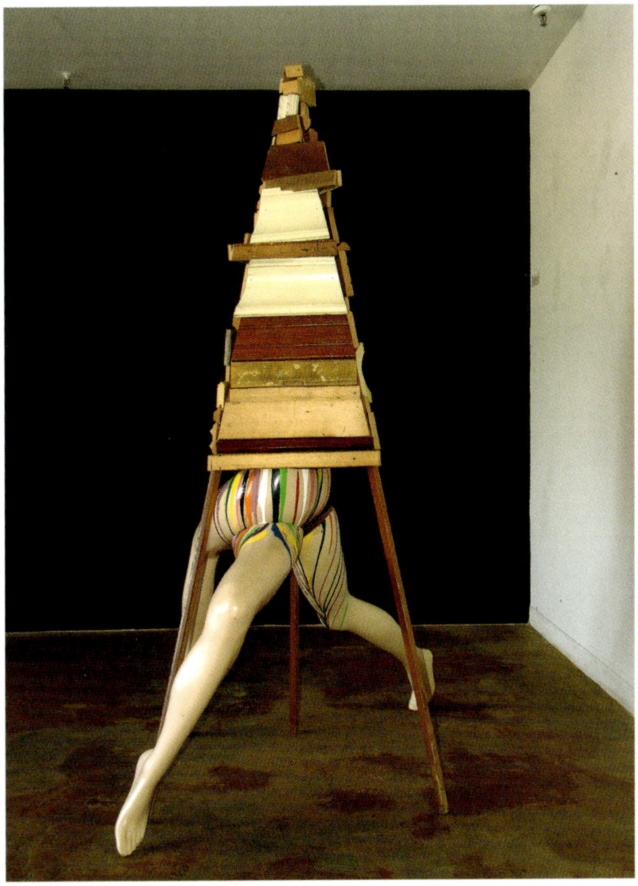

Anointment 2, 2005. Mixed media installation, 7′ x 4′ x 5′.

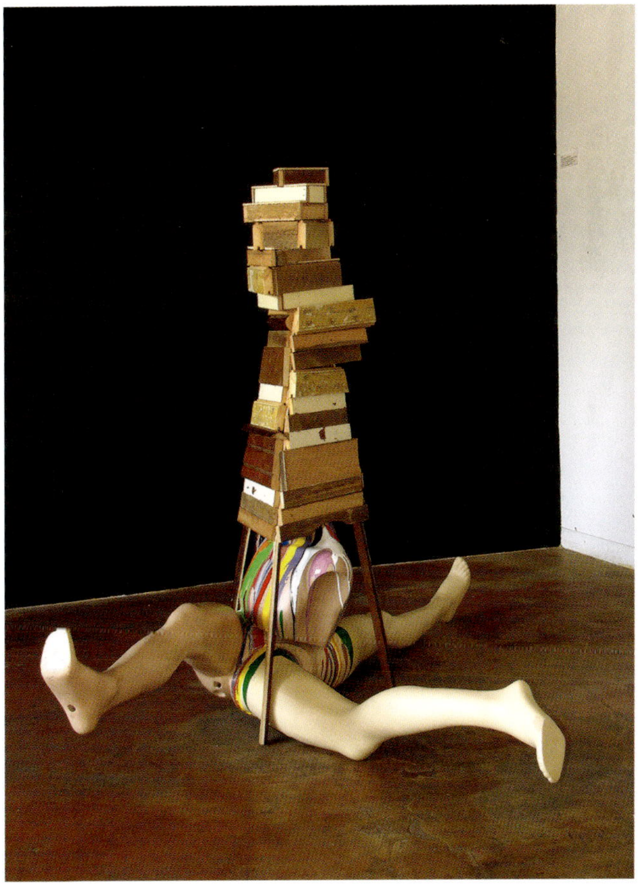

Anointment 3, 2005. Mixed media installation, 4′ x 8.5′ x 6′.

JONATHAN PECK

Much of my work to date has involved investigating conventional ideas of reality and truth, and the boundaries between fact and fiction. The life of "factual information" is often finite and short-lived; new information is continuously being generated that undermines or changes preceding ideas of how things are. I'm interested in the gray area that exists between "reasonable" and "eccentric" notions of realty, and how these notions are both formed and defied in contemporary cultures around the world. After spending the past year translating my ideas into paper sculptures and masks, the golden room, an image of the soul, showed up and I made it real in the installation "*Hopeless, but Not Empty*." This installation was the last in a series of self portraits that began by first depicting my body as dismembered, then as a shell (a costume), and finally as a space elaborately adorned with images and symbols from my past, but lacking any actual physical objects. Because I'm watching the process in myself I have become increasingly interested in the development and evolution of the self. Although, now, I am becoming less interested in investigating my personal self and more interested in investigating the notion of self as it relates to all of humankind.

I moved to Miami in November of 2004 after living in Kansas City, Missouri, for six years. What I've found since I've been here is that Miami and Kansas City are very comparable cities. Their sizes compare geographically as do their communities of artists. The talent amongst the artists in both cities is very strong as is the excitement and energy they provoke. The major difference between the two cities is money. Miami has it and Kansas City doesn't! Because of the fairs in December and great support of local art by members of the community Miami has made its way onto the world's stage, and the city's artists have been reaping the benefits. I'd like to see the same opportunities that have arisen in Miami make it to areas like Kansas City where the work is equally as strong and provocative. I plan to do what I can to create some bridges between the cities so such things may happen, but until then I'm glad to be in what I believe is the best place, right now, to be as an artist with a burgeoning career.

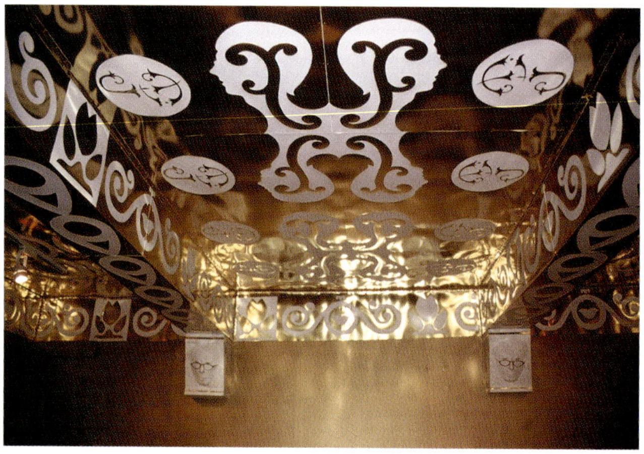

Hopeless but not empty (detail ceiling)

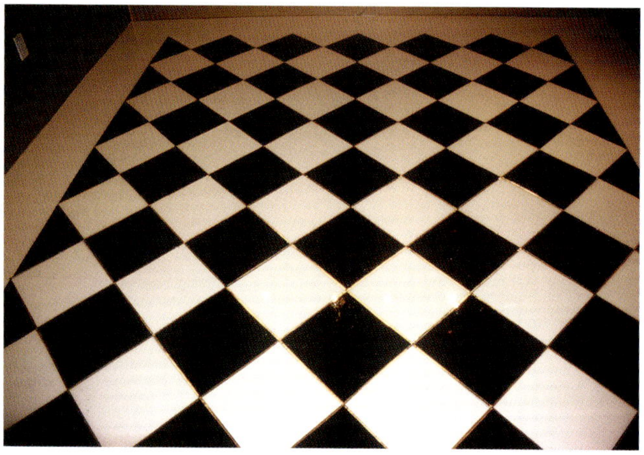

Hopeless but not empty (detail floor)

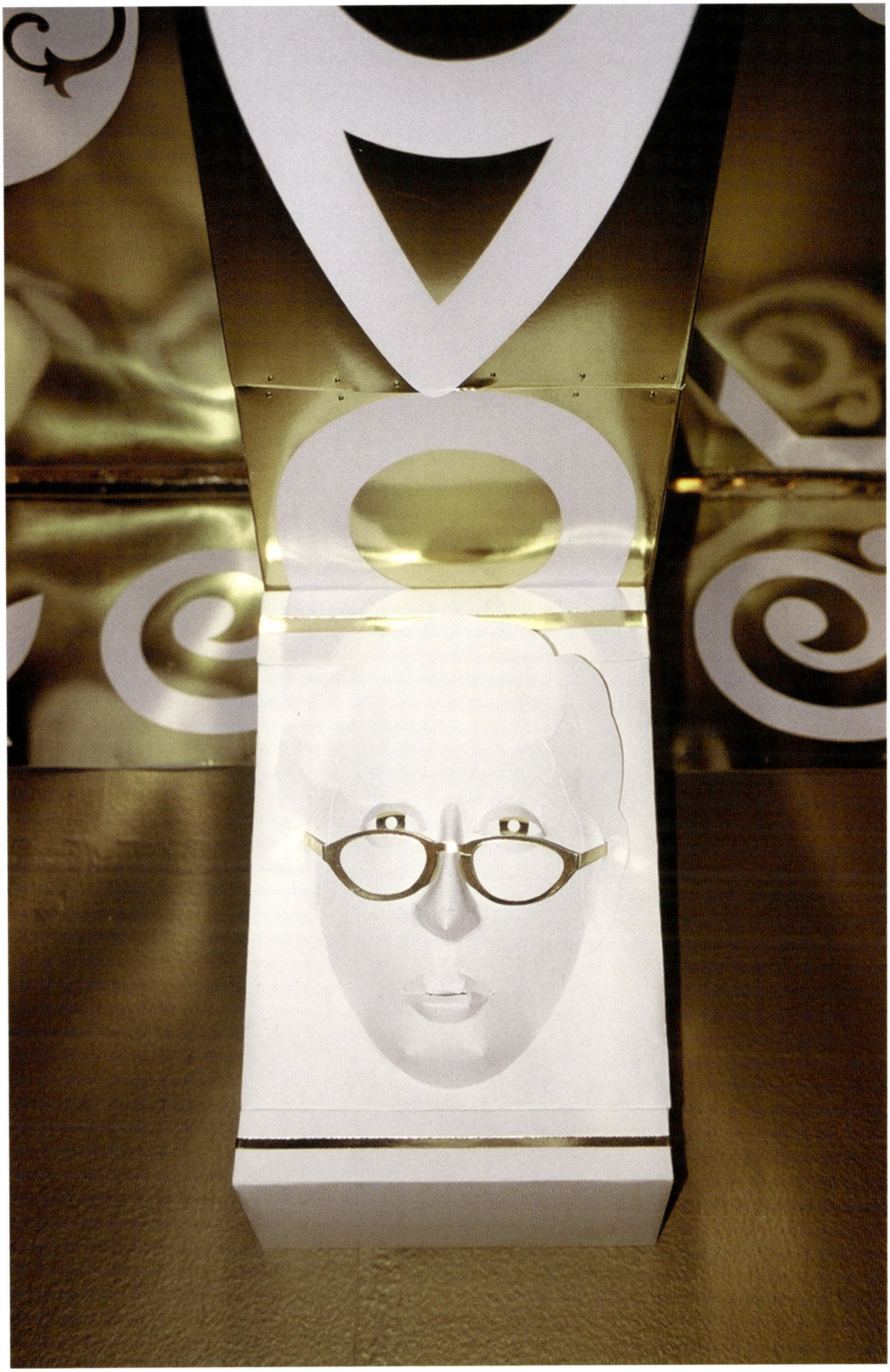

Hopeless but not empty (detail), 2005. White and black cardstock, gold poster board, gold wallpaper, and epoxy resin, dimensions variable.

GAVIN PERRY

Main Entry: cus·tom·ize
Pronunciation: 'k&s-t&-"mIz
Function: transitive verb
Inflected Form(s): -ized; -iz·ing
Date: 1923
: to build, fit, or alter according to individual specifications
– cus·tom·iz·er noun

The act of customizing is a subversive one. In every reigning civilizations effort to homogenize its culture, a wave of radical individuality is found left in the wake. With a desire to express their personal identity many people in our society have drastically and often violently altered mass-produced objects. Any number of things can and have been customized, including cars, furniture, and clothing to name a few. In all instances, mass produced objects have been modified to fit the requirements of the individual doing the customizing, be they aesthetic, utilitarian, or otherwise. My interests lie in the relationship between the object and the customizer. In particular, the obsession with finish is significant in that it reveals the devotion of the perpetrator. I believe these obsessive manipulations imbue the objects with a form of magic. I produce paintings and sculpture that are primarily constructed through the use of industrial materials and techniques. I work with the same methodical approach custom car builders' use. Laboring to get the surface pristine, making the piece seamless. By choosing these caveats I maintain my allegiance to the blue collar/DIY world that I grew up in. At the same time, I address implications of judgment, class and taste.

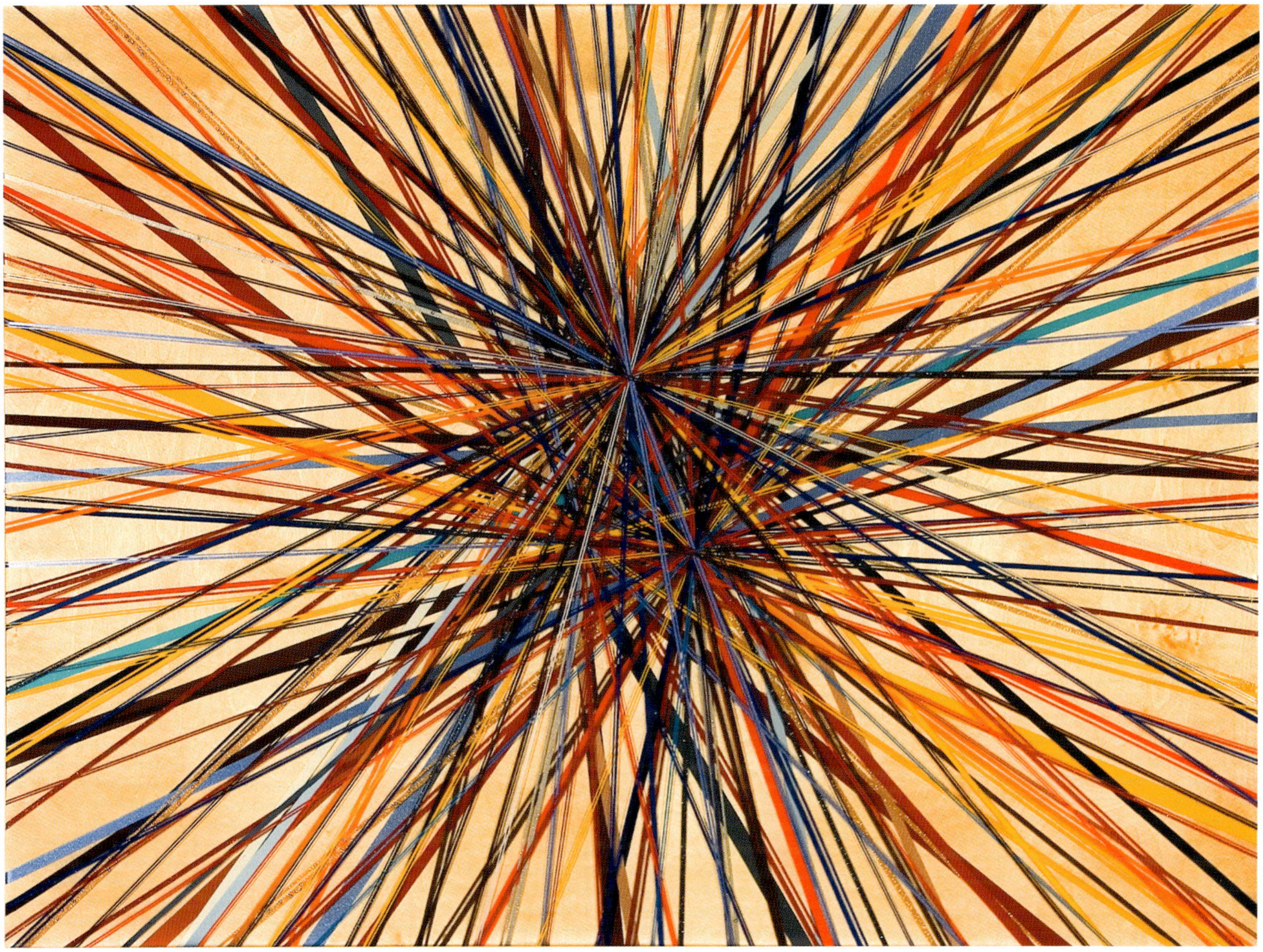

Set Me Down on the Earth, 2006. Vinyl tape and resin on board, 44" x 60".

Next page:
Untitled (Escape Plan), 2006. Vinyl tape and resin on board, 80" x 120".

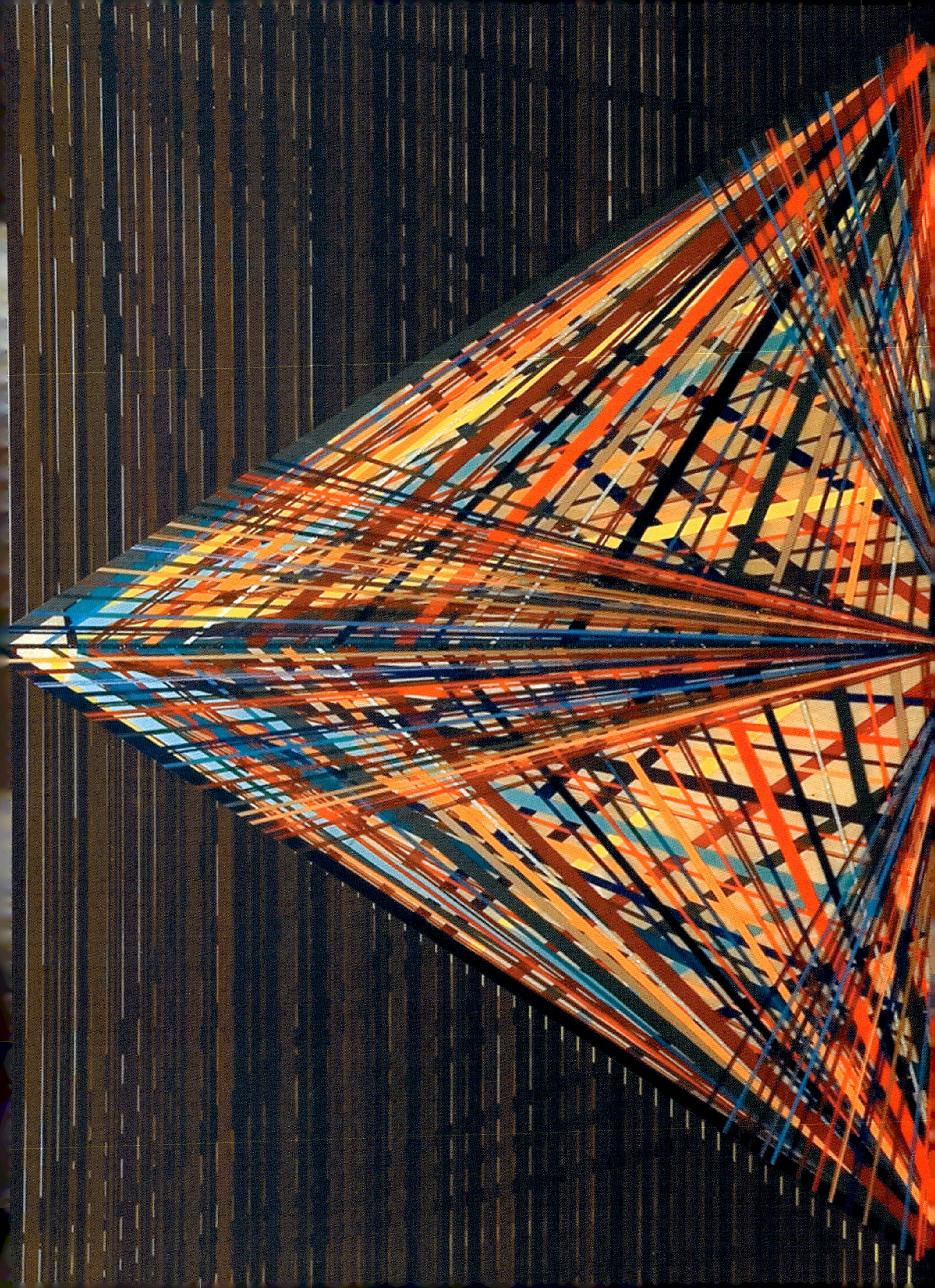

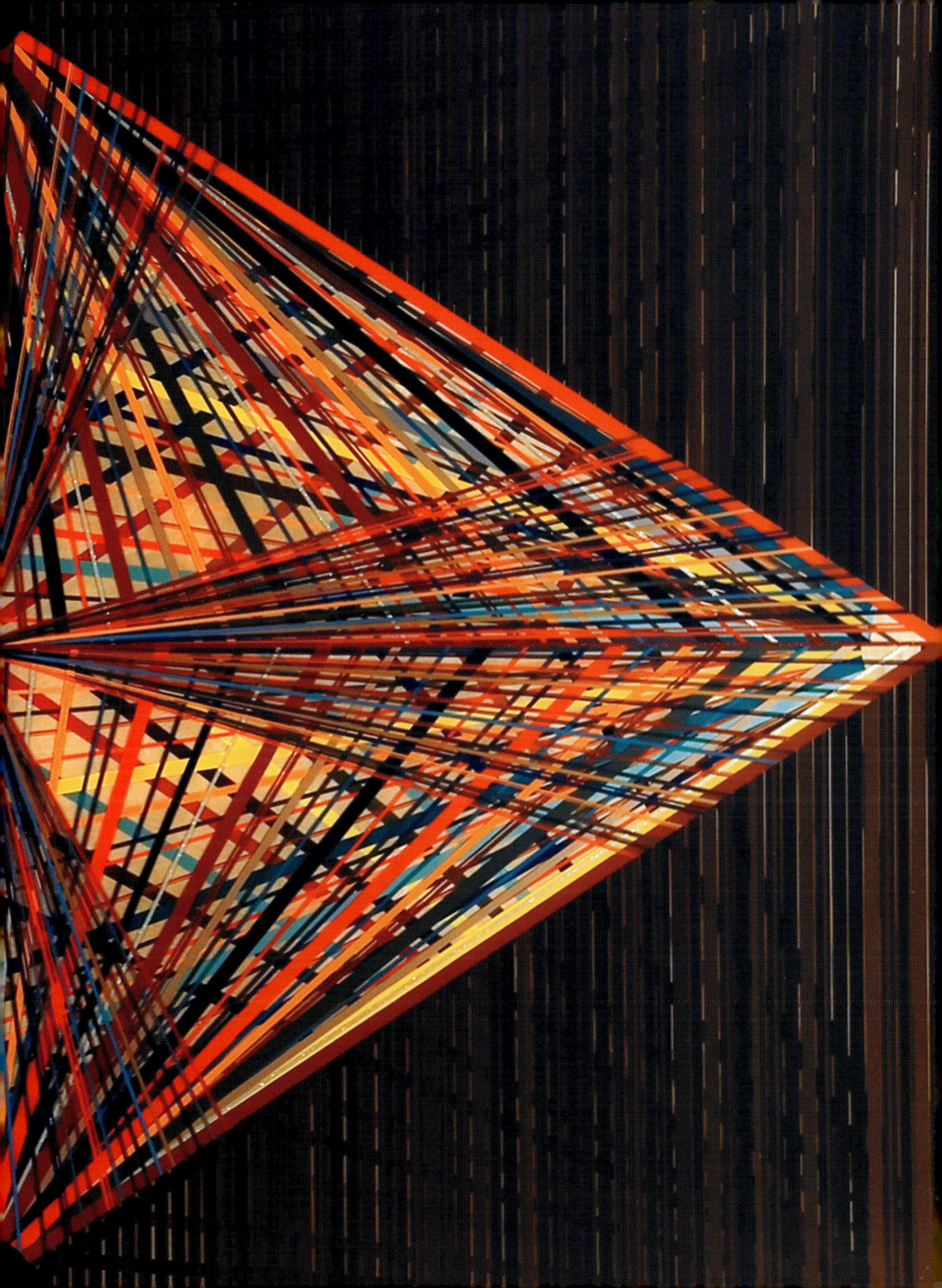

VICKIE **PIERRE**

The work of Vickie Pierre is informed and inspired by her collection of vintage children's books and textiles, childhood memories, fantasy and pattern and decoration. Pierre employs a range of techniques that include painting, wall drawing and installation, focusing on the exploration of form and structure through the use of appropriated source materials and feminine psychology. Pierre's current process converts rubber stamps of Disney female icons, ink and paint into a complex universe where space and movement are whimsically conveyed. The abstract landscape of this world is comprised of the dresses of the three graces of the fairy tale animation world: Snow White, Sleeping Beauty and Cinderella. In certain instances, the works are combined with text that expresses a reciprocal sentiment. The repetitive application of the stamps into clusters and groupings, along with the text, has become the basis of a connective network that alludes to identity, order, and desire; as well as the psychological implications of social conditioning occurring in popular culture. The text stems from song lyrics, overheard conversations, poetry or artist musings. It interacts and interferes with the biomorphic forms, allowing for a narrative of sorts to exist but also functions simply as mark, as line, as decoration. The deconstructed elements within the paintings and works on paper are transformed into characters with sensual and precious personalities that recall the abstractions and distortions of the body. They are playfully aggressive yet delicate, nudging and resting against one another, consumed with their own interior formal logic and color balance.

I moved to Miami Beach from New York in 1998. The transition was fairly easy: coffee in the morning, a walk to the beach for a swim, and then painting for hours. It was my daily routine. The energy of living on the beach impacted my daily creative process. I could see the change in my work almost immediately. The tropical surroundings and brilliant light really influenced the coloring in my paintings. The result was warmer and more inviting work. It has been 7 years now, and Miami has continued to prove itself as a growing and challenging place for me to make art. The artists here with different view points and techniques are creating thoughtful and honest work, and I am glad to be a part of that.

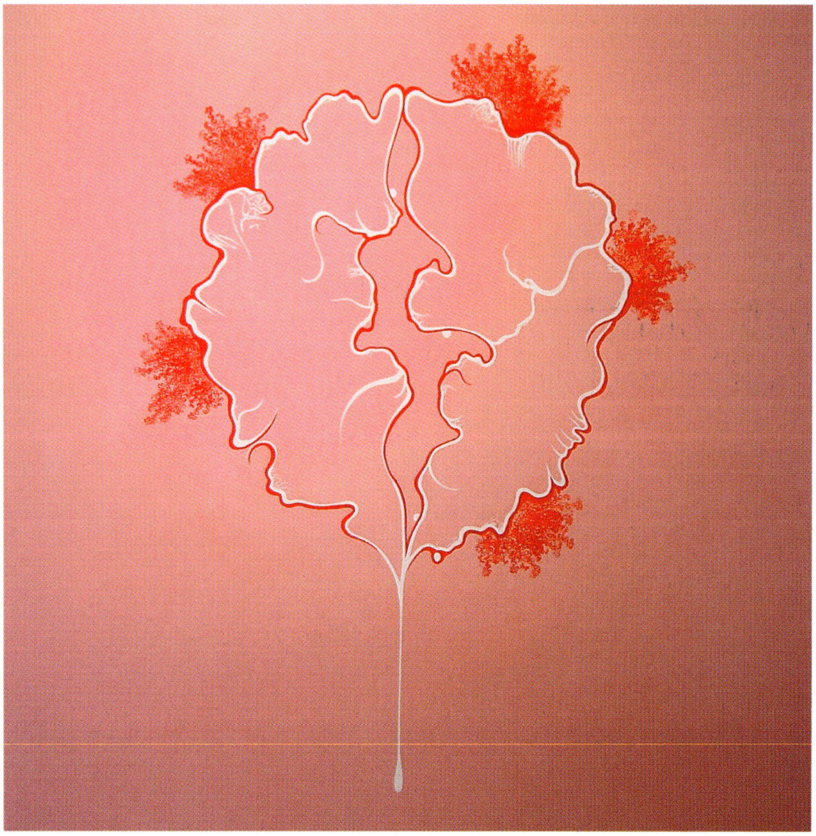

The Secret Pearls Inside of Me, 2006. Acrylic on canvas, 24" x 24".

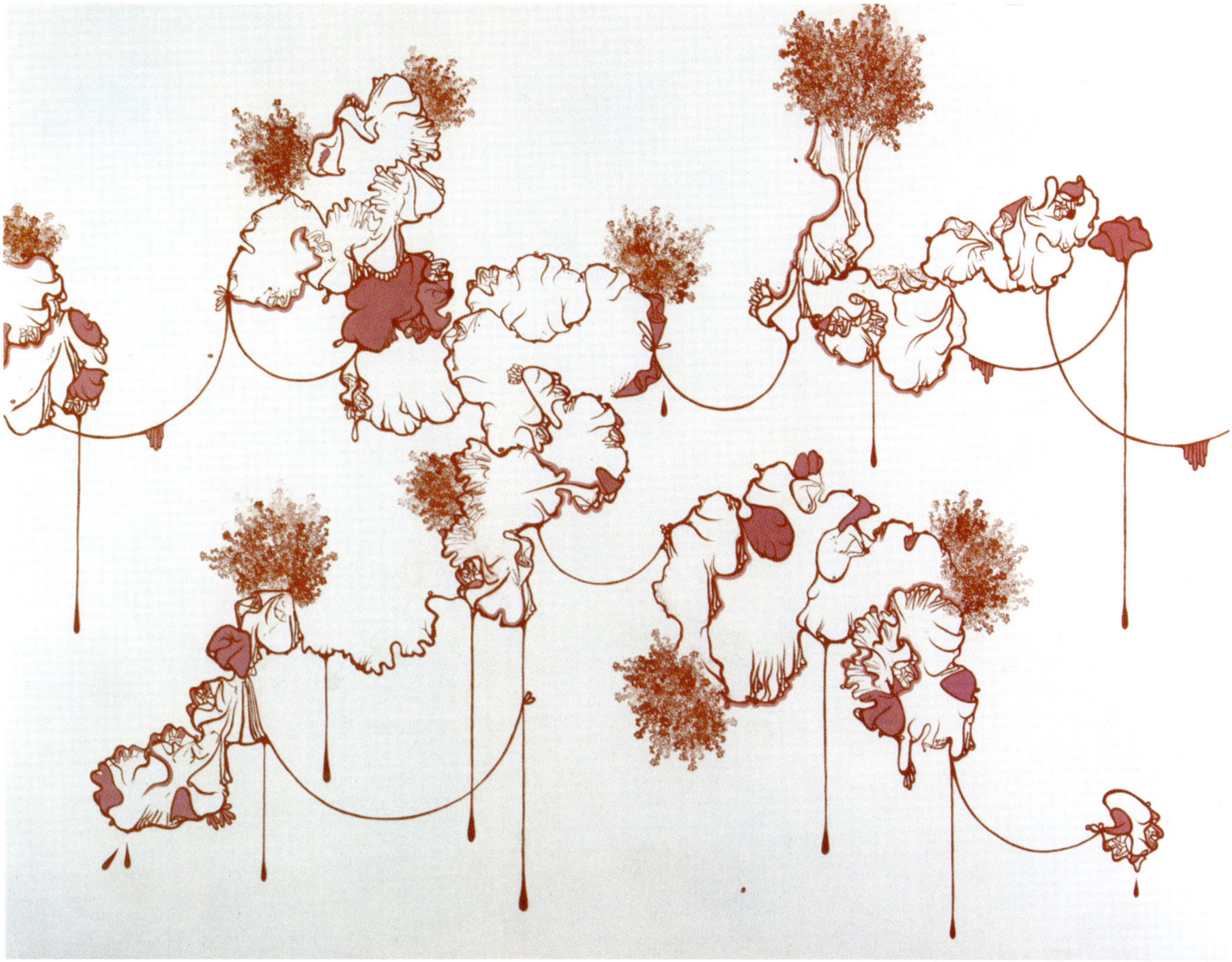

My Innermost Thoughts, 2006. Acrylic on canvas. 26" x 35".

ALISA PITCHENIK

Alisa Pitchenik's work focuses on the convergence of disparate media, patterns of human behavior, relationships, sports, language, and humor. Her pieces explore the balance of stability and instability born out of internal, natural, and technological modern-day environments. She conjures forms utilizing multimedia and cross-disciplinary collaborations in real time. Her experiments often develop into lesson plans and inspirations for her students. Presently, she has arrived at narrative dark comedies, documentaries demystifying the art making process and surreal time-lapse and stop motion animations. Currently she is an Associate Professor of Visual Arts and the Director of the Electronic Intermedia College BFA Program at New World School of the Arts in downtown Miami. She graduated from the University of Miami with a BFA in Painting and Art History. She then received her MFA from the School of Visual Arts in New York City where she focused on multi-media performance and installation, and continued her study of post-modern art. Alisa is a multi-media and interdisciplinary artist, curator, and educator. She has either personally exhibited, taught, curated and collaborated in Miami, New York, Los Angeles, Boston, London, Mexico, and Italy in a broad range of intriguing art institutions, such as museums, galleries, and alternative venues for art, animation, and film. She actively supports non-profit art and design spaces by aiding with technical assistance and recommending student artists for internships.

I find making art a worthy investment in Miami. The artistic process, for me, is difficult, highly personal, painful, hidden, and not particularly marketable. Having become so aware of "art" has made the task even more taxing. I enjoy when the process is over. This has always been the case as I moved through mediums of painting, performance/installation, composites, time-lapse animations, digital and collaborative experiments, and currently narrative films. My time in New York was incredible, but I missed Miami terribly and came back. Miami was clearly ripe for possibilities. Local artists came out and converged during the infamous "Faux Basel" of December 2001. It was a private, amazing, magical time full of possibilities without expectation. With Art Basel taking foothold, galleries have popped up in the crack of a sidewalk and real estate has been expanding, as well. I hope I can afford to stay. Artists, dealers, educators, collectors, and investors recognized a diamond in the rough and have been working overtime to secure Miami as a stronghold for art as a rich artistic community is developing here with stories galore. The process has been exhausting but worthwhile. I have personally experienced the hope and opportunities develop, and watched the flourishing of artists and dealers who have capitalized on the moment. I strive to contribute to the artistic growth of budding artists in Miami. The right opportunity is worth seeking right here in Miami, a city of extremes; to know it is to love it. Miami, after all, is warm, attractive, and edgy.

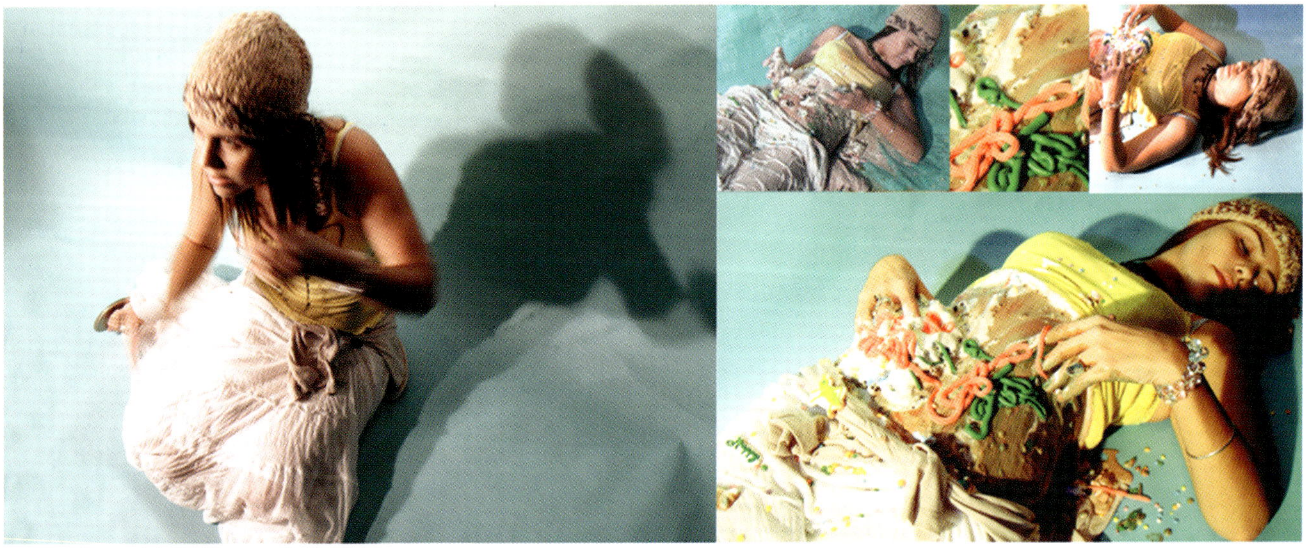

Someone Left the Cake out in the Rain, Now What?, 2005. Video still.

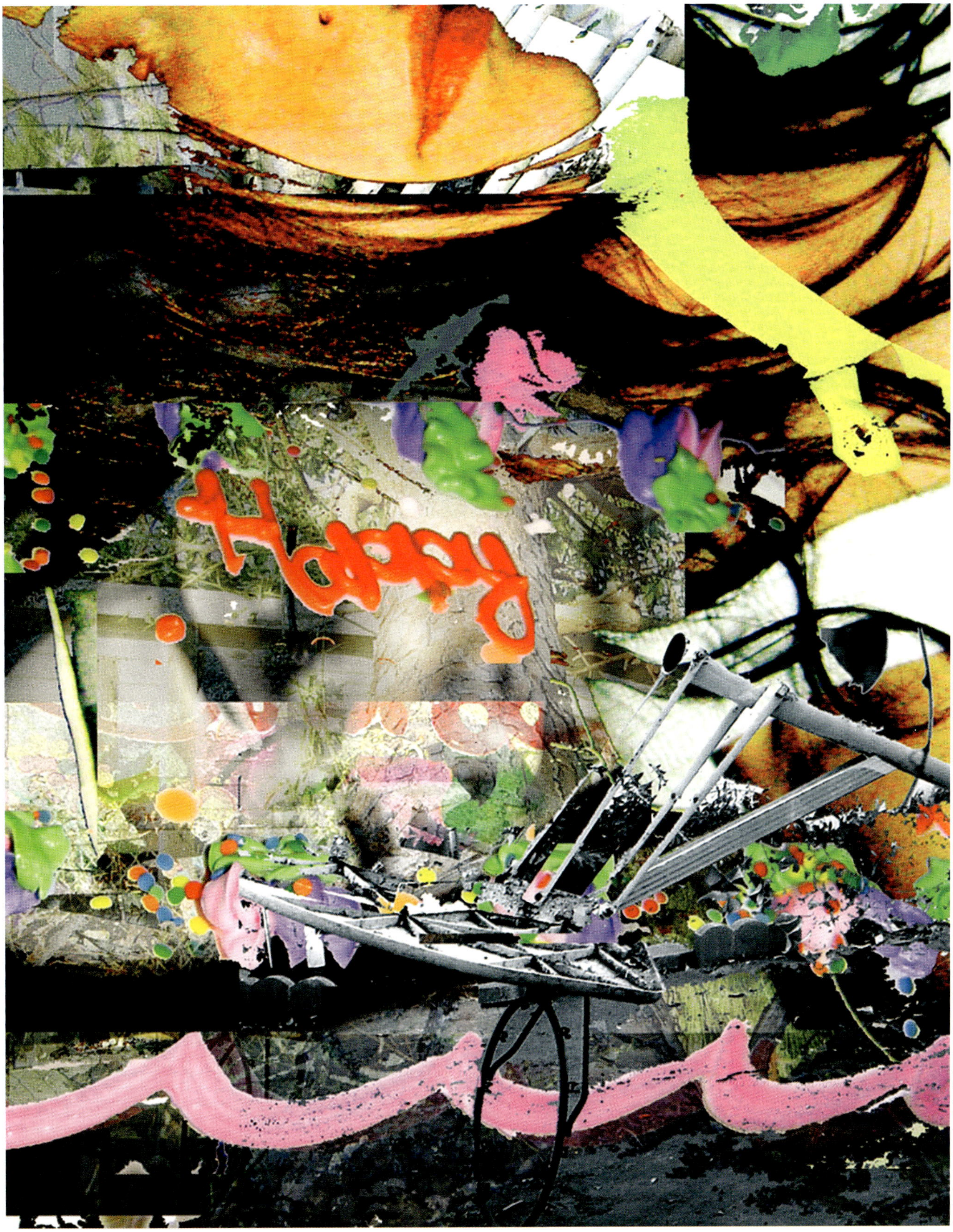

Hurricane cake (Experiment 5) The Aftermath, 2005. Digital composite of performance, 13.5″ x 17″.

MANNY **PRIERES**

For a long time I have been fascinated with visual languages that are often considered outcast forms of expression, i.e. tattoo, prison, flash, and punk rock flyer art. My work deals largely with combining various iconographies, from different classes or cultures, to create a new visual language. By appropriating logos, art, and ornate patterns the end result is a juxtaposition of ironic visual imagery. My new work takes this further with introducing more personal imagery such as family heirlooms or past memories.

Manny Prieres was born in Madrid Spain, 1972. He lives and works in Miami. Prieres co-founded the Miami alternative art space "BOX," in 1999 along with artists Jose Reyes and Leyden Rodriguez-Casanova.

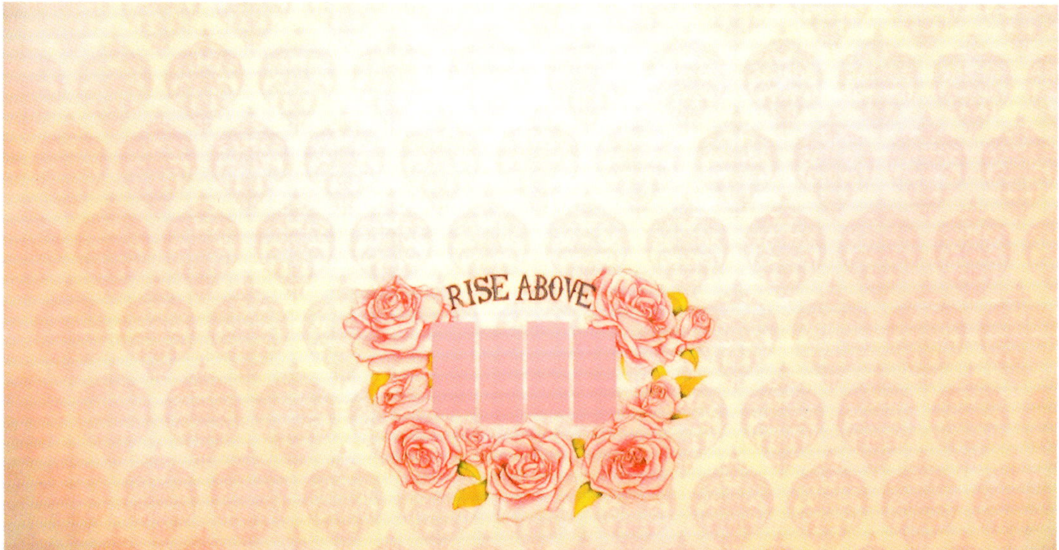

Rise Above, 2004. Colored pencils, acrylic on Mylar, 24" x 36".

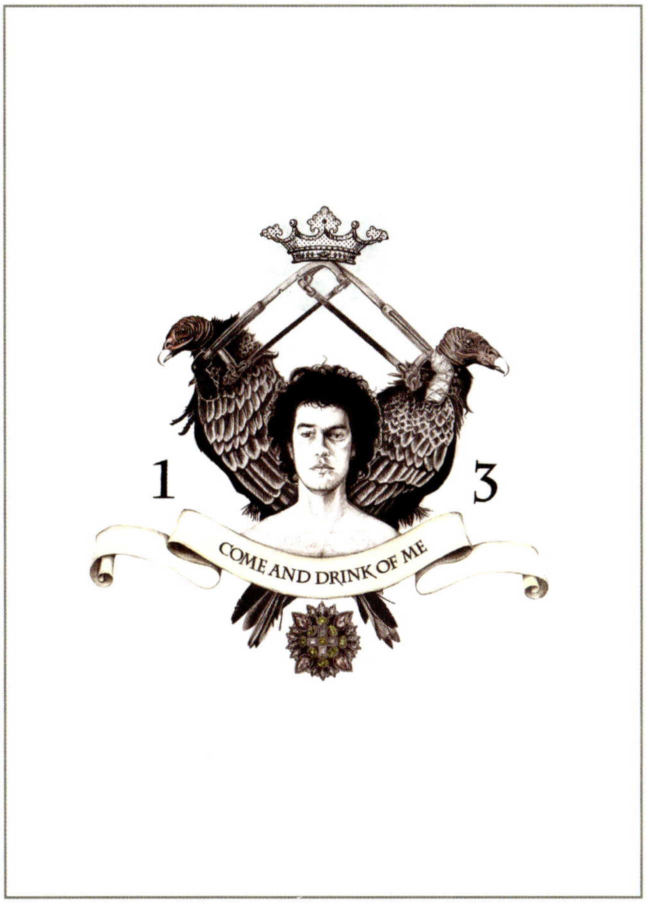

Untitled (Self Portrait), 2005. Graphite, watercolor on paper, 22" x 30".

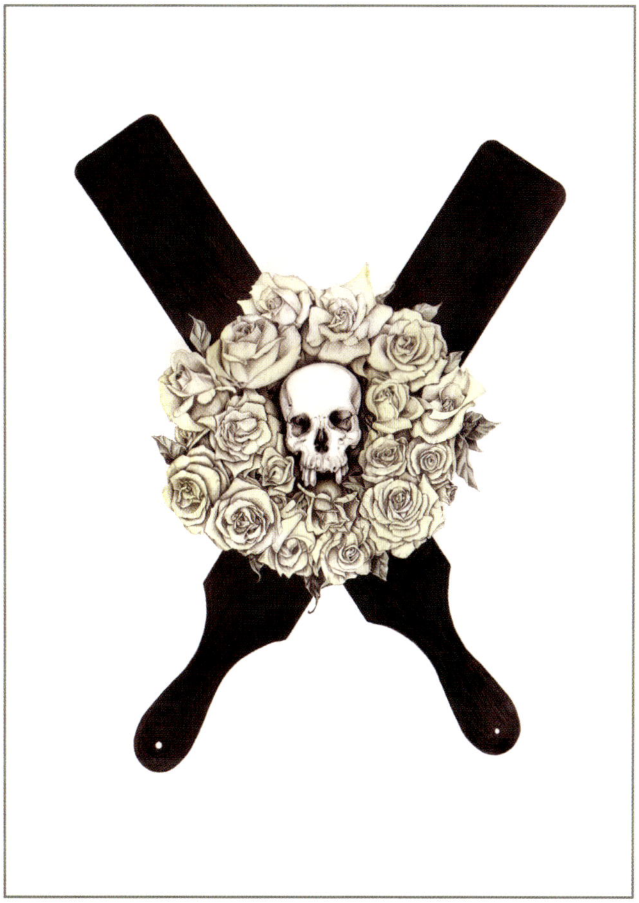

My Boy, 2005. Graphite, watercolor on paper, 22" x 30".

ALI PROSCH

My artistic efforts have centered on creating scenes that explore the destruction, beauty and desires that define human relationships and identity. By constructing short, fantastical narratives I seek to hyper-beautify moments that are emotionally potent. These narratives blend reactions and coping mechanisms to personal and social situations. I find coping mechanisms to be an intriguing phenomena, sometimes I laugh when I have nothing to say, sometimes I wish to hit you in the fucking face. *"Fight That Bitch and Win*," one of my early videos, was stylized after a video game. In the piece, I realized my desire to fight my nemesis by kicking her, slapping her, and shoving her into the ground. A shower of digitized stars would emerge on the screen each time I succeeded in making contact. This effect provided a gratifying "bang, boom, pow!" comic effect. Humor makes anger relatable in "*Fight That Bitch and Win*" and is an integral part of my practice. My work is driven by dichotomies that are manifested through photo, video, drawing and installation works. I want these works to behave like a plank on a see-saw, vacillating between fantasy/reality, destruction/charm, humor/ sobriety, choreography and spontaneity.

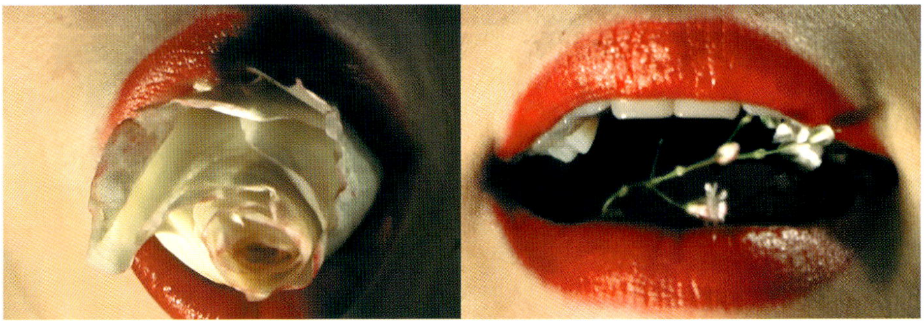

Forever (diptych), 2005. Still from color DV video.

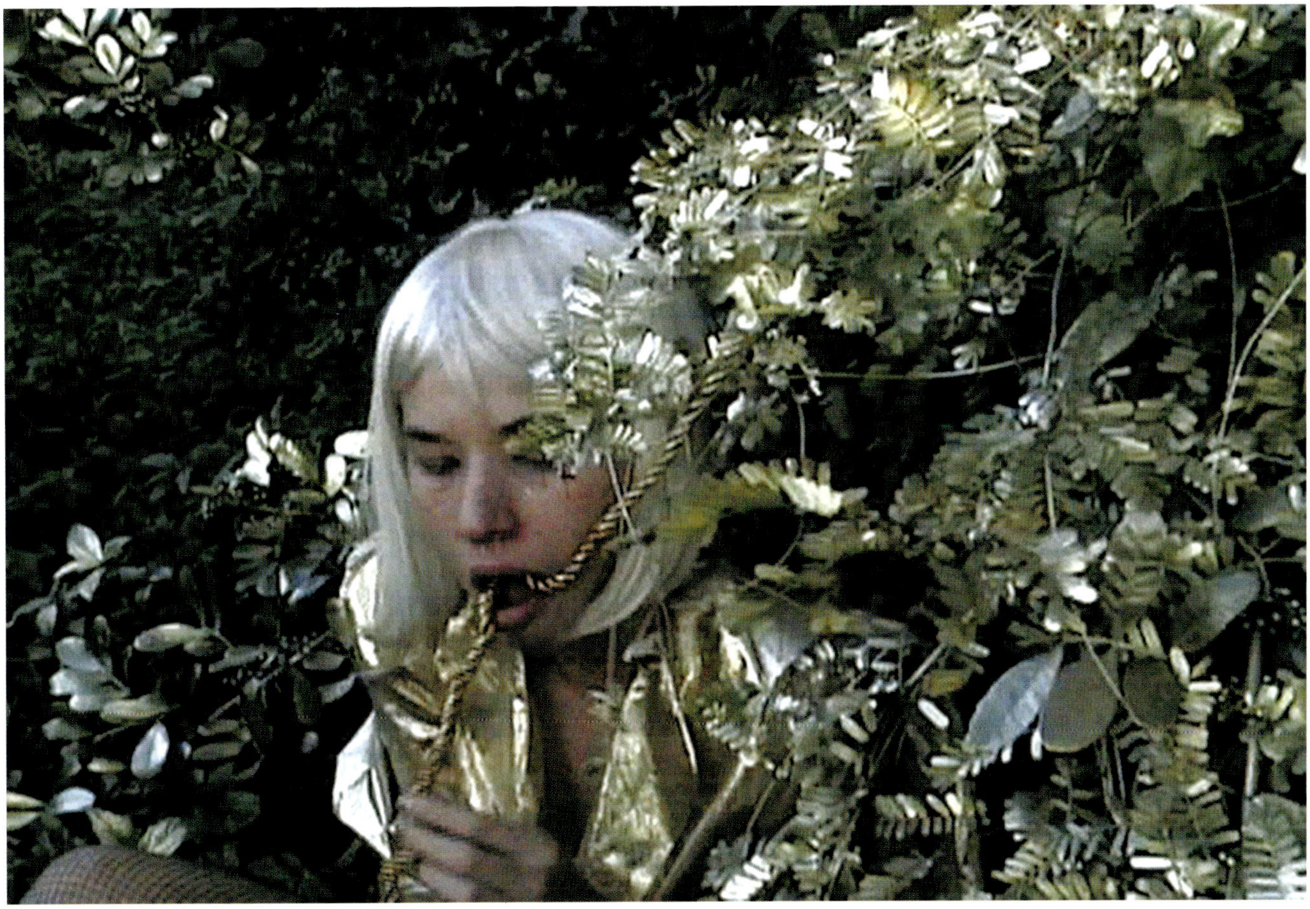

Consume, 2004. Still from color DV video, 2 minutes 49 seconds, ed. of 5.

RALPH PROVISERO

My interest in dynamic form and movement fuels a great deal of the visual aspects of my work. It is a style that on the surface is quiet yet strong, and ideas more deeply rooted than mere aesthetics are often indicated by subtle suggestion. Just as the balance of proportions and materials is weighted, so is that of concept and form.

It is an exciting time to be an artist in Miami. The rate at which Miami is currently growing and attracting members of other art communities makes it feel historic. There is a forward momentum evident with the growth of the population of artists and galleries, encouraged by what is possible. What is probably most exciting, though, is being part of an art community that is in progressive flux.

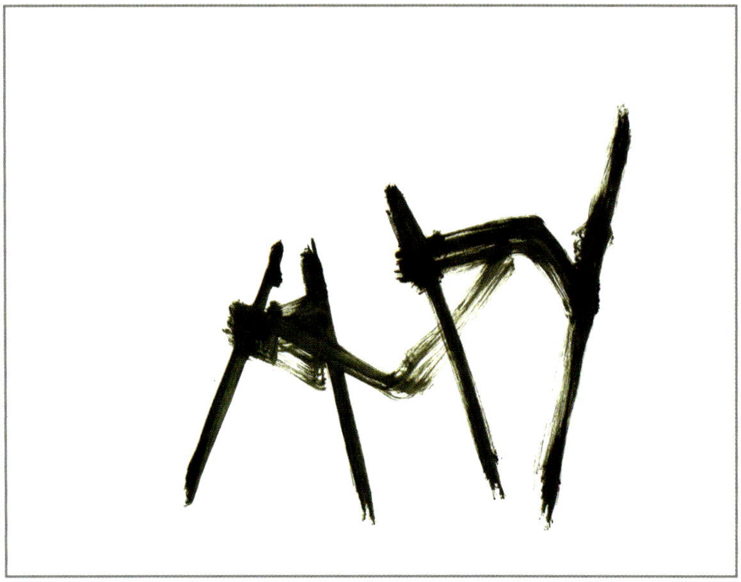

Study #1, 2004. Graphite, charcoal and shellac on paper, 32" x 40".

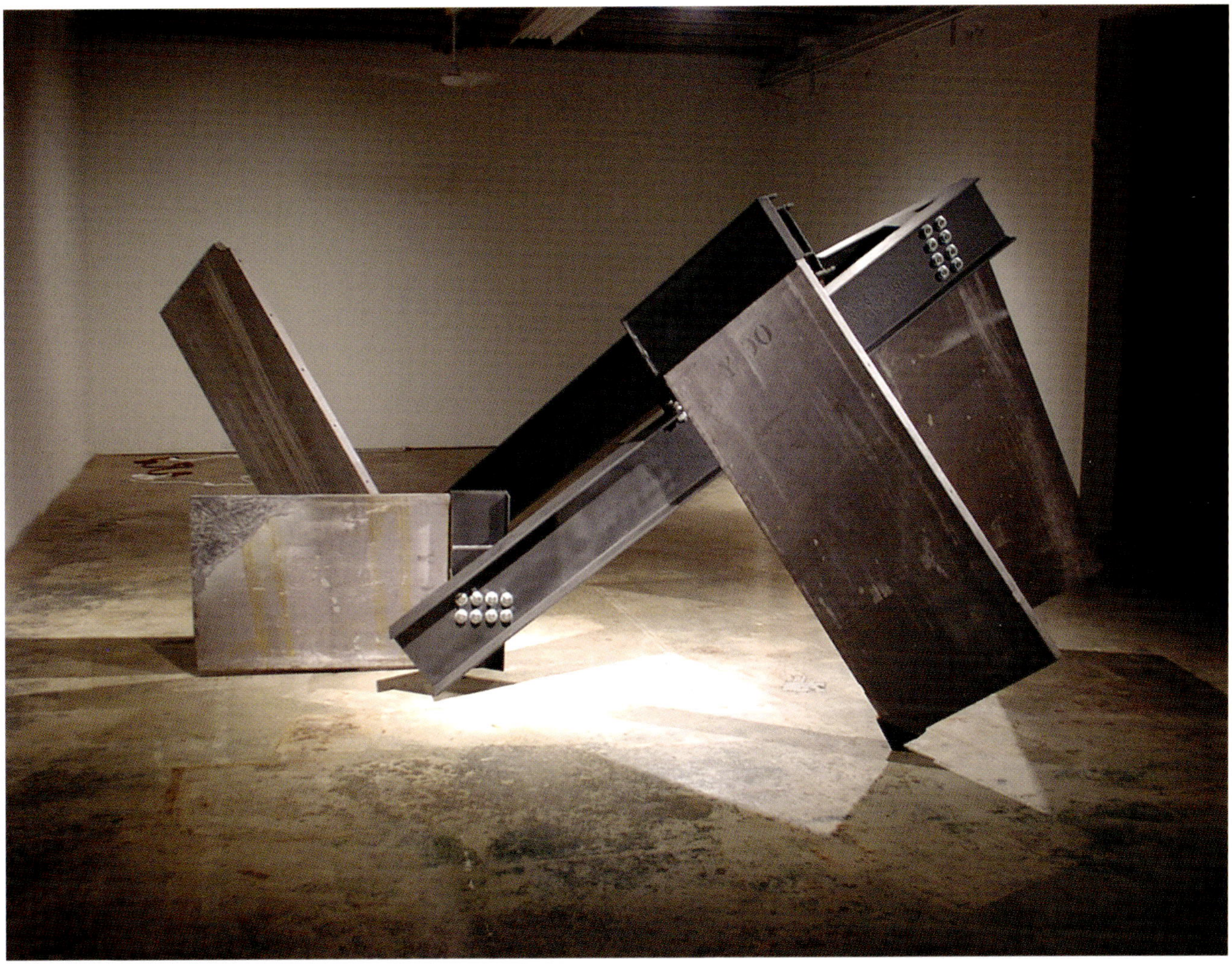

Pietra Veloce, 2003. Steel, slate, 8′ x 7′2″ x 16′.

CAROL **PRUSA**

These painted drawings are done in silverpoint with graphite on acrylic gesso on wood panel, heightened with titanium white pigment bound with acrylic polymer. *A constellation of possibilities delivers innies or outies – world belly buttons. Connection to disconnection is fleeting. A pregnant belly distends towards a potential big bang. Macro and micro scales collide into intimate exchanges. The chaotic abyss offers rebound. There are no answers but you feel alive and infinitely generous. (all states are becoming and disintegrating)* As a conceptual voyager I intuit a new picture of reality. Seeking to conjure a balance between expansion and collapse without asserting an absolute, making visible what is not seen, I quietly insist on being something more than an undifferentiated tumor – at least for a moment.

Miami is wonderful for its support of contemporary art. The feeding frenzy of Basel-Miami can overwhelm and the commodification of art can frustrate, but the flux of ideas and multiple art worlds in South Florida creates incredible opportunities to work and flourish as an artist. I moved to South Florida several months after reading the two-part article, spring of 1999, in Art in America on the developing vibrant Miami art scene. I was seeking an environment that embraced many ways of making art and had cultural institutions dedicated to exhibiting contemporary work. I felt my work would grow by working in an art community significantly different than the one I left. In the mid-west my work was colorful, involved performance and video and installation. In Florida I shifted to drawing and painting and my work is subtle and intricately adaptive. I think the bizarre plants outside my studio window account for this. What they do overnight is shocking. The hardest part of being a South Florida artist is staying informed because everything here is complexly dynamic.

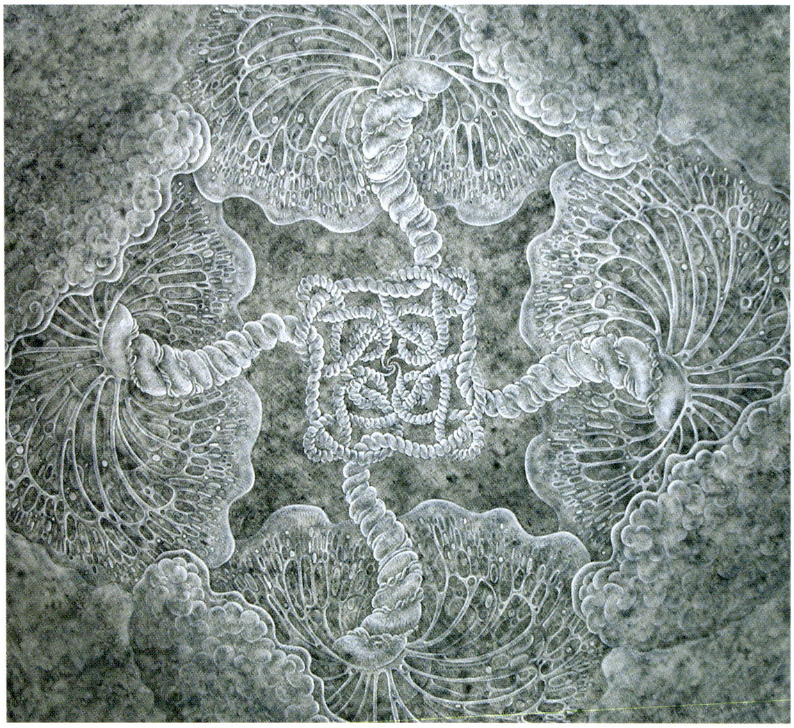

To Be All (detail),2006. Silverpoint, graphite, titanium white pigment with binder on wood panel, 37" x 37".

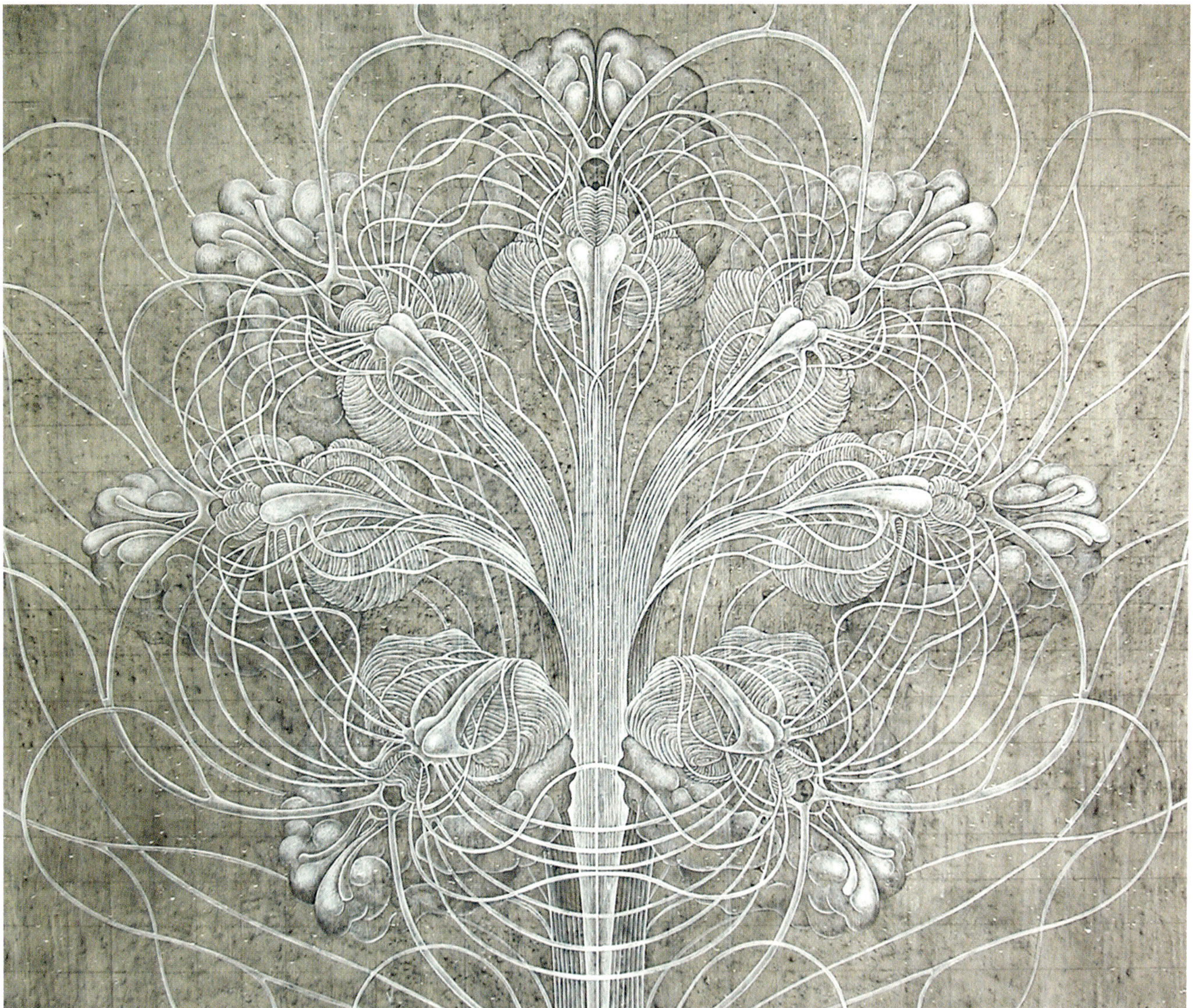

Web (detail), 2003. Silverpoint, graphite, titanium white pigment with binder on wood panel, 84" x 48".

TAO **REY**

Tao Rey's work breaks down the hegemonic hold of corporate and governmental style over the urban environment and the situations of daily life. As a form of aesthetic sabotage, it interrupts the pleasant, efficient uniformity of planned urban space and predictable urban living. As an example, graffiti survives as a creative playful response to a pre-fabricated culture, a response that subverts legal and political boundaries as well as the notion of public and private space. Graffiti exists as a public art outside the control of public officials, an alternative language outside the corporate style. Tao's work illuminates the city sporadically as evocative moments rather than as lasting monuments. Ultimately, it stands as a sort of decentralized and de-centered insubordination, a mysterious resistance to conformity and control, a stylish counterpunch to the belly of authority. *1.* Rey's work is informed by the city as a new lexicon of forms. He works with signifiers implicit in the urban landscape, some are supplied by the city (as in his street signs) and others are interjections into it (as in his works which use the vernacular of graffiti). By subverting both of these systems, he is able to create an idiosyncratic coalescence of urban space, a detournment in the lived space of the city. When applied to a "fine art" context, his interjections become hybrids, incorporating the predisposition of graffiti, urban iconography, and language itself. In this manner his work can be described as "socially curious," particularly as applied to the polarizations that have stretched us far beyond the definition of community, as well as the dysfunction of language as it alienates us, and joins us as a congregation: a congregation of alienated and alienating subjects.

1. See "Graffiti is part of us www.artcrimes.com/faq/graffiti-is-part-of-us.html

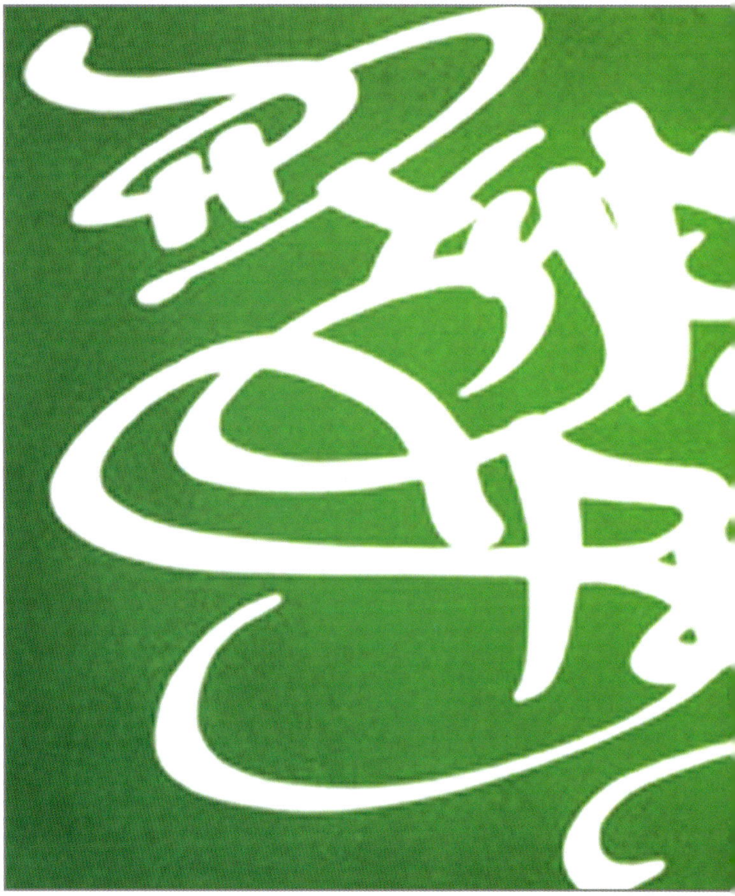

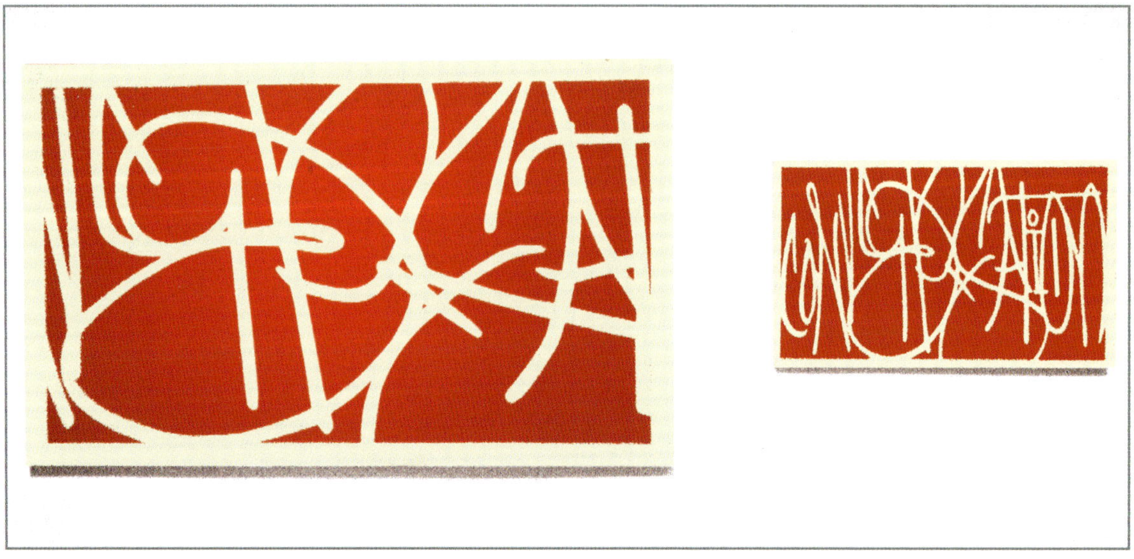

Conversation, 2001. Acrylic on canvas, 6′ x 10′, 3′ x 5′.

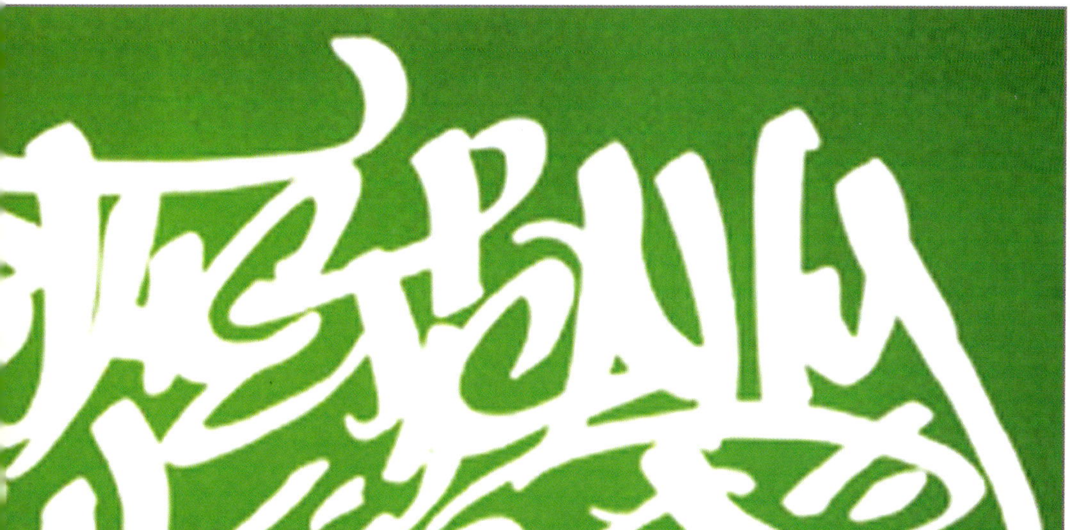

Hypothetically speaking, 2003. Acrylic and glass spheres on panel, 32.5" x 72".

TALL RICKARDS

My photographs are first and foremost cinematic and they can be appreciated as stills from a movie or life. Photography, video and sound are sources that I innately gravitate towards to illustrate ideas. My work also attempts to evoke a spiritual and poetic response to nature and its mysteries; the use of images as emblems of struggle which are metaphorical in the guest for manhood and the balance of inner power with the forces of the natural world. My concern is in pursuing art that can move beyond the conventional boundaries, offering something more intimate and transcendent. Though art occupies an exclusive environment, it can be a source of promoting new thinking and change. The good, the bad and the mysterious provokes us to question the nature of ourselves, and the world around us. The mystical, surreal, and the supernatural are common in my work, yet metaphorically and subconsciously the real rebellion has always been against the abuse of authority and the forces that makes us less human.

Working as an artist in Miami has always allowed me to explore and take advantage of new territories. The city and scene are active and emerging into something world wide. Though this city is transient, and I sometimes feel misplaced in it, I am aware of the contributions and strides I've made here as a person and an artist. Also, I've had numerous opportunities to exercise my vision as a curator/ organizer, for independent exhibitions and projects. Miami can be a place that we sometimes take advantage of, but when away it's well appreciated.

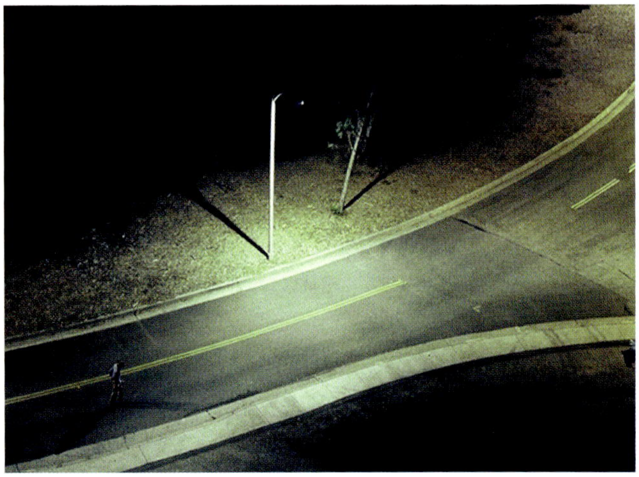

After the Noon #2, 2003. Lambda print, 24" x 36". Edition of 6.

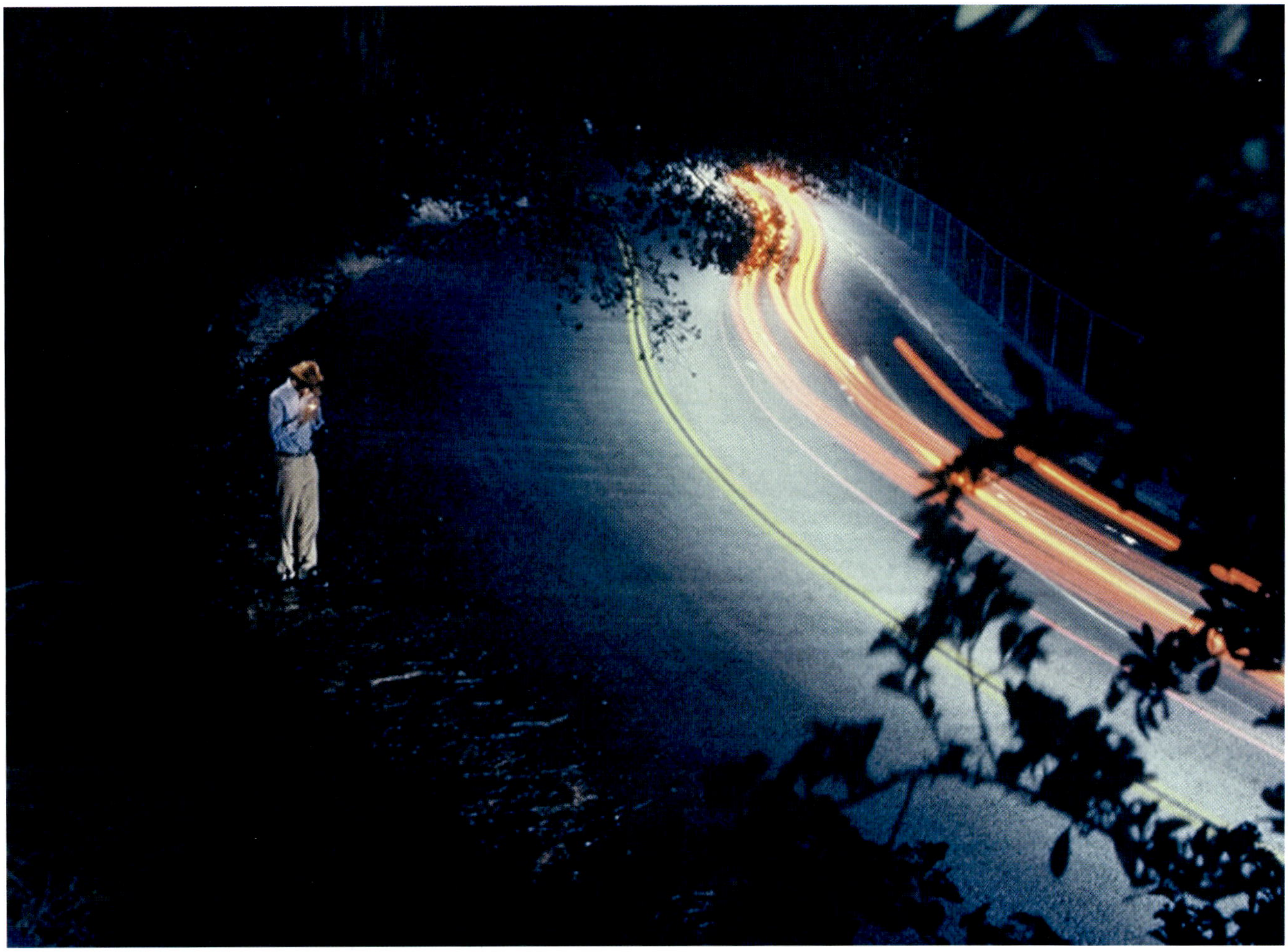

After the Noon, # 1, 2003. Lambda print, 24" x 36". Edition of 6.

KAREN RIFAS

I am seduced by
materials and form
order and chaos
geometry and chance
and my need to take ordinary materials and rearrange them into new contexts.

I was graduated in the late 1980s. Then most established artists made their living primarily by teaching at Miami-Dade College, Florida International University and The University of Miami which was the only institution granting an MFA at that time. Some artists taught at these institutions and then left to pursue careers at other institutions or high-tailed it to New York City along with their students. A few of us with family ties could not leave, or vowed to return to Miami and make it our permanent base. We exhibited with the handful of commercial galleries in town and at the few alternative spaces such as Sheldon Lurie-run Miami-Dade Galleries or ArtCenter/South Florida, Ground Level Gallery. We also realized that to stop the exodus of Miami artists we needed to provide young artists with an income, exhibition opportunities and an alternative educational source such as New World School of the Arts, and a sense that they were a part of a budding and exciting art community. It happened – with the international influx swelling and rejuvenating our city and South Beach regaining its rank as a prominent stomping ground. Then Art Basel Miami. Now... Wow!

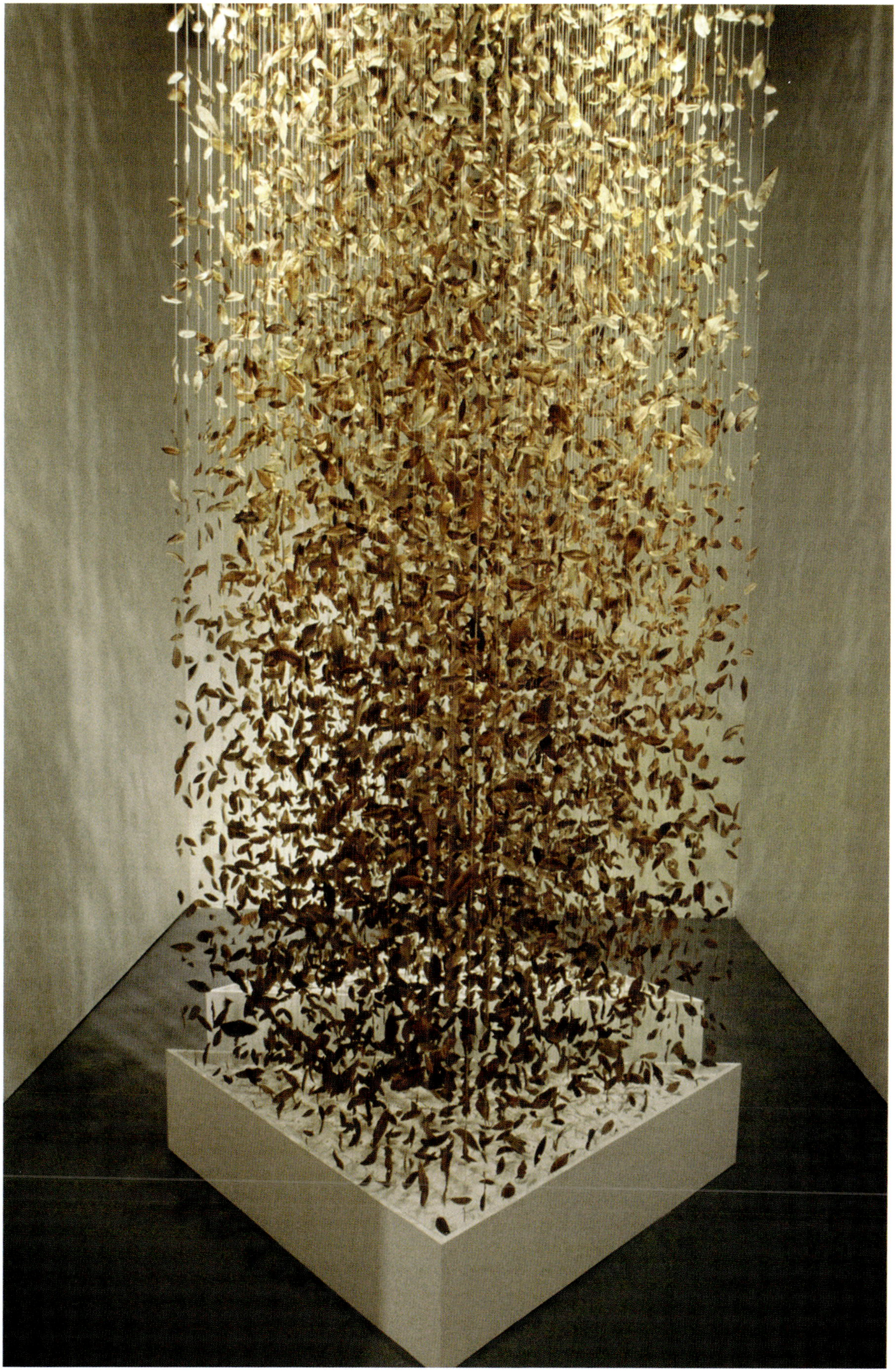

Reflection (detail), 2006. Stitched oak leaves, wood, 12′ x 56″ x 7″; Room 12′ x 11.5 ′ x 8′

LEYDEN **RODRIGUEZ-CASANOVA**

The aesthetic of suburban domestic objects and environments serves as inspiration for my work. The mundane, trivial process by which such objects and their environments are fashioned stands in contrast to traditional artistic production, with its associated intensification of meaning. By drawing attention to the aesthetic of the banal and its production methods, my work questions the complicit reduction of life's intensity to that of a trite existence. My work shows that ultimately, such products offered on a mass-scale are the highest abstraction of reality.

I have lived in Miami since I was twelve years old. My parents and I immigrated to this country from Cuba in 1980. We lived in Los Angeles for about five years before moving down here. For my family and me, it has been home ever since. I have been an artist in Miami for about ten years. In that time I have found plenty of inspiration in this city. The mixture of all the different nationalities offers a wonderful array of visual and conceptual information to react to. My work stems from this cultural blending of immigrants searching for the American dream and locals who were born here. The close proximity to where I come from, my family and the Cuban people that live here continues to inspire me on a daily basis. This is what makes Miami so special to me. I think Miami has many layers and is occasionally seen as a superficial vacation destination. I believe it is slowly moving away from these misconceptions and becoming known for the artistic community that lives and works here. Although the arts community is growing, for me, the cultural richness of Miami exists in the people and the way they live. I love this city, it's where I will continue to live and work for years to come.

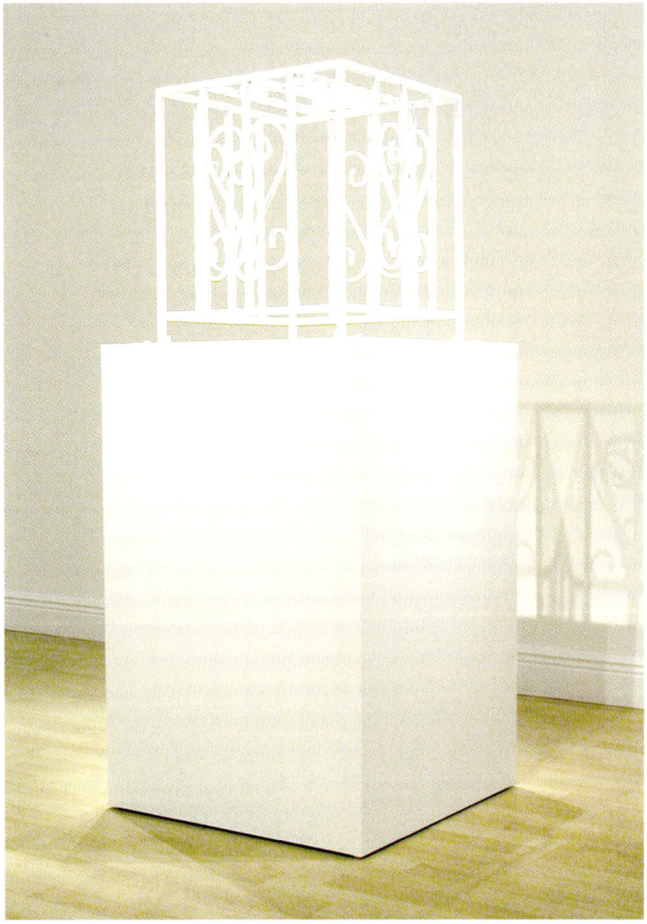

Gated Pedestal, 2003. Iron bars, plywood, paint, 24.75" x 24" x 60".

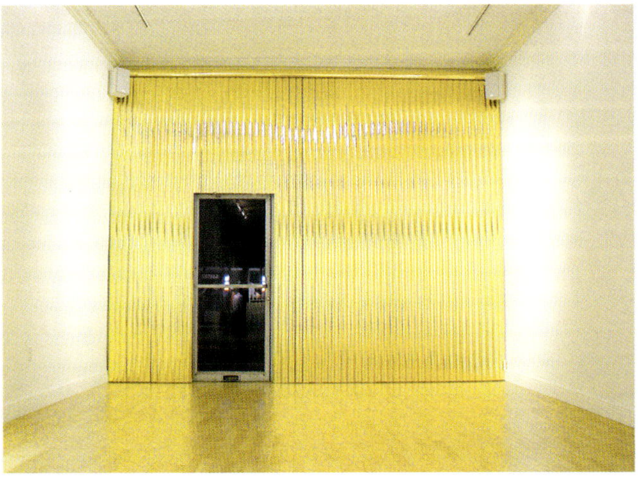

Golden Blinds, 2003. Vertical blinds, dimensions variable.

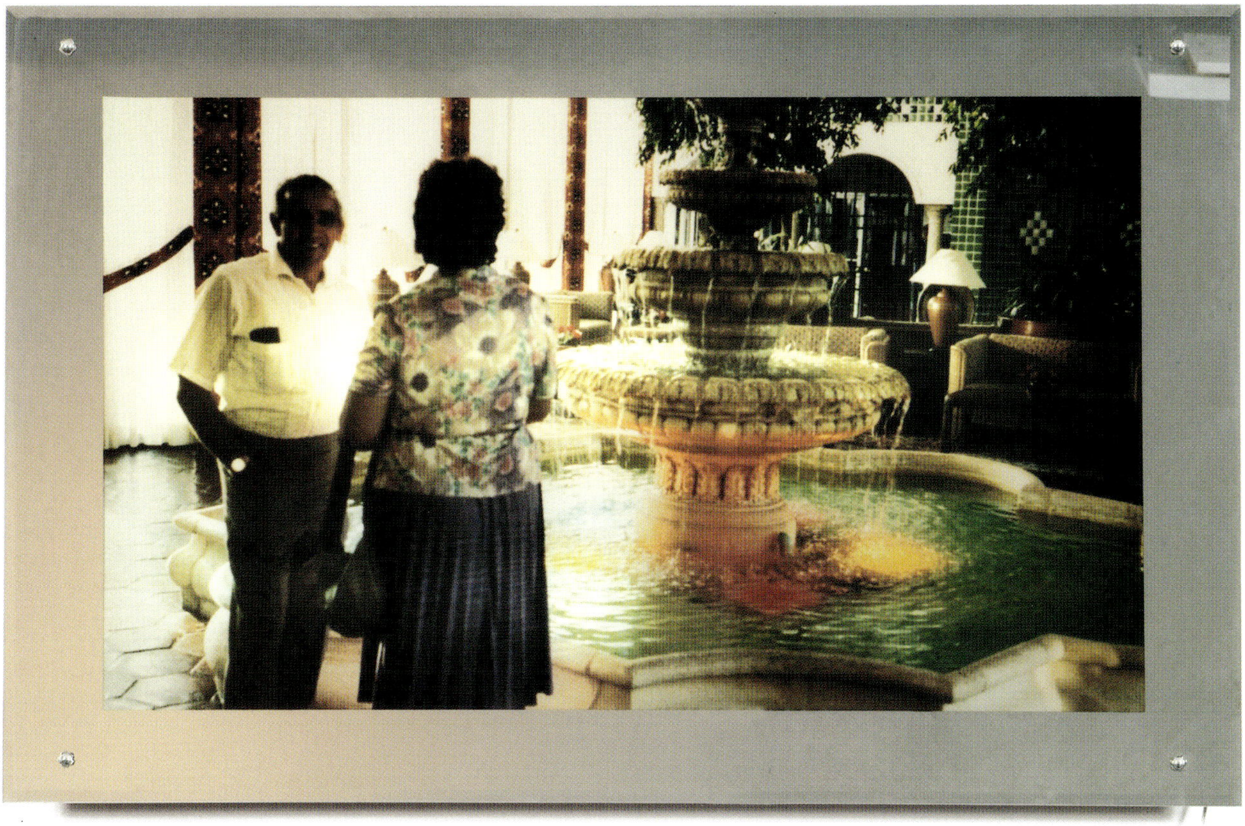

The Fountain, 2004. Dura-tran, moving light box, 24" x 18".

CRISTINA LEI **RODRIGUEZ**

The gardens I tend to are within my studio. I cultivate, prune and primp my sculptures to represent a moment in nature that is frozen in time. By staging an instant I can reveal and explore the complexity of life in different stages and environments. My art practice requires a combination of chance and control to sustain a resemblance to the natural world. I control my sculptures by considering and choosing objects, color, form, and content. Multiple layers of plastic, foam, paint, and glitter are then sprinkled and poured onto my sculptures to create a surface with history and complexity. I am influenced by the baroque and minimal, and I consider how these competing influences co-exist in my work. Gardens fulfill the human urge to control and enjoy nature. They are created to provide distraction from the realities of everyday life. The garden is also a place of display for the gardener to express her belief's and values through the type of garden that she keeps. They reflect the time and place in which they are made, and I am interested in how my artwork operates in this same way.

My studio is at a house in Miami, where I grew up and now live, that used to belong to my grandparents. I use the patio of the house, a well ventilated work space, to build my sculptures and safely use the plastics they are made with. For me, the materials and colors I use in my sculptures remind me of the Miami around me. Here, people are obsessed with the new. The newest car, club, sunglasses, condo, diet, whatever it is, in Miami we want to be a new city. This desire promotes non-stop construction so that we will never look old. This new city is in constant negotiation between the built and the natural environment. Both sides are backed with power and fury that support accelerated growth. We are about to begin a long humid summer here in our subtropical climate, which means constant hurricane threats, swarms of mosquitoes and termites, and an abundance of mangos and avocados. From my studio patio, I can see the landscape is lush, green and alive from getting so much rain. During the hot summer the built environment keeps me calm with air conditioning and pesticides. My sculptures imitate the wildness of nature, with the sterility of plastic consumer goods. Some sculptures are completely overrun by nature, fierce and chaotic and others are more maintained and manipulated and ornate.

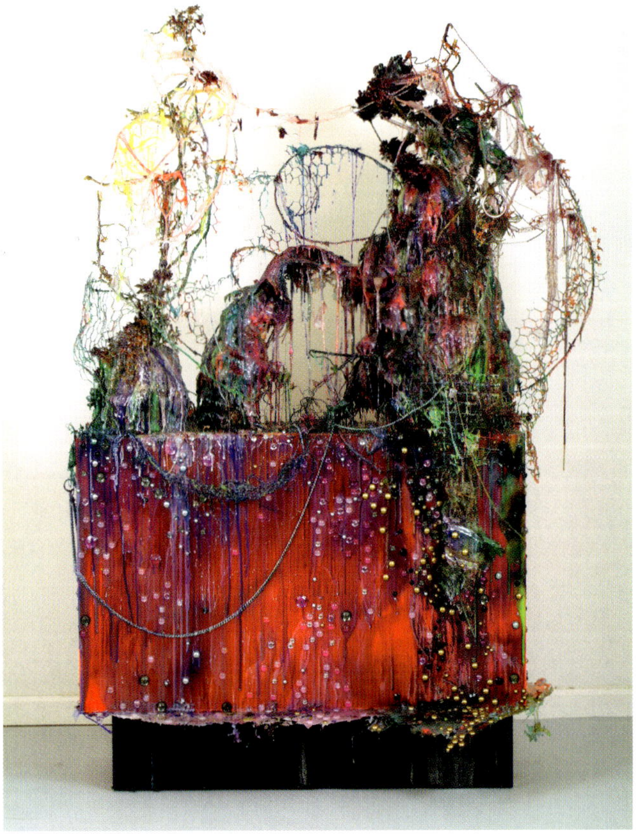

After the Storm (Rock Formations), 2005.
Plastic, foam, epoxy, paint, plexi and selected objects, 48" x 75" x 34".

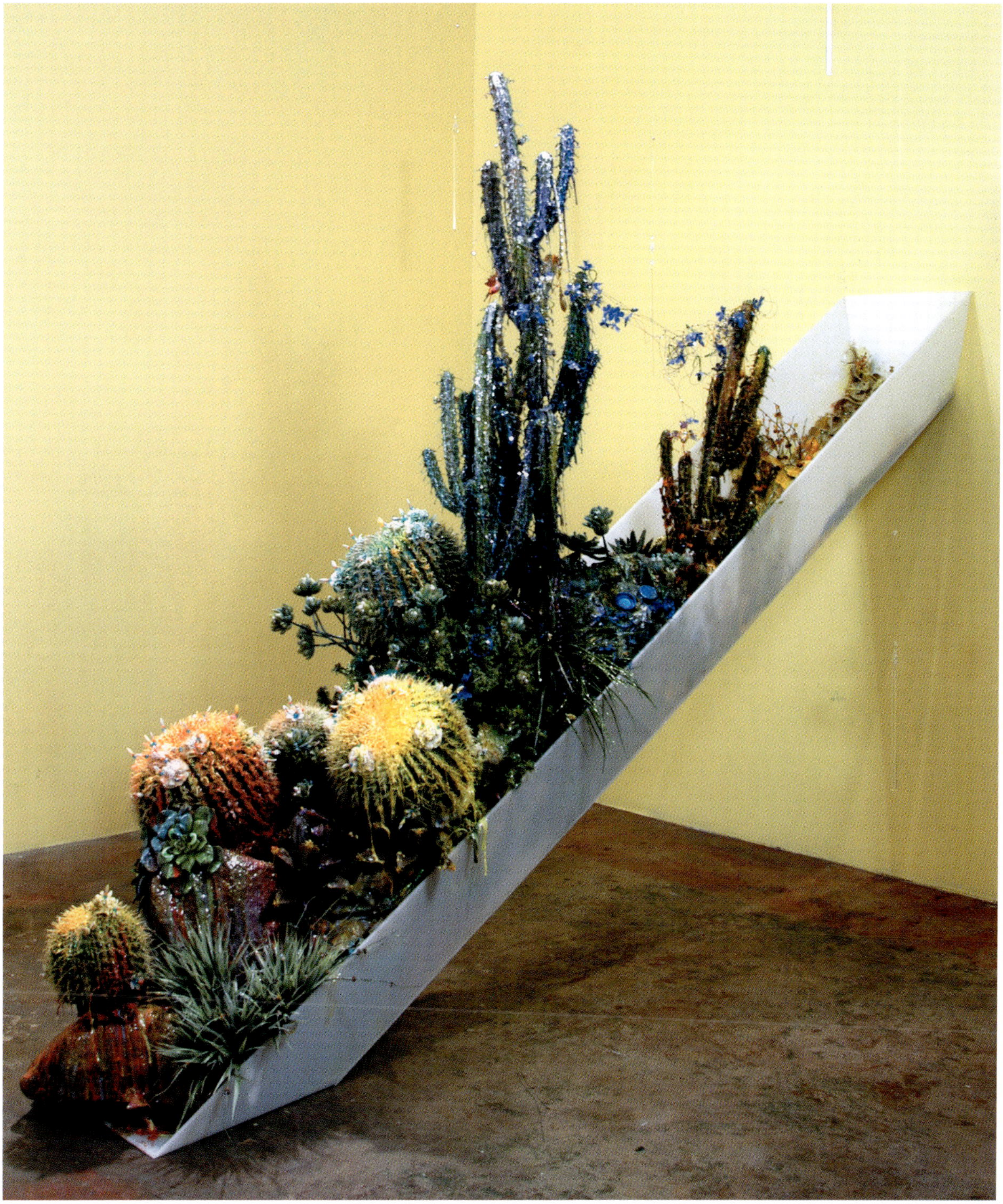

Experimental Garden (desert), 2005. Plastic, foam, epoxy, paint, plexi, and selected objects, 85" x 24' x 111". *Courtesy of the artist and the Rubell Family Collection*

NORBERTO **RODRIGUEZ**

My name is Bert (you can call me Norbs). I have a very soft beard and extraordinarily tender ways. I draw some of my undying inspiration from Sharif, toothless sweeties on Biscayne, pups, dipeys, and beef tartare. I hope that, through my work, I can get across that I am, above all, a peanut-headed man whose soul truly cries from the gutter.

I live here.

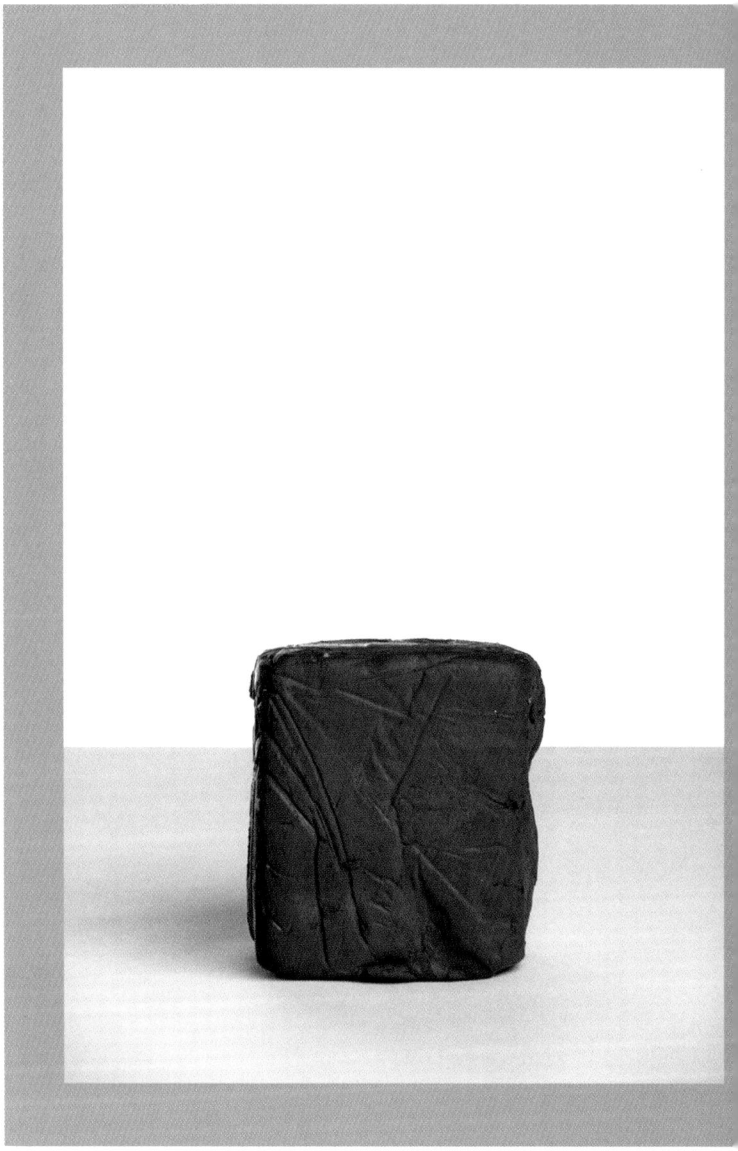

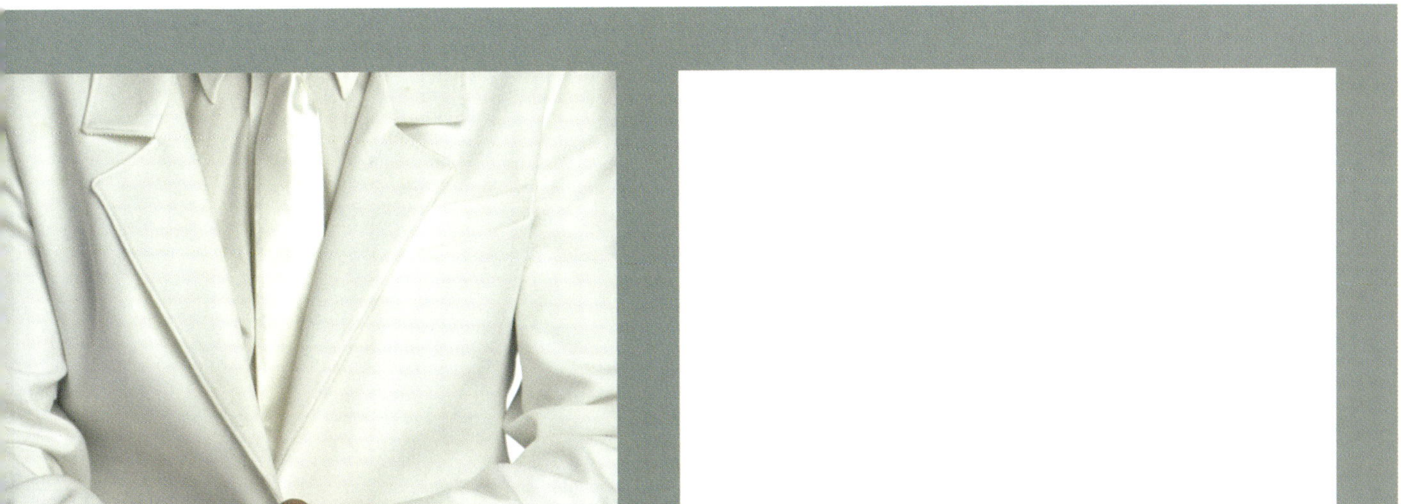

How God Makes Snakes, 2006. Cibachrome, set of three each, 30" X 20".

DAVID ROHN

Making art: painting, sculpture, drawing, or performance, for me is about trying to organize and integrate all the different elements of experience both internal and external, past and present, spiritual, mental and emotional, for my own satisfaction and peace of mind. I find there is a lot of complexity and paradox in my experience, and that trying to fit the pieces together that may or may not at first appear any more consistent or harmonious than life experience is basically what I am trying to do with "Art." That's the content. As for formal considerations, I am interested in working off or dialoguing with other artists past and present who have spoken to me through their work or who have developed things that seem like appropriate responses to experience. Sometimes you want to try to build on what they've done or maybe just walk your way through their path to see where it might lead you. Recently, that has included for me, Mondrian, Kandinsky, Bacon, David Smith, Robert Mangold, Phillip Glass, Frank Zappa, Beckmann, Robin Williams, Basquiat, and Haim Steinbach. For me Artistic work is not the repetition of the same exercise over and over. Instead it is like research, so it also becomes an exercise in openness and experimentation as well as frustration and perseverance. Getting the work out is not always possible, but it is important to participate at least with other involved artists.

I've been in Miami for 14 years and it's changed enormously since then. After a lot of evolution and devolution, things seem much more defined and commercial now though I think artists also have more opportunity to sell art and be seen by a wider audience than before. Earlier if you lived on the beach there was a good sense of creative community. Now it's all spread out. There is no artist neighborhood – wherever artists move to seems to become a site for massive real estate speculation. That coupled with the lack of public transportation and all the recent construction has made Miami a city where one has to combat a sense of isolation. That said, the existence of websites and blogs has in some ways countered this. Hopefully the disappearance or expropriation of the grass roots art venues like the House, the Box, the Home Shows, Locust Projects, (this was an especially creative phase) is also countered by grassroots internet activity. Having lived in other cities Miami is noticeably short in offering opportunity to see and assimilate past art. Both major museums are focused on art since World War II so the focus on Contemporary Art is particularly sharp. The lack of even any architecture from pre-1920 allows us to ignore whatever happened before 1920. This is a remarkable contrast to Rome, Italy for example where the Museum of Modern Art has scarcely any art made after 1940 in its collection. They're building a museum of contemporary art soon. I guess Miami seems like a brash and irreverent, young and flashy town brimming with energy that has shown it to be roughly the equal of any the other city focused on the contemporary art industry.

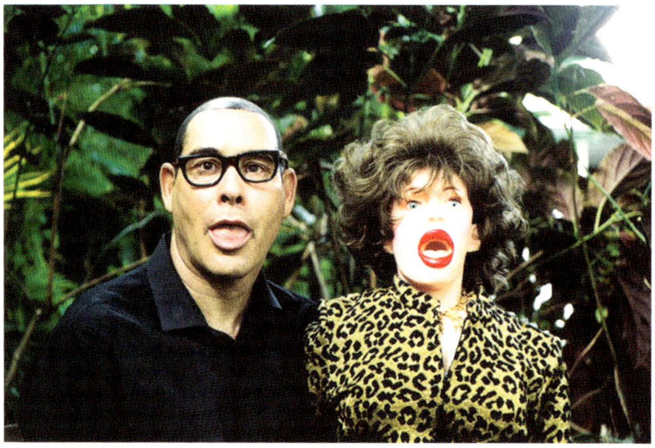

Herb and Kitty Katzenjammer Kontemporary Art Kollectors, 2002. Cibachrome photo on paper, 35" x 47".

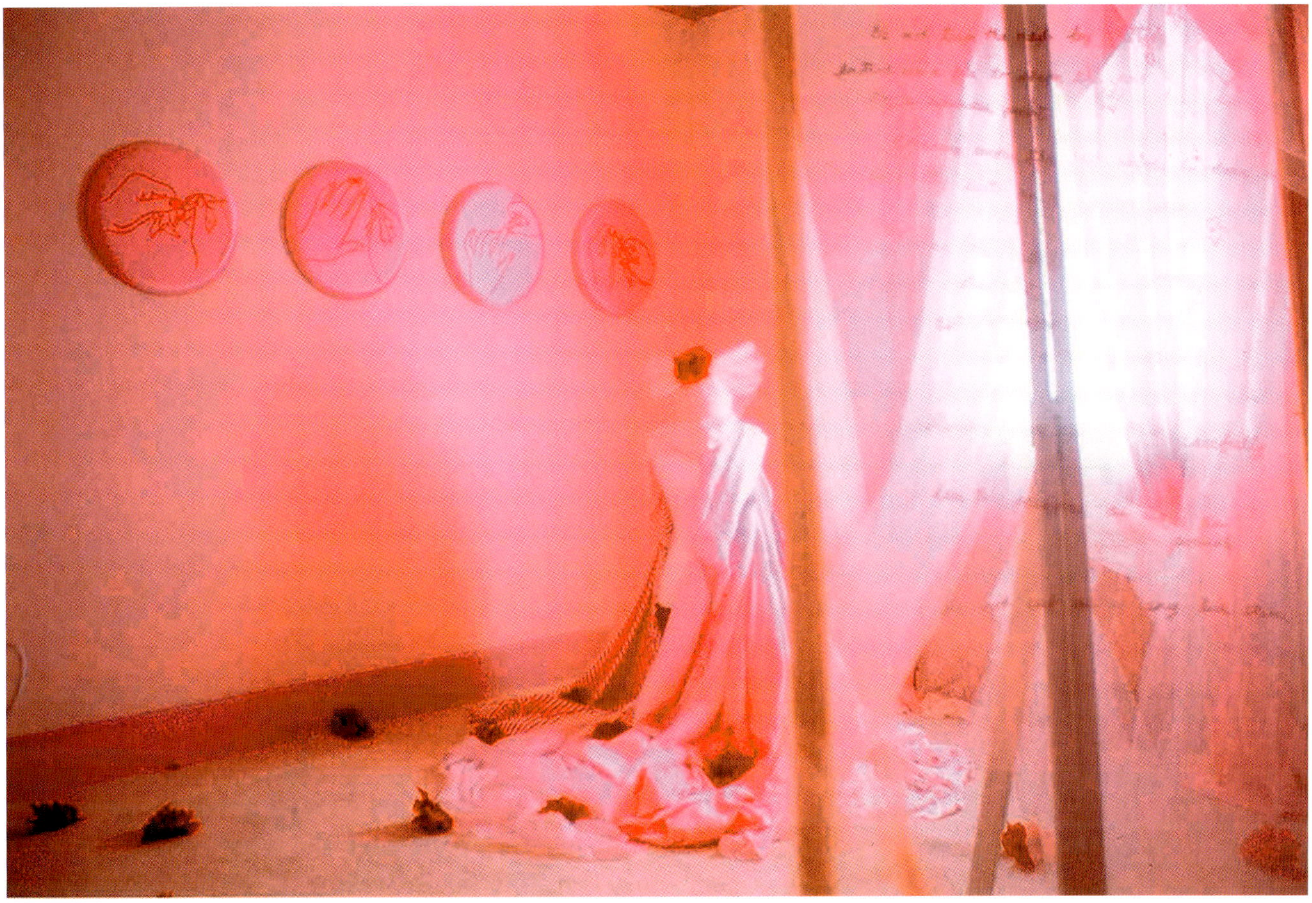

Le Chateau del Pueblo Model Home – Little Girl's Room, 2001. Mixed media including mannequin, manicure on glass (in foreground), manicure illustrations (on wall), variable dimensions. From performance and installation at Brooke Dorsch Gallery.

GUSTAVO **ROMÁN**

Sexual tension, gender ambiguity and the myth of male sexual prowess are some recurrent themes I explore. A lot of my work speaks of an exaggerated sexuality, which renders itself useless achieving a state of ridicule, anti-sensual at best. The work is a hyperbole of our cultural ideas of sex and sensuality. It comments on the sensual body as a projection of the self, of identity and our cult of it. The work's scale speaks of the private and personal, of intimacy and shyness, as well as the forbidden and taboo.

Worldwide attention is on our young city. It is exciting to be an artist in a town with international patronage. But unlike Paris, Rome and New York – Miami has no deep roots. It is often a transient place. People fly in and hurricanes blow them out again. But that is the allure; Miami has no real sense of identity. I believe it is my job, our job as artists to give this stop-over for the jet set a tangible self. We will make Miami real beyond the glitz. Art can create identity and permanence.

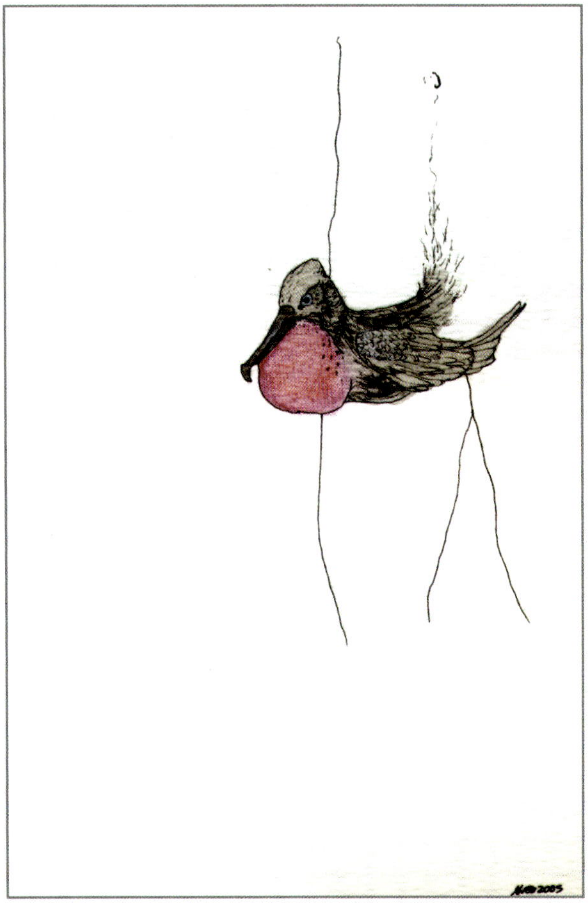

Untitled (Magnificent Frigate bird), 2005. Pen, ink, gouache on paper, 6" x 9".

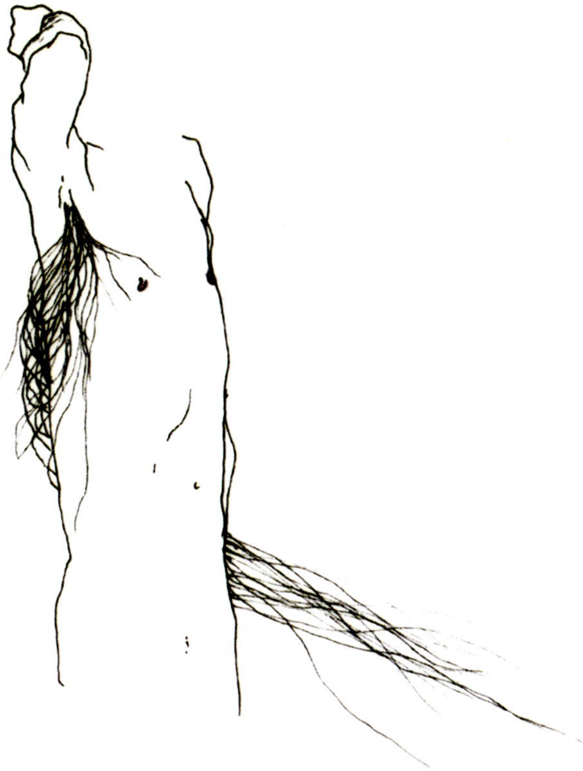

Erotic as an Ape, 2005. Pen and ink on paper, 11" x 14".

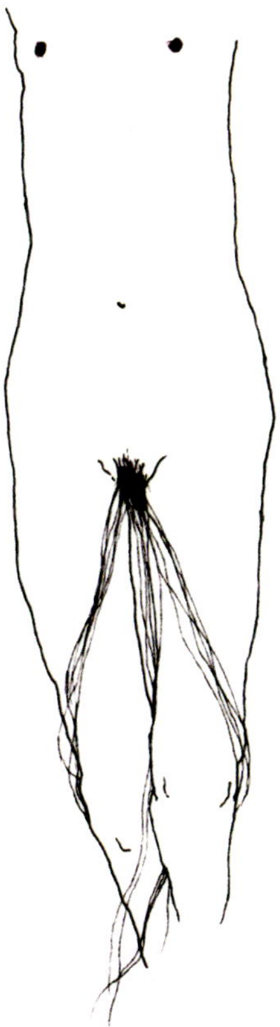

Erotic as an Ape 2, 2005. Pen and ink on paper, 11" x 14".

BETTY ROSADO

It started out as a simple idea: to shoot images of some of South Florida's established and emerging artists, folks who also happened to be friends of mine. I met them over the past few years while living and working in an electric, gentrifying Miami growing more interesting by the day. I made a few phone calls and they all agreed to sit for sessions. But something happened along the way. I realized the project could be about more than just shooting a few friends. It became clear to me that I was recording an evolving society, a city changing right before our eyes. The folks I was shooting all represented this new Miami. But I felt that to do justice to this project, more artists than the ones who were in my speed dial needed to be included. Everybody knows that South Florida's art scene is booming. The art world watches our every move as we continue to grow into a mecca in our own right. Many of my subjects have been a fundamental part of this movement from the very beginning. Long before there was a Performing Arts Center under construction, or an Art Basel Miami Beach, these artists were making names for themselves, and laying the groundwork for the vibrant arts community that we have become. My ideal is to be able to capture each and every one of these outstanding characters; the ones who have been at it for years, and the ones who are beginning to make waves now – because together, they represent a culturally maturing Miami ripe with new possibility. Once I realized that the moment we are living is an important moment in our history, it dawned on me the significance of documenting it all. It is a far larger undertaking than I had originally imagined, but it is my way to credit the people who are lending color and originality to a city on the verge of something big.

Betty Rosado is a photographer keenly adept at rendering the unspoken, searching her subjects and illuminating their truths with a keen sense for the intimate and the revealing. She is currently producing a portrait series on artists working in South Florida. What began as a simple project to photograph friends who happen to be artists has expanded into an ambitious five-year project of recording the seemingly endless ranks of emerging and established Miami

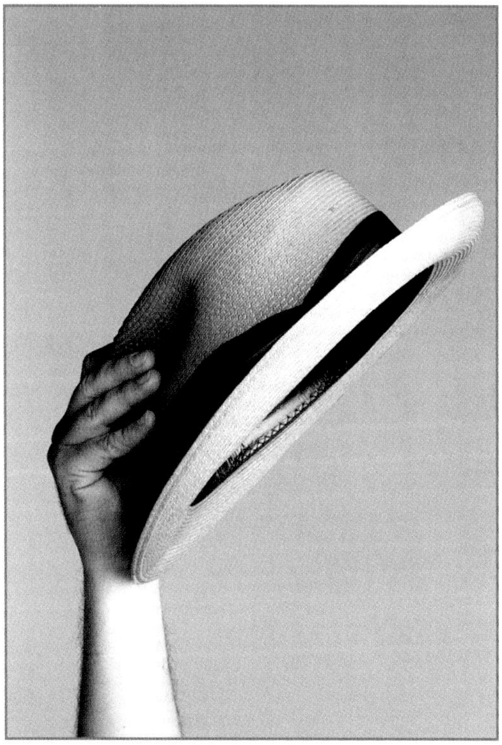

Roberto Behar, 2004. Black and white silver gelatin print, 40" x 60".

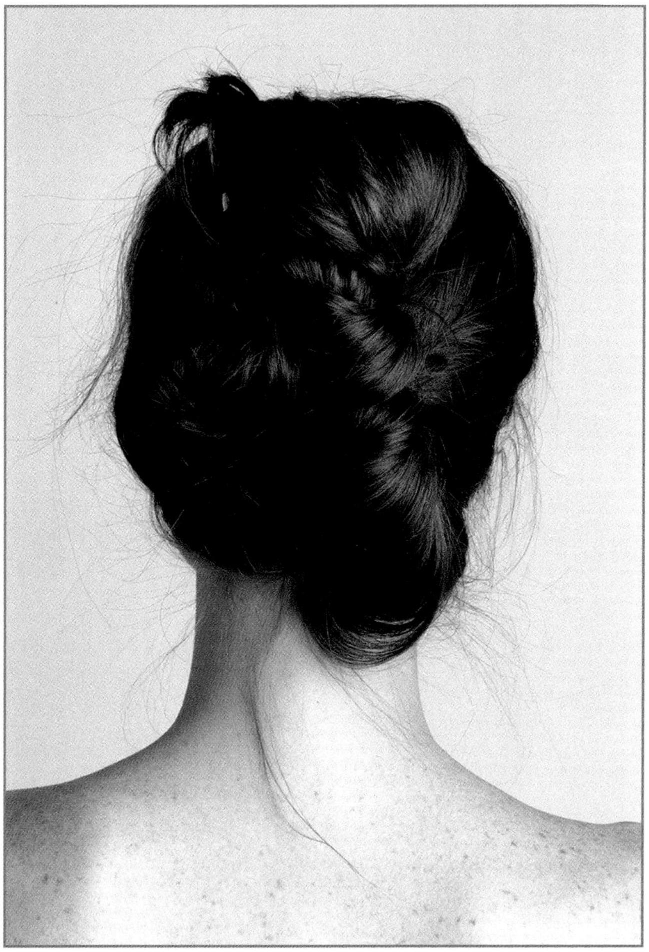

Frances Trombly, 2005. Black and white vintage silver Gelatin print, 20" x 24".

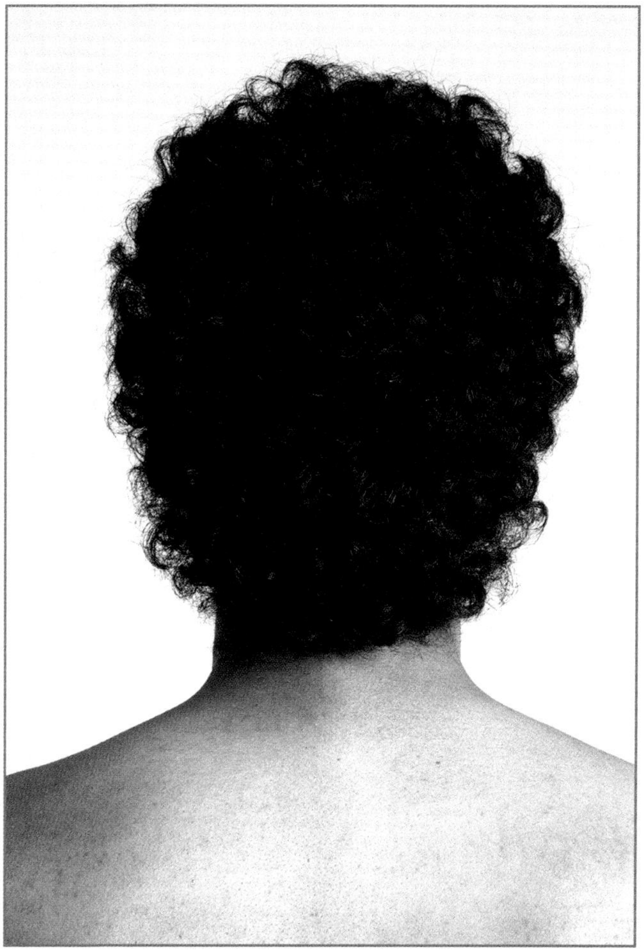

Leyden Rodriguez-Casanova, 2005, black and white vintage silver gelatin print, 20" x 24".

RAYMOND SAÁ

My work tries to show the experience of amalgamated living within an urban multi cultural city such as Miami, and the shared and secret spaces that different cultures inhabit. I approach this from a first generation American's point of view. Raised by my exiled mother and maternal grandparents, I experienced their feelings of displacement. My own came from a space in constant conflict, between the survival of their heritage and my experiences outside of the family.

The tropical floral imagery I use reveals a sometimes menacing feel that describes some of the dichotomy in the experience of immigrants living in America – the promised opportunities versus the confusion of a new and competitive culture, and the hitherto unrecognized strength of the now forsaken culture of ones home country.

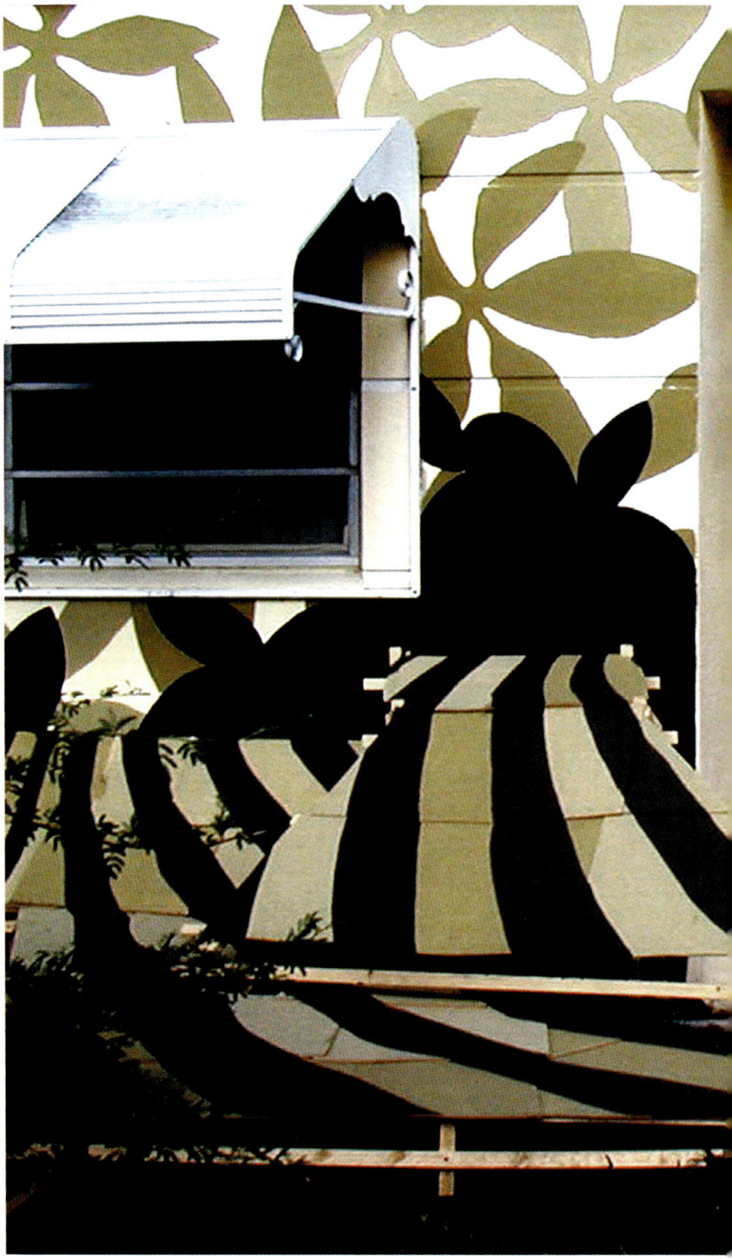

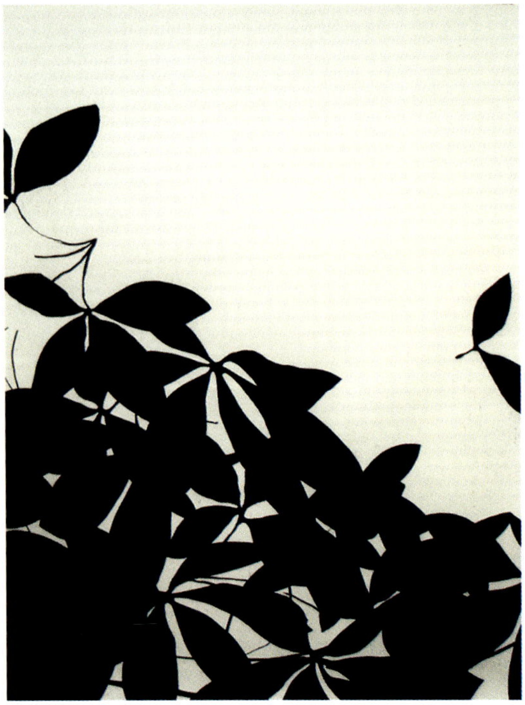

Untitled, 2006, charcoal on paper, 48" x 36".

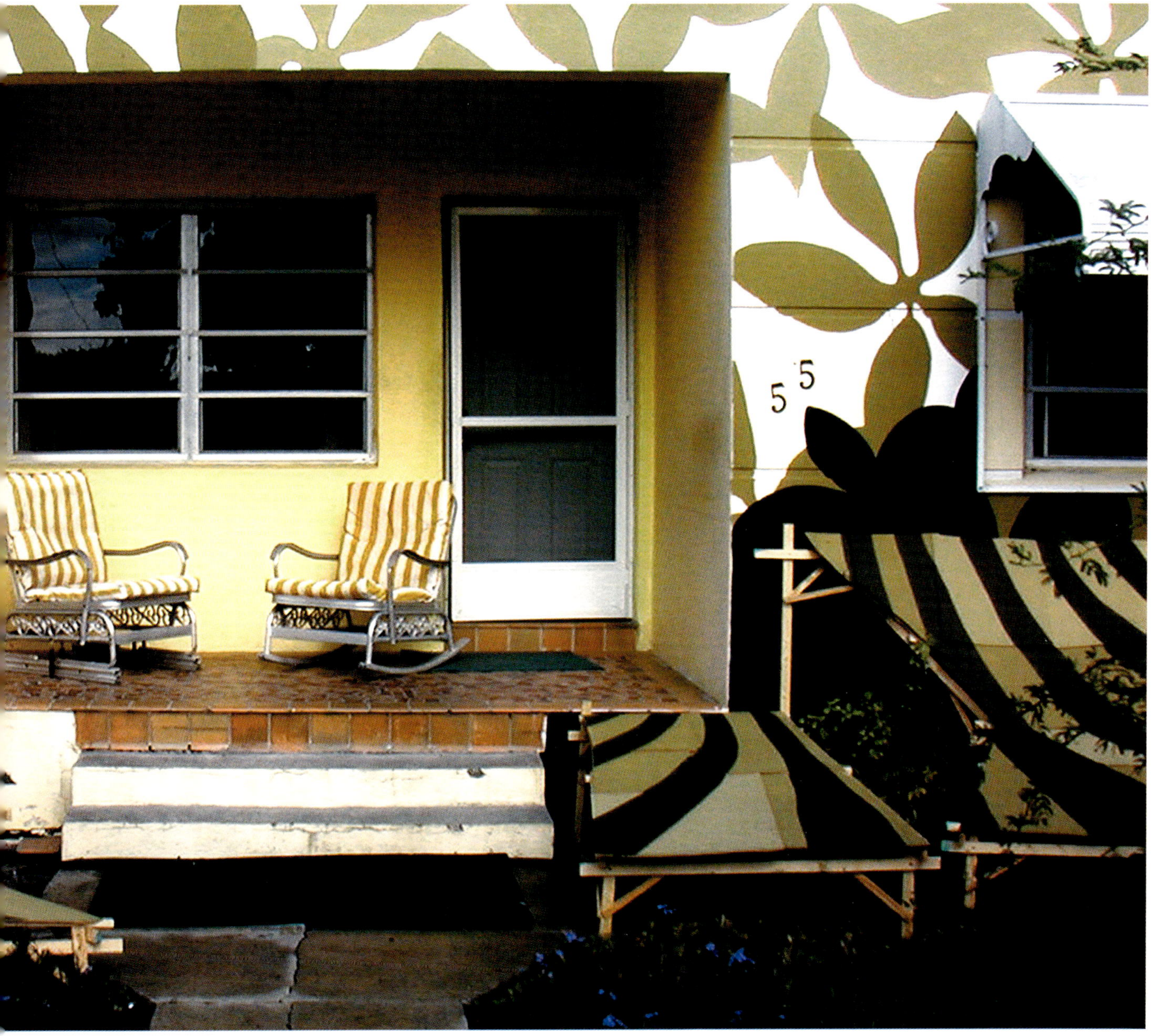

Si las casas pudiesen hablar(If Houses Could Talk), 2004 ,#2 of 2 painted houses. *The Yard at Casa Lin; Wynwood, Miami, FL*

GEORGE **SÁNCHEZ-CALDERÓN**

"La Bendicion" involved the re-creation in eighty percent scale of Le Corbusier's masterpiece the "Villa Savoye," under Interstate 395 in downtown Miami, Florida. The artwork called into question the goals of modernism by juxtaposing the quintessential modern home with the harsh realities of the blight-ridden area under interstate 395. The immediate area under the I-395 freeway where *"The Blessing / La Bendicion"* was placed is infamous for prostitution and the panhandling of crack-cocaine and heroin. *La Bendicion / The Blessing* remained lit every day from sunset to sunrise for three years. The only damage that ever came to the structure was due to the hurricanes and tropical storms that frequent South Florida. *"Plinth / Monument / Stoop"* involved recreating the Plinth of a Monument with a set of steps leading to the top of it. For those individuals that choose to, they rose to the top of the Plinth and became a sculptural work of art that frequently adorns cities. During the month that the sculpture was located on its site, individuals walking by rested on the steps of the sculpture thereby activating it as a stoop. *"Plinth / Monument / Stoop"* was originally executed out of plywood in Overtown, Florida adjacent to the I-395 Freeway in March of 2006. The participants were documented and images were printed and gifted them.

George Sánchez-Calderón was born in New York City in 1967 the son of Cuban exiles. His family re-located to Miami, Florida where Mr. Sánchez-Calderón has lived for the majority of his life. Mr. Sánchez-Calderón received his Bachelors in Fine Arts degree from Florida International University and Masters in Fine Arts degree from the Rhode Island School of Design in 1995. He had his first one-man exhibit at the Franklin Furnace Archive in New York City in 1996. Silvia Karmen-Cubiña has described Mr. Sánchez-Calderón's work as being "*context-driven public installations and architectural re-interpretations that confront the viewer due to their social and political content.*" His work is in the permanent collection of the Miami Art Museum, Museum of Contemporary Art, North Miami, Margulies Collection, Craig Robins Collection and the Carlos and Rosa de la Cruz collection. Mr. Sánchez-Calderón is the recipient of the Oscar B. Cintas Fellowship and the South Florida Cultural Consortium Award.

Coming back home to Miami after being in grad school was a conscious choice. I wanted to be near the family to spend quality time with them being they were getting older. I could drive a convertible in Miami and buy an apartment. As opposed to renting a studio in NY I could buy a building in Miami. Also, there is something about Miami, which makes me think of going out west, mid-nineteenth century. Miami is free of parameters. We are not re-creating anything but creating something anew. I love the ocean, the blue skies and Cuban Coffee. Most people I know don't understand what it is that I do, and that's alright. Explaining it to them is part of the process.

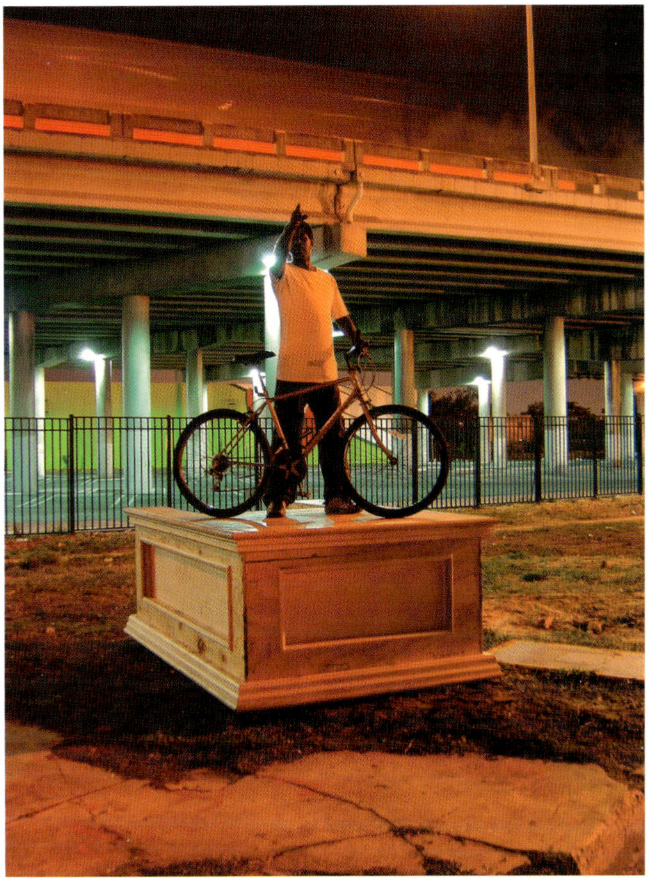

Plinth/Monument Stoop (Man with Bicycle), 2006. Wood, 3′ x 5′ x 8′.

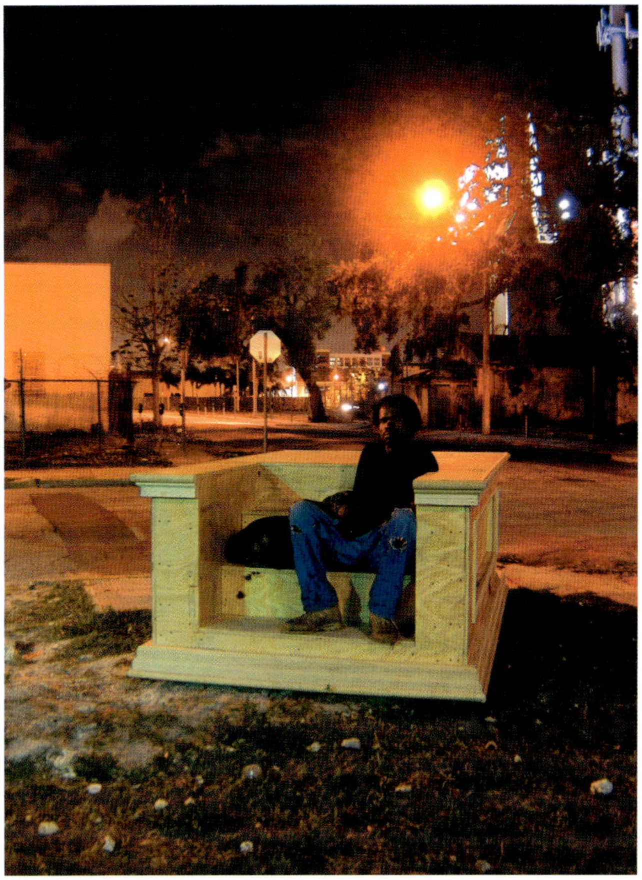

Plinth/Monument Stoop (Man Seated), 2006. Wood, 3′ x 5′ x 8′.

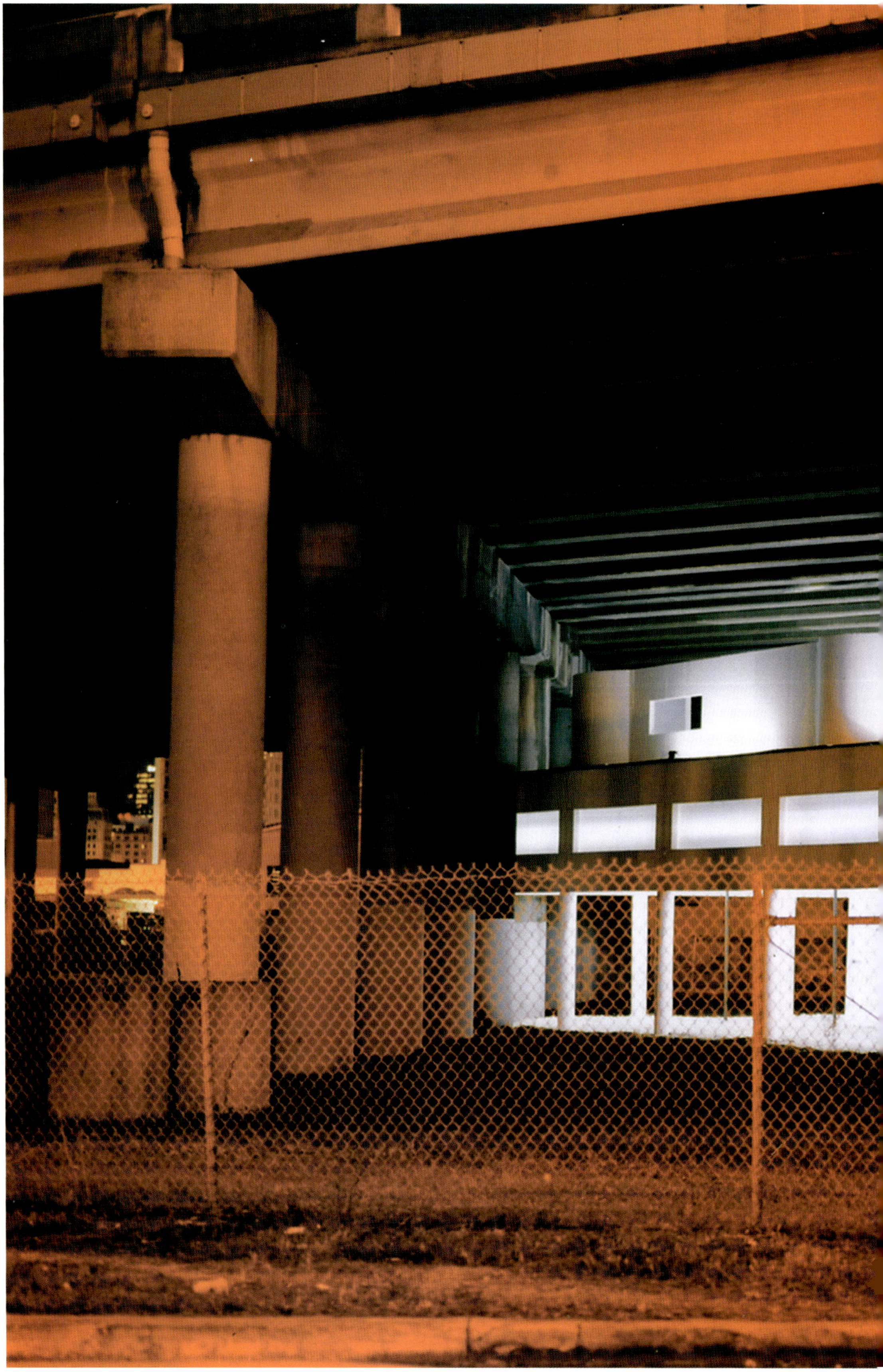

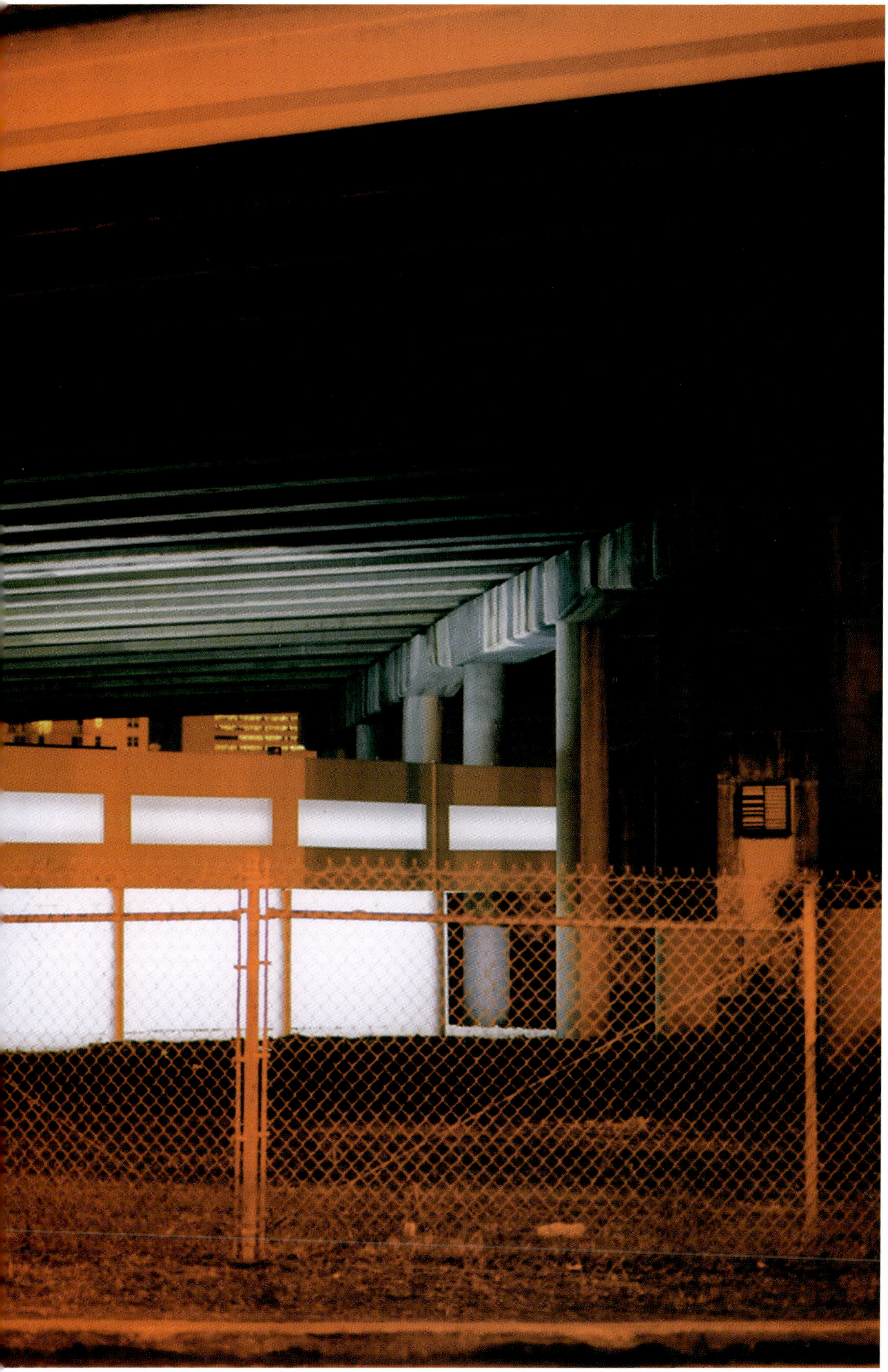

La Bendicion, 2001-2004, re-creation of Le Corbusier's Villa Savoye under the I-395 freeway. Steel, concrete, EPS foam, neon ,48′ x 48′ x 23′.

REEVE SCHUMACHER

Birthed into a cold world on a colder morning in 1981 was an artist known to few as Snug the Joiner. Although his spirit better resembles a Puck the Miter, most have come to know him as Reeve the Schumacher.

Born in Minneapolis, Minnesota Reeve Schumacher graduated from the University of Miami in 2003 with BFA in Sculptural Ceramics as well as a minor in Art History and Motion Pictures. Drawing is certainly the foundation of his art, but no means the final conclusion. His most recent series include record album manipulation and Polaroid transformations. Skilled and young, Schumacher creates mind-tripping evocations of unrestrained subconscious. Dreams and the duality of man are themes that his art frequently addresses. By molding quasi-grotesque and beautifully haunting clay masks to working with transferred drawings on acetate (transparency) of various figures on sundry Polaroid's for backdrops; or arranging human face/butterfly wing vinyl's on layered glass compositions. Seemingly independent elements are combined in layers as words of symbols in a poem. Inserted backgrounds serve as a schema for the subject. The Polaroid Cell Series offers the opportunity for lines of the artist's pen a place in reality with the unique photograph itself as the background. In the Mixed Media Cell Series, the photo is replaced by a more conceptual environment. The various printed papers like sheet music, maps, wall paper and drawing transfers imply a context, situating the drawn cell within. *(A. Hayes)*

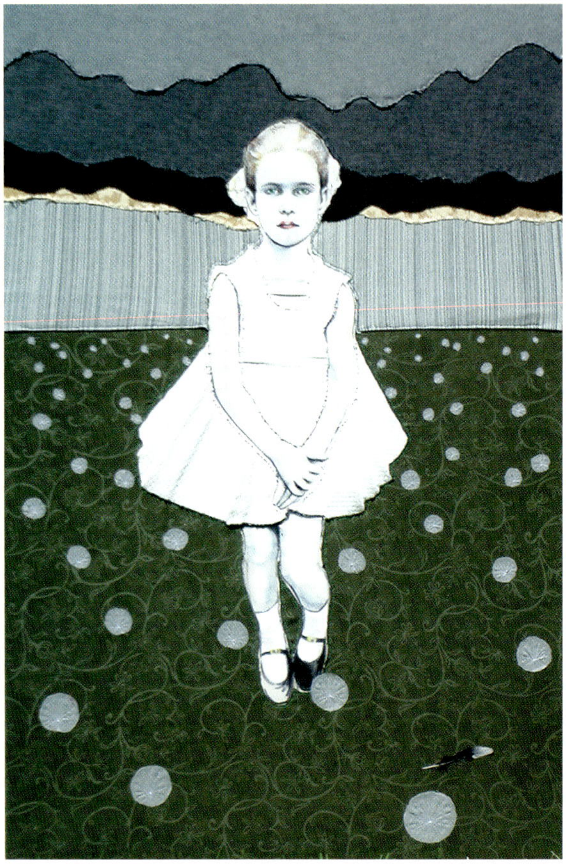

Lesley, 2006. Mixed media, 49" x 34".

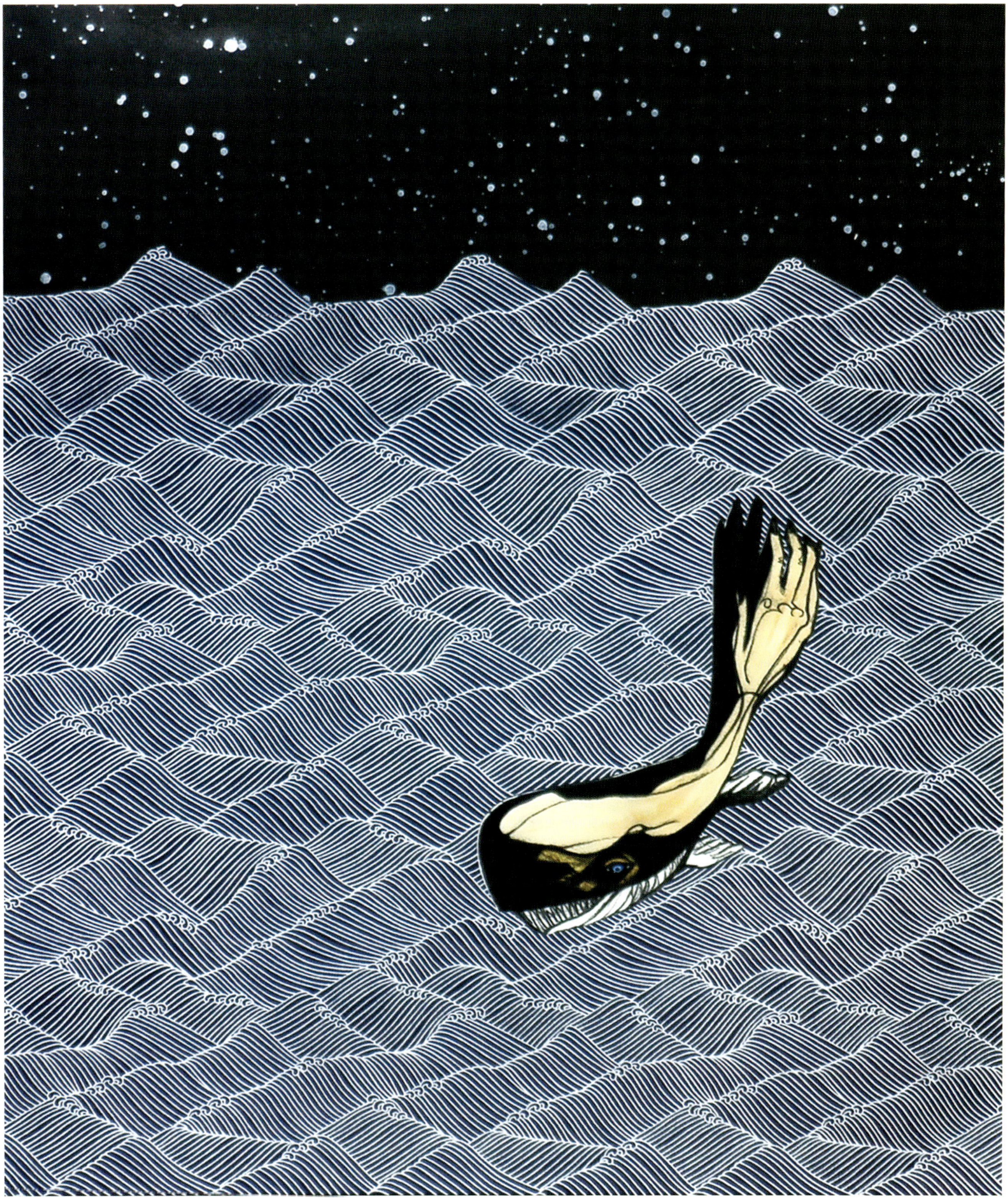

Inside the belly of the whale, 2006. Mixed media, 30" x 27".

ONAJIDE SHABAKA

Art is a language that communicates a certain type of knowledge and a perception of the world that matters. The premise that if one could do away with the exterior shackles that restrict ones development, then one could (and would) be freer to express one's innermost self, limited only by one's own talent and imagination. With such great freedom there is also a great responsibility, great discipline, and the obligation to channel that freedom into some coherent, meaningful expression. It also takes a masterful command of one's craft, so that one can in a moment of contemplation convincingly initiate an idea and respond in some creative, responsive way. This process is a journey much like working ones way through a mangrove forest, a mesh of both land and water, which in its fluidity and borderlessness is open to influence and change. Deleuze and Guattari suggest such border zones are sites of challenge and creation. With my art I want to outline a new or different site in which to center aesthetic investigations away from the resultant art image or object and, on to the entire context of life and our relationship to it. I have forged a path for my artistic interests that challenge the status quo of the mainstream art world, especially the hermeticism and austerity of the white cubic gallery space. At the same time, my work, in its engagement with nature, history, technology, and ritual, allows the viewers to experience a more holistic view of the world.

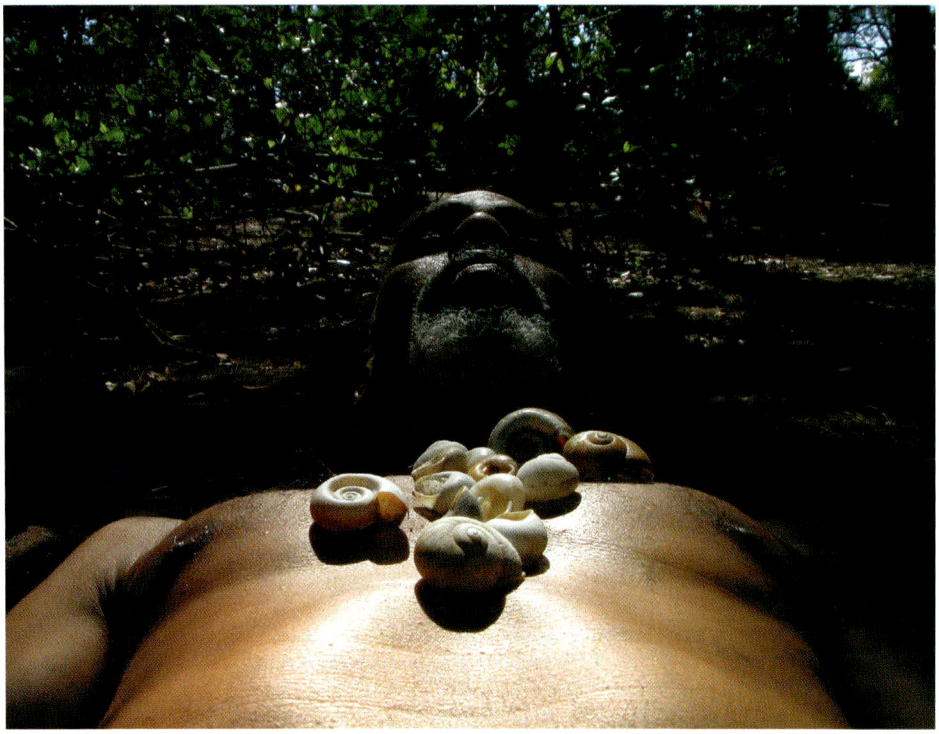

Untitled (shells on body) 2005. Light jet print on paper, 8" x 10".

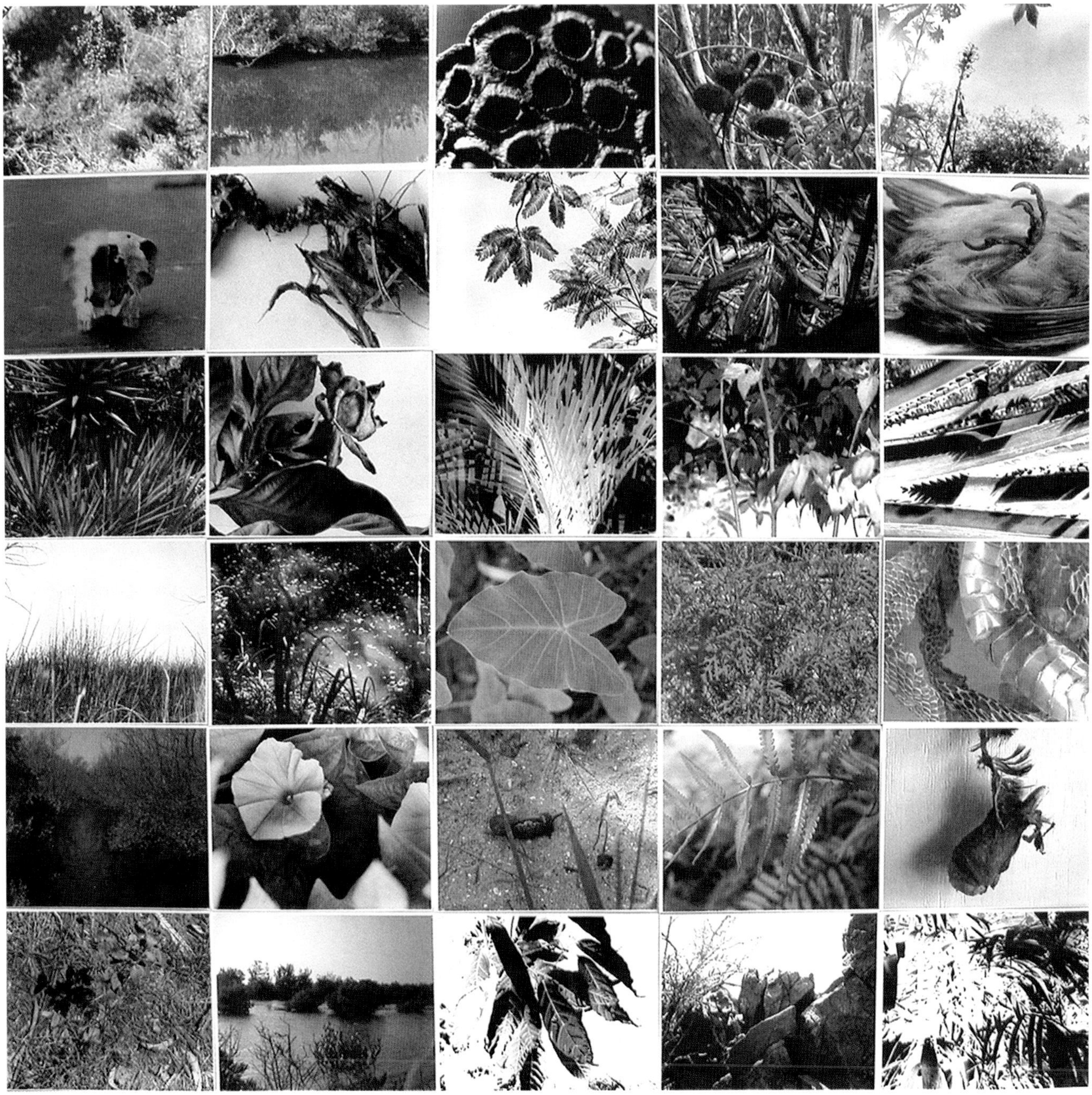
37 Years, 2005. Silver gelatin prints, 120" x 96".

TAWNIE **SILVA**, WITH LOU LAURITA

When people ask me "what is your medium," I say "language." My interest is in mastering the text, not the materials. The materials are critical in terms of conveying the message, not becoming it. Idealistically I use words or phrases that possess positive ideas, and realistically I tell truths with a sense of irony. These truths express the fortunate or unfortunate realities of existence. I have the same voice but in different tones. My work has no visual continuity. When I speak my voice comes out in different volumes, shapes, colors, luminosities, densities, sizes, and speeds. Words can manipulate us into many places depending on the content and where the emphasis is placed. That's how I think about sculpture. While using text there is an automatic connection in my brain's inventory to the experience and how I relate to the content. It is like reading a book that has no pictures. What I remember is a visual experience. The idea that one or multiple words, in their simplicity, combined with the diversity of viewers, creates a different individual experience for each person, from action to reaction. In works where I combine a digital image or a drawn image with language I try to create a visual vocabulary that engages the viewer the same way. In my collaborative work with Lou Laurita, we use image in language which allows us to add to a narrative or create two contradictory narratives within the same piece. In my Velcro pieces the drawings do not illustrate the language but act as a separate idea, challenging the viewer to see that language in different ways.

I found a really cool apartment that was a block away from the water. A little piece of paradise for a penny, the beauty of an island, the vibe of a city. The beautiful architecture and soothing palette of this once elegant resort had become an artist's colony with vacant store fronts as studios so the arts have always been integral to the reinvention of South Beach. And as the city became a resort destination so did it become a destination for artists and collectors. The city is constantly moving, shifting, and redefining itself providing fertile ground for artists. Despite the international attention, the art scene has maintained a lack of pretense and remains genial with risk that sustains a quality level equal to that of any major city. I feel a strong sense of optimism even with the fear of another wave of gentrification. Cranes from north to south map out the future sky line. Art Deco buildings and vintage signs, remnants of the city's hey days permeate the fringe of a beautiful rebirth of a stunning city that's nostalgic with a contemporary edge. Art is refreshing, youthful, and charged. Alternative spaces pop up constantly. Young curators turn their apartments into project spaces. To be an artist in the middle of this emergence is exhilarating. Is there another way of saying right place, right time?

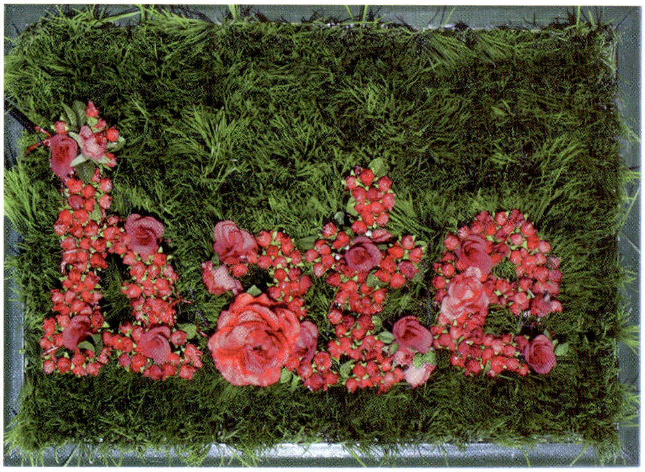

Welcome Home, 2005. Plastic, silk, LED lights, 24" x 32".

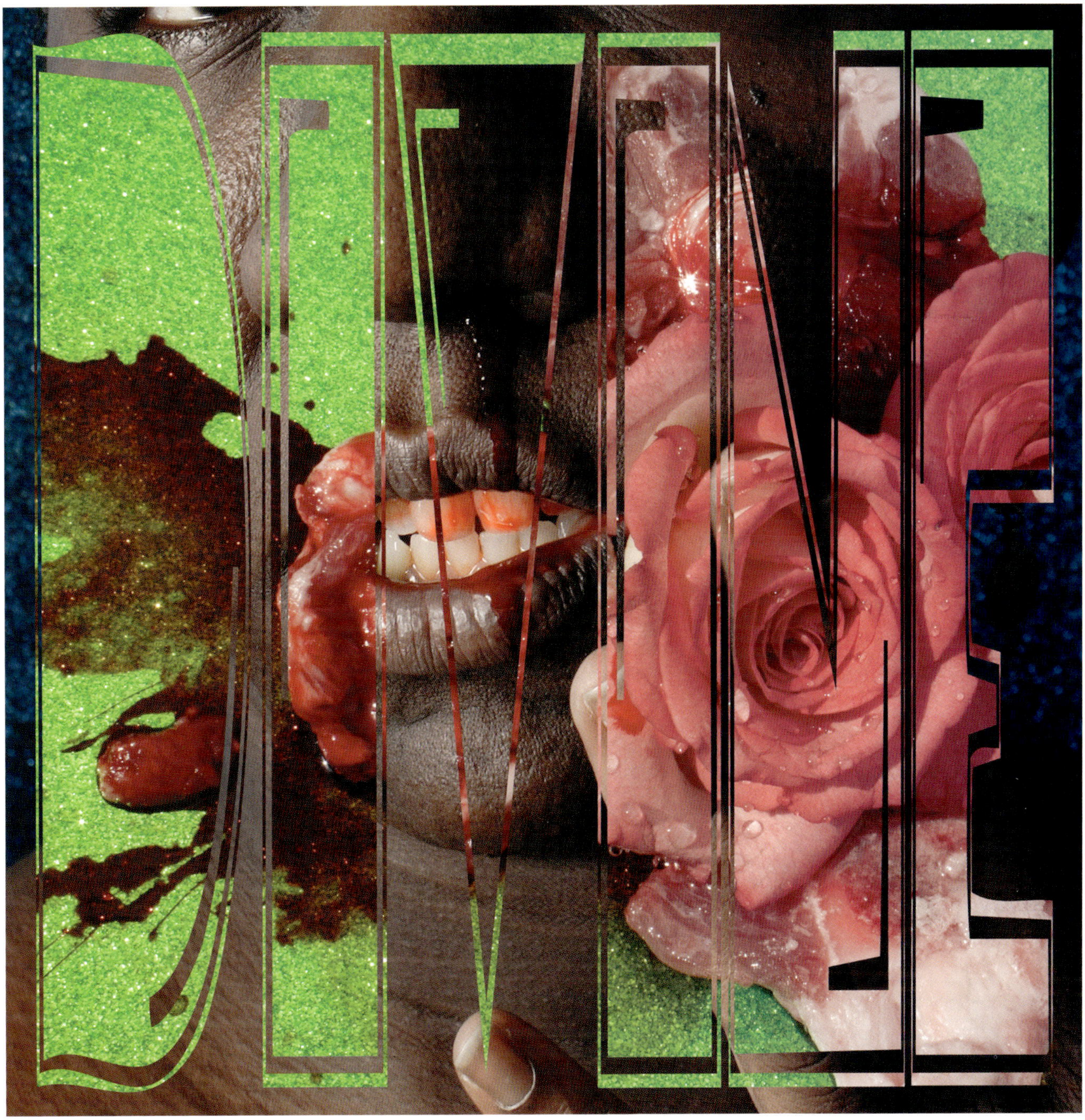

Divine, 2006. Photo collage, 24" x 24". Collaboration with Lou Laurita

ALETTE SIMMONS-JIMENEZ

From a family of mixed heritage, Polish Jews and German Lutherans, we were also like drifters, constantly packing and unpacking, setting up a new home every few months. My current home is #22. Consistency and stability are not the foundation of my personality. Line-curling, turning, angled or twisted, for me is the single most important element of expression. Lines figure strongly in my paintings, from the under drawings to scratched, cross-hatchings directly in the oil, or as symbolic elements patterned across the surface. They exist in my sculptural objects, from the sketches, to thin lines of wire woven to build a final form. In my video work line appears overtly or other times as a mental road map, leading the question "Who are we, where do we come from, and where are we going?" Rather than setting stylistic limitations, my working method is a wandering exploration. I enjoy experimenting with constructive and material aesthetics, socio-political perceptions, and the planned versus the accidental, using a dialogue of pluralism that engages and modifies divergent artistic practices. Wind, water, earth, and stone are frequently a point of departure. The idea evolves often with a bit of humor or whimsy, along with a crystal clear mental picture dictating the media to be used. I engage the viewer to consider the rushing, stumbling, twisting, & turning course of man's expedient manipulations.

For me it is important that my work is constantly changing, allowing for growth and improvement upon each previous body of work. Returning to the US and Miami, after 18 years working in the Dominican Republic, has had a profound impact on my work. I was forced to sharpen my focus and make hard critical judgments about my own work's direction. The competition and opportunities have been 90% positive and exhilarating, yet there is always, at least, a 10% of compromising for the consumer, that if left unchecked will swallow an artist whole. So much in an artist's career depends on luck. I have never had a lucky break and any achievement has been due to obsessive hard work. However, making the decision to relocate to Florida, and particularly Miami, 13 years ago seems to have been perhaps my lucky break. During these 13 years I have experienced the birth of a center of international cultural exchange and my work has found inspiration in the challenge. Still, only a very few can be chosen by that one fabulous gallery who handles it all while we retire to the studio and work. Just living in Miami, even at this time, will not bring an artist any measure of success. For most of us to have that happen, we must actively engage our community, become involved at whatever level is comfortable, get out there and get noticed.

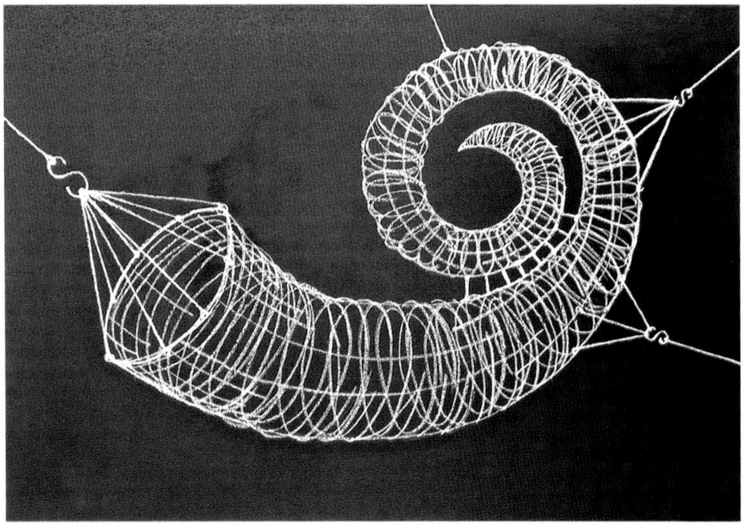

Clamorous Horn silenced & shackled, 2005. Oil stick on latex on canvas, varnished, 34" x 50".

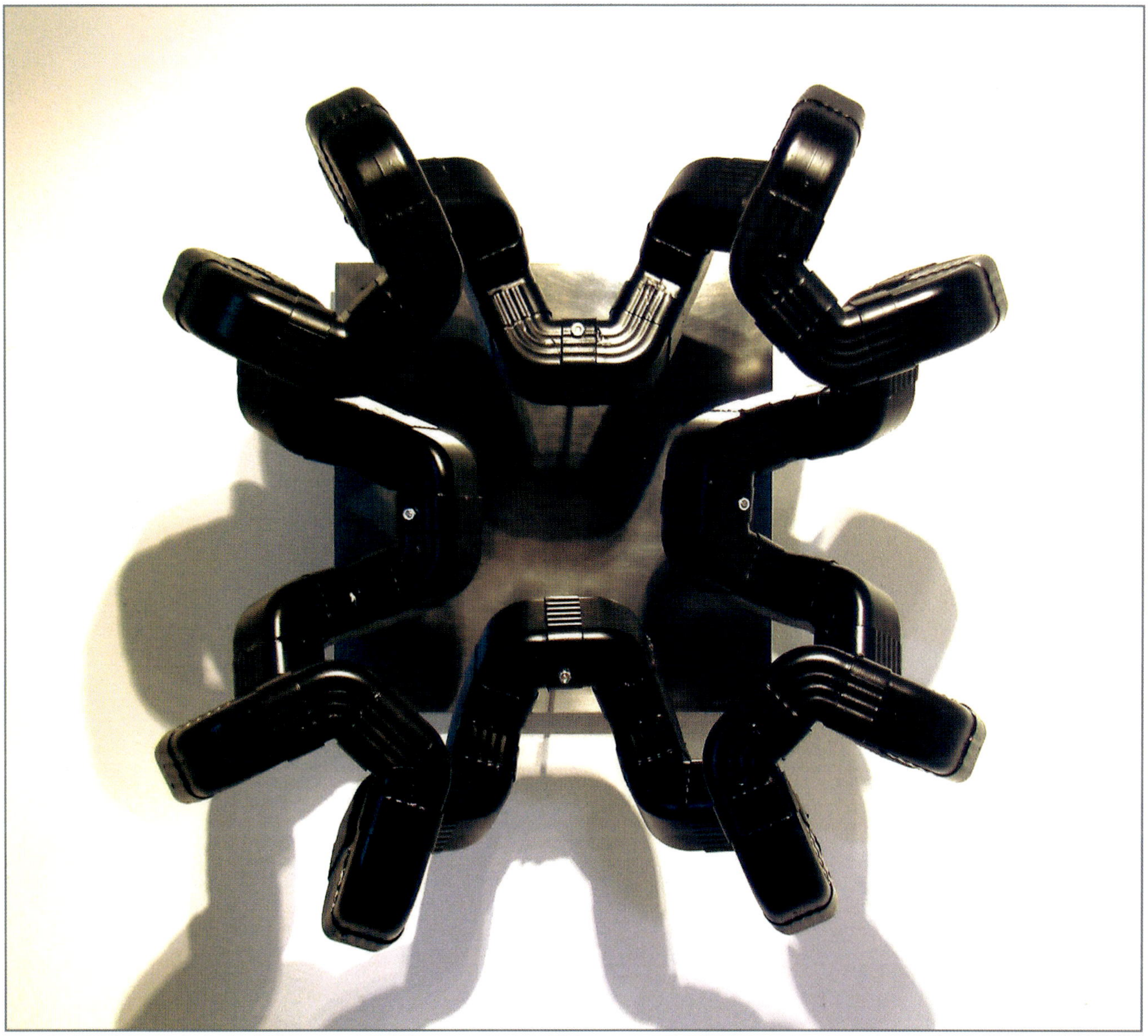

Claw, 2005. Vinyl rainspouts, acrylic, polyurethane, aluminum, 21″ x 32″ x 32″, mounted on wall.

DIEGO SINGH

We're up for what we can get. We've changed our names, our countries. We paint, advertise, and publish ourselves. We don't need a rising moon. We don't need anything but you. We thought no one was going to take us seriously. But people did. Dozens of them.

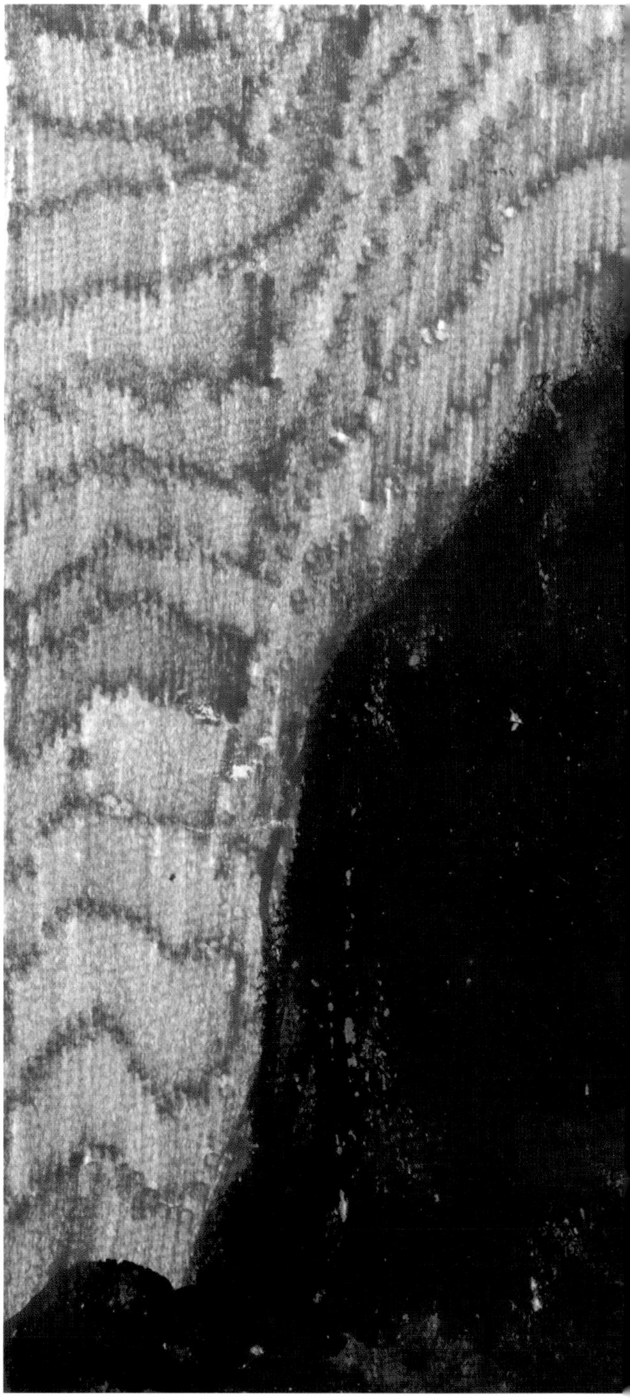

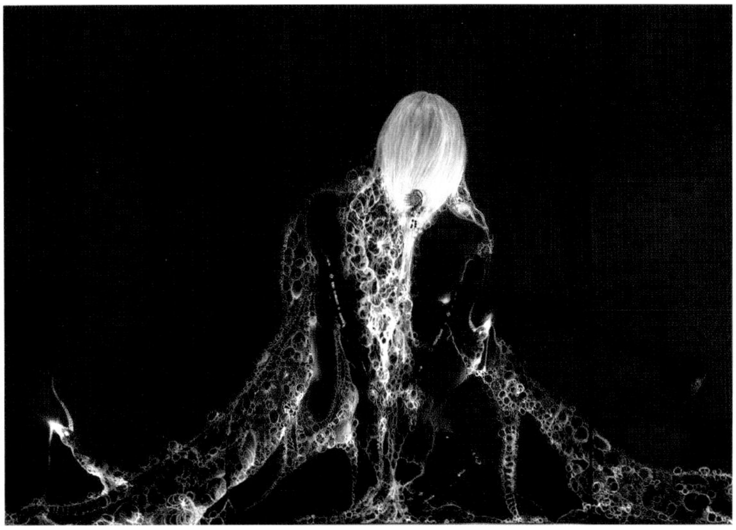

The Man is Gone, Anna, 2006. Pastel, ink, beads on paper, 44" x 72".

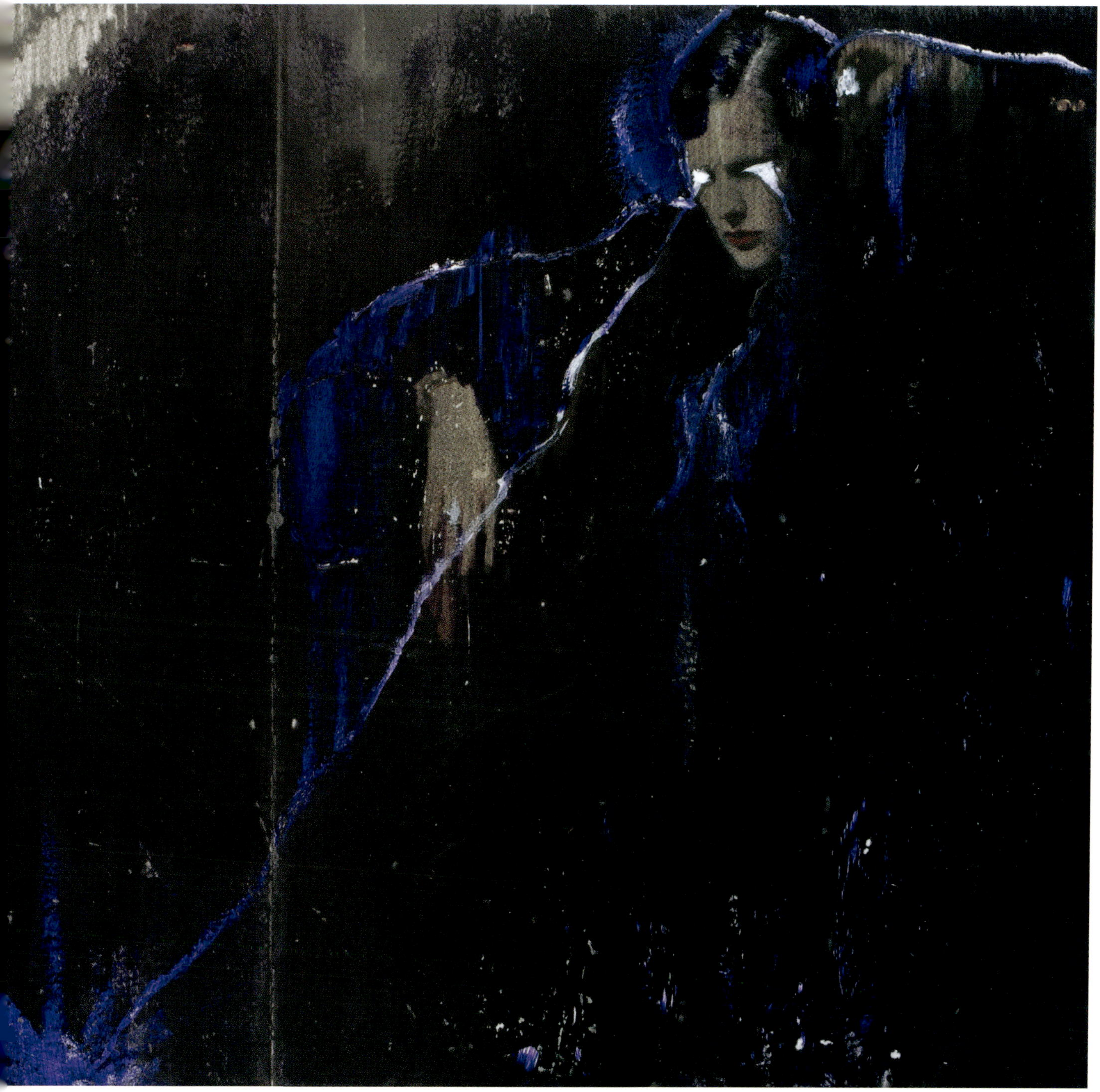

Breakup Letter to God #2, excerpt from the Green Book, 2006.
Mixed media on paper, 11" x 14".

KOL SOLTHON

The images included in this publication are from a series of works created during a six-month collaborative project with the artist Dash N., titled *"North American I."* Site-specific performances, sculptures and drawings were made throughout Canada and the United States. Miami was the starting and ending point for this project. This collaboration was a continuation of a similar exploration throughout Mexico in 2003.
Kol Solthon was born in Vancouver, BC in 1971. He currently lives and works in New Mexico.

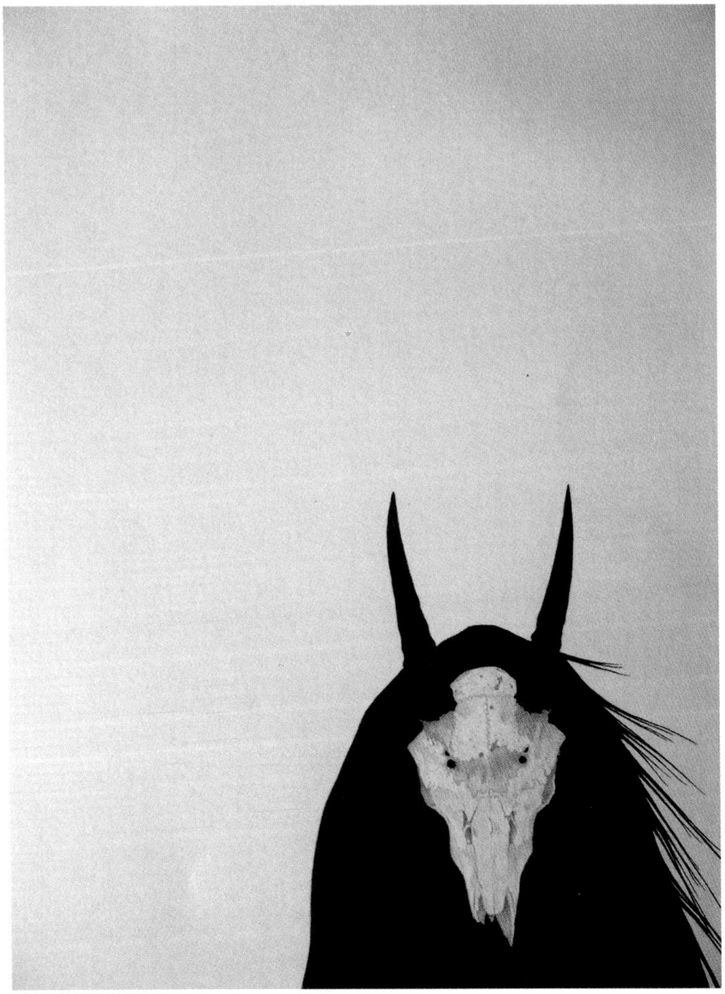

Untitled, 2005. Ink and graphite on paper, 7" x 10".

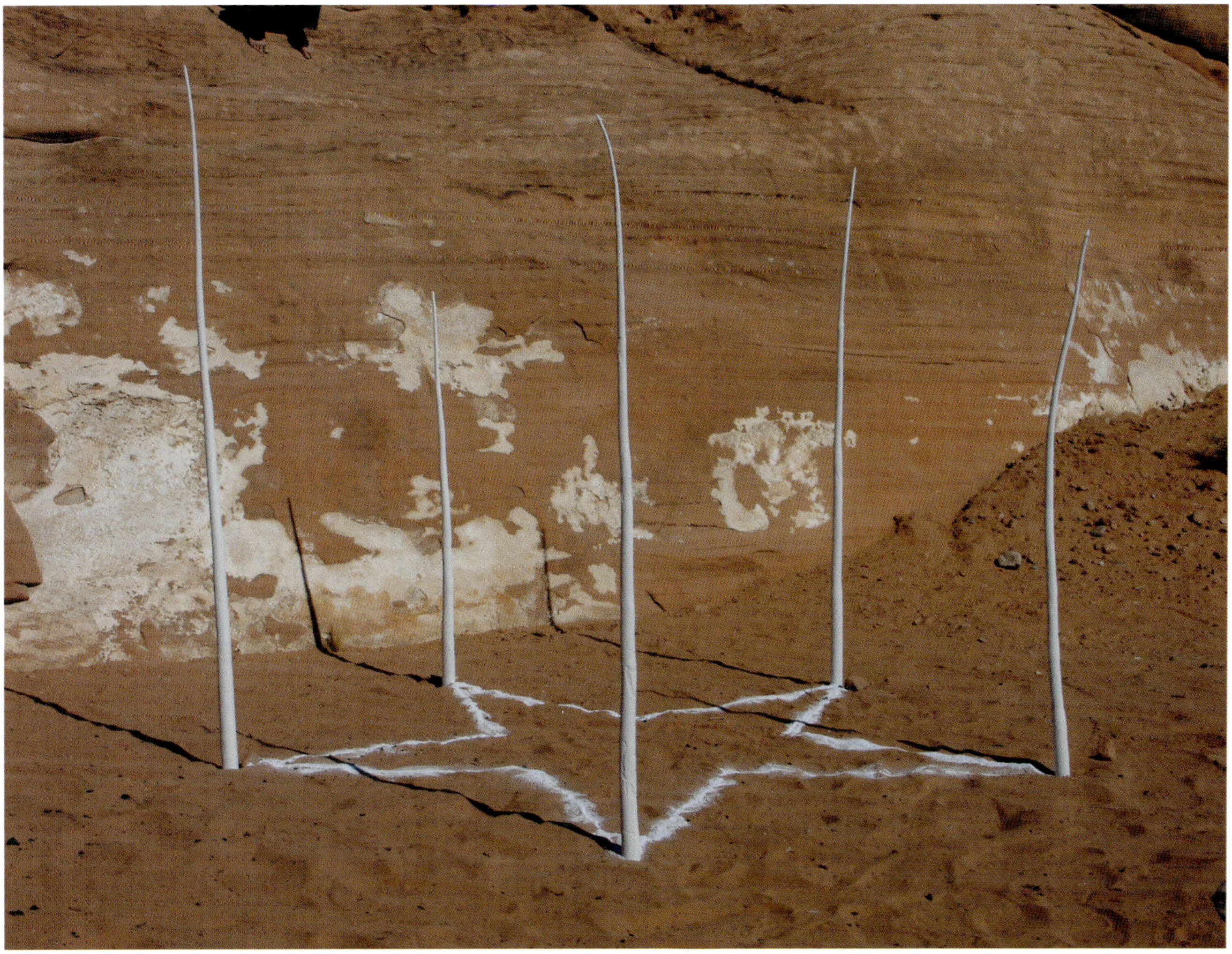

In the Valley of Fire, 2005. Production still, 16" x 20".

TINA SPIRO

My first project completed in Miami in 2000 was *"The Shekkinah Scrolls"* and tabernacle, a thirty-six foot diameter black canvas structure containing scribed and painted scrolls transported from Jamaica, my home for thirty years, This portable space for spiritual renewal was erected in the Design District complete with sound track and sculpted harps. My next project in Miami was *"Paint the Town,"* a large-scale urban intervention in the form of a Master Plan to paint the buildings of the Omni neighborhood adjacent to the Performing Arts Center in a coordinated color palette. The plan was approved and funded by the City of Miami and implemented over a two-year period. The success of this project moved the City of Miami to encourage me to produce a special event for Art Basel Miami Beach, and OMNIART was born. This encompassed sixty Miami and international artists, installations and artworks spread out over 40,000 square feet of vacant warehouse space in the Omni neighborhood. My own installation was a scaled down version of the changing streetscape outside, each building becoming a small gallery containing photos of the neighborhood transformed by color. For OMNIART III I created *"Mayaima,"* a twenty-four foot diameter installation based on the satellite mapping of the Miami Circle, an ancient Tequesta communal site in downtown Miami. This is one of an ongoing series of "Sacred Sites" with spiritual and environmental themes representing cycles of the past, future and community. Miami provides me with the opportunity to educate, curate and create...my favorite activities.

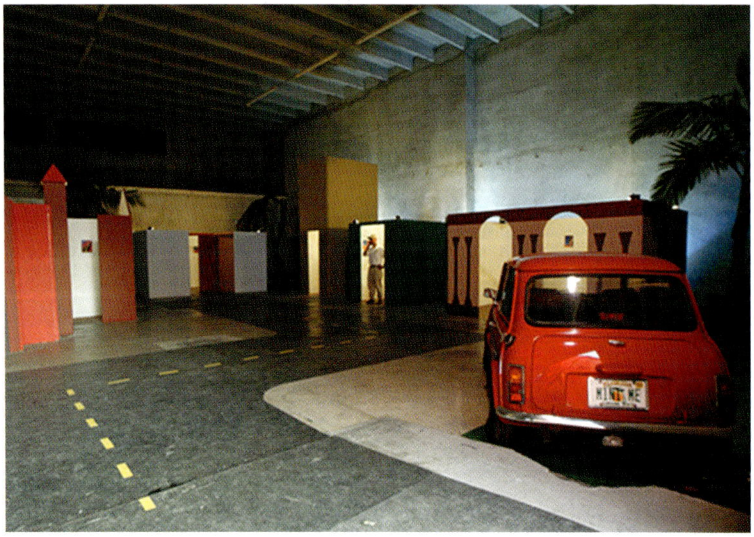

Paint the Town, 2003. Mixed media installation, 45′ x 65′ x 13′6″ with 50 photographs.

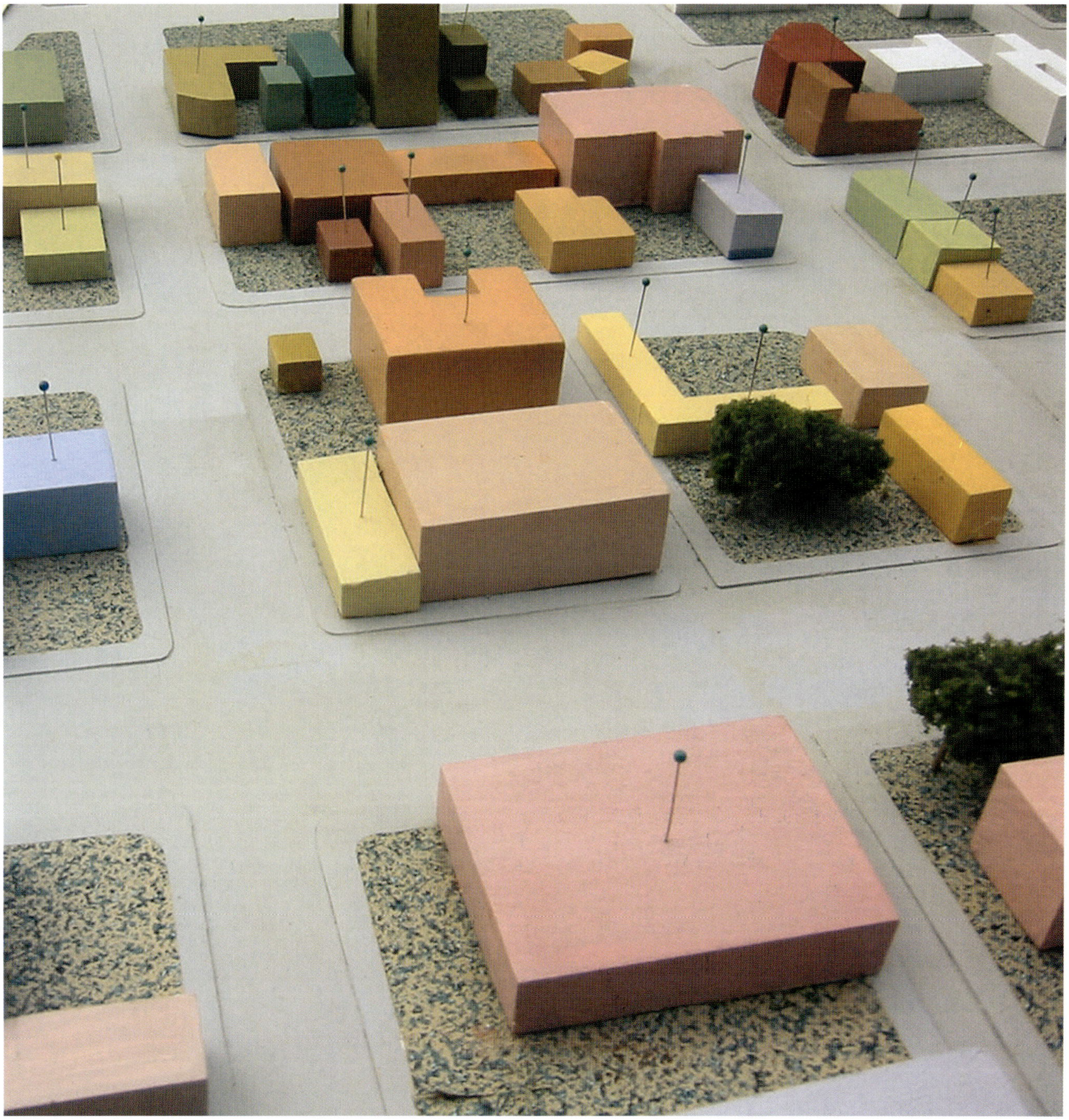

Paint the town, 2003. Maquette.

SARA STITES

A friend suggested I read The Marble Faun by Nathaniel Hawthorne after seeing my drawings of part-human, part-animal creatures. While I often have trouble pinpointing why I am driven to make these combined creatures which sometimes shock and disgust the viewer, I know there is a warmer, more visceral reason that they come tumbling out of my pen and brush. The character Donatello in the book, the human embodiment of the faun, a male figure with furry ears and a zest for life, resembles in many ways the sculpture made of marble in the book. Richard Brodhead describes him in his introduction as "*...half man, half faun, he is a kind of missing link between the civilized and natural orders, a civilized fantasy of a pre-civilized form of life in which the human is still in touch with its 'animal nature.'*" Yes, that is closer to my feelings than being driven to distort. Hawthorne concerns himself with the principle of virtue, simplicity, honesty, animal-nature versus characteristics of "higher ideals" and weaves them into a riddle: *"Neither man nor animal, and yet no monster, but a being in whom both races meet, on friendly ground!"*

I moved from New York to the Florida Keys, and when I'd had enough solitude, came to Miami. Soon after putting down roots here, I witnessed the blooming of Miami's art scene with the arrival of Art Basel. The symbiotic relationship of the greater art world with the local one has nourished me, too.

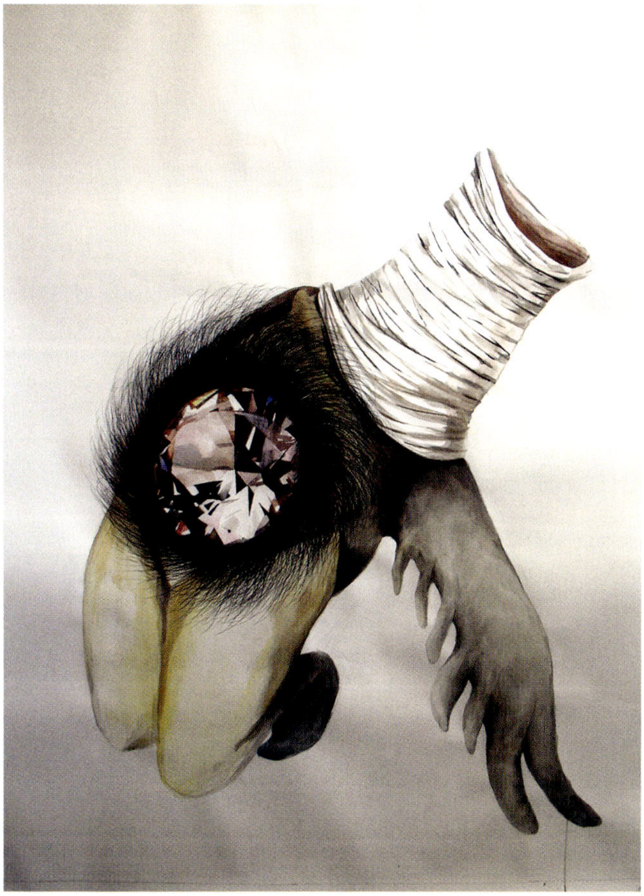

Gembelly Large, 2006. Watercolor and ink on paper, 60" x 65".

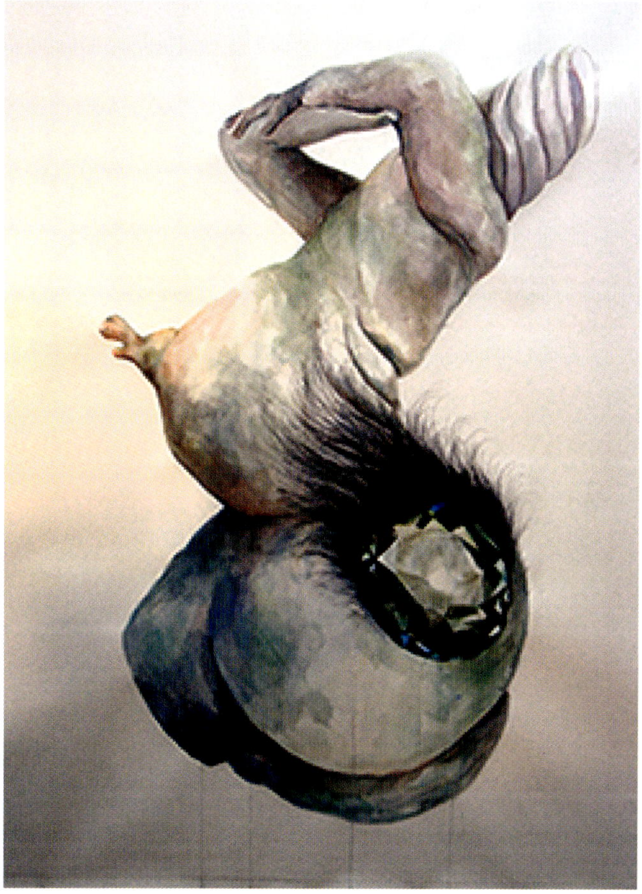

Wo-man Large, 2006. Watercolor and ink on paper, 60" x 72".

PAUL **STOPPI**

This isn't really a statement as much as it is a confession. What I do is not really art; it's really more of an obsession. I find planes sexy and I love flying in them and watching them move. The big, bulbous ones. The shiny aluminum ones, with wings like legs and engines like breasts, they can't help but pose. Always on show, always dancing and performing tricks, always entertaining without meaning to. Modest by design, shaped by the wind on the outside, they're all business on the inside. On brief yet satisfying occasions, I am granted access, accommodated, and it is then that I go to work, doing that which others call art, on my snug economy seat, recording experiences that few others see and fewer still appreciate, nuances of light, and the slow motion waltz with the ground. I gather my material like a squirrel nuts; to be enjoyed while grounded, head tilted back. I stare at them. Glisten in the sunshine. They were made for me to adore, take pictures of, and enjoy in all too infrequent stints aloft. It's for them that I have eyes.

Miami is like fly-paper for curious artists buzzing through. I was one seven years ago and I'm still here, lapping up the Kool-Aid; a convert of sorts. But it's not the geography and I can't credit the weather, I'm actually used to better. It's the people. Plain and simple. They are a very easy going bunch. Curious, adventurous and fun. No wonder a Miami opening is like a party. If you can't have fun with art in Miami, there are probably better books for you than this one.

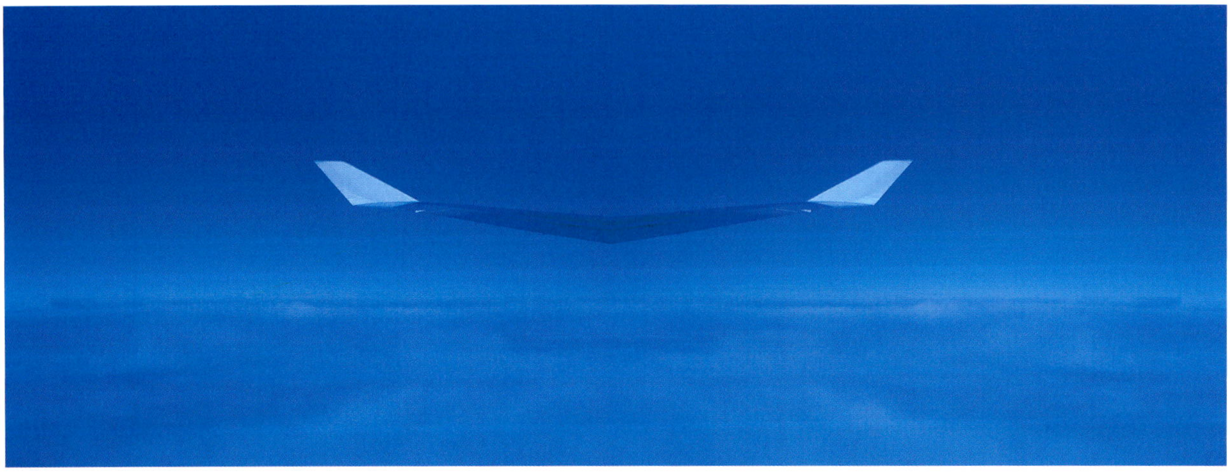

MIA-CDG 747, 2003. Light jet transparency in brushed-aluminum light box, 15" x 36" x 4".

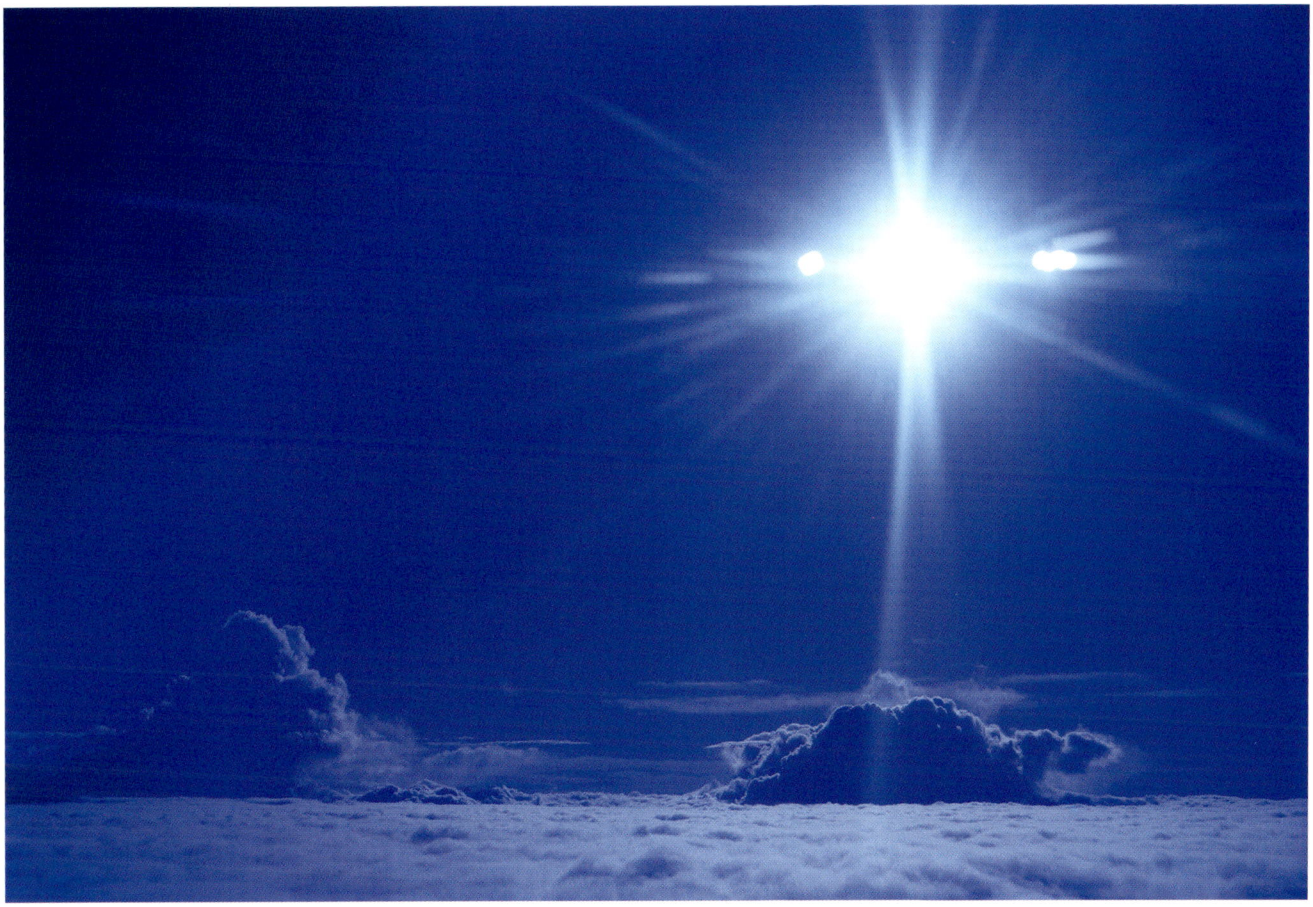

Bumboclat!, 2000. Light jet n PVC, 48" x 72".

KRISTEN THIELE

My current work "*Eye Candy*" is about composition, color, light, reflection, and transparency. This series is particularly about formal aspects of painting and painterliness itself.

I grew up in Miami. Both of my parents are artists that have been part of the art community since the late 60's. Miami has, in my experience, always been an artist community, though it has grown considerably in the last few years. The infrastructure that supports this has also grown; along with South Florida's increasing population, there are the galleries, schools for the arts, arts districts, centers, museums, collectors, etc. that have supported and accommodated the burgeoning art community. After living almost a decade in Chicago, I became a resident artist of the Art Center/ South Florida after returning to Miami in 2000. I feel extraordinarily lucky to have experienced Miami's changing scene first had, and to continue to be a part of it.

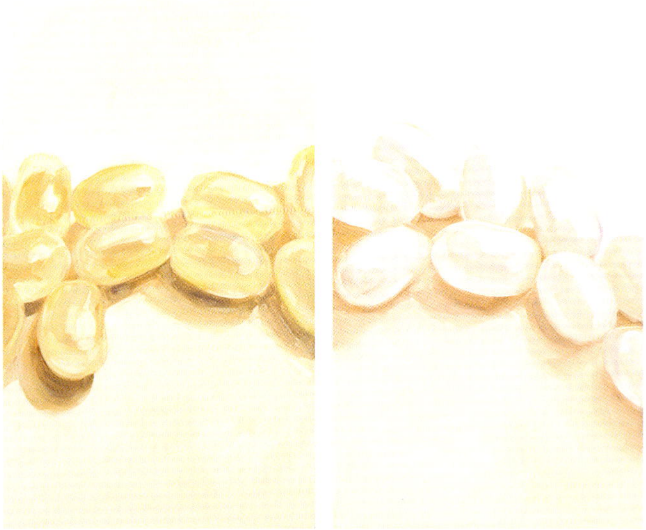

Clear and White Jelly Beans, (diptych), 2006. Oil on wood, 20 "x 12".

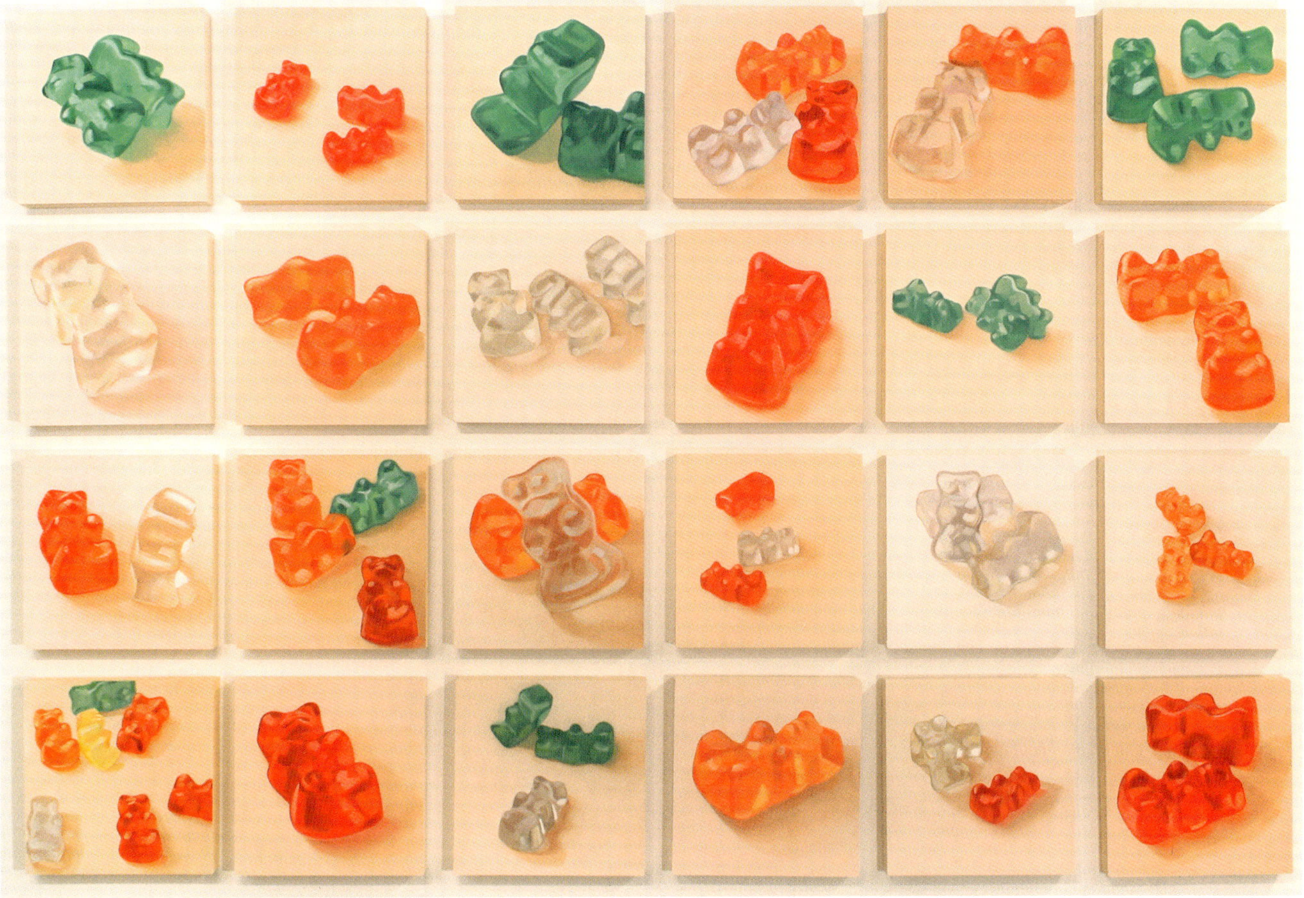

Group24 Gummies, 2006. Oil on wood, 12" x 12" each.

ROBERT **THIELE**

"The tension in an artist's work lies between what is revealed and what is concealed"

The writer Peter Frank observed in a recent conversation we had in New York, that the current art scene in Miami reminded him of L.A. in the 1970's and early 80's. A reach? Perhaps not. I would agree that Miami is experiencing the vitality of a robust adolescence. Few would long for the relative innocence of its early years, or the older complacency of the "advanced" scenes in New York or Los Angeles.

A-401 (diptych), 2006. Mixed media, 14.75" x 10" x 4.25" each.

A-388, 2006. Mixed media, 6.125" x 4.625" x 4.5".

TM SISTERS

Vibrations of super powered spiritual existence and colorful musical soundscapes drive us forward. Powerful and electric imagery are used by many bands to express the emotion in their songs. Videogames use flashes and bursts to enhance actions and movements of the characters, objects, and environment. Our videos, performances, sewn collages, xerography, animation, and video games visually investigate this extra presence and energy. People's interactions with these elements are entertaining, jagged, and beautiful. Although it is not visible to the eye, there is a lot of commotion moving in the space between the earth and the sky, particularly how lightning bolts create a connection between the heavens and the earth. Rays of light give reference to historical spiritual scenes. Lyrics in songs and wisdom from verses provide the insight and humor that fuel our work. As sisters, we have been involved in throwing punk concerts, creating fanzines, producing musical happenings, photocopying flyers, and sewing clothing. Our do-it-yourself ethic started with us being home-schooled by our parents. We were raised in Miami as the daughters of a pastor turned psychotherapist/ professor and grew up surrounded by intense spiritual and psychological discussion. Our family was thrown out of church. Despite this experience, our connection to God has only deepened, and is one of the main subjects within our work. Our brother, Samuel López De Victoria, also works with us in programming and conceptualizing video games.

Pink clouds... orange-smeared sky... pthalo waters... key lime and mango houses... humid nights... green, electric storms... sunny, clear sky breezes... crazy hurricanes... dancing people... audio beats... endless nights... everyone knows each other.

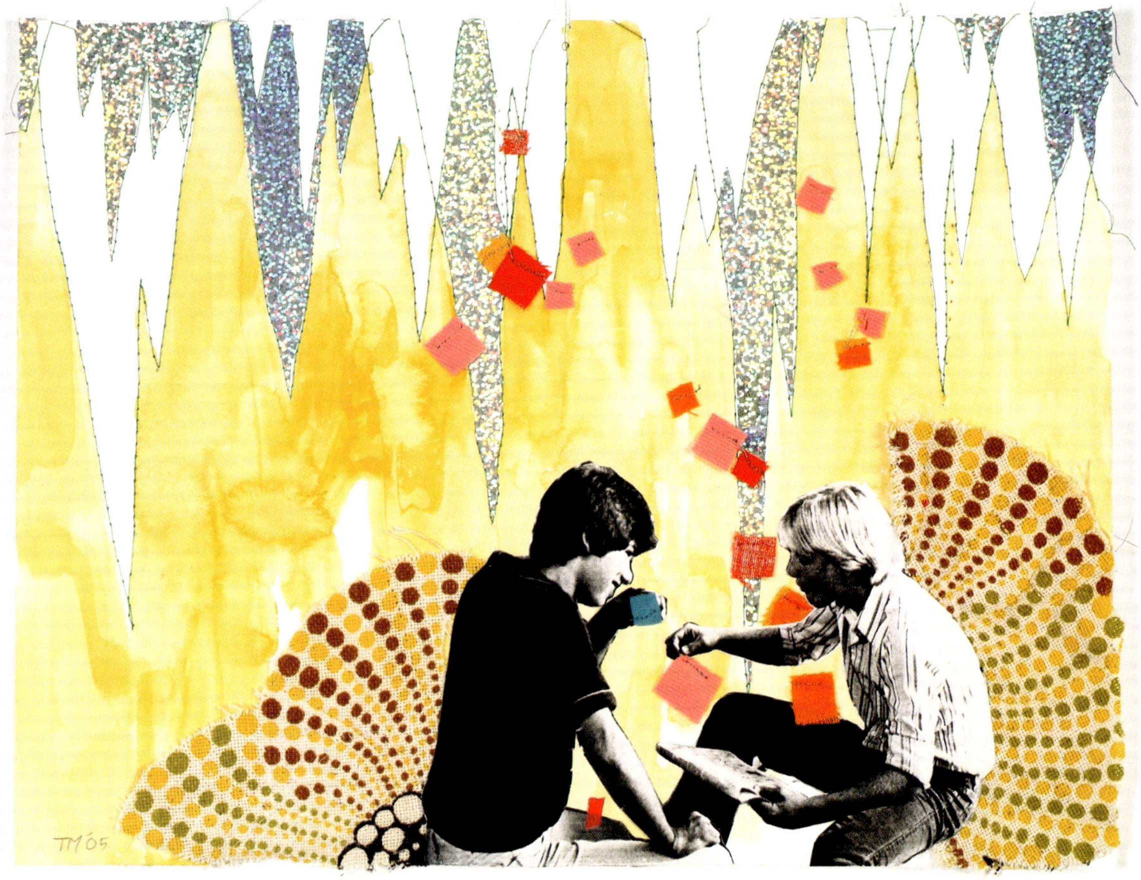

Evaporated, 2005. Xerox, fabric, thread, acrylic holographic adhesive paper on watercolor paper, 12" x 9".

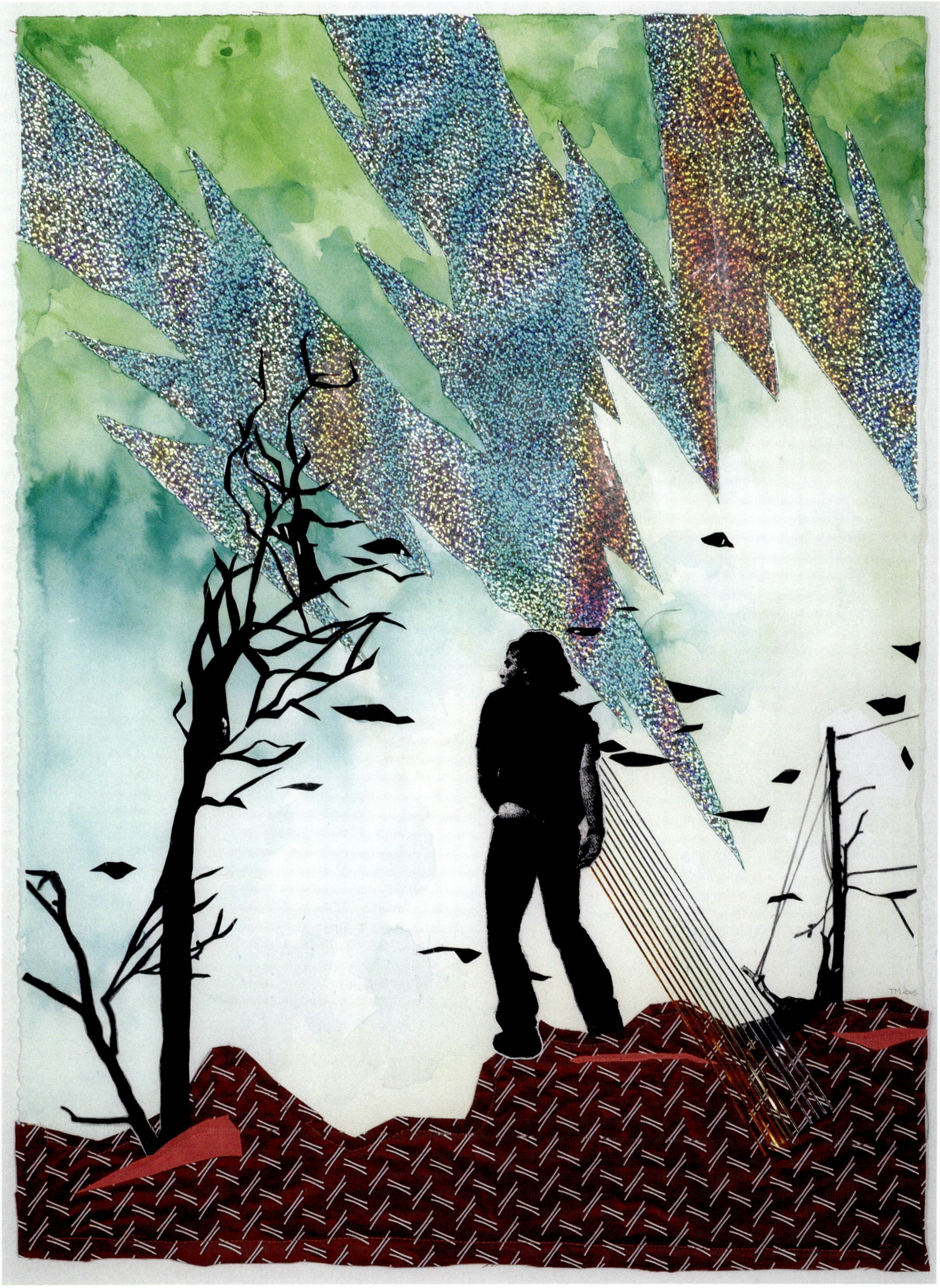

There is a Design, 2005. Xerox, fabric, thread, acrylic holographic adhesive paper on watercolor paper, 30″ x 22″.

METTE TOMMERUP

I am a native of Denmark and my work investigates themes of memory, history and nostalgia associated with my Danish relatives and upbringing. In particular, I am curious about morals and world representation described in older fairytales. One thing that is striking is the macabre passages found in many stories. These stories have haunting messages and images that I dissect and distort to create a new narrative so that the viewer can be cued to create new stories based on the digital manipulation of elements of suggestion. In the late 1990's I changed medium, from a painter into a digital artist. I realize that it is only a label since I still act like a painter, producing unique work and also capturing digitally the "artist hand." I want to show that the digital medium can act like a painting while using the latest computer software and hi-tech pigments. I find that with today's equipment, I can create intricate imagery with extraordinary detail and benefit from the ever progressing digital technologies and mediums.

."*.... It almost looks like a great plateful of spiders jumping about in a crowd. And how fierce they are! They tear off each other's legs and arms and bodies, before and behind; and yet they are merry and joyful in their way."* From "The Drop of Water" by Hans Christian Andersen (1848)

Miami is fortunate to have a great talent base of artists and passionate individuals working on a multitude of levels within the contemporary art scene. Individuals who have been here working diligently long before the contemporary art world and Miami would be on the map together. The local art scene here has changed dramatically since I started coming here from NYC in the late 90's. One of the nicest benefits of the explosive scene is that most artist friends from all over the world now find their way to Miami to visit and show. My first impression of the Miami art scene was that there was a real sense of community of people trying to help each other out. It was an inclusive scene with lots of opportunities and at a scale where everybody seemed to know each other. At an early stage I was fortunate to be involved with several curatorial projects with my husband, Robert Chambers and it was an instant way to get to know everybody who was producing or involved with art at that moment in Miami. It was an eye-opening lesson in how shows can come together and the importance of artist curated shows at a time where there seemed to be a real need for these events. If anybody had told us back then that people would come from all over the world later to see the latest trends in contemporary art we would have thought it a bit absurd. However, Miami was ready to accommodate a significant contemporary art audience and there are many visionary individuals to thank for these accomplishments. I feel very appreciative to be part of this ongoing transformation.

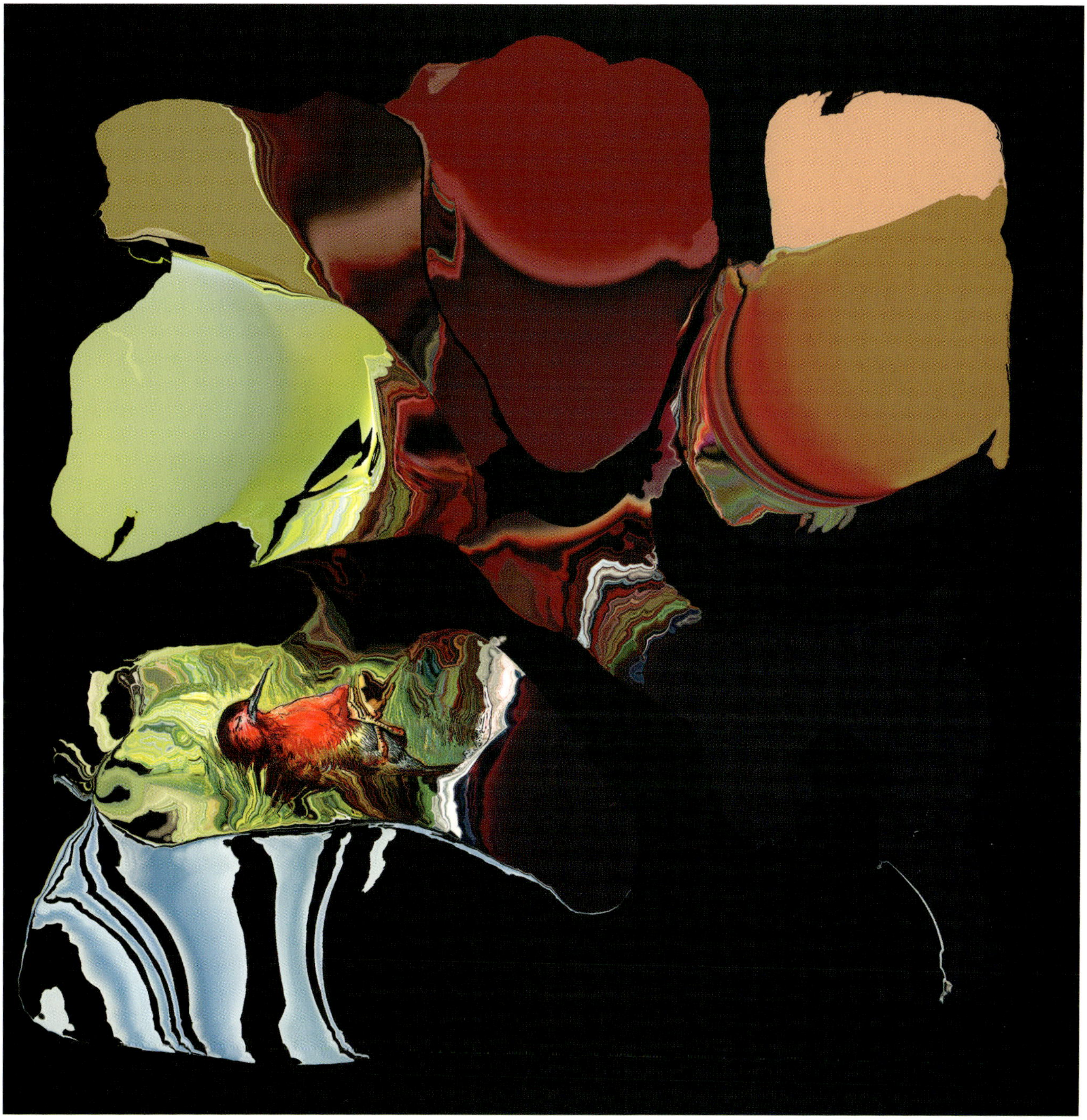

Far Near – Robin, 2005. Ink on watercolor paper, 12″ x 12″, unique.

RUBÉN TORRES **LLORCA**

Creo sinceramente que en cierto momento de la vida, un artista entre los 40 y los 50 años, debería detenerse y dejar de producir arte para el público. Es decir, tener un poco de pudor. Quizás, recibir un estipendio del estado por el sacrificio de tener que hacer obra para vender y de tener que convertir el placer de crear en un tedioso trabajo comercial. El ideal de mi vida sería, dedicarme a ver las viejas películas de samurai que ví de niño en Cuba, tener una casita frente a la playa o algo así. Desafortunadamente, tengo que pagar las cuentas, y esto es exactamente mi principal fuente de inspiración.

I sincerely believe that, at a given moment in the life of an artist, let's say between 40 and 50 years old, art should not be produced for the public. That is to say, to have a little *pudor*. He or she could maybe receive a stipend from the government in pay for the hard labor of producing work to sale, and to have to turn the pleasure to create in a tedious commercial work. The ideal of my life would be, to spend time watching old samurai films, to have a small house at the beach or something like it. Unfortunately, I must pay the bills, and this is exactly my main source of inspiration.

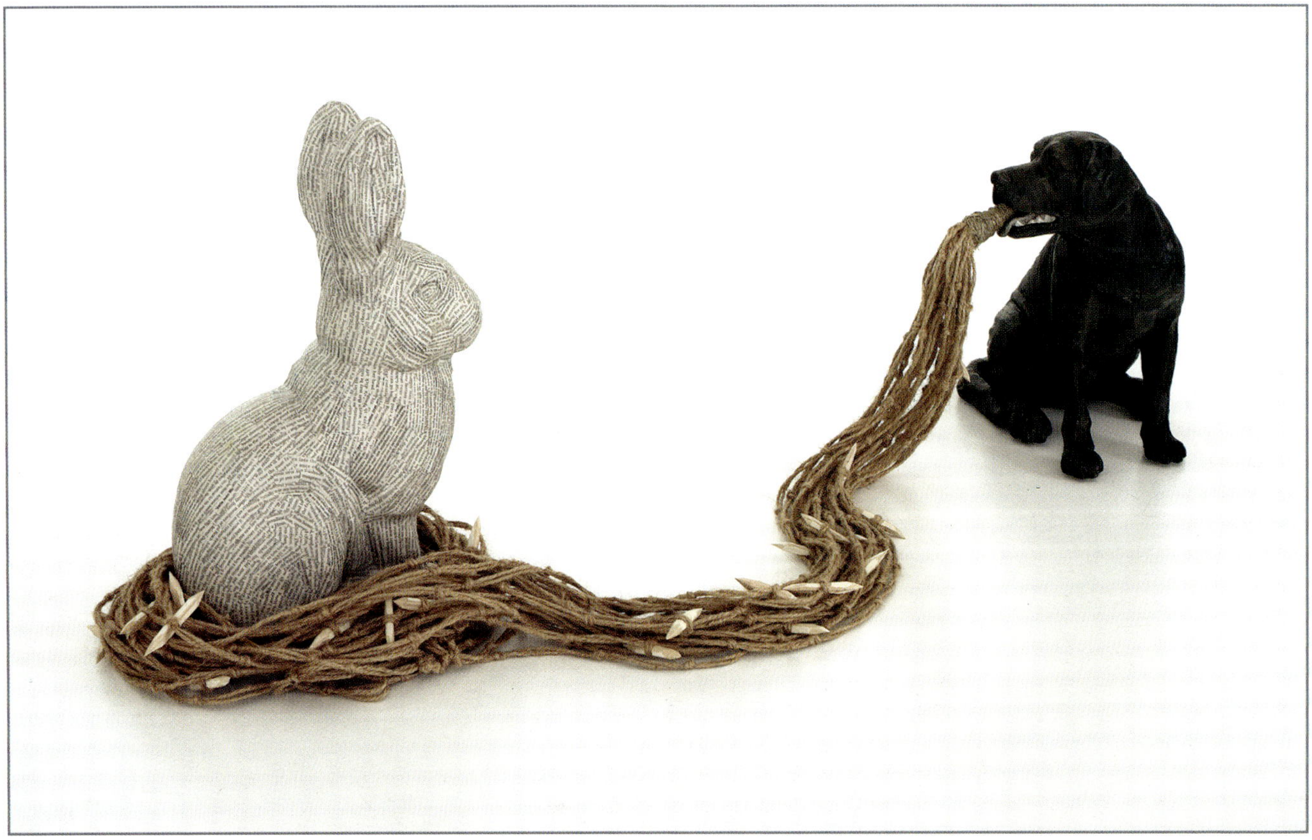

The Warning, 2005. Mixed media, dimensions variable.

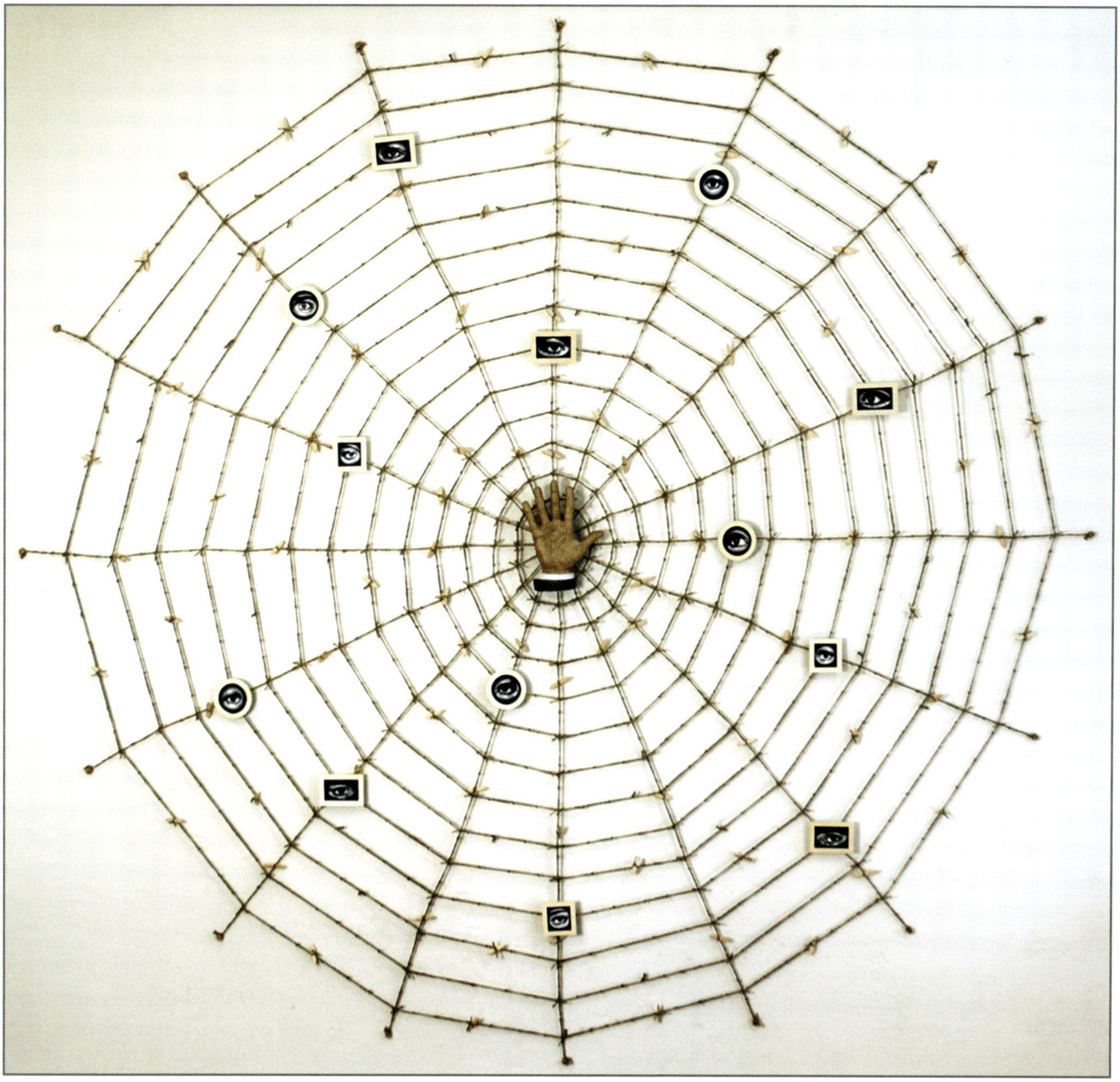

Remedio Para el Mal de Ojo (Remedy for the Evil Eye), 2004. Mixed media, 86″ diameter.

CÉSAR **TRASOBARES**

Working in Miami since 1974, I define my practice as an artist broadly: in the studio, I produce work in various media; in the art world, I serve as art activist, curator, educator and performer; in the institutional field, I work in education and art administration. Addressing broad audiences, I have often dissected and presented the social territories that shape and define individuals in our dynamically mutating society. Art and Life are inseparable in my world. My early studio work dealt with the Cuban quinceañera, her images and symbols and the significance of the rite-of-passage of young women as a metaphor for Miami's exile community at the time. Working with mixed media, video and performance, the 15 years of work with this subject were highlighted in the exhibition *"Quinceañera Works"* in 1984. Over the years I would recycle some of this material in installations. My Man Ring character served as an artistic alter-ego beginning in the mid 1980s. I made, collected and exhibited finger rings as objects of culture. Each ring was shaped and inspired in different social and stylistic sources, revealing a landscape of non-hierarchical, universal expression in myriad forms and materials. Comprising the personal side of my official work as public art administrator, I developed series of drawings and diagrams about power structures and struggles in the art world, culminating in the installation *"Museum of American Democratic Art: Tumbling Chairs"* at the Center for the Fine Arts in 1993. At the time I also worked with furniture as sculpture expressing interpersonal relations. I also began to embroider the many pillows featured in *"SOCIAL FABRIC: Old Pillows and Recent Money Works"* at the Green Gallery, Florida International University in 2003.In 2000 I developed a project about Elian González and the media spectacle surrounding the boy as a captive of political and social manipulation and his transformation into a polyvalent historical symbol. The work resulted in a major installation for the Bass Museum, *"Elian in Wonderland."* Since the mid-1990s, I have worked with money as my primary esthetic material. Money is implicated in nearly all aspects and spheres of contemporary life and culture. As man dollar I draw and stamp bills as well as use them in constructions and installations. Commissioned by the Wolfsonian-FIU, *"CONSERVATORIUM"* addressed the monetary atmosphere of Miami under the reign of the art fairs since the beginning of this century and the increasing place of art globally as commodity and status symbol. I live in my studio in Wynwood's flight path, cultivating a garden and occasionally cooking for friends as I continue to work with shredded and unused cash. Being a submerged artist in Miami's subtropical climate is OK with me. Born in Holguín, Cuba in 1949, I have lived in Miami since 1965 (41 years)

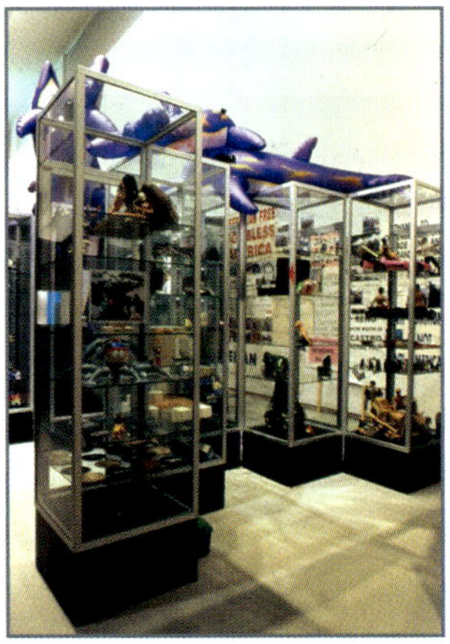

Elian in Wonderland,2001.
Mixed media installation from *globe>miami>island* at the Bass Museum of Art.

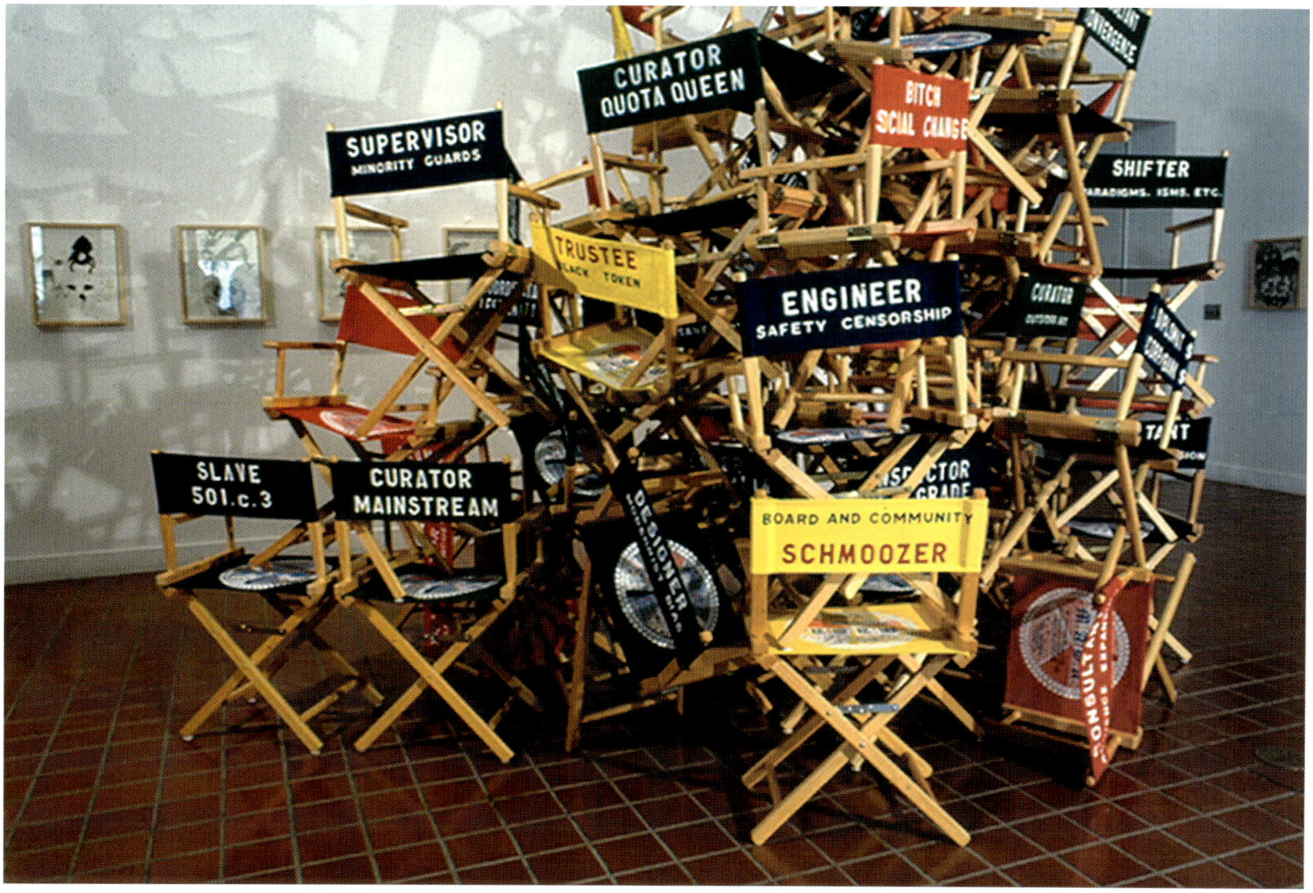

Museum of American Democratic Art, 1994. Solo installation as part of the National N.A.A.O. Conference. *Center for the Fine Arts.*

FRANCES TROMBLY

My work focuses around the process of making. The pieces all use different types of trompe-l'oeil effects in order to investigate issues concerning craft, identity, value and labor. Everyday mundane objects, knitted, crocheted and embroidered are seen at first glance to be nothing more than the worthless objects that they are. I am interested in the experience that takes place upon discovering or not discovering these objects.

Having grown up in Miami, I have a sentimental appreciation for where I live. No one can deny that things here are continually changing. That change is beautiful and certainly has and will continue to be a prominent influence.

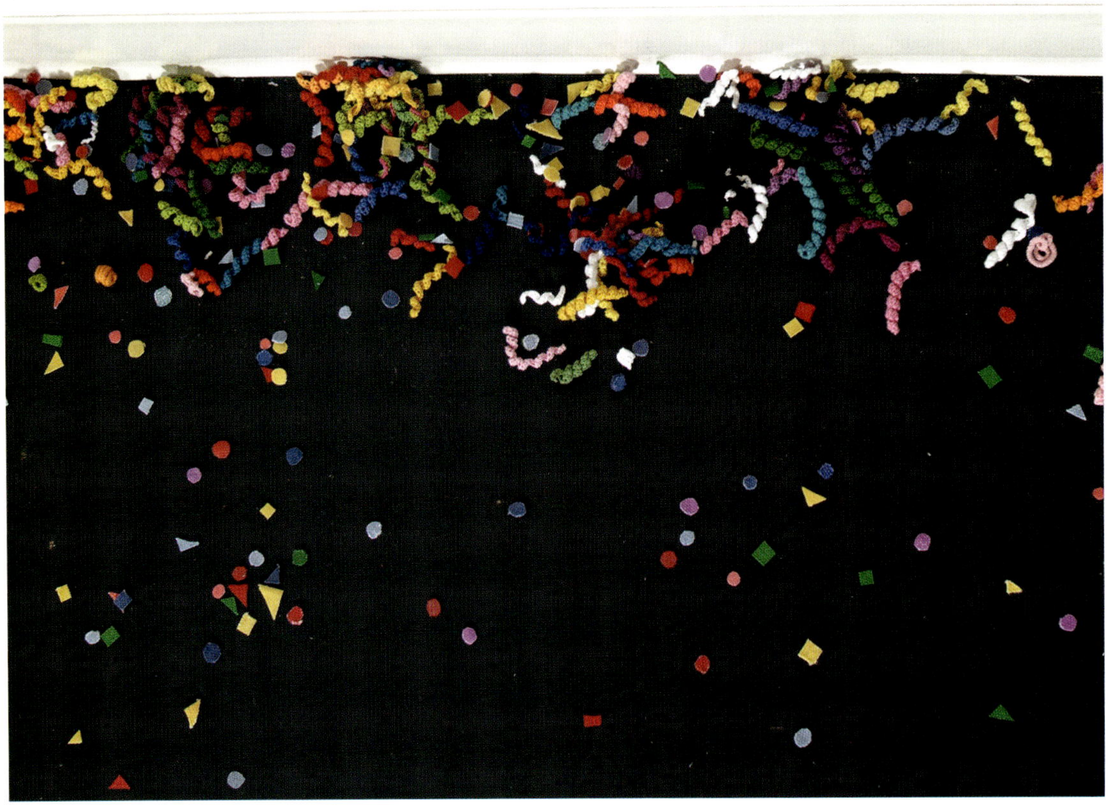

Confetti Border (detail), 2005-06. Crocheted cotton fabric, dimensions variable.

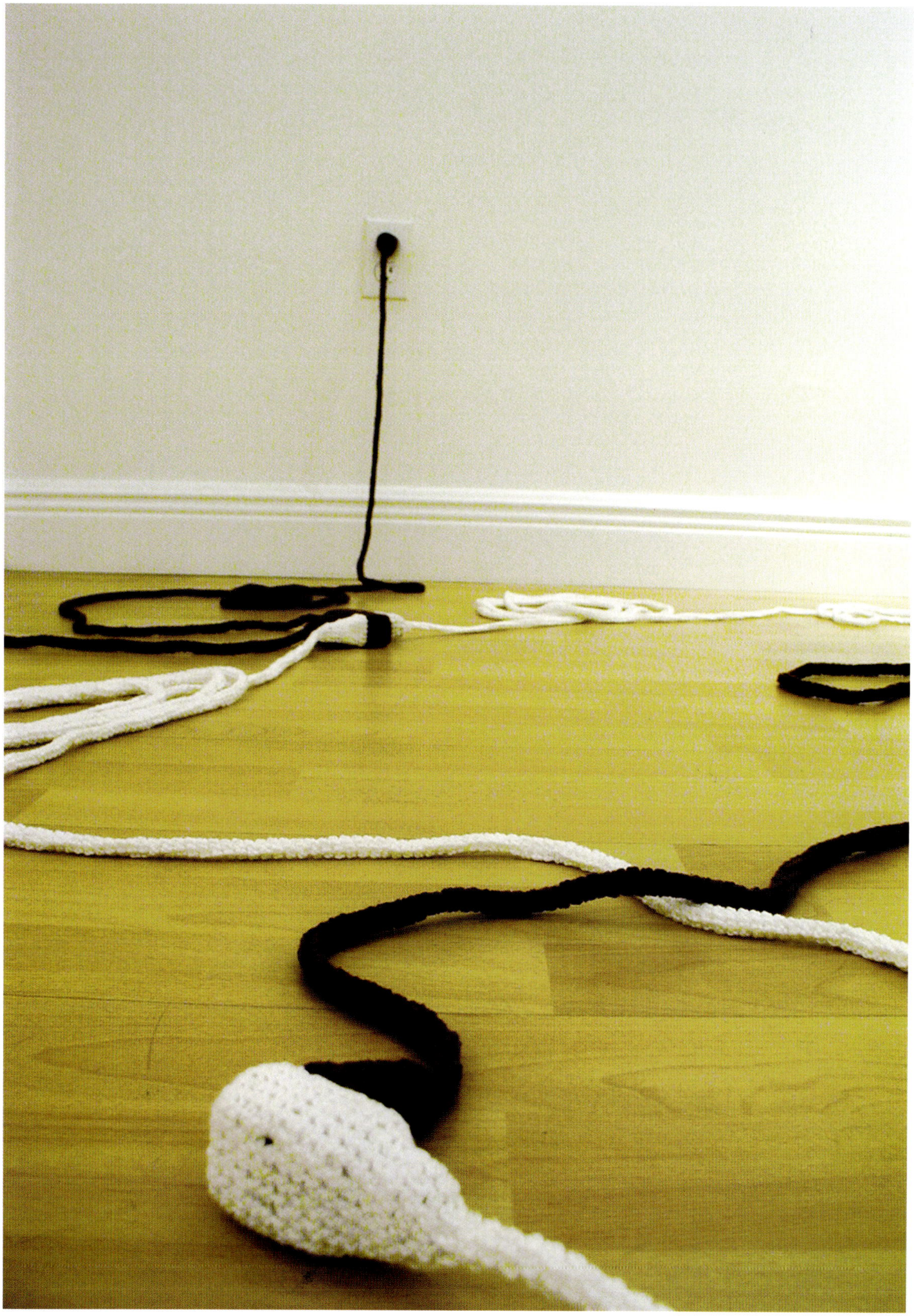

Connections (detail), 2003. Crocheted cotton, dimensions variable.

KYLE TROWBRIDGE

My current work explores the stereotypes of youth through the contrasting of fragility and aggression among children and teens attempting to find their place in society. Adolescence resonates with a woven duality of innocence and malevolent power, reminding us of where we come from and who we may become. These artworks function as a reminder of the world we were promised as children, and a visual record of my search for understanding in that world as an adult. This loss of innocence or purity clearly illustrates the ever-changing nature of life itself. This is where I feel my art survives.

Being an artist in Miami is a wonderful experience filled with great opportunity. The scene is fresh and alive and has yet to have been classified with a particular aesthetic label – allowing for new and exciting work from our local pool of talent. While the city itself does not inform my work, I believe the benefit of working in Miami, is the true sense of belonging. The art scene here is one large extended family where most of us know, support and work side by side with one another. Some may suggest this is dangerous – possibly the perfect recipe for becoming one large homogenized scene that would eventually earn that aesthetic label so many other cities suffer from. The difference here is, we [Miami artists] have a tendency to fly the Miami flag. We are not just artists; we are *Miami* artists. I truly believe this "gang" mentality will place our city at the forefront of the contemporary art world. One by one we will pull each other up the ladder.

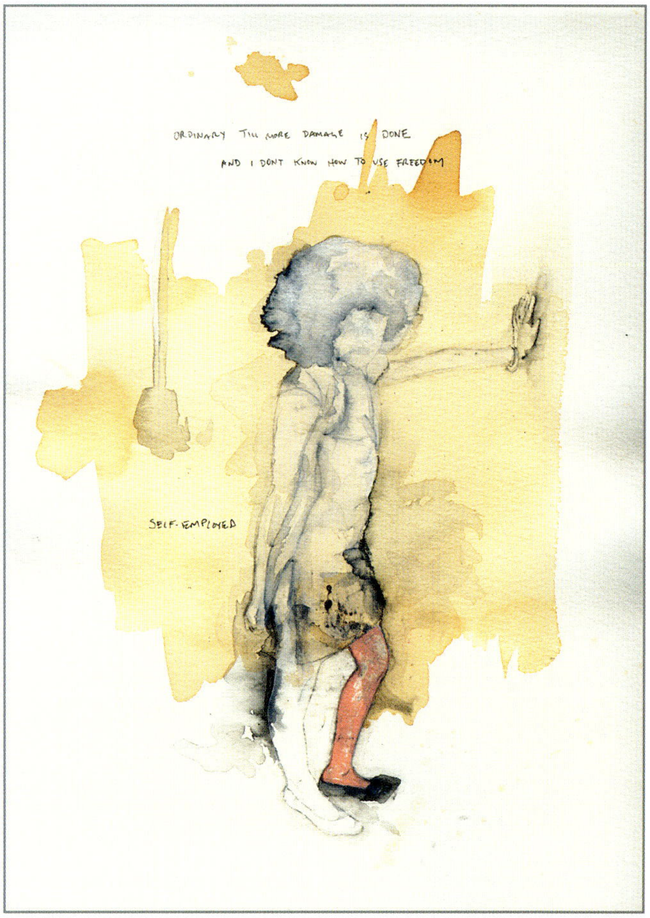

"Self-Employed" from the series 100 Punks, 2006. Graphite, acrylic paint and tea stains on paper, 9" x 12".

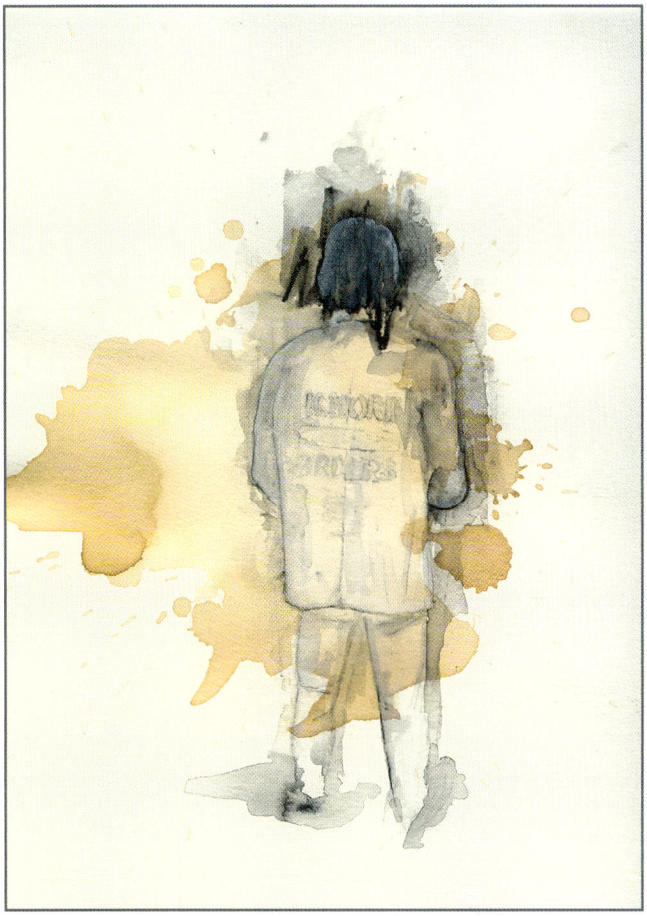

"*Ignore Orders" from the series 100 Punks*, 2006. Acrylic paint and tea stains on paper, 9" x 12".

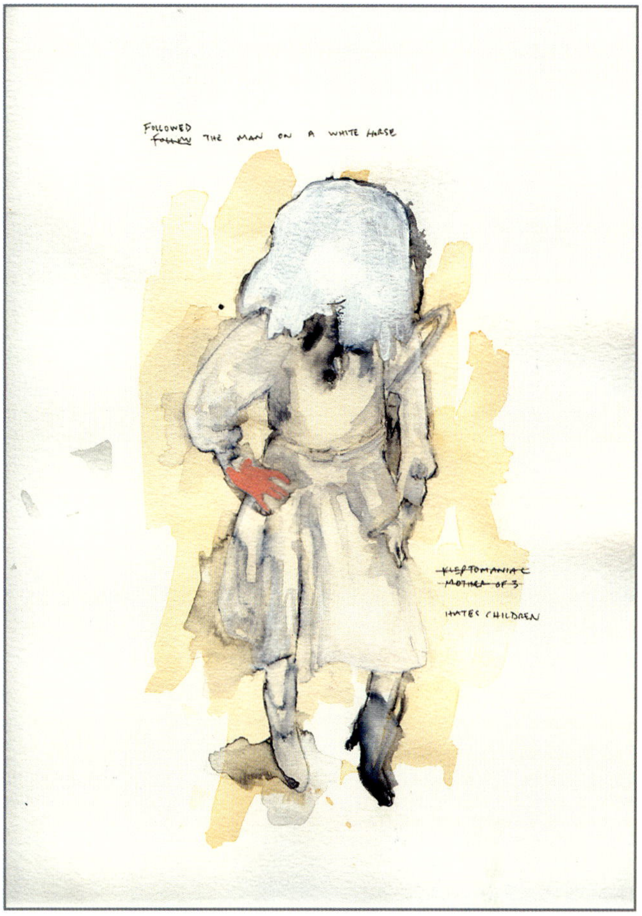

"Salvation" from the series 100 Punks, 2006. Graphite, acrylic paint and tea stains on paper, 9" x 12".

EUGENIA **VARGAS**

In the series *"The Longest Day"* through the medium of photography and video, I explore the relationship between girls and horses, and how this liaison has been depicted throughout the history of art. Myths, clichés, and their origins are present from the Caribbean, Taino Indian legends to Greek mythology. These archetypes have been exploited in the pop culture of Hollywood movies and advertising. Young girls clad in beautiful flowing dresses and long silky hair charge across the screen on beautiful horses. In the video *"Girls and Horses,"* through the appropriation of Hollywood, MTV, and independent film clips, scenes of very young girls, to young women and horses, are always highly charged with eroticism. Together with their horses, young women are capable of taking great risks, facing grave danger, and even defying death. The Girl is willing to go all the way with her horse.

What does it mean to be an artist in Miami? It is not a very easy question to answer because it means many things on many different levels. Just to mention a few, I would say that, being an artist, it has meant starting over, learning a new environment, redefining my identity and my work. It has been a great challenge. I have let myself be influenced by the city in the sense that things I once thought of as mundane, or superficial, have become new and interesting to explore in Miami. I guess this is true whenever you move to a new place, but Miami is unique because the city is constantly redefining itself, reinventing itself, and growing. Being an artist in Miami has allowed me to be a part of that growth and those changes.

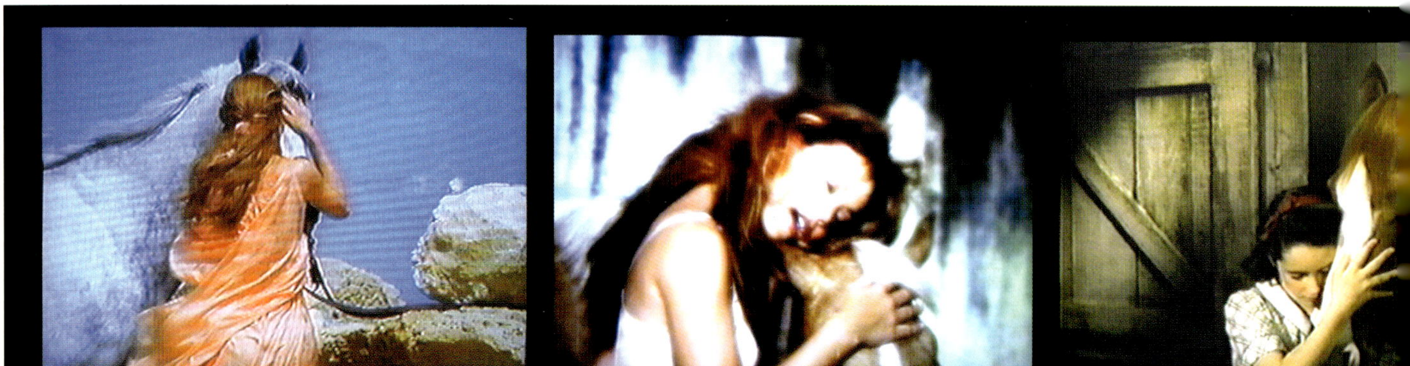

Girls and Horses, 2003. Video still.

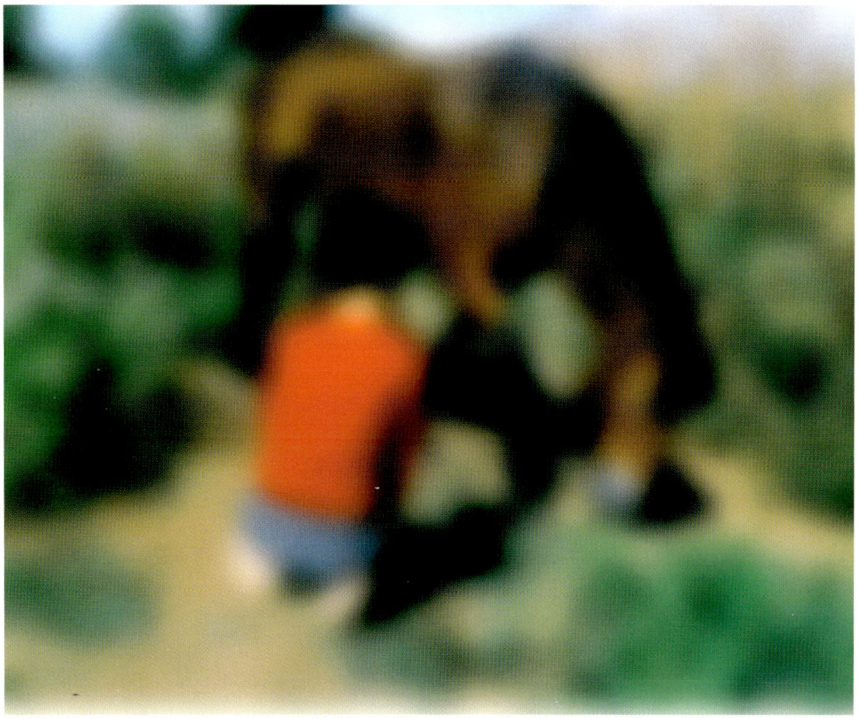

From The Longest Day series, 2001. Chromogenic print, 40″ x 40″.

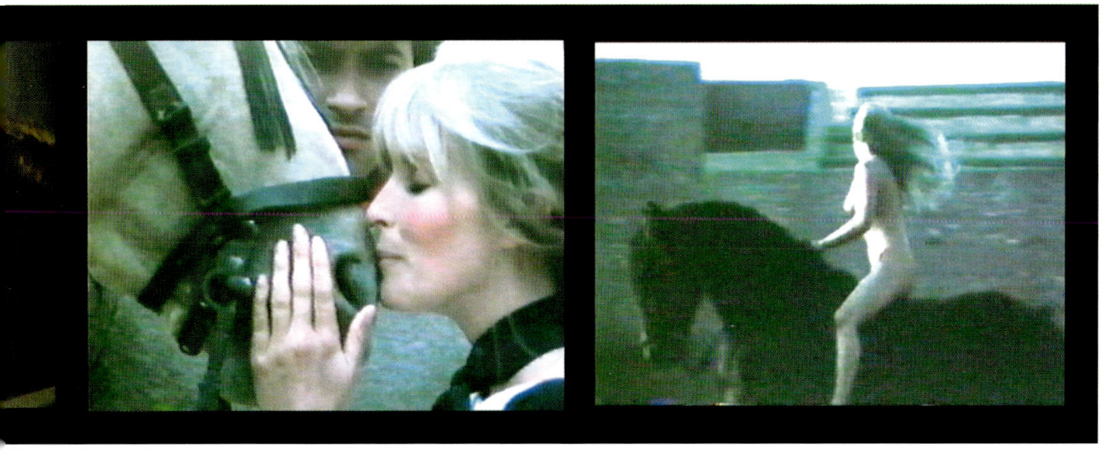

CARLOS DE VILLASANTE

I use graphic reduction to capture presence in portraits. This method bridges the gap between the handmade and photographic image, the mechanized and the manual. The hand made occurs after the image has been edited, photographed and reduced to its essential characteristics (one color separation). My process is to apply the paint in a manner that highlights the evidence of the hand. I do this to explore the possibility of intimacy in a mass produced language. I paint on three dimensional surfaces such as car hoods and theater seats to further undermine our expectations of the graphic image. I use these materials for the beauty of their form, not as a reference to their previous existence. These once utilitarian objects, when removed from their function are free to reveal their object characteristics. The hood becomes a shield, the seat becomes a mask, and the symbol becomes the represented.

Miami has had a very positive impact on my development. It is sunny which fits my disposition and helps me stay in balance. It is warm all year which keeps me from becoming too rigid. I can speak Spanish or choose to use English (sometimes). Cuban coffee keeps my eye twitching and hand working, and the "cuisine" here has compelled me to become a better cook. Most of all, I enjoy its citizens, while a tiny fraction of the population, the small minority of people I know and love, make Miami an exceptional place to be.

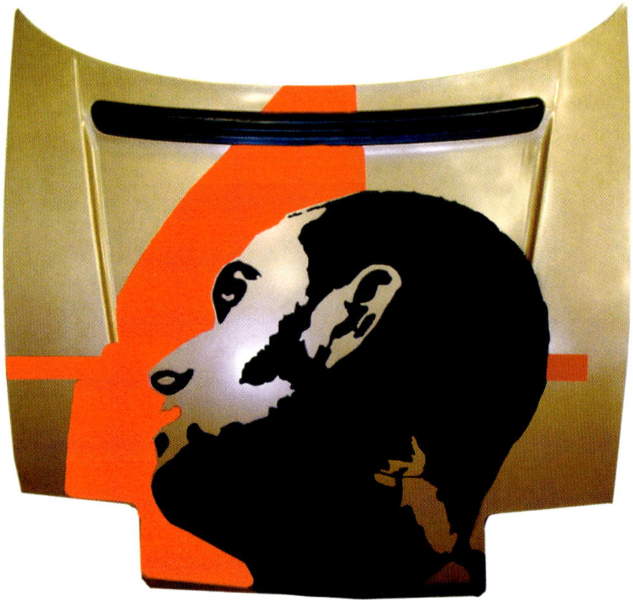

Profile West, 2005. Enamel on car hood, 64" x 56".

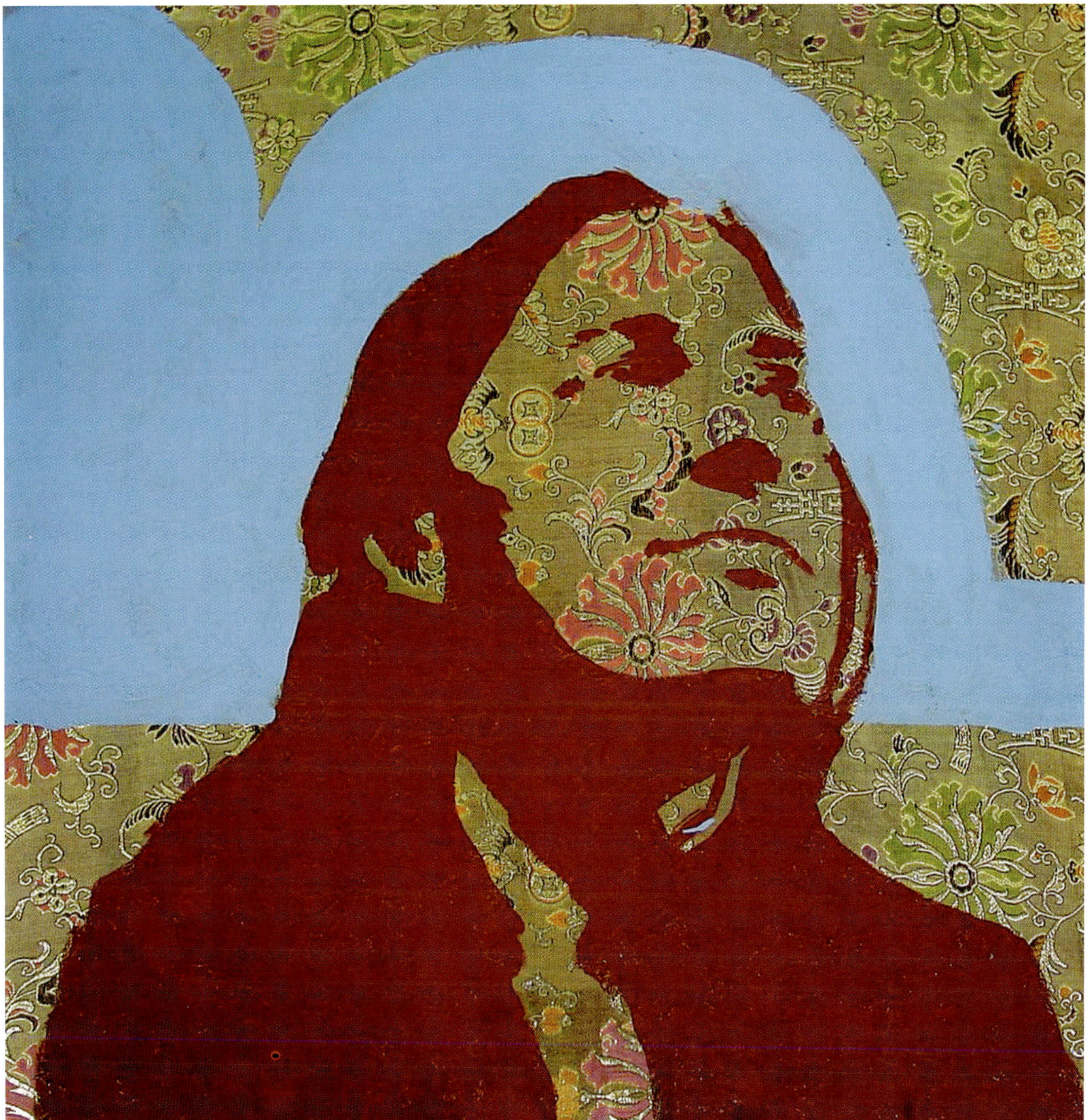

Rebecca on Gold Silk, 2005. Acrylic on silk, 24" x 24".

MICHELLE **WEINBERG**

My goal as an artist is to use imagery to penetrate the veneer of everyday appearances, to activate and bring to the surface latent and surprising possibilities within. Primarily, my work is about the freedom derived from rearranging a set of givens from the visible world. I am inspired by settings in nature and the urban environment, and in them I see a vivid contemporary folklore. By re-fashioning these elements according to my own narrative, I can animate them with new meaning. I can levitate elements, patch flat fields of color together, and paste phrases from commercial signage to building facades like poetry on paper. Pattern is central to my imaginations, and provides a pulse, a visual rhythm to all my work. My collage process is mediumistic in that I respond to found printed matter gathered from varied sources. The color and print quality of the 1960s and 1970s particularly attracts me. A major source for my work has been hand painted manuscripts from Persia and India. Each of my collages comprises a single scene edited out of a larger continuum, a page from an endless book or a frame from an animated movie. In all my work, I'm interested in achieving a grand decoration using economic means.

Miami has created opportunities for me that have afforded me a great deal of personal freedom. Miami's unique live/work economics plus the social solitude have created an equation that allows me time to pursue new outlets such as video, public commissions, and hand-made rugs, and to write on art. I've found an incredible group of artists to collaborate with who challenge me aesthetically and technically. The look and the structure of the physical city of Miami has provided great raw material for my work, because I look at it with an outsider's eyes. Also, the modernist architecture and flat color treatments on warehouse dovetail with my own aesthetic. The experience of driving through blighted and abject thoroughfares of Miami have absorbed me in a way I hadn't experienced before, coming from a walking city full of street life like my hometown of New York.

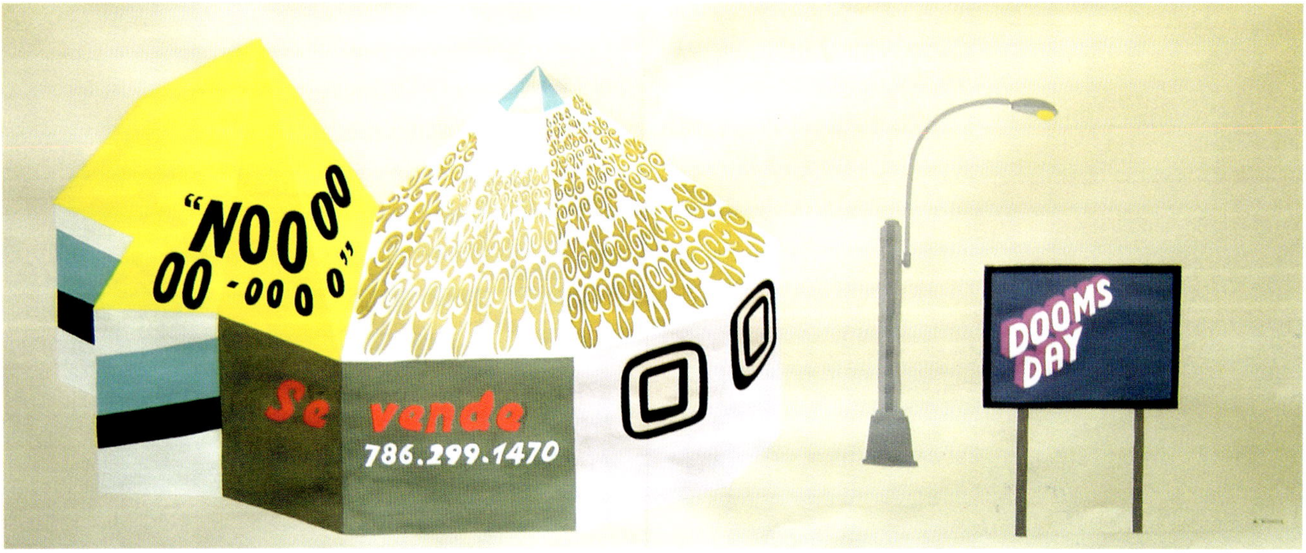

Doomsday, 2005. Gouache on paper, 18" x 38".

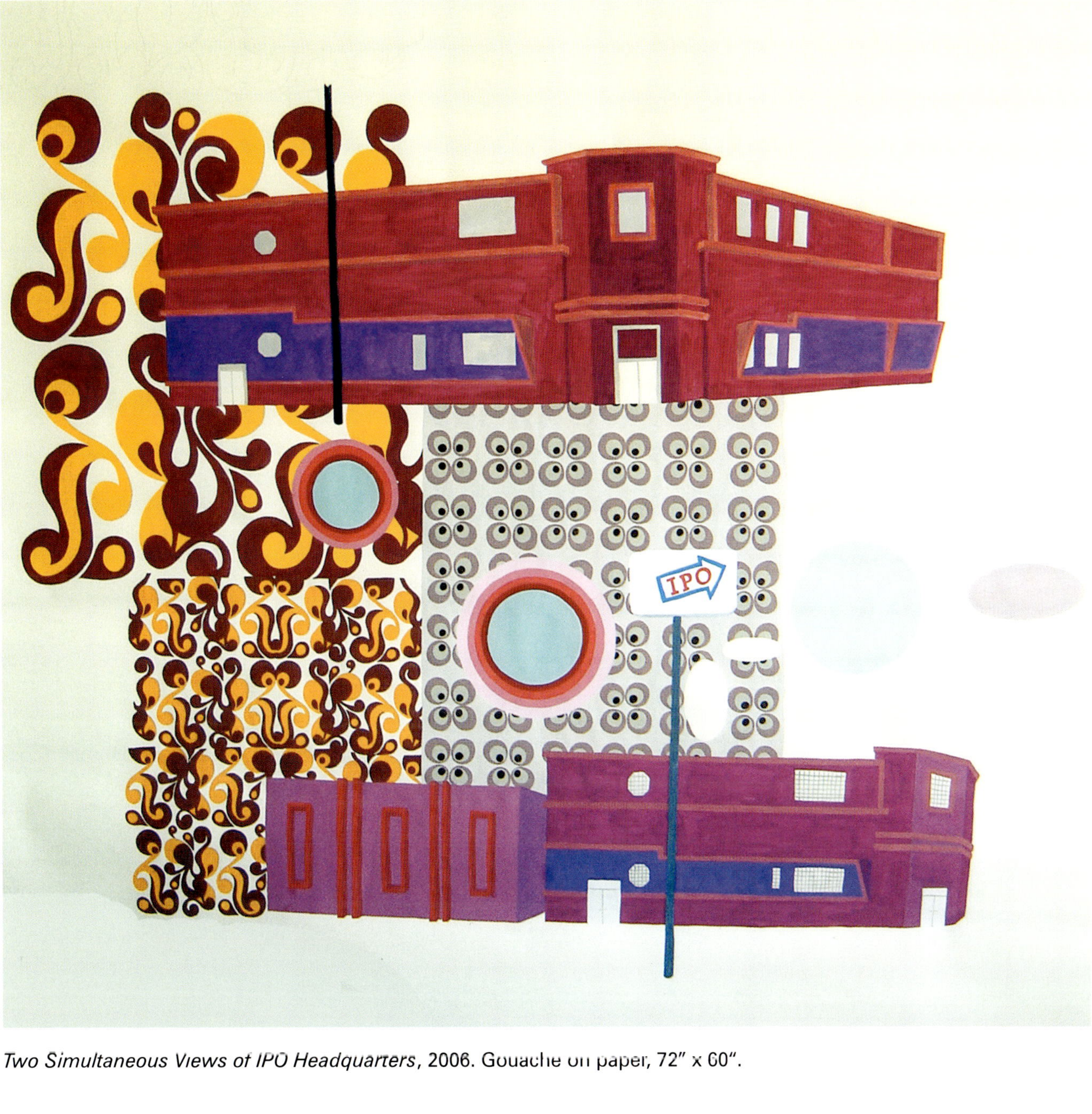

Two Simultaneous Views of IPO Headquarters, 2006. Gouache on paper, 72" x 60".

HELENE WEISS

I try to paint both the feeling inside and outside us. Energy is invisible, untraceable, and undetectable; it is a million atoms that are inside each and every one of us: a tremor, a beat, a glance. If you can feel my paintings you can feel the immaterial source of all that is.

Miami: The landscape, the horizons…the city allows my mind clearness to paint. The colors, the spaciousness, the rhythm: all combine to give way for my inspiration to flow.

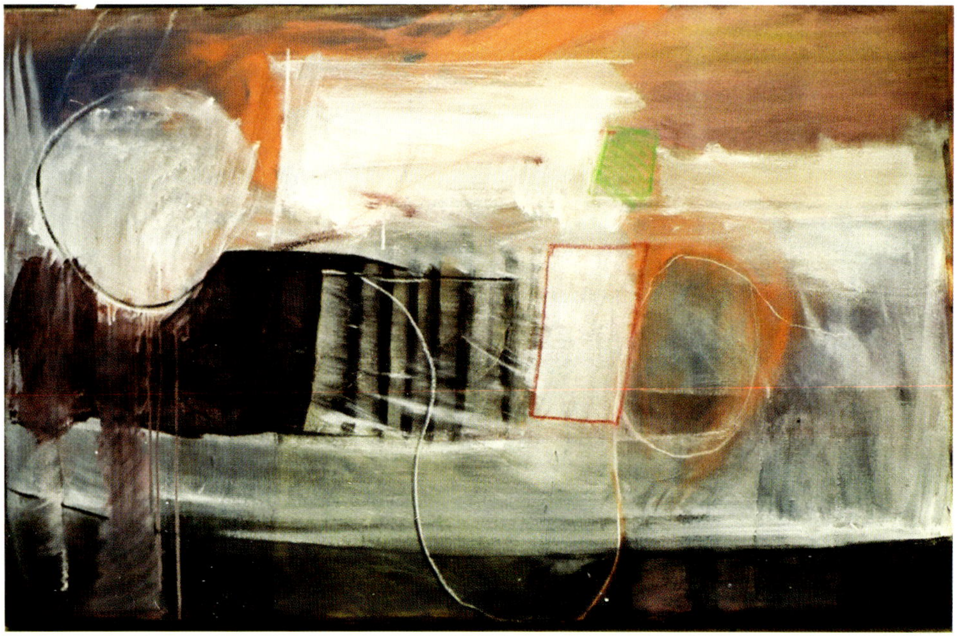

The Piano, 2000. Acrylic on canvas, 26" x 48".

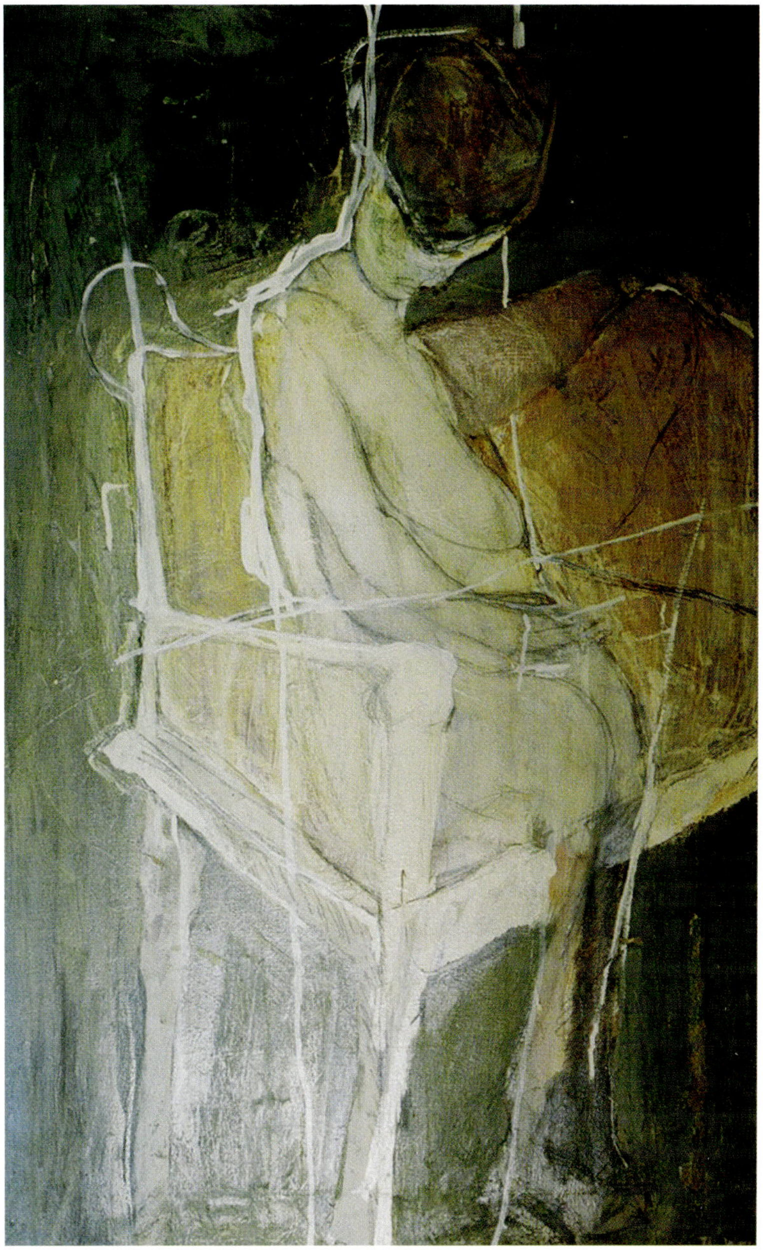

Meditation, 1992. Oil on canvas, 30" x 40".

ANNIE **WHARTON**

I'm really interested in the juxtaposition between exigent beauty, ironic configurations, and clandestine experiences. I am especially inspired by the banal (including objects like kitchen appliances and muscle cars) and the exquisite (fairies, Asian material culture following a fellowship in Japan, and sparkly jewels). I make my own paints from a blend of pigments, plastic, and metallic compounds, and manipulate color and composition to inform and saturate the process. Originally trained in sculpture, I am very interested in the structure and the three-dimensionality of my media...and use it to create abstract depictions of a fancy and sometimes fantastic world, rife with idiosyncrasies.

While I love Los Angeles, I do miss working in Miami, as it really is the perfect place to be an artist. It's quite surreal to work in the land of perpetual vacation, and South Beach, with its insouciant decadence and impenitent bling-bling, provides a utopian backdrop for an art world. Miami's art scene, once marginalized, is now receiving its due recognition. This growth and stature is helping to further a dialogue peripheral to Art Deco, Miami Vice, posh VIP lounges, and beautiful, thong-clad people on sandy beaches. Not that there's anything wrong with those things...but there is also an incredible wealth of creative minds working in all aspects of visual art.

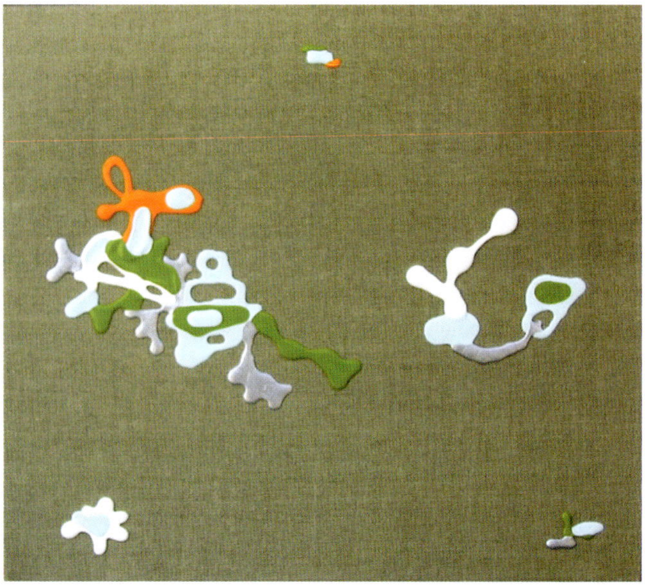

Smeltrocket, 2005. Acrylic, urethane, pigment dispersions, and aluminum on Belgian linen, 16 " x 20".

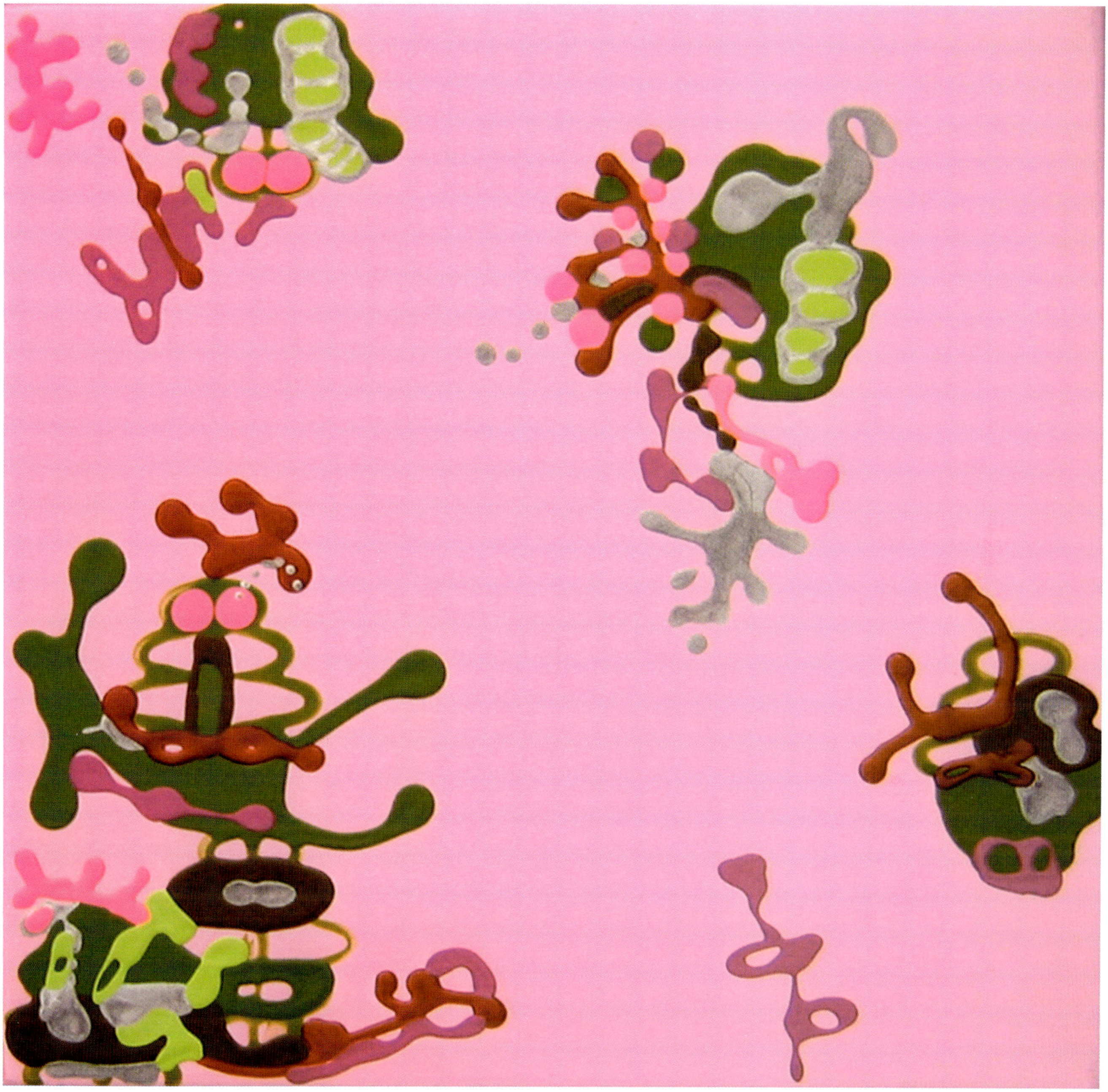

Prickle, 2005. Acrylic, urethane, pigment dispersions and aluminum on patent vinyl, 18" x 18".

WENDY WISCHER

Living in both rural and urban settings has brought two worlds together. The exposure to Ellen Dissanayake's *Homoaestheticus,* created a great interest in Earth Art, as the natural world stirs a nostalgic affection and strong sense of identity while at the same time, the excitement of an urban environment and refined technology prove to be equally intoxicating. With a minimalist approach to form and reflection on process, I am lured to re-define the term environment and explore the impact of surroundings. Including the use of technology in my vocabulary, links that which is man made to the natural elements, and in certain cases propose technology as environment. Much of the work is based on blurring the separation between the spirituality of working with nature, the cutting edge of "New Media" and the common place of the familiar object, while also connecting mysticism and scientific discovery. Light as a medium has proven to be a strong voice as it is easily identifiable in both the real and the artificial, it is both tangible and intangible at the same time. I am interested in re-directing attention to the smaller things in life. I seek to expose the sacred within the mundane, the monumental within the minute, unraveling boundaries created by culture and language and revealing common ground in the "in-betweens" of established categories through a dichotomy of concepts. Thoughts and memories, experiences and environments continuously appear and reappear in overlapping fragments. The images create resting spots, visceral places of contemplation.

Living in Miami has proven to be very exciting for me as an artist. Since my first exhibition in 1999, the art community has changed significantly. While the Miami art scene was growing, there was the incredible opportunity to have work seen and studios visited by curators and museum directors. The new international exposure for Miami's art scene has continued to provide important growth and opportunities for everyone. With galleries and artists moving to Miami from all over the world, the scene continues to provide anticipation and diversity. Personally, Miami continues to inspire with its natural surroundings and expanding urban environment.

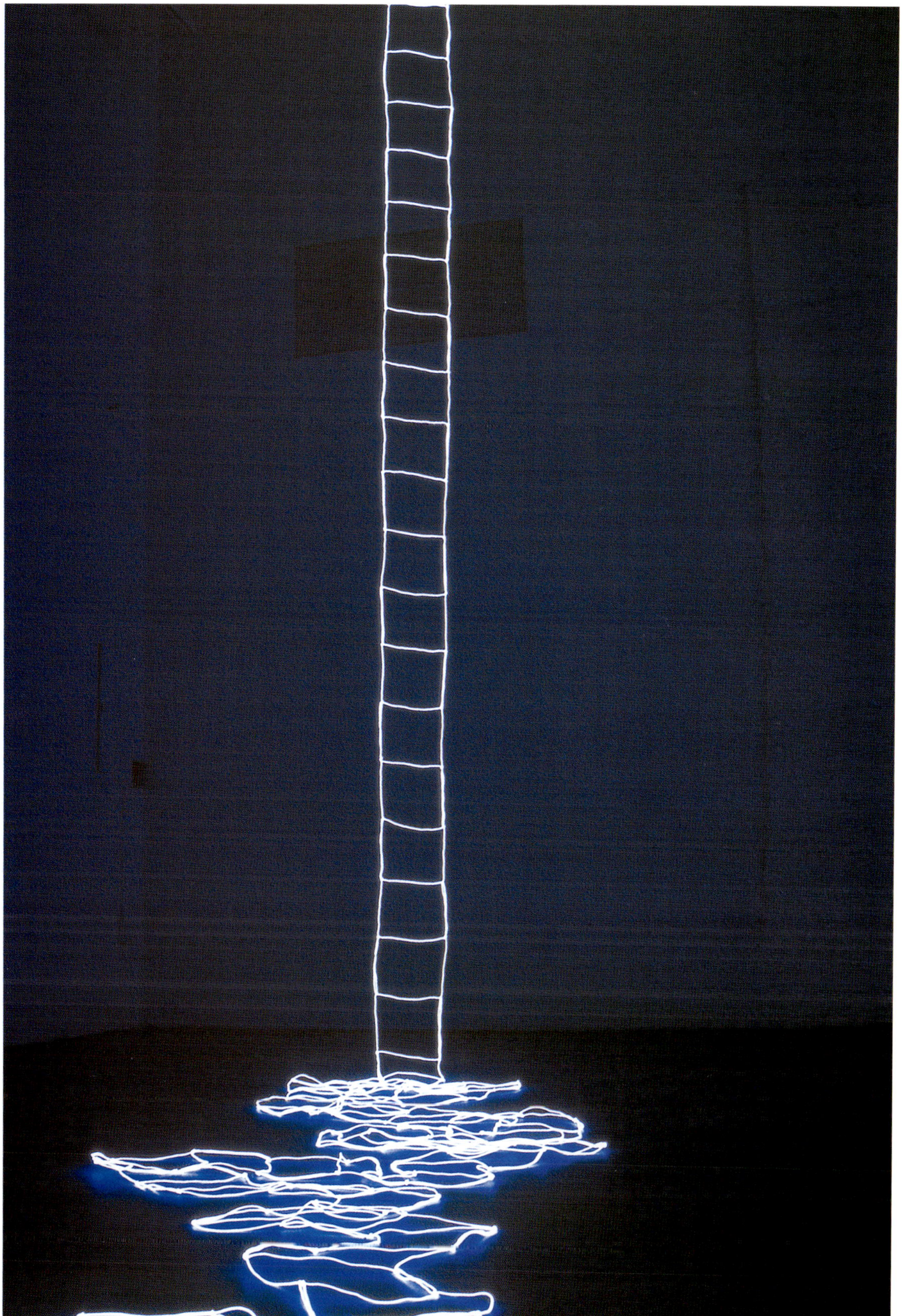

Ariadne's Thread, 2004. E.L. wire, 70" x 12".

PURVIS YOUNG

"I paint what I see" – Purvis Young, 2006.

Purvis Young was born and raised in Miami, living most of his life in Overtown. Completely self-taught, he began painting at 23 finding his art education on the shelves of the main branch of the Miami-Dade Public Library. He studied books on the old masters like Rembrandt, Rubens and Van Gogh, and supplemented his reading with programs on public television. Young's choice of medium and materials were those that he could find or were given to him – primarily old books, notebooks, wooden crates, discarded plywood and house paint. The socio-economic plight of his immediate neighborhood has been an endless source of inspiration for the content of his work. His interest in world events and politics find their way into his brilliantly hued and emotionally charged paintings; commenting on the injustices suffered by man: the struggles of war, oppression, prejudice, and economic strife. But Young's paintings are not without hope, and the images of angels both black and white, of crowds of people with arms reaching skyward, and warriors astride proud wild horses figure prominently, suggesting salvation and freedom from these social ills. Purvis Young has exhibited widely throughout the United States and abroad. His work can be found in many public and private collections, and is part of a permanent exhibition at the Smithsonian Institution in Washington, DC. Many books have featured the artist, and he is the focus of an award winning documentary film *"Purvis of Overtown."*

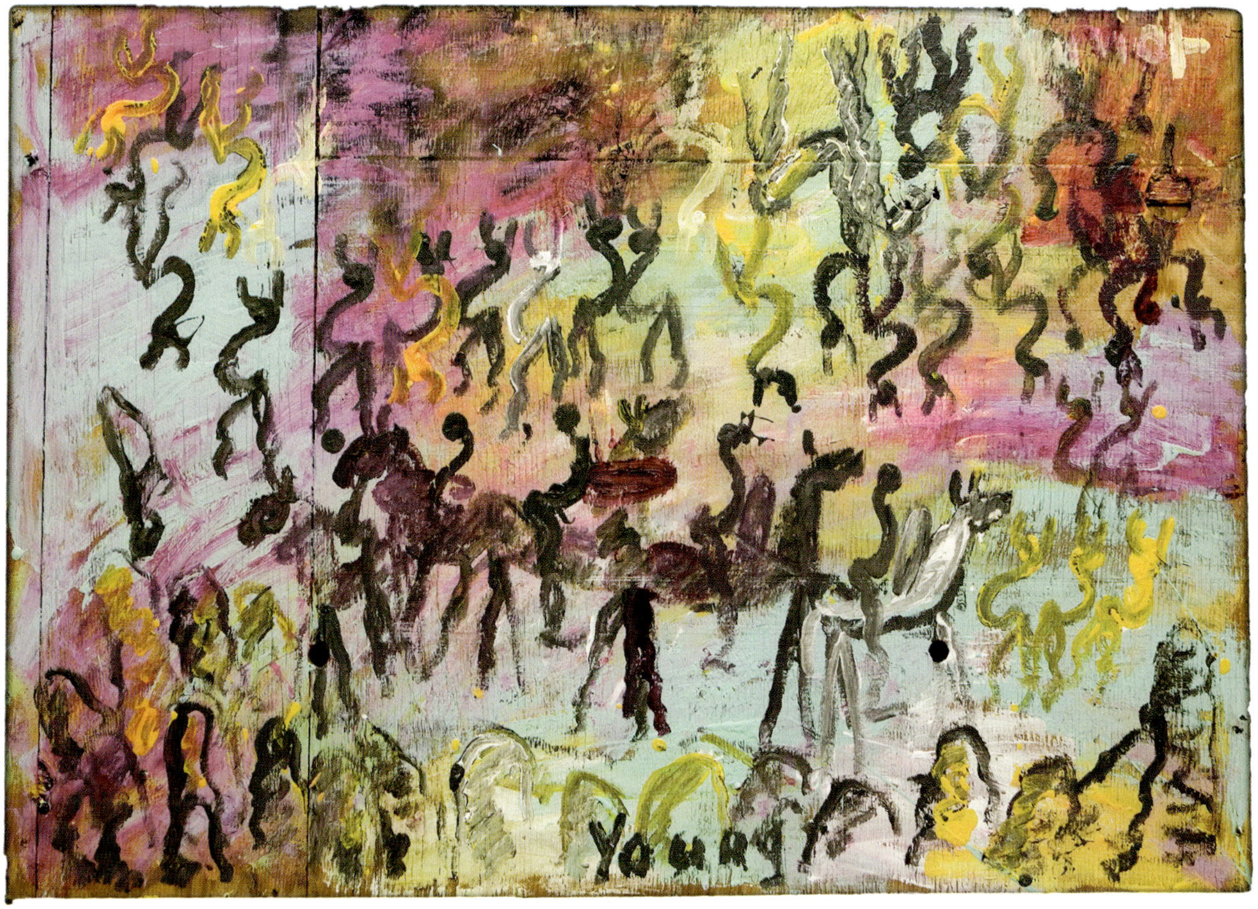

Untitled. Paint on plywood, 39″ x 45″ x 38.5″

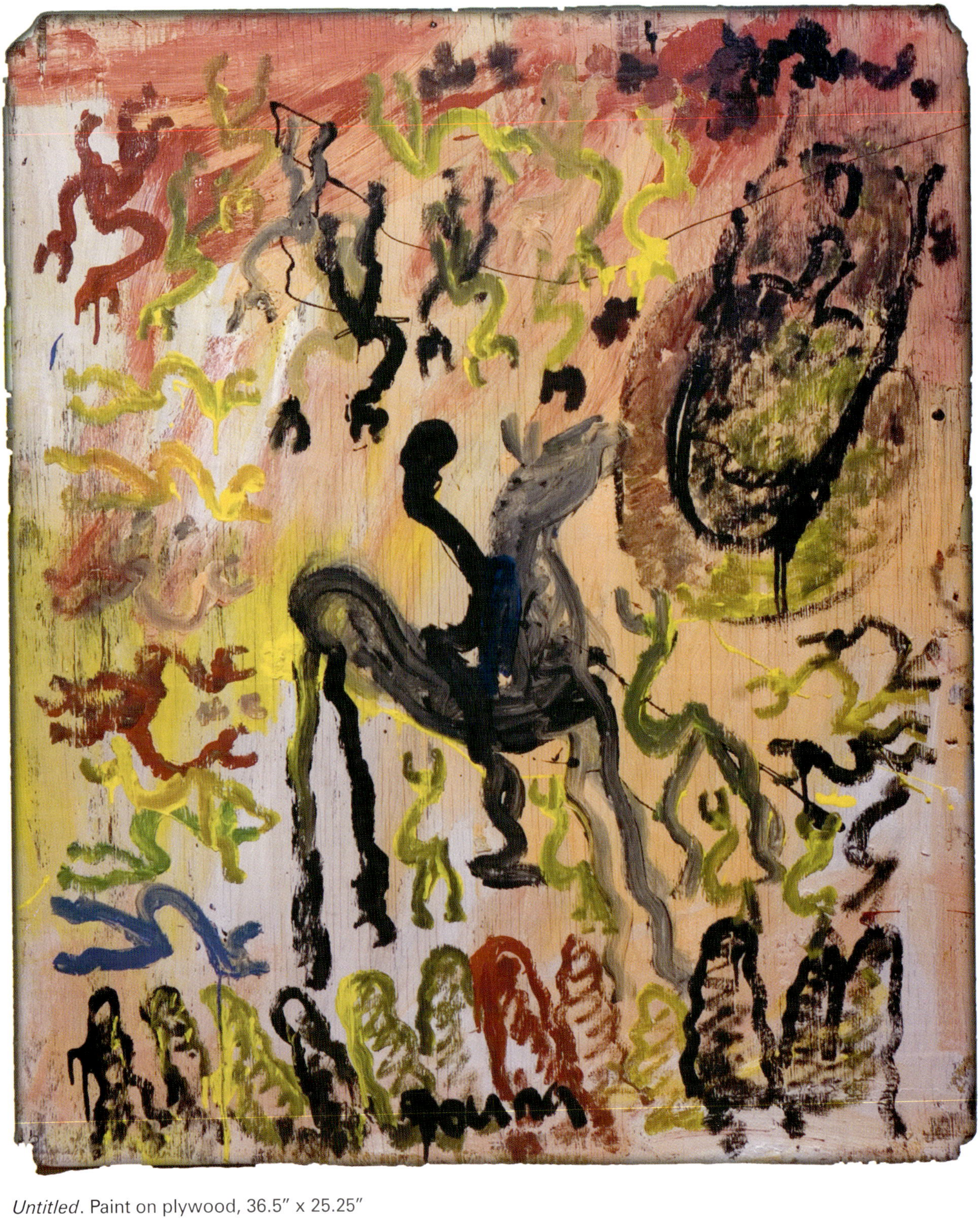

Untitled. Paint on plywood, 36.5″ x 25.25″

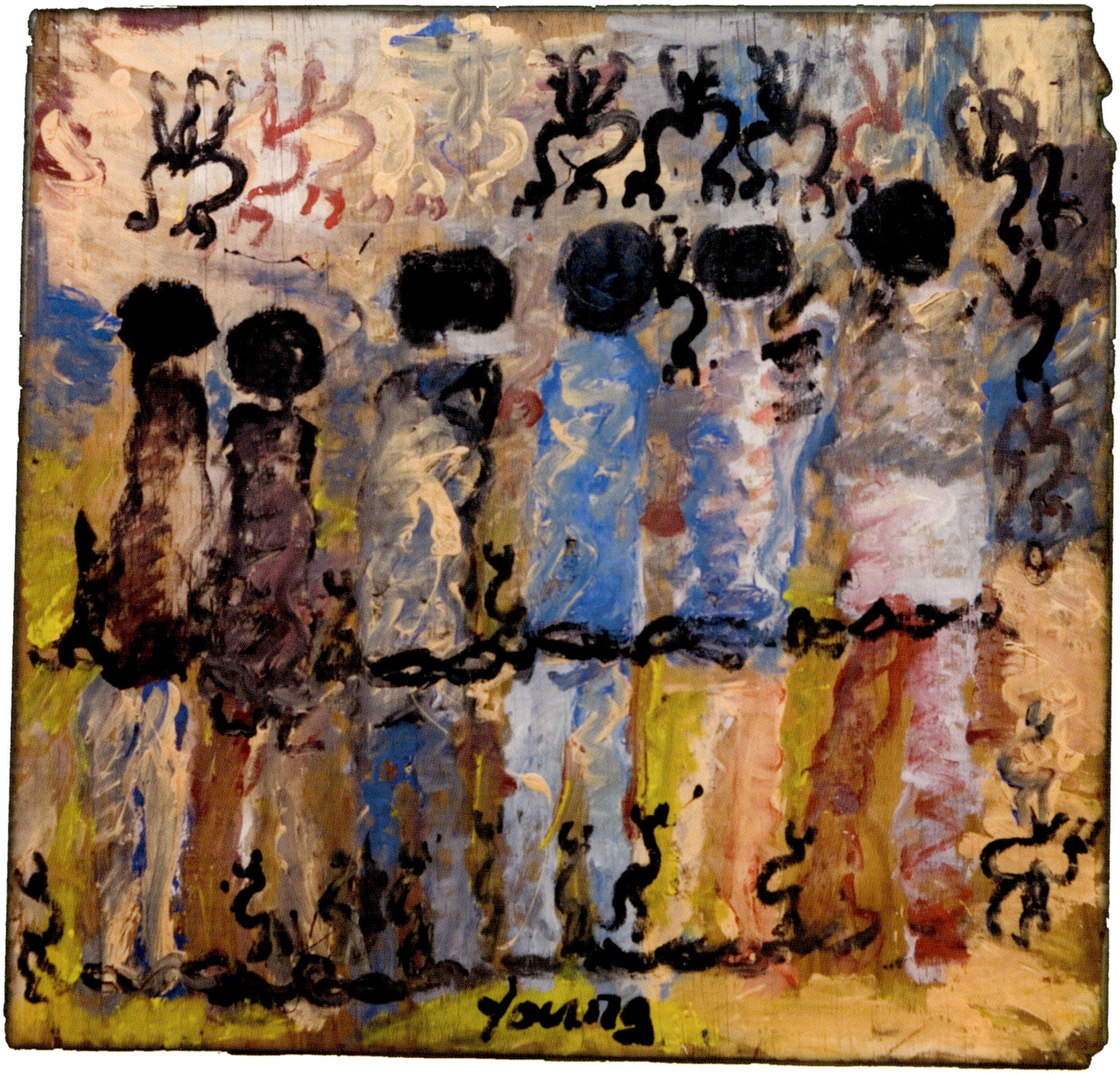

Untitled. Paint on plywood, 47.5" x 45" x 47" x 44.8".

ARTISTS INDEX

Years in Miami: 5
Gallery: n/a
Web: www.theflew.com

Lou Anne Colodny pp 66 - 67
Born: Denver, CO
Years in Miami: 40
Gallery: n/a
Web: www.cjazzart.com

Cooper pp 68 - 69
Born: Miami, FL
Years in Miami: 25
Gallery: Fredric Snitzer Gallery
Web: www.snitzer.com/cooper

Christian Curiel pp 70 -71
Born: 1977, Ponce, Puerto Rico (from Cuban heritage)
Years in Miami: 26
Gallery: Lehmann Maupin Galley, NY
Web: www.christiancuriel.com,
www.lehmannmaupin.com

Dash N pp 72 -73
Born: 1980, Miami Beach, FL
Years in Miami: off and on 26 years
Gallery: Ingalls & Associates
Web: www.ingallsassociates.com

Ivan Toth Depeña pp 74 -75
Born: n/a
Years in Miami: n/a
Gallery: Ingalls & Associates; Miami, FL.
Web: www.passingeye.com,
www.ingallsassociates.com

Christian Duran pp 76 -77
Born: 1976, Hialeah, FL
Years in Miami: 6
Gallery: Ingalls & Associates, Miami, FL
Web: www.christianduran.com,
www.ingallsassociates.com

Edouard Duval-Carrié pp 78 - 81
Born: 1954, Port-au-Prince, Haiti
Years in Miami: 14
Gallery: Bernice Steinbaum Gallery
Web: www.edouard-duval-carrie.com,
www.bernicesteinbaumgallery.com

Franklin Einspruch pp 82 - 83
Born: 1968, Dallas, TX
Years in Miami: 30
Gallery: Dorsch Gallery, Miami; Scott White Contemporary Art, San Diego, CA
Web: www.einspruch.com,
www.dorschgallery.com

John Espinosa pp 84 - 85
Born: Bogota, Colombia
Years in Miami: 1993-1999
Gallery: Fredric Snitzer Gallery, Miami; Sandroni Rei, Los Angeles
Web: www.john-espinosa.com,
www.snitzer.com,
www.sandronirey.com

Charles Falarara pp 86 - 87
Born: 1966, Sao Paulo, Brazil
Years in Miami: 10
Gallery: n/a
Web: www.falarara.com

Jason Ferguson pp 88 - 89
Born: 1972, Trinidad & Tobago
Years in Miami: 12
Gallery: n/a
Web: www.fecuop.com,
www.freemarketsociety.com

Teresita Fernández pp 90 -93
Born: 1968, Miami, FL
Years In Miami:
Gallery: Lehmann Maupin, NY
Web:www.lehmannmaupin.com

Naomi Fisher pp 94 - 95
Born: 1977, Miami, FL
Years in Miami: 29
Gallery: Fredric Snitzer Gallery
Web: www.snitzer.com

Robert Flynn pp 96 -97
Born: 1967, Manhasset, NY
Years in Miami:11
Gallery: Barbara Gillman Gallery
Web: www.robert-flynn.com,
www.barbaragillman-gallery.com

Lynne Golob Gelfman pp 98 - 99
Born: 1944, Waukegan, IL
Years in Miami: Since 1972
Gallery: Fredric Snitzer Gallery; Miami, FL ; Newman Popiashvili Gallery; New York, NY
Web: www.snitzer.com

Jacin Giordano pp 100 - 101
Born: 1978, Stamford, CT
Years in Miami: 24
Gallery: Fredric Snitzer Gallery
Web: www.snitzer.com

Luis Gispert pp 102 - 103
Born: 1972, New Jersey
Years in Miami: Growing up
Gallery: Zach Feuer Gallery (LFL)
Web: www.zachfeuer.com

Guerra de la Paz pp 104 - 105
Born: 1968, Havana, Cuba
Years in Miami: 11 years
Gallery: Creative Thrift Shop, Brooklyn, NY
Web: www.guerradelapaz.com,
www.creativethriftshop.com
www.cjazzart.com

Adler Guerrier pp 106 - 107
Born: 1975, Port-au-Prince, Haiti
Years in Miami: 18
Gallery: Fredric Snitzer Gallery
Web: www.thenextfewhours.com,
www.snitzer.com

Jason Hedges pp 108 - 109
Born: 1978, Hollywood, FL
Years in Miami: 27
Gallery: n/a
Web: www.placemaker.org

Quisqueya Henríquez pp110 - 111
Born: 1966, Havana, Cuba
Years in Miami: On and off, since 1993.
Gallery: David Castillo Gallery
Web: www.castilloart.com

Alexander Heria pp 112 - 113
Born: 1961, Elizabeth, NJ
Years in Miami: 35
Gallery: n/a
Website: www.ultralex.com

Robert Huff pp 114 - 115
Born: 1945, Kalamazoo, Michigan
Years in Miami: 38
Gallery: Bernice Steinbaum Gallery
Web: www.bernicesteinbaumgallery.com

Jiae Hwang pp 16 - 117
Born: 1981, Seoul, Korea
Years in Miami: 6
Gallery: Fredric Snitzer Gallery
Web: www.snitzer.com

Julie Lara Kahn pp 118 - 119
Born: Miami, FL
Years in Miami: 10
Gallery: n/a
Web: www.juliekahn.com

Bayunga Nsimba Kialeuka pp 120 -121
Born: 1974 Kinshasa, Congo
Years in Miami: 25
Gallery: Bikeko Gallery
Web: www.bayungakialeukastudio.com

Susan Lee-Chun pp 122 - 123
Born: 1976, Seoul, Korea
Years in Miami: 2
Gallery: n/a
Web: www.re-title.com/artists/susanlee-chun.asp

Mira Lehr pp 124 - 125
Born: Brooklyn, NY
Years in Miami: 45
Gallery: Elaine Baker Gallery, Boca Raton, FL; Flomenhaft Gallery
Chelsea, NY
Web: www.miralehr.com

Joshua Levine pp 126 - 127
Born: Boston, MA
Years in Miami: 1979-1991, 1994-1998
Gallery: Ambrosino Gallery, Miami ;
Irvine Contemporary, Washington, DC
Web: www.copyright1972.com;
www.ambrosinogallery.com;
www.irvinecontemporary.com

Petra Liebl-Osborne pp 128 - 129
Born: Munich, Germany
Years in Miami: Since 1995
Gallery: Ambrosino Gallery
Web: www.petra-liebl-osborne.de,
www.ambrosinogallery.com

Francesco Locastro pp 130 - 131
Born: 1976
Years in Miami: 6
Gallery: n/a
Web: www.francescolocastro.com

Michael Loveland pp 132 - 133
Born: 1973, Miami, FL
Years in Miami: On and off about 20.
Gallery: n/a
Web: www.michaelloveland.com

Pepe Mar pp 134 - 135
Born: 1977, Reynosa, Mexico
Years in Miami: 6
Gallery: David Castillo Gallery
Web: www.castilloart.com

Jordan Massengale pp 136 - 137
Born: Orillia, Canada
Years in Miami: 12
Leonard Tachmes Gallery
Web: www.jordanmass.net,
www.leonardtachmesgallery.com

Maritza Molina pp 138 - 139
Born: Havana, Cuba
Years in Miami: On and off 19
Gallery: n/a
Web: www.maritzamolina.com

Beatriz Monteavaro pp 140 -141
Born: 1971, Havana, Cuba
Years in Miami: 29
Gallery: Fredric Snitzer Gallery
Web: www.snitzer.com

Gean Moreno pp 142 - 143
Born: 1972, New York, NY
Years in Miami: 18
Gallery: Fredric Snitzer Gallery, Miami;
Derek Eller Gallery, NY
Web: www.snitzer.com

Victor Muñiz pp 144 - 145
Born: 1978, Brooklyn, NY
Years in Miami: 15
Gallery: Leonard Tachmes Gallery
Web: www.victormuniz.com,
www.leonardtachmesgallery.com

Glexis Novoa pp 146 - 149
Born: 1964 Holguín, Cuba
Years in Miami: 11
Gallery: Bernice Steinbaum Gallery
Web: www.bernicesteinbaumgallery.com

Brandon Opalka pp 150 -151
Born: Virginia, USA
Years in Miami: 15
Gallery: n/a
Web: www.fecuop.com,
www.brandonopalka.com

Martin Oppel pp 152 - 153
Born: 1976, Buenos Aires, Argentina
Years in Miami: 15
Gallery: Galerie Emmanuel Perrotin
Web: www.placemaker.org,
www.galerieperrotin.com

Charo Oquet pp 154 - 155
Born: Santo Domingo, Dominican Republic
Years in Miami: 17
Gallery: Edge Zones
Web: www.edgezones.org

Jonathan Peck pp 156 - 157
Born: 1980, Boston, MA
Years in Miami: 3
Gallery: Ambrosino Gallery, Miami; Boots Contemporary, Kansas City
Web: www.ambrosinogallery.com,
www.bootscontemporary.com

Gavin Perry pp 158 - 161
Born: 1971, Philadelphia, PA
Years in Miami: 10
Gallery: Fredric Snitzer Gallery
Web: www.snitzer.com

Vickie Pierre pp 162 - 163
Born: 1970, Brooklyn, NY
Years in Miami: 8
Gallery: Ambrosino Gallery
Website: www.ambrosinogallery.com

Alisa Pitchenik pp 164 - 165
Born: 1971, Lafayette, LA
Years in Miami: 25
Gallery: n/a
Web: n/a

Manny Prieres pp166 - 167
Born: 1972, Madrid, Spain
Years in Miami: 31
Gallery: Diana Lowenstein Fine Art
Web: www.dlfa.com

Ali Prosch pp 168 - 169
Born: 1979, Fairfax, CA
Years in Miami: 5
Gallery: n/a
Web: n/a

Ralph Provisero pp 170 - 171
Born: 1967, South Miami, FL
Years in Miami: 38
Gallery: Dorsch Gallery, Miami
Web: www.provisero.com,
www.dorschgallery.com

Carol Prusa pp 172 - 173
Born: 1956, Chicago, IL
Years in Miami: 7
Gallery: Bernice Steinbaum Gallery, Miami
Web: www.bernicesteinbaumgallery.com

Tao Rey pp 174 - 175
Born: 1978, Buenos Aires, Argentina
Years in Miami: 28
Gallery: n/a
Web: www.placemaker.org

Tall Rickards pp 176 - 177
Born: 1971, Kingston, Jamaica
Years in Miami: 15
Gallery: n/a
Web: n/a

Karen Rifas pp 178 - 179
Born: 1942, Chicago, IL
Years in Miami: 50
Gallery: Bernice Steinbaum Gallery, Miami
Web: www.bernicesteinbaumgallery.com

Leyden Rodriguez-Casanova pp 180 - 181
Born: 1973, Havana, Cuba
Years in Miami: 19
Gallery: David Castillo Gallery, Miami; Casas Reigner Gallery, Colombia.
Web: www.iamleyden.com; www.castilloart.com

Cristina Lei Rodriguez pp 182 - 183
Born: 1974, Miami, FL
Years in Miami: 21
Gallery: Galerie Emmanuel Perrotin, Miami and Paris
Web: www.galerieperrotin.com

Norberto Rodriguez pp 184 - 185
Born: 1975, Miami, FL
Years in Miami: 30
Gallery: Fredric Snitzer Gallery, Miami, FL ; Monte Clark
Gallery Toronto, Canada
Web: www.minegro.com, www.snitzer.com

David Rohn pp 186 - 187
Born: 1951, Englewood, NJ
Years in Miami: 15
Gallery: n/a
Web: www.davidrohn.net

Gustavo Román pp 188 - 189
Born: 1974, Santurce, Puerto Rico
Years in Miami: 7
Gallery: n/a
Web: www.gustavoroman.com

Betty Rosado pp 190 - 191
Born: 1966, New York, NY
Years in Miami: 12
Gallery: Ambrosino Gallery
Web: www.b2studio.com/brosado

Raymond Saá pp 192 - 193
Born: 1972, New Orleans, LA
Years in Miami: 20
Gallery: Ambrosino Gallery
Web: www.ambrosinogallery.com

George Sánchez-Calderón pp 194 - 197
Born: 1967, New York, NY
Years in Miami: 33
Web: www.sanchezcalderon.com
Gallery: n/a

Reeve Schumacher pp 198 - 199
Born: 1981, Minneapolis, MS
Years in Miami: 7
Gallery: Damien B. Contemporary Art Center, Miami.
Web: www.damienb.com

Onajide Shabaka pp 200 - 201
Born: 1948, Cincinnati, Ohio
Years in Miami: 21
Gallery: n/a
Web: www.art3st.com

Tawnie Silva, with Lou Laurita pp 202 - 203
Born: 1965, Stoughton, MA
Years in Miami: 20
Gallery: Spinello Gallery, Miami, FL
Web: www.spinellogallery.com

Alette Simmons-Jimenez pp 204 - 205
Born: 1952, Madison, Wisconsin
Years in Miami: 13
Gallery: Artformz Alternative, Miami, FL
Web: www.artformz.net

Diego Singh pp 206 - 207
Born: 1977, Argentina
Years in Miami: n/a
Gallery: Fredric Snitzer Gallery, Miami ; Tomio Koyama Gallery, Tokyo
Web: www.snitzer.com, www.tomiokoyamagallery.com

Kol Solthon pp 208 - 209
Born: 1971, Vancouver, British Columbia
Years in Miami: off and on
Gallery: Ingalls & Associates, Miami
Web: www.ingallsassociates.com

Tina Spiro pp 210 - 211
Born: New York, NY
Years in Miami: 7
Gallery: Chelsea Galleria
Website: www.chelseagalleria.com

Sara Stites pp 212 - 213
Born: New York, NY
Years in Miami: 5
Gallery: n/a
Website: www.sarastites.com

Paul Sto ppi
pp 214 - 215
Born: 1966, Kingston, Jamaica
Years in Miami: 7
Gallery: n/a
Website: www.sto ppi.com

Kristen Thiele pp 216 - 217
Born: 1969, Honolulu, Hawaii
Years in Miami: 28
Gallery: n/a
Website: www.kristenthiele.com

Robert Thiele pp 218 - 219
Born: 1941, Milwaukee, Wisconsin
Years in Miami: 40
Gallery: Barbara Gillman Gallery, Miami
Website: www.barbara-gillmangallery.com

TM Sisters pp 220 - 221
Born: 1983, Gainesville, FL
Years in Miami: 18
Gallery: Filter, Hamburg, Germany
Website: www.tmsisters.com

Mette Tommerup pp 222- 223
Born: 1969, Kalundborg, Denmark
Years in Miami: 9
Gallery: Fredric Snitzer Gallery, Miami
Web: www.mettetommerup.com, www.snitzer.com

Rubén Torres-Llorca pp224 - 225
Born: 1957, Havana, Cuba
Years in Miami: 13
Gallery: Praxis Int'l Art, Coral Gables, FL; Byron C. Cohen Gallery, KS City, MO; GDS, San Jose, Costa Rica
Web: www.praxis-art.com, www.gdsgallery.com

César Trasobares pp 226 - 227
Born: 1949, Holguín, Cuba
Years in Miami: 41
Gallery: n/a
Web: www.cesartrasobares.com

Frances Trombly pp 228 - 229
Born: Miami
Years in Miami:
Gallery: Kevin Bruk Gallery
Web: www.francestrombly.com,
www.kevinbruk.com

Kyle Trowbridge pp 230 - 231
Born: 1973, Miami, FL
Years in Miami: 27
Gallery: Dorsch Gallery
Web: www.dorschgallery.com

Eugenia Vargas pp 232 - 233
Born: Chilean, Chile
Years in Miami: 10
Gallery: Ingalls & Associates
Web: www.imagenfoto.com,
www.talkingheadstransmitters.com,
www.ingallsassociates.com

Carlos de Villasante pp 234 - 235
Born: Mexico City, Mexico
Years in Miami: 6
Gallery: Heriard Cimino Gallery, New Orleans, LA ; Kathleen Cullen Gallery, New York;
Web: www.carlosdevillasante.com

Michelle Weinberg pp 236 - 237
Born: 1961, Brooklyn, NY
Years in Miami: 8
Gallery: n/a
Web: www.michelleweinberg.com

Helene Weiss pp 238 - 239
Born: 1945, Brooklyn, NY
Years in Miami: 11
Gallery: n/a
Web :n/a

Annie Wharton pp 240 - 241
Born: 1969, Tallahassee, FL
Years in Miami: 11
Gallery: Ambrosino Gallery
Web: www.anniewharton.com,
www.ambrosinogallery.com

Wendy Wischer pp 242 - 243
Born: 1971, Waukesha, WI
Years in Miami: 11
Gallery: David Castillo Gallery
Web: www.wendywischer.com,
www.castilloart.com

Purvis Young pp 244 - 247
Born: 1943, Liberty City, FL
Years in Miami: 63
Gallery: Purvis Young Studio, Miami
Web: n/a

PHOTO CREDITS

COVER: Courtesy of Gavin Perry and Frederic Snitzer Gallery

FOREWORD:

City Sky, courtesy of Alex Heria
"Making Art in Miami: Travels in Hyperreality," courtesy of MOCA and © Steven Brooke
"At this time: 10 Miami artists from the Rubell Family Collection," courtesy of the artist and the Rubell Family Collection
"Humid," courtesy of the artist
"Departing Perspectives," courtesy of the artist
"Goodbread Alley," courtesy of Purvis Young Studio and The Vasari Project
"Front and Center," courtesy of BOX and Leyden Rodriguez-Casanova
"The Home Show," courtesy of Guerra de la Paz
"The House" courtesy of The House
"Sears Building at The House," courtesy of Natalia Benedetti
The House demolition, courtesy of The House
"10 Floridians", courtesy of Miami Art Central
From "Miami in Transition," courtesy of Michael Loveland
"Daniel Arsham set design–downstage left" courtesy of the artist
"Full to Wailing and Back Again," courtesy of the artist

ARTISTS LAYOUTS

Kevin Arrow, courtesy of the artist
Daniel Arsham, courtesy of Galerie Emmanuel Perrotin
Asandra, courtesy of the artist
John Bailly, courtesy of Gloria Leigh O'Connell
Bhakti Baxter, courtesy of Fredric Snitzer Gallery
Hernan Bas, courtesy of Fredric Snitzer Gallery
José Bedia, courtesy of Fredric Snitzer Gallery
Roberto Behar & Rosario Marquardt, © R & R Studios
Natalia Benedetti, courtesy of the artist
Rakel Bernié, Courtesy of the artist and Jenny Brillhart
Carlos Betancourt, Studio CB
Francie Bishop-Good, Francie Bishop-Good
Pip Brant, courtesy of the artist
Jenny Brillhart, courtesy of the artist
Carol K. Brown, courtesy of the artist
Ernesto Burgos, courtesy of the artist
Pablo Cano, courtesy of the artist
Elizabeth Cerejido, courtesy of the artist
Robert Chambers, courtesy of the artist
Westen Charles, courtesy of the artist
Clifton Childree, courtesy of the artist
Lou Anne Colodny, courtesy of the artist
Cooper, courtesy of Fredric Snitzer Gallery
Christian Curiel, courtesy of the artist
Dash N, courtesy of the artist
Ivan Toth Depeña, © Ivan Toth Depeña, All Rights Reserved
Christian Duran, courtesy of the artist
Edouard Duval-Carrié, courtesy of Bernice Steinbaum Gallery
Franklin Einspruch, courtesy of the artist
John Espinosa, courtesy of the artist, MOCA, and Kevin Arrow
Charles Falarara, courtesy of the artist
Jason Ferguson, courtesy of the artist
Teresita Fernández, courtesy of the artist and Lehmann Maupin Gallery, New York
Naomi Fisher, courtesy of Fredric Snitzer Gallery
Robert Flynn, courtesy of the artist
Lynne Golob Gelfman, courtesy of Frederic Snitzer Gallery and © Oriol Tarridas
Jacin Giordano, courtesy of the artist
Luis Gispert, courtesy of Luis Gispert and Zach Feuer Gallery
Guerra de la Paz, courtesy of Douglas Voisin
Adler Guerrier, courtesy of the artist and Frederic Snitzer Gallery
Jason Hedges, courtesy of the artist
Quisqueya Henríquez, courtesy of David Castillo Gallery
Alexander Heria, courtesy of the artist
Robert Huff, courtesy of the artist
Jiae Hwang, courtesy of Fredric Snitzer Gallery
Julie Lara Kahn, courtesy of the artist
Bayunga Nsimba Kialeuka, courtesy of Bikeko Gallery
Susan Lee-Chun, courtesy of the artist
Mira Lehr, courtesy of the artist
Joshua Levine, courtesy of the artist
Petra Liebl-Osborne, courtesy of the artist
Francesco Locastro, courtesy of the artist
Michael Loveland, courtesy of the artist
Pepe Mar, courtesy of Juan Cabrera Photography
Jordan Massengale, courtesy of Mirna Massengale
Maritza Molina, Maritza Molina © All Rights Reserved
Beatriz Monteavaro, courtesy of Frederic Snitzer Gallery
Gean Moreno, courtesy of the artist and Fredric Snitzer Gallery
Victor Muñiz, courtesy of the artist
Glexis Novoa, courtesy of Bernice Steinbaum Gallery
Brandon Opalka, courtesy of the artist
Martin Oppel, courtesy of Galerie Emmanuel Perrotin
Charo Oquet, courtesy of the artist
Jonathan Peck, courtesy of the artist
Gavin Perry, courtesy of the artist and Frederic Snitzer Gallery
Vickie Pierre, courtesy of the artist

Alisa Pitchenik, courtesy of the artist
Manny Prieres, courtesy of the artist
Ali Prosch, courtesy of the artist
Ralph Provisero, courtesy of Brook Dorsch, the artist, William Keddell
Carol Prusa, courtesy of the artist
Tao Rey, courtesy of the artist
Tall Rickards, courtesy of the artist
Karen Rifas, courtesy of the artist
Leyden Rodriguez-Casanova, courtesy of the artist
Cristina Lei Rodriguez, Mariano Peuser and Galerie Emmanuel Perrotin
Norberto Rodriguez, courtesy of the artist and Fredric Snitzer Gallery
David Rohn, courtesy of the artist
Gustavo Roman, courtesy of the artist
Betty Rosado, Betty Rosado © All Rights Reserved
Raymond Saá, courtesy of the artist and Ambrosino Gallery
George Sánchez-Calderón, courtesy of the artist
Reeve Schumacher, courtesy of the artist
Onajide Shabaka, courtesy of Onajide Shabaka
Tawnie Silva, with Lou Laurita, courtesy of the artists
Alette Simmons-Jimenez, courtesy of the artist and Artformz Alternative, Miami
Diego Singh, courtesy of the artists, Frederic Snitzer Gallery and Tomio Koyama Gallery
Kol Solthon, courtesy of the artist
Tina Spiro, courtesy of the artist and Chelsea Galleria
Sara Stites, courtesy of the artist
Paul Stoppi, courtesy of the artist
Kristen Thiele, courtesy of the artist and Francesco Casale
Robert Thiele, courtesy of the artist and Francesco Casale
TM Sisters (Tasha and Monica Lopez de Victoria), courtesy of the artists
Mette Tommerup, courtesy of the artist and Frederic Snitzer Gallery
Rubén Torres-Llorca, courtesy of the artist and Liliam Dominguez
César Trasobares, courtesy of the artist
Frances Trombly, courtesy of the artist and Kevin Bruk Gallery
Kyle Trowbridge, courtesy of the artist
Eugenia Vargas, courtesy of the artist and Ingalls & Associates
Carlos de Villasante, courtesy of the artist
Michelle Weinberg, courtesy of the artist
Helene Weiss, courtesy of the artist
Annie Wharton, courtesy of the artist and Ambrosino Gallery
Wendy Wischer, courtesy of the artist
Purvis Young, courtesy of Purvis Young Studio and Daniel Aubry

CREDITS

FOREWORD

For many years award-winning writer Elisa Turner has written reviews, news reports, and essays as The Miami Herald art critic and Miami correspondent for ARTnews. For the Miami Herald, she has traveled to write about art in Havana, Venice, and Basel. A former editor in the college division of Random House, she has a B.A. from DePauw University and a M.A. in Comparative Literature from University of North Carolina at Chapel Hill. She is a member of the International Association of Art Critics and Art Table. While growing up in the Midwest she studied ballet and, thanks to a film she saw in high school, fell in love with the rose windows of Chartres.

This foreword was prepared with research from Miami Herald archives. I thank art historian Roni Feinstein, Julie Davidow, and Paul Clemence for commenting on drafts of this foreword. All quotations, unless otherwise noted, are from my Herald articles and reviews or from interviews and e-mail correspondence that I initiated. – *Elisa Turner*

GRAPHIC DESIGN

Alexander Heria was born in Elizabeth, New Jersey in 1961. He moved to Miami, Florida at age ten. Heria received a BFA in photography from Florida International University, Miami in 1992, and his MFA from Massachusetts College of Art and Design, Boston in 1994. He has taught photography and graphic design for seven years at FIU, Miami-Dade College, and the Art Institute Miami. His photography has been exhibited locally and is in numerous private collections. He is a recipient of the South Florida Cultural Consortium Award and is currently an artist-in-residence at the ArtCenter/South Florida.

COVER IMAGE

Gavin Perry was born and raised in Philadelphia, PA. He received his BFA from Tyler School of Art at Temple University, Philadelphia in 1996. He moved to Miami after graduation, where he now lives and works. Perry is an emerging artist who has exhibited nationally and internationally. He has been reviewed in numerous publications including Art Papers, Flash Art, Art News and Zing magazines. He is represented by Frederic Snitzer Gallery in Miami.

AUTHORS

PAUL CLEMENCE

American born and raised in Brazil, Paul Clemence is now based in Miami Beach, Florida. After graduating from the School of Architecture at Universidade Federal do Rio de Janeiro, Clemence took his design sensibilities and applied them to photography, creating award-winning avant-garde photos of modern and contemporary buildings throughout the world. His work has appeared in both domestic and international design and lifestyles magazines. He is the author of *"South Beach Architectural Photographs,"* a black and white photographic essay of South Beach's unique architecture; and *"Mies van der Rohe's Farnsworth House,"* a detailed visual exploration of Mies' iconic residential design. Selections of these photos are now part of the Mies van der Rohe Archives, housed in the Museum of Modern Art, in New York. In addition to his fine art work, he is also a freelance architectural photographer, and a publishing creative and design consultant.

www.paulclemence.com

JULIE DAVIDOW

Julie Davidow was born and raised in Miami, Florida. Her path to the arts was circuitous. She first received her BA in advertising from the University of North Florida in Jacksonville. After ten years as a small business owner, she returned to her first passion and attended New World School of Arts in Miami to study painting. Her work has since been exhibited at The National Museum of Women in the Arts in Washington D.C.; The Fort Lauderdale Museum of Art in Fort Lauderdale, FL; The Tampa Museum of Art; Tampa, FL; and the Southeastern Center for Contemporary Art in Winston-Salem, NC. Locally, she has exhibited her work at ArtCenter/South Florida Gallery, lemon sky: projects + editions, Ambrosino Gallery, and Rocket Projects. She is a recipient of the Leo and Raye Chestler Visual Arts Awards and is currently an artist-in-residence at the ArtCenter/ South Florida in Miami Beach.

www.juliedavidow.com